Merry Christmas
Cathie, Love Doug
1981

Cooking with Michael Field

Also by Michael Field:

Michael Field's Cooking School
Culinary Classics and Improvisations
All Manner of Food

Cooking with

Michael Field

EDITED BY

JOAN SCOBEY

Holt, Rinehart and Winston   New York

Published simultaneously in Canada by Holt, Rinehart and Winston
of Canada, Limited

Library of Congress Cataloging in Publication Data
Field, Michael, 1915–1971.
    Cooking with Michael Field.
    Includes index.
    1. Cookery.   I. Scobey, Joan.   II. Title.
TX651.F53   1978   641.5   78-752
ISBN 0-03-018501-7

FIRST EDITION

Designer: Joy Chu
Printed in the United States of America

10 9 8 7 6 5 4 3 2 1

For Frances and Jonathan

Contents

A Personal Note   ix

Equipment and Utensils   1

BOILING, POACHING, AND STEAMING   11

FRYING, DEEP FRYING, AND SAUTÉING   73

BROILING   141

BRAISING: A BIT OF KITCHEN MAGIC   209

ROASTING: MOST ANCIENT OF
    CULINARY ARTS   241

BAKING: BREADS AND BISCUITS   273

BAKING: CAKES   325

BAKING: PIES, TARTS, AND CHOU PUFFS   355

A FEW VERSATILE SAUCES   429

Culinary Glossary   443

Metric Equivalents of Weights and Measures   459

Menus   463

Index   477

A Personal Note

As a student some years ago, I frequently enjoyed the musical presentations of Michael Field at his duo piano concerts. As a professional writer and amateur cook, I happily met up with him again in his second career as Master Cook. To his cooking he brought the same grace, refinement, and taste that distinguished his music. Both were grounded in careful precise technique and illuminated by a marvelous sense of style and showmanship and vitality.

As devotees of Michael Field's cooking instructions already know, when you follow a Field recipe, you learn why you are using each ingredient, what the cooking process looks like at every stage, and what it will look like if done improperly. You find not only explicit, clear, and exact instructions, but also the comforting presence of Michael Field at your elbow, lending support and encouragement. You find yourself making four-handed kitchen magic, playing a culinary duet, as it were, with this gifted pianist-cook.

This book was drawn from a series of eight volumes available only to members of the Doubleday Book Clubs. Though Michael Field intended to use these as the basis for a new cookbook, he died before he was able to compress the original nine hundred pages into a single volume. Doing that obviously required editorial choices and making these posthumously in the name of another—let alone in the name of an authority—demanded particular care, especially when the intent was to keep the authenticity, integrity, and tone of the original.

All the recipes and glossary information appeared in the original books, but in order to make this volume as useful as possible, I have added fuller menus and included wines. From close readings of Michael Field's three other cookbooks, ramblings through many other volumes for which he was a consulting editor, and talks with his friends and cooking associates, I detected certain guidelines: Meals should be simple, sometimes even spare, often just one dish at a time. A vegetable course is an excellent way to start a meal, rather than accompanying the meat dish. The best desserts are frequently the simplest—often fruit, sometimes with cheese. The most appropriate wines may come from the region rather than a great vineyard. In this way, I devised the menus and wine recommendations.

In his first book—*Michael Field's Cooking School*—Michael Field wrote, "Tradition, taste, technical skill, and respect for ingredients are the standards of good cooks everywhere." While all his books honor these four standards, the first book may be said to focus on taste, the next—*Culinary Classics and Improvisations*—on tradition, and the third—*All Manner of Food*—on ingredients. Technical skill is an appropriate approach for this fourth book.

Michael Field has always dedicated his books to his wife, Frances, and his son, Jonathan; in his name I make the same dedication. In addition, had he lived, Michael Field would, I know, have wanted to acknowledge Helen McCully and Mary McCabe Gandall for their work on the original volumes. For myself, I raise a glass to Frances who enthusiastically supported my editorial decisions, and to Ed Fogel who brought us together.

JOAN M. SCOBEY

Cooking with Michael Field

Equipment and Utensils

The following equipment and utensils, grouped according to their basic functions, are used to prepare the specific recipes in this book. They also constitute a useful checklist of basic kitchen equipment.

Kitchen Appliances

Electric mixers. The ones with a whip, a paddle, and a dough hook, such as the heavy-duty KitchenAid mixers made by Hobart, are the most versatile. The large balloonlike whip will whip egg whites to great heights, and the dough hook is invaluable for mixing and kneading heavy doughs. In fact, I consider an electric mixer—whatever the brand—so useful that I have written the cake recipes assuming that you own, or at least plan to purchase, one.

Electric blender. These purée, pulverize, grate, crumb, and blend foods with ease and speed, simplifying the making of many dishes. Latest models have push-button controls and a variety of speeds for specific jobs, but older models with only a low and a high speed work successfully.

Food processor. These new "miracle" machines, of the type made by Cuisinart and Farberware, have taken over most of the functions of the electric blender and have added a few of their own: they shred, slice, and julienne vegetables, grind meat, make pie crusts and bread and cake doughs, and chop just about everything, all almost instantaneously. They come with chopping and mixing blades and slicing and shredding disks, and usually at a high price.

Electric deep-fat fryer. The most convenient fryers are thermostatically controlled—that is, they reach and hold the temperatures at which their thermostats are set.

Pots, Pans, Casseroles, and Baking Dishes

Tea kettle. This can be made of any material, but should hold at least 2 quarts of water.

Double boiler. The inset (top pan) should be of 3-quart capacity. Stainless steel is ideal, but it is expensive and sometimes difficult to find. Considerably less expensive enameled pans, while they may chip and tend to be lightweight, can be quite satisfactory. Avoid aluminum pans, which will discolor sauces containing egg yolks and certain acid ingredients like wine, and Pyrex glass double boilers, which are not only breakable, but retain heat so persistently that they make cooking control difficult.

8- to 10-quart pot with close-fitting cover. The weight of material of this pot is unimportant because it will be used primarily for boiling and blanching foods which require large amounts of water.

Heavy saucepans with tight-fitting covers. Pans of enameled cast iron, stainless steel, or tin-lined copper are all satisfactory. You will find the 2- and 4-quart sizes most practical, and the 1- or 1½-quart size useful for making sauces.

Heavy frying pans with tight-fitting covers. The best domestic pans are made of heavyweight aluminum and have sloping sides and nonstick linings. Attractive and useful imported enameled cast-iron pans are also available, but they tend to be quite expensive. The most useful sizes are the 12-inch pan (with 10-inch bottom) and the 10-inch pan (8-inch bottom) or 8-inch pan (6-inch bottom).

10-inch sauté pan with cover. Usually made of heavy-duty cast aluminum, this is the classic pan (in French, a *sautoir*) used by professional cooks. The one I recommend is made by Wear-Ever. It has straight sides, is 2¼ inches deep, and is unlined, a desirable characteristic for my sautés—and, in fact, for all classic sauté recipes—because the exposed metal surface will help build up the glaze, or golden-brown encrustations, in a way almost impossible to achieve in a pan with a nonstick surface.

Enameled cast-iron casseroles with tight-fitting covers. The heavier the casseroles are, the better they will perform and the easier it will be to control the temperature of their contents. Buy the heaviest ones you can afford. The 2- or 3-quart size is ideal for braising vegetables; the 5-quart round is an all-purpose pot and the best choice for many dishes that are braised, poached, and steamed (it is just the right size to hold a 3-legged collapsible steamer); the 7- and 9-quart ovals are recommended for some of the braised and simmered dishes.

Roasting pan with rack. An all-purpose roasting pan about 16 by 11 by 2 inches with its own rack is perfect for most roasting jobs;

only rarely will you need a larger pan. The rack lifts the roast up so that the heat circulates to all sides, including the bottom. The rack also keeps the meat from sitting—and stewing—in its own juices. The pan is also an ideal size for a water bath (bain-marie) in which to bake some creams and custards.

Deep fryer. Sometimes called a frying kettle, a deep fryer should be fairly heavy, flat-bottomed, and well constructed, with its own wire basket and a capacity of at least 4 to 5 quarts. An alternative would be any heavy, deep, 4- or 5-quart pot—a Dutch oven, for example—into which you can fit a separately purchased frying basket. If your electric range has a thermostatically controlled burner, it is imperative that you use the type of pot recommended by the manufacturer.

8-quart fish poacher with tight-fitting cover. A typical 8-quart poacher has a removable rack and is about 20 inches long, 6 inches wide, and $4\frac{1}{4}$ inches deep. It can be made of stainless steel, tin-lined copper, plain enameled steel, or, if you have no alternative, of aluminum. It can also be used for poaching a fillet of beef, a leg of lamb, and many other foods.

Heavy ovenproof baking dish. I recommend one about 9 by 13 by $1\frac{3}{4}$ inches for baking Yorkshire Pudding. It is also useful for marinating steaks and chops.

Shallow flameproof baking dish. One that is 9 inches square and 2 inches deep is handy for braising certain foods.

Au gratin dish. A dish, 10 to 12 inches long and preferably oval, that is also useful for braising some foods.

$1\frac{1}{2}$-quart soufflé dish. A dish precisely 3 inches deep and $7\frac{1}{2}$ inches in diameter (inside measurement) that is specified for the Deep-Dish Chicken Pie. There are many uses for this dish; one of them, obviously, is for soufflés.

Cutting and Chopping

Cutting slab. The best have a cutting surface of polyethylene, which won't chip or retain odors, or of durable hardwood like maple. A good size is about 16 by 20 inches.

Knives. They can be made of carbon steel or stainless steel but must be of high quality to take a sharp cutting edge; get the best you can afford. Stainless steel resists most stains; carbon steel holds its cutting edge longer but stains and rusts easily. You will need a small paring knife, about 3 inches long; a medium-size utility knife, about 5 inches long; a heavy 10-inch French chef's knife or 8-inch chopping knife; a narrow 10-inch slicer; and a 10-inch bread knife with serrated edge.

Carving knife and fork.

Knife sharpener. Among the best is the Zip-Zap, which is made of special ceramic and looks like a miniature sharpening steel.

Carving board.

Food mill. This round, hand-cranked mill fits snugly over small mixing bowls and saucepans and purées soft foods easily and efficiently. Some models have three removable disks, for fine, medium, and coarse puréeing.

Ricer. It eliminates the need for peeling potatoes that are to be mashed.

Stand-up four-sided grater.

Rotary-type (Mouli) grater. This is available with fine and coarse shredders and a slicing cylinder, and is useful for grinding hard cheeses and nuts.

Vegetable peeler with swivel-action blade.

Zester and/or citrus peeler. Use the first to remove strips and the second to shred fine pieces of citrus rind without the underlying bitter pith.

Measuring Utensils

Timer. It should mark minutes and a few hours.

Measuring spoons. A set of four holds 1 tablespoon and 1, ½, and ¼ teaspoon.

Stainless steel measuring cups. For measuring dry ingredients, cups should hold 1, ½, ⅓, and ¼ cup.

Ovenproof glass measuring cups. For measuring liquids, the most useful are the 2-cup (pint) and 4-cup (quart) sizes. The newer ones have a liter scale as well as a cup scale.

Oven thermometer. It is worth the small investment to buy an accurate oven thermometer. Because thermostatically controlled ovens vary and frequently need adjustment, always test the oven temperature each time you cook, and place the thermometer as near as possible to the baking or roasting pan without touching it.

"Spot-check" meat thermometer. I have a decided preference for those expensive pocket testing thermometers—I call them "spot-check" thermometers, although they are not sold under the name— that almost instantaneously register the internal temperature of any food, hot or cold. Such a thermometer has a 1- or 2-inch dial with a clear window atop a 5-inch shaft that is as slender as a knitting needle, has a range of 0° to 220° F., and can be manually adjusted for pinpoint accuracy. Keep it standing upright in a tall glass on your work counter where it is both protected and available. There are two brands that I know of and use: one is the Bi-Therm from Taylor Instrument Companies; the other is made by Weston Instruments, Inc.

Candy thermometer. I prefer a candy thermometer encased in stainless steel, with a bulb guard that keeps the sensor of the thermometer from touching the side or bottom of the pan, that is fairly easy to read, and whose stem need only be immersed 1 inch in the liquid for a reliable reading.

Deep-frying thermometer. Unquestionably, this is the most important utensil for successful deep frying. Any number of reliable thermometers are on the market, none of them overly expensive.

Baking Pans and Utensils

Square 8-inch aluminum cake pan, 2 inches deep.

Round 8-inch aluminum cake pan, 1½ inches deep.

Three round 9-inch aluminum cake pans, 1½ inches deep.

Round 10-inch aluminum cake pan, 1½ inches deep. This is useful for shortbread, but is optional.

Aluminum Gugelhopf pan (turkshead mold). Choose 8-cup (8-inch) and 10-cup (9½-inch) sizes.

Two aluminum loaf pans, about 9 by 5 by 3 inches. Variations up to ½ inch in any dimensions are of no consequence.

Aluminum 6-cup ring mold.

Two small muffin pans with nonstick linings. These 12-cup pans, with cups ¾ inch deep and 2 inches across the top, are used for tartlets.

Heavy cast-iron popover pan with 11 cups. Muffin tins or custard cups may be substituted.

Two aluminum pizza pans with nonstick linings. The ones I like best are 12 inches in diameter and made by Wear-Ever.

Aluminum jelly-roll pan. Select one about 12 by 18 inches with a rim about 1 inch high. The best are made of heavy aluminum and are usually available in restaurant-supply houses.

Two aluminum baking sheets. They should be about 18 by 14 inches with rims about ½ inch high.

Two cookie sheets. Choose sheets about 18 by 14 inches with slightly turned-up ends and no rims on the long sides. Heavy cookie sheets are preferable to light ones because thin pans sometimes warp or buckle during baking.

Pie pans. In metal pie pans I firmly recommend dull-finished aluminum ones. Unlike pans with gleaming surfaces, these absorb heat evenly and therefore produce deeper browning. I prefer those made by Wear-Ever which are 9 inches in diameter at the top (inside measurement) and 1¼ inches deep. Their extended rims, about ½ inch wide, make for securely constructed pies.

A 9-inch ovenproof glass pie plate is recommended for my deep-dish fruit pies, and it can be used for the chilled crumb crust as well. But if you prefer individual deep-dish fruit pies, choose 8 small (5- or 6-ounce) or 4 large (10-ounce) heatproof dishes made of glass or pottery.

Because glass retains heat so persistently, I do not recommend glass pie plates for standard single-crust or double-crust pies. The bottom crust seldom browns as evenly as I like and the filling frequently overcooks. Moreover, glass pie plates are generally deeper than the 9-inch aluminum pans for which my recipes have been devised.

Fluted, loose-bottomed tart pan. Imported from France, Germany, or Belgium, tart pans are 9 inches in diameter and 1 inch deep. They are usually inexpensive and are available in shops that specialize in cooking equipment or in housewares departments. Since pan sizes sometimes vary, measure the pan directly across the bottom; my tart recipes are designed to fill a 9-inch tart shell to the brim.

Flour sifter. You should have both 1- and 5-cup sizes.

Pastry blender. This is especially useful in making my pastry for American pies. Try to find one with a handle that is welded to the wire blade. If you have one that is secured with a small nut and bolt, tighten the nut from time to time.

Pastry board. It should be a wooden board at least 20 by 30 inches. You can dispense with it if you have a large marble slab or a Formica counter top.

Rolling pin. Buy a heavy one with a pin about 10 inches long and 2 inches in diameter, either an old-fashioned but excellent one-piece design or a ball-bearing pin that revolves between its handles.

Pastry cloth and rolling pin sleeve. To prevent your pastry from sticking to the rolling surface, I recommend a heavy canvas pastry cloth, about 20 by 24 inches, and an open-ended stockinette rolling pin sleeve. Both are washable and are usually sold as a set. If you are gadget-minded, the Foley Manufacturing Co. makes a cloth that has circles outlined on its surface to guide you when rolling out the pastry and pockets that hold stabilizing rods at either end.

Baker's dough scraper. Buy one of rigid plastic or stainless steel about 6 by 3 inches with one long side embedded in a wooden handle.

Pastry cutters. Choose one with a smooth cutting edge to cut rounds or strips of dough, and another, called a jagger, with a jagged or serrated edge to produce decorative strips for lattice pie tops. Both cutting edges are also available in one double-wheeled pastry cutter.

Pizza cutter. A pastry wheel can be substituted.

Cookie or biscuit cutters. Get 2- and 3-inch sizes, plain or fluted. They are used for cutting out pastry for tartlets and dough for biscuits.

Pastry bags and tips. These are available in nylon or canvas, in sizes from 10 to 24 inches. You should have at least three, ranging from small to large, but if you only have one, make it a 16-inch one. Nylon bags are easy to clean and do not retain odors. A canvas bag is preferable for whipped cream; unlike the smooth and slippery nylon, the canvas takes firm hold on the whipped cream and gives you more control as you pipe it out.

Pastry tips are designated by name and number. If you can't buy a complete set of decorative and plain tips, settle for Star Tip No. 9 and Plain Tips Nos. 3, 6, and 9.

Pastry brushes.

Cake tester. This small skewerlike device is much handier than the traditional toothpick.

Two wire cake racks. About 10 by 14 inches, they are inexpensive and need not be heavy in weight. In addition to cooling cakes, the racks are indispensable for broiling a whole fish or scallops, or for draining fried foods.

Miscellaneous Equipment

Mixing bowls. A set of three is recommended—small, medium, and large—preferably of stainless steel, heavy heatproof glass, or ceramic ware but definitely not aluminum because it may discolor eggs.

1-quart heatproof glass bowl with curved sides. This is used in my recipe for remolding a head of boiled cauliflower.

Large copper bowl. This is for beating egg whites, if you use a balloon whip.

Balloon whip. Called a *fouet* in French, this whips egg whites to spectacular volume.

Small- and medium-size wire whisks or whips. You need these for making sauces, for incorporating small amounts of beaten egg whites into mixtures, and for countless other mixing, stirring, and beating jobs.

Rotary or electric beater. Either does an effective job of whipping egg whites or heavy cream, although many French chefs prefer to use the balloon whip.

Collapsible steamer. It usually measures 9 inches in diameter when fully opened, and fits into round pots that are 4 to 5 inches deep, such as the 5-quart enameled cast-iron casserole. Because of its folding sides, it can be used in pots of various diameters, all of which should, of course, have tight-fitting covers.

Colander. Buy the largest size you can find, and make sure it is the stand-up type that rests on three legs.

Fine-meshed sieves, large and small.

Two-pronged fork. Choose one with long tines and a long handle.

Kitchen tongs. Those about 8 inches long, preferably with smooth rather than serrated clamps, are needed to turn fried and sautéed foods. Longer tongs are useful when broiling sizable pieces of meat or poultry.

Long-handled metal spoons, slotted and unslotted.

Wooden spoons.

Ladle.

Wooden spatulas. They resemble spoons but have a flat oval blade in place of a bowl and are excellent for mixing.

Rubber spatulas, wide and narrow. Use these for scraping and mixing.

Large flat spatulas. Both slotted and unslotted spatulas are essential for turning and lifting foods.

Metal icing spatula. Choose one with a 6- or 8-inch blade.

Pepper mills. You need one for black pepper, one for white, both with adjustable grinding mechanisms.

Garlic press.

Nutmeg grater.

Hammer or mallet or lobster cracker and picks.

Broiling skewers. They should be about 10 to 14 inches long and about $\frac{1}{4}$ inch wide, with ring-shaped handles for turning skewered foods easily. Steel skewers come in a variety of types and sizes. Bamboo skewers—6, 9, or 12 inches long—are surprisingly strong and sharp and can be used to skewer and broil kidneys and shellfish.

Trussing skewers. Several sizes will prove indispensable for stuffing and shaping roasts, fish, and poultry: the wooden butcher-type skewers; slender metal skewers 3 to 4 inches long; and poultry pins.

Kitchen or poultry shears.

Small scissors.

Larding needle. Choose one with a wooden handle and grooved blade for inserting strips of fat into roasts. The larding needles French chefs use are tapered metal tubes 8, 10, or 12 inches long and $\frac{1}{8}$, $\frac{1}{4}$, or $\frac{3}{4}$ inch in diameter at the top. The larger the piece of meat, the larger the larding needle used to lard it.

Bulb baster. A stainless steel one is preferable for basting and removing grease from pan drippings.

Aluminum dredger or shaker. Use it for dispensing powdered sugar.

Small funnel.

String. This is used for tying and shaping roasts.

Sturdy needle and kitchen thread. Use it for lacing or sewing up openings of meat, fish, and poultry.

Parchment paper. While this is good for sealing the braising pot so no moisture escapes, heavy-duty foil or wax paper may be used instead.

Heavy-duty aluminum foil.

Wax paper.

Plastic wrap.

Cheesecloth. This is for tying up seasonings in bouquets garnis and for lining sieves and colanders when sauces or gravies are to be strained.

Corkscrew.

Ruler. You need one at least 15 to 18 inches long to measure the diameter of your pastry.

Paper frills. To decorate crown roasts or drumsticks, you can make your own paper frills (see page 454.)

Boiling, Poaching, and Steaming

*I*f I were asked to name three words in the culinary lexicon least likely to stir your gustatory imagination, I would have to admit they would be boiling, poaching, and steaming. Yet these three cooking methods have produced some of the world's greatest dishes. What can compare with the moist, tender texture and the intensified natural flavor of "boiled" beef, the velvety character of a slice of simmered tongue, the succulence of a poached striped bass?

Unfortunately, the terms "boiling," "poaching," and "steaming" are used interchangeably and inaccurately, and thus, their culinary applications are often misunderstood. Without a doubt, the confusion arises because the processes are so closely related. All three are top-of-the-stove procedures and all use water as a basic cooking medium.

Boiling. This is probably the most misused of culinary terms. In the truest sense, boiling is a rapid and uninterrupted procedure, and it is used mainly for vegetables and shellfish that can truly be boiled from start to finish. Few other foods lend themselves to such straightforward treatment. Consider our New England "boiled" dinner—or its international counterparts, the Italian *bollito misto* (mixed boil) or Austrian boiled beef. Were any of these—or even so-called boiled tongue or boiled corned beef—really boiled, the results would be disastrous. These dishes, when properly prepared, are, in fact, simmered: that is, the liquid in which they are to be cooked is brought to a boil, the food is immersed, and the heat is adjusted so that the surface of the liquid merely ripples—or, as the French put it, "shivers" or "smiles"—throughout the entire cooking time.

Unlike simmering, blanching and parboiling are inseparable from true boiling. *Blanching* is the process of leaving food briefly in boiling water. It is done to facilitate removing skin (as for peaches, almonds, or tomatoes); or to free the food of excess salt (as for some cured meats); or to remove strong or bitter flavors (as for certain vegetables). *Parboiling*, although similar to blanching, is the process of boiling food for a brief preiod in order to prepare it for complete cooking by other means.

Poaching. This procedure is more difficult to understand because it is so closely related to simmering. In fact, the French use the word "poaching" as a synonym for simmering and, as usual in culinary matters, they are perfectly right.

Most of us, in America at least, think of poaching primarily in terms of eggs. And, interestingly enough, it was the egg that inspired the very word "poach." *Poche*, in French, means a pocket or pouch, and that is precisely what is created when the white of an egg snugly envelops its yolk in a silky white pouch as the egg is poaching.

One might deduce that the term "poaching" came to be used to describe the simmering liquid of any delicate food, not eggs alone. To me at least, the fragility of the food being cooked is the significant difference between poaching and simmering. It is with that definition in mind that I use the term "poach" in my recipes for dishes made with such foods as a comparatively fragile whole fish, a tender young chicken, a fillet of beef, delicate fresh peaches, and ephemeral meringues.

Poaching, even more than simmering, demands special vigilance on the part of the cook, who must see not only that the cooking liquid never even approaches the boil, but also that the food is timed with scrupulous accuracy and tested for doneness as described in each recipe. The slightest overcooking would do poached dishes irreparable harm.

Steaming. This is the cooking of food by entrapped steam alone and is perhaps the most neglected of culinary procedures in American cooking today. Even the French, incomparable masters in other culinary areas, never give the virtues of steaming their due. I know of only two steamed French dishes: one, *poularde vapeur*, was a famous specialty of the great French chef Alexandre Dumaine and is, simply and gloriously, a truffled chicken steamed over a fragrant broth; the other is *pommes vapeur*, or steamed potatoes.

The Chinese, however, have through the centuries raised the art of steaming to Confucian heights, and although it is not my intention to explore the often intricate steaming techniques they have devised, the simpler Chinese techniques are the base upon which my steaming recipes are built.

Pressure cooking—that is, steaming food in hermetically sealed pots in which temperatures as high as 250° F. can be generated—admittedly takes less time than conventional steaming methods, but I find the procedure so tedious and mechanical that I prefer not to use it at all. Classical steaming is not only simpler but produces superior results.

The Essential Ingredient: Water

Water, either alone or as part of another liquid, is absolutely essential for boiling, poaching, and steaming. And despite the common assumption that water is simply water, its characteristics often vary from locality to locality. It can contain any of a long list of substances that may affect its quality—its "flavor"—as well as affecting the color of pots or even the color of foods. Nitrogen or phosphorus in water, for example, can badly discolor your food or pots. Although neither of these substances is at all dangerous, to avoid discoloration you can use bottled or "spring" water for boiling or poaching. Hard water contains more minerals, especially calcium and magnesium, than soft water, but these substances will have no adverse effect upon the food you cook. In fact, green vegetables cooked in hard water containing magnesium and cobalt will be more brightly colored than those cooked in softer water.

Hot water from the tap? A question that has perplexed many novice and experienced cooks alike is whether it is desirable to use hot water from the tap for cooking. The time- and fuel-saving advantages are obvious, especially if large amounts are needed for boiling or simmering; the disadvantages involve the effect of the mineral deposits that have built up in your hot-water heater. Although eminent chemists and food scientists do not offer conclusive answers either way, I prefer to play it safe and start every dish that requires boiling water with cold water from the tap.

How water behaves as it heats. "A watched pot never boils" relates more to patience than to culinary truth. Of course, a watched pot will boil, and if you watch it carefully, you will recognize from the movement of the water what the crucial terms "simmer" and "boil" really mean. In the following description of a pot of pure cold water coming to a boil over high heat, I have included the sea-level temperature of the water at each stage. The first two stages have little or no practical culinary value, but the third and fourth—simmering and boiling—are the very foundations on which every recipe in this section is built.

COLD WATER. As it begins to heat, the water at the bottom of the pot will have the appearance of slowly fizzing soda water. About 150° to 160° F.

HOT WATER. The sodalike bubbles will begin to encompass the entire mass of water in the pot. About 180° F.

SIMMERING WATER. Around the sides of the pot, the water will begin to form very small, then occasionally larger, bubbles that break and move slowly toward the center. About 202° to 205° F.

BOILING WATER. Larger and larger bubbles will form until they encompass the mass of water, which begins to churn, then to bubble and heave violently in a full boil. Precisely 212° F. No matter how fierce the heat under the pot or how actively the water boils in the pot, the temperature of the boiling water will remain the same—212° F. Raising the heat will merely make the boiling action more vigorous; it will not shorten the cooking time.

The seemingly immutable physical phenomenon of boiling described above does undergo changes, depending on your height above sea level. The temperature at which water boils lowers by about one degree F. for every 550 feet of increased altitude. Therefore, water will boil at 208° F. at 2,200 feet above sea level; at 203° F. at about 5,000 feet; at 198° F. at about 7,500 feet, and so on.

Those who live at high altitudes have no doubt already learned to increase cooking times to compensate for lower boiling temperatures (which also, of course, affect foods cooked by other methods). Less experienced cooks must gain experience and rely on my testing-for-doneness methods.

Techniques for Boiling

An uncovered pot. All the boiled dishes in this book should be cooked in an uncovered pot. Foods that are to be truly boiled are cooked in large amounts of water and require a comparatively short cooking time; the loss of liquid by evaporation from the open pot is minimal and not worth worrying about. Leaving the pot uncovered when boiling vegetables will not only help retain the original color (chlorophyll) of the vegetables, but in many cases will actually intensify their greenness. This is in marked contrast to vegetables boiled in a covered pot; the cover traps chemical gases given off by the vegetables, causing green vegetables to turn gray. That the French know this well is clearly evident from the brilliant color of the vegetables they boil.

However, there is no reason, especially if you are pressed for time, why you shouldn't cover the pot to hasten bringing the water to the boiling point.

Heat control. Boiling requires little or no heat control, except in the matter of timing. However, in a few recipes, I will indicate when to lower the heat a bit—but never so far that the water falls below the boiling point of 212° F.—to prevent fragile foods from being buffeted about too violently and possibly bruised.

Techniques for Simmering and Poaching

Heat control. Arriving at and maintaining the simmering point of water—202° to 205° F.—is a far more crucial matter than maintaining the boiling point, and it requires constant attention on your part. Short of using a thermometer, your main guide must be your eye.

All the simmering and poaching recipes require that you first bring the cooking liquid to a full boil before you lower the food into the pot. Because uncooked food will be cold, or at least at room temperature, it will lower the water temperature instantaneously. In many cases, the water will stop boiling completely. You will have to watch the pot carefully until the boiling point is approached again, then lower the heat, cover the pot if the recipe so directs, and again adjust the heat as necessary until you have established a simmer. You will be wise to check the pot every few minutes until you are sure the correct water temperature and rate of cooking are being maintained.

An occasional cooking range will refuse to maintain a heat low enough for correct simmering or poaching. If your cooking liquid is hotter and the cooking action more vigorous than it should be, use an asbestos mat, a "flame-tamer," or other similar insulating device under your pot. Or, lacking any of these, move the pot slightly to one side on the burner, watching the cooking carefully until you find a position where the pot receives just enough heat to maintain a simmer.

A partially covered pot. While it is perfectly possible to poach almost any food in an uncovered pot—indeed, poached eggs are never covered while they cook—most of my poaching recipes direct you to cover the pot partially. Setting the cover slightly askew during poaching fulfills two purposes: it allows excess steam to escape, and it enables you to maintain the liquid at the simmering point. Were you to cover the pot fully, the entrapped steam would eventually cause the liquid to boil, no matter how low the heat beneath the pot. At the same time, a lid set slightly askew allows a certain amount of steam to collect under the lid, causing drops of liquid to continually fall back into the pot; this helps cook the exposed surface of the food, especially pieces that tend to float to the top.

A poacher. I consider a fish poacher indispensable for poaching a whole fish, but it can also be used for poaching a fillet of beef, a leg of lamb, and many other foods. It is the rack that makes the poacher so invaluable. In poaching, one of the major difficulties is that certain foods float to the top as they cook. You can wrap the food in cheesecloth and tie the ends of the cloth to the handles of a deep roaster or ordinary pot, but nothing works quite so well as loosely tying a whole fish or fillet of beef to the rack itself so that the food is properly immersed in the poaching liquid.

Turning meat. In simmering, meat will almost invariably float to the top as it cooks. Although the steam caught by the cover will fall back in the form of moisture onto the meat, thus keeping it from drying out, you would be wise to turn the piece of meat every half-hour or so to make certain it cooks through evenly.

Skimming. In almost every boiling, simmering, and poaching procedure, after food has been added to the pot and boiling or simmering resumes, foam and scum will begin to rise to the surface in varying amounts, depending on the food being cooked. These substances, unattractive as they may appear, are harmless (in fact, nutritious) protein elements. You may skim them off or not, as you prefer.

In many cuisines, though by no means in all, skimming is a traditional procedure. However, aside from its aesthetic aspects— it clarifies the cooking liquid—it really serves no purpose in any of my recipes. The foam will dissolve, and the solid particles either will be dissolved by the cooking liquid or will sink harmlessly to the bottom of the pot.

If you prefer to skim, it is simple enough to do. Slide a long-handled slotted or perforated spoon under the foam and scum as they accumulate. Lift them off carefully, spoonful by spoonful, until the top of the liquid is clear.

Techniques for Steaming

Steaming, as I use the technique in this book, must be done in a tightly covered pot; it is the steam produced by the boiling water—which never touches the food—that does the cooking. Therefore, you must be absolutely certain that the pot is not only covered, but covered so securely that not even a wisp of steam escapes. If the lid of your pot is ill-fitting, you can help reinforce the seal by covering the pot with heavy-duty foil before placing the lid on top.

Meats and Chicken

The dishes for which I give recipes are firmly anchored in culinary traditions extending far back into the past. Yet it is not tradition alone that has kept them among the culinary classics; they are superlative dishes because "boiling," poaching, and steaming give them tenderness, moistness, and succulence that would be impossible to achieve by any other means. They also call for appropriate sauces and/or condiments, since while retaining their natural flavor they tend to be somewhat bland. Serving any of these foods alone is carrying simplicity too far.

These foods fall into two categories. In the first—and this includes boiled beef and poached chicken—the cooking liquid provides a full-flavored, fine stock that can be used either to moisten the food before serving or to form the base for a sauce. In the second category—corned beef and smoked tongue, for example—

the strong-flavored cooking liquid must be discarded altogether, leaving the meats stark and unadorned. I feel that these meats profit by being served with condiments, such as mustard, pickles, horseradish, or relishes of various kinds, which provide colorful and flavorful accents.

Serving Meats and Poultry

Keeping food hot. After a food has finished cooking, you may sometimes find it necessary to keep it hot before serving. Except for the rare or medium-rare fillet of beef and the poached leg of lamb, both of which must be removed from their broth lest they overcook, there is no reason why the other dishes in this section can't be kept warm for 15 or 20 minutes in their cooking liquid. Of course, you should remove the pot from the heat and keep it partially covered during that time.

Letting the meat rest. Before carving, all "boiled," simmered, or poached meats and fowl should be allowed to rest on a carving board or serving platter for the length of time each recipe directs. During cooking, collagen, a protein contained in the connective tissue of meat, softens to a gelatinous state, and this interval allows it to firm up. Firmer-textured meat and fowl will be far easier to carve than if they had been taken directly from the pot.

Leftovers. One of the major dividends of foods that have been "boiled," simmered, or poached is that there are so many ways to use leftovers. If you want to serve the food hot, the simplest way, of course, is to reserve some of the original cooking liquid and simmer the food in it only long enough to heat it through. Or, if you have turned your cooking liquid into stock (see "The Soup Pot," page 34), you can cut up the meat or chicken and add it for a heartier soup.

If, however, you prefer to eat the leftover food cold—or, more properly, at room temperature—enhance it with an appropriate sauce. Serve the chicken, for example, with freshly made Herb-Flavored Mayonnaise (page 436), the beef with Horseradish Sauce (page 437) or your choice of condiments.

Leftover meat and chicken, with skin and any sauce removed, can be cut up for a salad and dressed with either Mayonnaise (page 436) or highly seasoned Vinaigrette Sauce (page 439). Even this treatment can be improved upon by allowing the food to marinate for a few hours before serving.

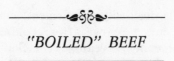

"BOILED" BEEF

In this recipe, I have specified boneless chuck as the cut of beef I prefer for "boiling." But the recipe is a generic one—that is, it can serve as a model should you prefer to use any of the following cuts of beef, which also serve 6. The amount of water to use and the cooking time will vary for the various other cuts as I have indicated; otherwise, follow the basic recipe.

Boneless chuck. Choose a piece of boneless chuck—sometimes called top chuck, middle chuck, or plate chuck—which is uniform in thickness, no less than 4 and no more than 5 inches in diameter, and weighs 3½ to 4 pounds. Whatever the cut, have the butcher tie the meat securely with string at 1-inch intervals so that it will hold its shape while simmering.

Fresh brisket. This cut is not often available in its fresh state because brisket is usually corned. However, it has distinctive qualities all its own: it is moist, grainy, and of incomparable flavor.

There are three cuts of brisket to choose from: The first cut is very lean and quite expensive; the second cut contains more fat; and the third cut is composed mainly of fat and gristle. I prefer the second cut for the flavor its fattiness gives it, but if you are most concerned with appearance, the first cut is preferable, although it tends to be dry.

Buy 3 pounds of the first cut, or 3 to 3½ pounds of the second cut, and simmer in about 3 quarts of water and 1 tablespoon of salt for approximately 3 hours for the first cut, perhaps a little longer for the second cut if it is quite thick.

Short ribs. These rib ends have robust flavor, but there is a large amount of fat and bone per pound. However, the fat and bone lend flavor to the meat; the bones can easily be removed and the fat cut away after the ribs have been cooked. Slicing the meat will be easier, too, if you don't allow the butcher to crack the bones or cut the ribs in half. Normally, each short rib is about 6 to 7 inches long, about 3 inches thick, and 2 inches wide. Buy 5 pounds and simmer in about 3 quarts of water and 1 tablespoon of salt for 1½ to 2 hours.

Rump of beef. This is decidedly the firmest, most symmetrical and manageable of beef cuts to carve after cooking, but the least desirable cut for simmering; because it lacks marbling (that is, streaks of white, firm fat running throughout the meat), its texture when cooked is far too firm and dry. You may, however, disagree and decide that the advantages of rump outweigh its disadvantages. Like the chuck, this cut should be tied at 1-inch intervals.

Buy 4 pounds and simmer it in about 4 quarts of water and 1½ tablespoons of salt for 3 to 3½ hours.

SERVES ABOUT 6

The Beef:
4 quarts water
2 tablespoons salt
3½ to 4 pounds boneless beef chuck, or another cut of your
    choice
3 large ribs celery with leaves, washed and cut crosswise in half
3 medium carrots, trimmed and scrubbed or scraped
1 medium white turnip, peeled
1 large leek, with 2 inches of green stem, split and washed
    free of sand
1 medium parsnip, scrubbed or scraped
3 medium onions, peeled
3 large cloves garlic, unpeeled
8 sprigs parsley with stems
1 medium bay leaf
1 teaspoon black peppercorns

The Garnish and Accompaniment:
Parsley sprigs
Horseradish Sauce (page 437)

Simmering the beef. Pour the water and salt into a heavy 7-quart enameled cast-iron casserole and bring to a boil over high heat. At the same time, bring water to a boil in a separate kettle and reserve, keeping it at a simmer, in case you need more liquid.

Lower the meat into the casserole and add celery, carrots, turnip, leek, parsnip, onions, garlic, parsley, bay leaf, and peppercorns.

If the water doesn't cover the meat by 2 inches, add boiling water from the kettle. Adjust the heat so that the water barely simmers. Partially cover the casserole and simmer the meat for 2 to 3 hours, depending upon its thickness. Turn the meat every half-hour or so. If at any point during simmering the liquid reduces to more than an inch below its original level, add enough boiling water from the kettle to compensate for the loss.

After 2 hours, test the meat by piercing it deeply with a long-tined fork. When the fork meets no resistance, the meat is definitely done. Simmered chuck, or any of the other cuts of beef described above, should be cooked to a well-done state but should not be over-done—overcooked "boiled" beef will shred unattractively and be almost impossible to slice.

Serving the beef. When the beef is done, transfer it to a carving board and let it rest for about 6 to 8 minutes before slicing it. Reserve the cooking liquid.

While the meat rests, warm a serving platter and plates.

If your meat has been tied during cooking, cut away the string. Carve the meat across the grain into symmetrical slices about ¼ inch thick. Arrange the slices, slightly overlapping, on the heated platter and moisten them with 2 or 3 tablespoons of the cooking liquid.

Surround the meat, if you like, with Boiled New Potatoes (page 58) intersected with sprigs of parsley, and serve it with Horse-radish Sauce.

BEEF TONGUE: SMOKED, PICKLED, OR FRESH

Europeans have long known as delicacies the freshly cooked tongues of beef, veal, pork, and lamb. In America, however, freshly cooked tongue is a comparative rarity on our tables. Admittedly, cooking a tongue is a time-consuming project. A beef tongue weighing about 4 pounds, for example, requires at least 4 hours of simmering, to say nothing of the time required to peel and trim it before serving. But I assure you that the expenditure of time and effort is more than worthwhile.

Most uncooked tongues available today are beef tongues, fresh, smoked, or pickled (these are actually salt-cured or "corned," like other cuts of beef). Pickled beef tongue, which is a light gray-pink in its uncooked state, is my favorite. It has an extraordinarily subtle flavor and unusual tenderness. Smoked tongue, a dark brownish red before cooking, is more readily available throughout the country, and for that reason I have used it in this recipe. Both types of tongue, after cooking, turn the same rich deep-red color. And, because of the intensity of flavor the particular curing process gives each type of tongue, it is a waste of time to cook either in anything but plain water.

If you prefer to simmer a pickled (corned) tongue, follow the recipe for simmering a smoked tongue, below, but simmer it for only about 3½ hours.

Fresh tongue, a deep red in its uncooked state, is something else again. When cooked, its color and texture are almost indistinguishable from those of a fine-grained cut of "boiled" beef. Not surprisingly, you should treat fresh tongue as if it were beef for boiling. A fresh beef tongue typically weighs about 4 pounds and will serve 6. Follow the preceding recipe for "Boiled" Beef and simmer it about 3½ hours.

Serve tongue with Horseradish Sauce (page 437) or a variety of prepared mustards and pickles.

SERVES ABOUT 6

3 to 5 quarts water
1 smoked beef tongue weighing 4 to 4½ pounds

Simmering the tongue. Pour 3 quarts of water into a 7-quart enameled cast-iron casserole and bring the water to a boil over high heat. At the same time, bring water to a boil in a separate kettle in case you need more liquid.

Add the tongue to the casserole; if the water doesn't cover the tongue by about 2 inches, add more boiling water from the kettle. Then adjust the heat under the pot so that the water barely simmers. Partially cover the pot and simmer the tongue for 4 to 4½ hours, turning it over every hour or so. If at any time during the simmering the liquid reduces to more than an inch below its original level, add enough boiling water to compensate for the loss.

Test the tongue after it has simmered for 4 hours, then repeat the test every 10 minutes or so until you can easily pierce the fleshiest part with a long-pronged fork. If in doubt about its doneness, continue to simmer the tongue; an undercooked tongue will be slightly tough and rubbery.

Peeling, carving, and serving the tongue. Transfer the tongue to a carving board and let it cool for about 5 minutes. Don't allow the tongue to cool too much, or you will find it difficult to peel.

Meanwhile, warm a large serving platter and plates.

With a small sharp knife, starting at the base, strip away the skin until the entire tongue is peeled. Then ruthlessly cut away and discard all the fat, bits of bone, and cartilage from the root of the tongue and trim the base as evenly as possible.

To carve the tongue, first set it firmly on its base on a carving board. With the knife held at a slight angle, begin at the tip and cut thin diagonal slices. Arrange the slices, slightly overlapping, on the heated platter, and serve at once.

POACHED FILLET OF BEEF
IN THE FRENCH MANNER

The thought of poaching an expensive fillet (tenderloin) of beef may surprise you, but cooking it in this manner gives the beef an extraordinary quality. I find a braised or roasted fillet of beef delicious but, oddly enough, too tender. I much prefer poaching a fillet because the meat has a firmer texture.

In France, this treatment is called *boeuf à la ficelle*, that is, "beef on a string." The usual method is to cradle the beef in the poaching liquid by tying the strings at each end to the handles of the pot, but, despite this ingenious device, the fillet will inevitably float to the top. To circumvent this phenomenon, I use a fish poacher equipped with a rack.

And, to protect your investment further—fillet of beef is always formidably expensive—you must use a meat thermometer. A fillet of beef poached to the rare or medium-rare stage is superb, but a well-done fillet is a disaster.

SERVES **6**

The Beef:
3-pound fillet of beef, trimmed weight, measuring no less than
    3 inches in diameter at its center
5 quarts beef stock or canned beef broth

The Garnish and Accompaniment:
1 tablespoon finely chopped fresh parsley
Béarnaise Sauce (page 432)

Preparing the fillet. Have your butcher trim the fillet of any excess fat and ask him to tie it with string, spacing the loops at about 1½-inch intervals. Using a scrupulously well-scrubbed fish poacher, securely tie the fillet to the rack of the poacher with 2 or 3 loops of string.

I prefer to use a "spot-check" thermometer in testing the fillet for doneness, but if you do not have one of these rather expensive instruments, insert a short-stemmed roasting thermometer upright into the fillet, leaving its dial above the liquid level and making sure that the tip reaches the center of the thickest part of the meat. Set the meat-laden rack aside.

Poaching the fillet. Place the poacher over two burners of your stove. Pour in the beef stock or canned broth and bring to a boil over high heat. If you have some additional stock available, bring it to a boil and keep at a simmer in a 2-quart saucepan. Or, lacking additional stock, bring water to a boil in a separate kettle and reserve, keeping it at a simmer, in case you need more cooking liquid.

Slowly lower the meat-laden rack into the boiling stock in the poacher. The liquid should cover the fillet by 1 inch or more; if it does not, add as much hot stock or water as you need.

Watch the poacher carefully. As soon as the liquid returns to the boil, lower the heat and simmer the meat, uncovered, for 25 to 35 minutes, or until your meat thermometer reaches a temperature of 120° F. If you are using a "spot-check" thermometer, test the meat for doneness after 20 minutes of poaching and continue to check every few minutes, inserting it halfway into the thickest part of the fillet. The fillet should reach the rare stage after 25 to 30 minutes of simmering.

Serving the fillet. As the end of cooking approaches, warm a serving platter and dinner plates.

Using potholders, remove the rack from the stock and hold it above the poacher for a moment or so to allow the fillet to drain. Then place the rack on a foil-lined work surface and, with a pair of scissors, cut away all the string. Reserve the stock (see "The Soup Pot," page 34, for its many uses).

Transfer the fillet to the heated serving platter and let the beef rest for 5 to 10 minutes. This will allow the meat to become slightly firmer and make slicing it easier.

You may serve the fillet in one of two ways. The first—and I consider it the better choice—is to place the meat on a board and carve it in the kitchen into slices not more than 1/4 inch thick. Arrange the slices, slightly overlapping, down the center of the warmed platter, and dust them with finely chopped parsley. Or you may dust the entire fillet with the chopped parsley and carve the beef at the table, either on its platter or, preferably, on a carving board. In either case, a perfectly poached fillet of beef demands an accompanying sauce of equal magnificence. With its rich, velvety texture and tarragon flavor a Béarnaise fulfills this requirement admirably.

POACHED LEG OF LAMB WITH DILL AND CAPER SAUCE

As an American, you may very well wonder: Why poach a leg of lamb? The English or French would never ask such a question. The French have been poaching lamb and the English have been "boiling" it for centuries.

Poached lamb—which must be cooked, as the French prefer, to the medium-rare stage (the English, alas, are hopelessly addicted to overdone lamb)—has several merits. Not the least of them is that poaching produces moist lamb with textural characteristics impossible to achieve by any other culinary method.

In this recipe, the lamb must be partially boned, making it fit more easily into a pot as well as facilitating carving. And the lamb bones themselves will be added to the poaching liquid, thus intensifying its flavor to the point where it can be used as the base for a soup as well as for the accompanying dill and caper sauce. You need not, of course, be limited to that sauce alone. Poached lamb can just as appropriately be served, as the French so often do, with a Béarnaise Sauce instead (page 432).

The Lamb:

1 untrimmed leg of lamb weighing about 6½ to 7 pounds
1 teaspoon salt (for the meat)
4 medium garlic cloves, peeled and cut in half lengthwise
4 quarts water
1 tablespoon salt (for the poaching liquid)
4 large ribs celery with leaves, washed and cut into about
    4 pieces each
4 medium carrots, trimmed and scrubbed or scraped
3 medium onions, peeled and cut in half
6 sprigs parsley with stems
½ teaspoon crumbled dried leaf thyme
1 medium bay leaf
1 tablespoon black peppercorns

The Dill and Caper Sauce:

3 cups lamb stock from the poaching liquid
3 tablespoons butter, cut into bits
4 tablespoons flour
2 egg yolks
¼ teaspoon salt
2 teaspoons white wine vinegar or cider vinegar
2 tablespoons finely cut fresh dill, or 1 tablespoon dried dill
    weed
2 tablespoons whole capers, drained in a sieve, rinsed under
    cold running water, and drained again

The Garnish:

1 tablespoon finely chopped fresh parsley or finely cut fresh dill

Preparing the lamb. Choose a leg of lamb that has not been trimmed; it should be a whole leg, with the leg and shank bones intact.

Have the lamb boned in the following fashion. Ask your butcher to remove the thin leg bone where it is attached to the shank, but don't let him remove the shank bone or crack it as is usually done. Then ask him to carefully remove the hip bone, the tail bone, and the main leg bone (the middle bone), thus creating a pocket in the upper section of the leg. If your butcher should balk at creating the pocket in this manner (which does call for some skill), resign yourself to letting him split the leg to remove the bones. In that event, you will have to reconstruct the pocket at home by sewing the split together with strong thread. The lamb bones should be saved and sawed into pieces about 2 inches long.

As a further refinement, all possible extraneous fat must be cut away from the lamb, but the thin parchmentlike covering, called the fell, should be left intact over the lean areas. Should you be concerned about the purple grade stamp on the meat (a harmless vegetable dye), you may ask the butcher to remove it, or cut it away yourself with a very sharp knife.

Using your fingers, rub the inside of the pocket with the teaspoon of salt. Then place the garlic in the pocket, scattering the pieces around. Reshape the meat by patting and molding it into its original shape and sew up the split (if there is one) and the open flaps of the pocket with strong thread. Set the lamb aside.

Preparing the poaching liquid. Pour 4 quarts of water into an oval 7-quart enameled cast-iron casserole or a thoroughly scrubbed fish poacher, add 1 tablespoon of salt, and bring to a boil over high heat, using one or two burners of your range, as necessary. At the same time, bring water to a boil in a separate kettle in case you need additional liquid.

When the poaching liquid boils, add the sawed-up lamb bones, then drop in the celery, carrots, onions, parsley sprigs, thyme, bay leaf, and peppercorns. When the liquid returns to the boil, reduce the heat to low and simmer the bones and vegetables, with the pot partially covered, for about 30 minutes.

Poaching the lamb. Carefully lower the leg of lamb, fell side up, into the pot, pushing the bones and vegetables aside with a wooden spoon. The poaching liquid should be sufficient to cover the lamb to a depth of 1 or 2 inches; if it doesn't, add more water from the simmering kettle. When the broth returns to the boil, partially cover the pot and regulate the heat so that the liquid barely simmers.

For medium-rare lamb, estimate the poaching time at 1 hour and 20 minutes. After 30 minutes of poaching, turn the lamb over, using a long-tined fork. Partially re-cover the pot and simmer the lamb for 30 minutes more, then turn the lamb back to its original position and simmer it for about 20 minutes longer. If you have kept the water at a proper simmer for the entire time, your lamb should be perfectly poached—that is, cooked to the point where its interior is still pink.

The most efficient way to test the lamb for doneness is to use a "spot-check" thermometer. After 1 hour and 10 minutes of poaching, test the lamb by inserting the thermometer stem into the center of the thickest part of the lamb. Remove the thermometer, partially re-cover the pot, and continue poaching, repeating the testing at 5-minute intervals until the dial registers 130° F.

If you insist on having your lamb well done, you will have to poach it for at least 20 minutes longer than I recommend, or until your thermometer reads 160° F.

When the lamb has been poached to your taste, place it on a carving board and let it rest for about 10 minutes. Reserve the stock and refer to "The Soup Pot" (page 34) for its many uses.

Meanwhile, warm a large serving platter, a sauceboat, and your dinner plates, and prepare the sauce.

Making the dill and caper sauce. Set a small fine-meshed sieve over a quart-size glass measuring cup and ladle enough of the lamb stock through the sieve to reach a little above the 3-cup mark. Let the stock rest for a moment or two, then tip the cup slightly and with a small spoon remove and discard as much of the surface fat as you can.

Place the butter bits in a heavy 2-quart saucepan and set it over moderate heat. When the butter has melted (don't let it brown), remove the pan from the heat; with a wooden spoon, stir in the flour to make a smooth paste, or roux. Then, stirring the roux constantly with the spoon, pour in 2½ cups of the measured lamb stock. Return the pan to moderate heat and stir the sauce with a whisk until it comes to a boil, thickens, and becomes smooth. Lower the heat and let the sauce cook slowly, stirring it occasionally, for 3 to 4 minutes to remove any taste of raw flour.

Remove the pan from the heat and beat in the egg yolks, one at a time, making sure that the first yolk is thoroughly absorbed before adding the second. Then return the pan to moderate heat and, whisking constantly, simmer the sauce for a minute or two. Do not let it boil.

Remove the sauce from the heat and add the ¼ teaspoon of salt, the vinegar, and the dill and capers. Taste for seasoning and add more salt, vinegar, or dill if you wish.

If the sauce is too thick for your taste, thin it with as much of the remaining ½ cup of stock as you wish.

Serving the lamb. You may serve the lamb in one of two ways: Present it whole, fell side up, on the heated platter, and carve it at the table, preferably on a board. Or carve the lamb in the kitchen into slices no more than ¼ inch thick, cut slightly on the diagonal, and arrange the slices, slightly overlapping, on the warmed platter.

However you serve it, dust the lamb lightly with the parsley or dill. Accompany it with a sauceboat of the dill and caper sauce.

POACHED CHICKEN WITH IVORY SAUCE

A chicken meant to be poached must be of the highest quality; it is to be so simply cooked that it must, in effect, stand on its own. Unlike a chicken masked with a distinctively seasoned sauce such as the red-wine sauce used in a coq au vin, which could conceivably disguise the flavor of an inferior bird, the poached chicken in this recipe is accompanied by a sauce of extreme delicacy. If the chicken you choose for poaching should lack flavor to begin with, the velvety sauce—based on the classic French *sauce ivoire*—will do nothing to camouflage it.

As you read this recipe you will discover that the white meat of the chicken will be added to the pot after the dark meat has been partially poached. The reason for this is simple: the white meat of a chicken takes less time to poach than the dark meat, and were you to cook them together from the start, the white meat would be overdone.

SERVES 4 TO 6

The Chicken:
3½- to 4-pound chicken
2 quarts freshly made Chicken Stock (page 36) or canned
    chicken broth
Salt (optional)

The Ivory Sauce:
2 cups chicken stock from the poaching liquid
3 tablespoons butter, cut into bits
4 tablespoons flour
1 egg yolk
¼ cup heavy cream
¼ teaspoon fresh lemon juice
⅛ teaspoon curry powder
Salt

Preparing the chicken. Have the butcher cut the chicken into 3 main sections—a single breast section and 2 leg sections—as follows: Ask him first to remove and reserve the back, then to cut the thighs from either side of the breast, using a knife, not a cleaver, and to leave the thighs attached to the drumsticks. The breast section should be left whole, with the wings attached, but the wing tips cut off and saved. The spoon-shaped breastbone should be removed to facilitate the sectioning of the breasts in the manner described below after the chicken has been poached.

Poaching the chicken. Pour 2 quarts of fresh chicken stock or canned chicken broth into a 5-quart enameled cast-iron casserole and bring it to a boil over high heat. Taste the stock and add salt if you think it needs it.

Add the back and neck, gizzard, heart, wing tips, and leg-and-thigh sections of the chicken to the casserole, then partially cover the pot and regulate the heat so that the liquid barely simmers.

Poach the pieces of chicken undisturbed for 20 minutes, keeping the liquid at a simmer. Then add the breast and, if necessary, rearrange the chicken in the casserole so that the breast section is completely immersed in the simmering stock.

Again cover the pot partially and adjust the heat so that the liquid simmers gently. Poach the chicken for about 20 minutes longer. After this time the breast should be firm but juicy, and a small sharp knife, inserted into the fleshiest part of the thigh, should meet no resistance at all.

Turn off the heat, remove the cover, and let the chicken remain in the stock to keep warm while you make the sauce.

Making the sauce. Quickly ladle enough stock from the pot to fill a 2-cup glass measuring cup to the brim. Set it aside for a moment or two. Then, with a small spoon, skim off and discard all the fat that has risen to the surface. You should have about 2 cups left. Reserve the remaining stock and see "The Soup Pot" (page 34) for its many uses.

Place the butter in the top pan of a double boiler and set the top directly over moderate heat. When the butter has melted (don't let it brown), remove the pan from the heat and with a wooden spoon stir in the flour to make a smooth paste, or roux. Then, stirring the roux constantly with a whisk, pour in 1¾ cups of the stock.

Return the pan to moderate heat and continue to whisk until the sauce comes to a boil and thickens heavily. Lower the heat until the sauce barely simmers. To remove any taste of raw flour, let the sauce cook slowly for about 5 minutes, stirring it occasionally to keep it smooth.

Meanwhile, bring about 2 inches of water to a simmer in the bottom section of the double boiler.

In a small bowl, beat the egg yolk and cream together with a whisk. When they are well combined, whisk in about ¼ cup of the hot sauce. Then pour the mixture into the simmering sauce, whisking constantly, and raise the heat to high. The sauce will come to a boil almost instantly. Let it boil for about 30 seconds, still stirring, then immediately remove the pan from the heat.

Stir in the lemon juice and curry powder, and taste for seasoning, adding as much salt as you think the sauce needs and perhaps a drop or two more of lemon juice. If the sauce is too thick for your taste, use the remaining ¼ cup of chicken stock, whisking in a tablespoonful at a time until the sauce reaches the consistency you like.

To keep the sauce hot, cover it and set the top pan into the lower section of your double boiler over low heat.

Warm a large serving platter and a sauceboat.

Serving the chicken. With tongs, transfer the chicken from the remaining broth to a carving board; discard the back, neck, and giblets, or save for another use.

Using a sharp knife, separate the legs from the thighs; separate the halves of the breast and cut each half in two diagonally. Arrange the 8 pieces of chicken, skin side up, as attractively as you can on the large heated platter.

Spoon about half the sauce over the top of the chicken pieces, masking them completely. Serve the remaining sauce separately in the warmed sauceboat.

VITELLO TONNATO

To anyone who has never tasted this delectable dish, poached veal served cold with a sauce of tuna and capers may seem a singular combination. But the flavor of the tuna is not perceptible as such in the velvety sauce, taking on another dimension entirely when combined with the other ingredients.

One of the most distinguished dishes in the Italian cuisine, Vitello Tonnato is usually served in spring or summer as a main course, but it can be served throughout the year, garnished with sliced tomatoes, scallions, hard-cooked eggs, and black olives.

You might note that an electric blender or food processor is indispensable for giving the sauce the velvety texture it must have, and that the cooling and marinating of the meat requires that the dish be made at least a day ahead.

The Veal:
3 pounds boneless veal from the rump or leg, in one solid piece
3 quarts water
1 tablespoon salt
2 large ribs celery with leaves, washed and cut crosswise in half
2 medium carrots, trimmed and scrubbed or scraped
1 large leek with 2 inches of green stem, split and washed
    free of sand
2 medium onions, peeled
2 large cloves garlic, peeled and crushed with the flat of a knife
6 sprigs parsley with stems
2 medium bay leaves
1 teaspoon black peppercorns

The Tuna Sauce:
1 egg yolk
1 can (3½ ounces) tuna fish packed in oil, preferably imported
    Italian tuna in olive oil
¾ cup olive oil
5 flat anchovy fillets, rinsed, drained, and patted dry with
    paper towels
2 tablespoons fresh lemon juice
⅛ teaspoon white pepper
⅓ to ½ cup heavy cream
3 tablespoons whole capers, drained in a sieve, rinsed under
    cold running water, and patted dry with paper towels

Preparing the veal. Your piece of boneless veal should be as solid and as symmetrical in shape as possible. Have the butcher trim off any external fat and ask him to tie the meat with string, spacing the loops at about 1-inch intervals.

Poaching the veal. Pour the water and salt into a 7-quart enameled cast-iron casserole and, over high heat, bring the water to a boil. At the same time, bring water to a boil in a separate kettle in the event you need additional liquid.

Lower the veal into the casserole and add the celery, carrots, leek, onions, garlic, parsley sprigs, bay leaves, and peppercorns.

When the liquid returns to the boil, reduce the heat at once, partially cover the casserole, and adjust the heat so the water barely simmers. Then poach the veal for about 1½ hours; it may require 10 minutes, more or less, depending on its diameter.

Turn the veal over every half-hour or so to make sure it

poaches evenly. If at any point during the poaching the liquid reduces to more than an inch below its original level, add enough boiling water from the kettle to make up the difference.

After 1 hour and 15 minutes of poaching, begin to test the veal every few minutes by piercing it deeply with a long-tined fork. When the fork meets no resistance, the veal is done.

Turn off the heat, remove the cover, and let the veal cool in the casserole to room temperature. Then remove the veal from the stock, pat it dry with paper towels, wrap it in plastic wrap, and refrigerate it for at least 6 hours, or until it is thoroughly chilled. Reserve the poaching liquid, which has now become a white veal stock, and see "The Soup Pot" (page 34) for some of its uses.

Making the tuna sauce. Drop the egg yolk into the container of your electric blender or food processor and add the broken-up tuna fish and its oil, the olive oil, the anchovy fillets, the lemon juice, the white pepper, and ⅓ cup of the heavy cream, reserving the rest.

Cover the container and process at high speed for about 30 seconds in a blender or about 5 seconds in a food processor, using an on/off motion. Scrape down the sides of the container with a rubber spatula, re-cover, and process again, as above. Be careful not to overblend the sauce or it will liquefy instead of becoming a thick, smooth purée.

Pour the sauce into a glass or stainless steel mixing bowl. If the sauce seems too thick—it should flow off the spoon fairly easily —thin it with some or all of the remaining cream, beating the cream in by the tablespoonful until the sauce reaches the desired consistency.

Now stir in the capers and taste the sauce for seasoning. Add salt if you think it needs it, and more pepper and lemon juice if you like.

Cover the bowl with plastic wrap and refrigerate the sauce until you are ready to use it.

Assembling and serving the veal. Remove the strings from the chilled veal. Then, with a large sharp knife, cut the veal into slices about ¼ inch thick and trim off any fat or gristle.

Arrange the slices, not overlapping them, on a large platter. Spoon the sauce over the veal, spreading it with a rubber spatula to mask each slice completely. Then cover with plastic wrap and refrigerate it for at least 8 hours, or as long as overnight, before serving. In this way, the veal has a chance to marinate in the sauce.

The Soup Pot

Volumes have been written on the subject of soups. It is not my intention to traverse that same territory in the recipes in this section, or to involve you in the subtleties of sophisticated and classical soups. Instead, I hope to provide a basic concept of how to make fairly simple soups, using chicken, beef, lamb, and veal stocks. The possible variations of these soups are endless.

Making a stock. The culinary cornerstones upon which most soups and many sauces are constructed are known, more or less interchangeably, as stocks and broths, and you can make them in a number of ways. A stock can be made from scratch, as is the Chicken Stock on page 36, in which the less expensive parts of the bird (or parts not needed for other chicken recipes), together with appropriate vegetables and seasonings, are simmered in water to achieve a rich, full-flavored base for soups or sauces.

A stock can also be a dividend, as it were, from cooking large pieces of meat in aromatically flavored liquid, as in such dishes as "Boiled" Beef (page 19), Poached Leg of Lamb (page 25), or the poached veal of Vitello Tonnato (page 31).

It is also easy enough to make a beef, veal, or lamb stock without cooking a large cut of meat. Use the same ingredients, procedures, and timing as you would for "Boiled" Beef, poached lamb, or poached veal, but instead of the main-dish meats that are described in the original recipe, substitute approximately 2 pounds of any inexpensive cut of meat, such as shin, plate, chuck, or short ribs (of beef); shanks or neck (lamb); shoulder or knuckles (veal), together with at least 3 pounds of bones.

Straining and degreasing stock. However you have arrived at your stock, strain and degrease it before using it. To strain a stock effectively, remove the large pieces of meat, fowl, or bones, then pour all the liquid and the vegetables or herbs into a large, fine-meshed sieve set over a large bowl. With the back of a large spoon,

34

press down hard on the vegetables to extract their liquid before throwing the pulp away. Now degrease the stock in one of two ways:

The first way is to let the stock rest for 5 to 10 minutes to allow the fat to rise to the top. Then tilt the bowl slightly and, with a large spoon, skim off and discard as much of the surface fat as you can.

The second way—and the one I prefer—is to refrigerate the stock without skimming it until the fat rises to the top. After about 5 or 6 hours, the fat will solidify into an airtight seal over the liquid beneath; it can remain in place until you wish to use the stock. If the stock was made of lamb, veal, or beef, the fat will be so rigid that you can remove it in large pieces with a spoon or your fingers. Chicken fat will have a softer consistency, and you will have to remove it carefully with a spoon.

Reducing stock. If your stock lacks sufficient flavor after it has been strained and degreased, you can reduce it to give it more character. To do this, boil the stock rapidly in an uncovered pot, thus intensifying the flavor by evaporation alone. Naturally, the longer you boil stock the more evaporation will occur. You would be wise to taste the stock from time to time until it reaches the concentration you want.

Storing or freezing stock. If you do not plan to use stock immediately and want to refrigerate it, strain it but do not degrease it. Allow it to cool uncovered, then refrigerate it. It will keep safely in the refrigerator, under its airtight seal of fat, for at least 3 or 4 days.

To prepare stock for freezing, strain, cool, *and* degrease it. Then pour it into freezing containers, cover it securely, and freeze it. Stock may be kept in this state for up to 3 months at a temperature below 0° F.

Canned broths. When you are pressed for time and require a base for a soup or sauce, or a flavorful cooking liquid for such dishes as Poached Fillet of Beef or Poached Chicken, canned broths will do. (Beef broth is sometimes labeled "beef bouillon.") Always remove and discard the clumps of fat usually floating on top of canned broths. And if you buy the condensed type of broth, make certain you dilute it with an equal amount of water, or it will be far too salty and strong.

I must caution you not to use canned beef or chicken consommé in place of stock or broth. Consommés usually contain added gelatin and are often unpleasantly sweet in flavor.

CHICKEN STOCK

Apart from its uses in poaching and saucemaking, this chicken stock can in minutes be transformed into interesting and delicate soups. When you have any suitable leftover vegetables, add them, singly or in combination, to simmering stock, letting them cook only long enough to heat through. Just before serving, embellish the soup by sprinkling it with any chopped fresh herbs you have at hand.

MAKES ABOUT 2 QUARTS

3 pounds chicken parts (necks, backs, wing tips, gizzards, and hearts)
3 quarts water
1 tablespoon salt
2 medium onions, peeled and quartered
1 large leek with 2 inches of green stem, split and washed free of sand
2 medium carrots, trimmed and scrubbed or scraped, and cut into 2-inch pieces
Leafy tops of 2 ribs celery
6 sprigs parsley with stems
½ teaspoon crumbled dried leaf thyme
¼ teaspoon whole black peppercorns

Preparing the chicken. In addition to the chicken parts specified above, you can use any cooked or uncooked pieces of chicken you may have at hand or in your freezer, as well as the frame of the chicken. (Cooked chicken should have the skin removed.) A preponderance of backs and wings will produce a stock of finer flavor than the choicer portions will.

Whatever parts you use, place them in a sieve and wash them thoroughly under cold running water. This is a necessary departure from my usual admonition not to wash chicken; when you are using chicken pieces, there may be bone splinters or other unwanted bits clinging to the meat.

Making the stock. Pour the water into a 5-quart enameled cast-iron casserole, add salt, and bring to a boil over high heat. Then add the chicken parts, onions, leek, carrots, celery tops, parsley sprigs, thyme, and peppercorns.

When the water returns to the boil, reduce the heat, partially cover the pot, and adjust the heat to allow the stock to simmer undisturbed for about 1 hour. Remove the cover, and simmer the stock for another 30 minutes; this will reduce the liquid and intensify its flavor.

At the end of 1½ hours of simmering, the chicken parts will be soft, as will all the vegetables, and the stock should have a light, delicate chicken flavor. If, at this point, the taste of the stock pleases you, simply turn off the heat. However, if you want a more robust flavor, simmer the stock, uncovered, for another 15 minutes or so.

Straining and degreasing the stock. Follow the procedures for straining and degreasing stock that are described on pages 34–35. You can now use the stock in any way you wish, or store it in the refrigerator or freezer.

VEGETABLE SOUP: A BASIC RECIPE

As you read this recipe for Vegetable Soup, you will notice that I offer you a choice of stocks to use. I have done this deliberately, because the recipe is essentially a generic one; it can be used as a reliable model for other soups. Veal stock, because of its delicate flavor, can be combined with beef, lamb, or chicken stock in any proportions you like and used in any of the recipes that follow.

If you use lamb stock, the soup becomes a traditional Scotch Broth; or, by using beef stock and substituting pastas or grains for the barley, you can easily create A Version of Italian Minestrone. Chicken stock, naturally, is the base for American Chicken, Rice, and Vegetable Soup. I have given basic directions for these soups following the Vegetable Soup recipe, but you should consider them only a beginning. Once you understand the simplicity of the procedures involved, you can freely improvise many distinctive soups of your own.

SERVES 4 TO 6

2 quarts chicken, beef, or lamb stock, strained and degreased
1/3 cup quick-cooking pearl barley
2 medium onions, peeled and coarsely chopped (about 3/4 cup)
1 medium carrot, trimmed, scraped, and cut into 1/4-inch dice
    (about 1/2 cup)
2 medium white turnips, peeled and cut into 1/4-inch dice
    (about 3/4 cup)
1 large leek, white part only, split, washed free of sand, and
    thinly sliced
1 large rib celery with leaves, coarsely chopped (about 1/2 cup)
Salt
Freshly ground black pepper
2 tablespoons finely chopped fresh parsley

Cooking the barley. Pour the stock of your choice into a 5-quart enameled cast-iron casserole and bring it to a boil over high heat. Add the barley to the boiling stock, partially cover the pot, and adjust the heat to allow the stock to simmer. Simmer undisturbed for 30 minutes.

Making the soup. Raise the heat to high and add to the simmering stock the onions, carrot, turnips, leek, and celery. When the stock has begun to boil again, partially cover the pot and adjust the heat so that the soup returns to a simmer.

The vegetables should be tender and fully cooked after they have simmered for about 30 minutes, but you would be wise to test them after 25 minutes to make sure that they are not being overcooked.

You will probably discover that the soup needs no salt if the stock you have used was fully seasoned at the start. However, if you like, add salt and a few grindings of pepper to your taste.

Serving the soup. You may serve the soup directly from its casserole or from a large heated tureen. In either case, sprinkle the soup with the chopped parsley just before serving.

VARIATION: SCOTCH BROTH

SERVES 4 TO 6

Follow the preceding Vegetable Soup recipe precisely, but use lamb stock. If you have any leftover lamb, trim it of all fat and gristle, cut it into ½-inch dice, and add as much as you like to the finished soup. Simmer the soup for 5 minutes after adding the lamb to heat it through.

VARIATION: A VERSION OF
ITALIAN MINESTRONE

SERVES 4 TO 6

Use beef stock or a combination of beef and veal stock, if you have it; omit the barley; and simmer the soup with the vegetables listed in the Vegetable Soup recipe (page 37).

Five minutes or so before the soup is done, stir in ½ to 1 cup of fully cooked pasta of any kind and simmer the soup 5 minutes longer to heat the pasta through.

Serve the minestrone with freshly grated Parmesan cheese.

VARIATION: CHICKEN, RICE,
AND VEGETABLE SOUP

SERVES 4 TO 6

Follow the recipe for Vegetable Soup (page 37) but use chicken stock (or part chicken and part veal stock) and omit the barley. Add the vegetables listed in the Vegetable Soup recipe, then add ¼ cup uncooked rice as well. Simmer until the rice is done.

Fish and Shellfish

What is more reasonable than to cook shellfish and fish in their natural element, water? Certainly, New Englanders understand this when they use the water of the sea itself to boil huge pots of lobsters, or when they employ steaming (as I do in my recipe for steamed fish fillets) for their traditional clambakes.

Recognizing both these affinities of seafood—for water and for salt—is precisely what I have done when I boil lobsters and shrimp and poach a whole fish in water almost as heavily salted as the sea. Nothing preserves the purity of flavor of thick-shelled lobsters, thin-shelled shrimp, or delicate-skinned fish as well as boiling or poaching them in this fashion.

The French always poach fish in what they call a court bouillon, an aromatic, quickly made broth composed of water, vegetables, seasonings, and sometimes wine. I never use a court bouillon when I poach fish unless I intend to use the broth as the base of a soup or sauce; I find the exquisite flavor of a truly fresh fish somewhat muted, rather than enhanced, by a court bouillon.

BOILED SHRIMP: HOT OR COLD

Plain boiled shrimp are seldom served hot, straight from the pot. There is no reason why they shouldn't be—in fact, a somewhat original first course might be hot boiled shrimp served as you would lobsters, accompanied by wedges of lemon and separate bowls of hot melted butter. Or, in place of the butter, you might serve a rich Hollandaise or Béarnaise sauce (pages 430 and 432).

Americans have a decided preference for chilled boiled shrimp served with a sauce—a sauce usually made of ketchup liberally spiked with horseradish and other spicy condiments. I find ketchup

40

sauce, however skillfully made, a most unfortunate choice because it masks the delicacy and special flavor of the shrimp. A far better alternative is to accompany chilled shrimp with freshly made mayonnaise, either plain or seasoned with herbs, or with a tuna sauce.

But in whatever manner you choose to serve your shrimp—hot or cold—you must know how to boil them properly. I do not believe in flavoring the water for boiling shrimp with anything but salt and white vinegar. The salt accentuates the natural flavor of the shrimp, and the vinegar eliminates any fishy odor. Because boiling shrimp is so rapid a process, I feel that using any other seasonings, whatever they may be, are a waste of time and materials; only salt is potent enough to penetrate the shrimp, and the amount I use may seem inordinate to you when you first read the recipe. I would suggest that you boil a batch of shrimp with the amount of salt I recommend, and then, if you are daring, that you cook shrimp another time with double the amount of salt and compare the flavor. If the truth be known, that is what I personally do.

SERVES 4 TO 6

The Shrimp:
1½ pounds medium shrimp, preferably fresh; if frozen, thoroughly defrosted
3 quarts water
2 tablespoons distilled white vinegar
3 tablespoons salt

Accompaniments for Hot Shrimp:
½ pound (2 quarter-pound sticks) hot melted butter, preferably clarified
Lemon quarters

Accompaniments for Cold Shrimp:
Shredded lettuce
Mayonnaise (page 436), Herb-Flavored Mayonnaise (page 436), or the tuna sauce of Vitello Tonnato (page 31)

Preparing the shrimp. There are two ways you may shell the shrimp. You may either remove the shells of the shrimp with your fingers or by prying with a small knife, leaving the tail and the segment of shell next to it intact; or you may remove all the shell, including the tail. The first way, to my mind, is more attractive for boiled whole shrimp to be served hot or cold.

Once you have shelled the shrimp, make a shallow incision all along the outer curve of each one with a small sharp knife or a pair of small scissors. Use the point of the knife to lift out the intestinal vein that runs the length of the shrimp's body about ⅛ inch under the surface. (Depending upon the kind of shrimp, the veins will be black, white, or yellow.)

Rinse each shrimp under cold water; because they are extremely perishable in their raw state, refrigerate them if you do not wish to boil them at once.

Boiling the shrimp. Pour the water into a 5-quart enameled cast-iron casserole, add the vinegar and salt, and bring the water to a full boil over high heat.

Handful by handful, drop the shrimp into the pot; the boiling action of the water will drop momentarily, then almost immediately resurge. When it does, foam may also appear. Should the foam threaten to overflow the pot, immediately lower the heat and it will subside at once. Then raise the heat again and boil the shrimp undisturbed for 3 to 4 minutes, depending upon their size; they should be pink and firm to the touch. If you are in doubt as to their doneness, cut one in half; the flesh should be opaque, not glossy.

Serving the shrimp hot. The moment the shrimp are done, drain them in a large sieve or colander and serve them at once, accompanied by wedges of lemon and individual dishes of hot melted butter.

Serving the shrimp cold. If you prefer the shrimp cold, let them come to room temperature after draining, spread them out on a platter, cover the platter with plastic wrap, and refrigerate them until they are thoroughly chilled.

Serve the shrimp in shrimp-cocktail glasses or in small bowls on a bed of shredded lettuce, accompanied by your choice of the listed accompaniments for cold shrimp.

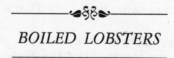

BOILED LOBSTERS

Make sure that the lobsters you buy are not only alive but lively. However, do not attempt to keep the lobsters alive by placing them in cold water, either from the tap or from the sea, because they will most assuredly drown. If you don't intend to boil the lobsters immediately, keep them in the coldest part of your refrigerator, loosely wrapped in a large paper bag or unwrapped in a deep box or in the crisper pan, where they may remain for a day or so with little danger of expiring. But even if they should perish, you may safely cook them within the day (despite misconceptions to the contrary) because you will know the time, the place, and the circumstances under which they met their end.

When you buy a lobster, usually the larger claw is pegged. If you still consider the lobster a fearsome creature, ask the fishman to peg the smaller claw as well. This entirely eliminates the risk of your being nipped. The lobsters are easier to handle and their claws won't tangle in the pot if you extend the two claws forward, crossing them, and tie them by looping a string firmly through and around the crossed claws. Ask your fishman to do this for you—or, if he is uncooperative, courageously do it yourself.

SERVES 4

The Lobsters:
6 quarts water
6 tablespoons salt
4 live lobsters weighing about 1¼ to 1½ pounds each

Accompaniments for Hot Lobsters:
½ to ¾ pound (2 to 3 quarter-pound sticks) hot melted butter, preferably clarified
Lemon quarters

Accompaniment for Cold Lobsters:
Mayonnaise (page 436) or Herb-Flavored Mayonnaise (page 436)

Boiling the lobsters. Pour the water into an 8-quart pot, add the salt, and bring the water to a full boil over high heat. If you are using a 9- or 10-quart pot, increase the amount of water and salt proportionately. At the same time, bring water to a boil in a separate kettle and reserve if, keeping it at a simmer.

Drop the lobsters into the pot of boiling water. The water should cover them by about 2 inches; if it does not, add boiling water from the kettle.

Time the boiling from the moment the lobsters enter the pot. Boil 1¼-pound lobsters, uncovered, for precisely 15 minutes, 1½-pound lobsters for 17 minutes.

You may discover after a few minutes of boiling that the water begins to foam and froth. Should this occur, simply lower the heat a bit until the foam subsides, but never allow the water to drop below the boiling point.

Testing for doneness. If you follow my timings precisely, your lobsters will be perfectly cooked. But if you have the slightest doubt as to their doneness, the most reliable way to test them is to use a "spot-check" thermometer.

With tongs, remove one of the lobsters from the pot and insert the tip of the thermometer through the underside into the center of the fleshiest part of the tail. A reading of 160° F. indicates that the lobster is thoroughly cooked.

When all the lobsters are done, use your tongs to place them side by side, right side up, on the largest deep platter you own and let them drain while you melt the butter, or reheat it if it has been clarified ahead of time.

Serving the lobsters hot. The most considerate way to serve lobsters to your family or guests, unless they are true adepts, is to prepare them in the kitchen in the following efficient manner:

Working as quickly as possible to prevent the lobsters from cooling too much, grasp each lobster firmly at head and tail with two small, clean kitchen towels. Holding the lobster over the platter, slowly bend the head back toward the tail until the tail, in its entirety, snaps away from the body.

Then, with a pair of scissors, cut the translucent sheath of the underside of the tail lengthwise up the middle without cutting into the meat of the tail—thus making it a simple matter for your family or guests to extract the tail meat in one piece at the table.

Snap off the large claws and crack them with a lobster cracker; or, with the sharp edge of a heavy knife, split the convex side of each claw with a swift heavy blow.

Using scissors, cut off and discard the antennae and eyes from the head of each lobster.

With the body of the lobster lying on its back, cut the underside in half lengthwise with a knife, but don't cut through the back shell. Firmly spread the body apart and remove and discard the small sac behind the eyes (despite its singular location, this is actually the stomach) and the intestinal vein attached to it, if you can find it. (If you can't, it doesn't matter a bit.) Do not, however, tamper with the delicious green or grayish-brown mass (the liver, called the tomalley) or any red clumps of coral (the eggs often found in female lobsters); simply leave them in place.

Now arrange each partitioned lobster as fancifully as you like on large individual plates and place 1 or 2 lemon quarters at the side of each. Serve the lobsters at once, accompanied by small individual dishes or cups of hot melted butter.

If you have them, small lobster forks and a nutcracker or two are invaluable aids for extracting the meat of the lobster from the tail and claws.

Serving the lobsters cold. Prepare the lobsters for serving while they are still warm, or let them cool if you wish. If you dissect them while warm in the manner described above, arrange the prepared lobsters on individual plates, let them cool completely, then cover the plates securely with plastic wrap and refrigerate them until serving time. Or, if your refrigerator space is limited, you can wrap each whole lobster (first cooled to room temperature) in plastic wrap, then refrigerate all of them until thoroughly chilled. The lobsters may then be dissected just before serving.

In either case, accompany the lobsters with a bowl of freshly made mayonnaise, either plain or seasoned with your choice of herbs.

POACHED STRIPED BASS

Because whole fish vary so in size and shape, most cooks, experienced or otherwise, find poaching them a considerable challenge. There is nothing quite so disconcerting as cutting into what you think is a fully cooked fish and finding the flesh close to the bone to be virtually raw. And even more distressing is an overcooked fish.

But both undercooking and overcooking are problems that are easily solved. It is the thickness of the body of the fish and not its length or weight that determines how long or how short a time it should be poached. Based on demonstrated fact, the Canadian Bureau of Fisheries has formulated a foolproof rule for determining the exact poaching time for a fish of any type. Without any equivocation, the Bureau recommends a poaching time of 10 minutes per inch of thickness of the fish at its fleshiest part. The timing starts the moment the poaching liquid returns to a gentle simmer after the fish has been added to the pot.

The thickness can be measured in various ways, but I have devised my own method which ensures the precision you need. Lay the fish on its side and insert a skewer directly through its fleshiest part so that the point of the skewer touches the table under the fish.

Then grasp the skewer, placing your thumb and forefinger at the exact point where it enters the body of the fish. Remove the skewer and measure the distance between the tips of thumb and finger and the point of the skewer. Then calculate the poaching time on the basis of 10 minutes per inch of skewer.

SERVES 4

The Fish:
3- to 3½-pound striped bass, scaled and eviscerated, preferably
  with head and tail left on; or a similar-sized salmon trout,
  sea bass, or any other fish of your choice
2 tablespoons salt (for the fish)
5 quarts water
5 tablespoons salt (for the water)
5 teaspoons distilled white vinegar

The Garnish:
Parsley sprigs

Sauce for Hot Poached Fish:
Hollandaise Sauce (page 430), or Béarnaise Sauce (page 432),
  or Lemon Sauce (page 434)

Sauce for Cold Poached Fish:
Mayonnaise (page 436), or Herb-Flavored Mayonnaise (page
  436), preferably freshly made

Preparing the fish. Cut a piece of cheesecloth about 10 inches longer than the fish you want to poach. Spread the cheesecloth out in a single layer. Rinse the fish thoroughly inside and out under cold running water and center it lengthwise on the cheesecloth. With the fish lying flat, determine the required cooking time, using the method of measuring with a skewer that is described in the introduction to this recipe.

With your fingers, spread 2 teaspoons of salt in the cavity of the fish, then wrap the fish securely in the cloth, leaving the ends of the cheesecloth free.

Place the fish on the rack of your fish poacher. To prevent the fish from floating to the top as it cooks, tie it loosely—never tightly, which would leave unattractive indentations on the cooked fish—to the rack with string, spacing the loops at about 2-inch intervals. Set the fish-laden rack aside.

Poaching the fish. Pour 5 quarts of water into your poacher and add 5 tablespoons of salt and the vinegar. Place the poacher over two burners of your stove and bring the water to a boil over high heat. At the same time, bring water to a boil in a separate kettle and keep it at a simmer.

Carefully lower the rack and fish into the poacher. The water should cover the fish by at least 1 inch; if necessary, add more boiling water from the kettle. When the water returns to a simmer, partially cover the pan, reduce the heat of both burners, and check and adjust the heat to allow the fish to poach undisturbed for the exact time you have estimated, starting the timing the instant the simmering resumes.

Meanwhile, if you intend to serve the fish hot, warm a large serving platter and your dinner plates.

At the end of the poaching time, remove the rack from the poacher at once, using potholders, and set it slightly askew atop the pan to allow the fish to drain for a minute or so.

Serving the fish hot. Place the preheated serving platter on your work surface. Then set the rack holding the fish parallel to the platter. Cut away the strings and carefully open the cheesecloth without disturbing the fish. Using the ends of the cheesecloth, gently lift up the cradled fish, and ever so carefully and slowly turn it onto the platter. Discard the cheesecloth.

With a small sharp knife, carefully strip off the skin from the upper side of the fish, cutting it away from the gills to the base of the tail. Surround the fish with a wreath of parsley and serve it at once with a bowl of the sauce of your choice.

At the table, use a broad-bladed serving utensil to cut the upper half of the fish crosswise into portions, but don't attempt to cut through the backbone—simply lift each serving free of the bones. When all the cut portions have been served, remove the backbone in one piece and serve the bottom half of the fish in the same fashion.

Serving the fish cold. To serve poached whole fish cold, first let the hot fish cool to room temperature on its serving platter. Then cover the platter with plastic wrap and chill the fish for 4 to 6 hours, or as long as overnight, before serving it.

Garnish the platter with parsley sprigs and accompany it with a bowl of Mayonnaise or Herb-Flavored Mayonnaise.

———— ❧§❧ ————

VARIATION: POACHED FISH STEAKS

Steaks of codfish, halibut, or salmon, cut 1 inch thick and weighing about ½ pound each, may be poached in the manner described in the preceding recipe. Using the timing method based on thickness, 1-inch steaks will require only 10 minutes' poaching time.

Be sure your poacher contains enough salted and acidulated water to cover the steaks by about 1 inch.

The steaks should be individually wrapped in cheesecloth but because they will not float to the top, it is not necessary to tie them to the rack. For that reason you needn't use a poacher at all; a 5- or 7-quart enameled cast-iron casserole will serve equally well. You can poach as many steaks at one time as your poacher or pot will accommodate in a single layer.

Serve hot or cold with the desired sauce as listed in the preceding recipe for Poached Striped Bass.

———— ❧§❧ ————

ROLLED FILLETS OF SOLE

Fillets of sole, rolled with seasonings and steamed in this rather unusual fashion, are a dish of great delicacy and visual appeal.

SERVES 4

The Fish:
1½ pounds fillets of sole, or fillets of any other white-fleshed fish, prepared as described below
3 tablespoons butter, softened at room temperature
1 teaspoon salt
¼ teaspoon white pepper (optional)
1 tablespoon finely chopped fresh parsley
2 cups water

The Sauce:
Lemon Sauce (page 434), or Hollandaise Sauce (page 430), or Béarnaise Sauce (page 432)

Preparing the fish. Ideally, the fish you buy not only should be the freshest you can find, but should be filleted before your eyes. And because they are to be rolled, the fillets should be of equal thickness and length; rolls of disparate sizes cook unevenly. Therefore, choose fillets about ⅜ inch thick and have them split lengthwise in half and trimmed to a uniform 6-inch length.

Quickly rinse the fillets under cold running water, then pat them thoroughly dry with paper towels. Lay the fillets side by side on a sheet of wax paper and, with a pastry brush, coat them lightly with 2 tablespoons of the softened butter. Sprinkle the fillets evenly on one side only with the salt and, if you like, with the white pepper. Then sprinkle the same side evenly with the chopped parsley.

Starting at the narrow tapered end, roll up each fillet loosely and secure the ends by inserting 1 or 2 toothpicks crosswise into each roll. The rolls may be steamed at once, or may be covered with plastic wrap and refrigerated for as long as 3 or 4 hours.

Steaming the fish. Pour the water into a 5-quart enameled cast-iron casserole and bring it to a full boil over high heat. Then open your folding steamer and, using a pastry brush, coat the inner surface evenly with the remaining tablespoon of softened butter.

Set the steamer into the pot over the boiling water and place the fillets upright in it, side by side. Immediately cover the pot tightly and lower the heat to moderate.

Let the fillets steam undisturbed for 5 to 6 minutes; they will then be fully cooked if you have followed my specifications precisely as to their size. These size specifications—and precise timing —are crucial because there is no other way to make sure the fish is done.

While the fillets are steaming, warm a serving platter that is just large enough to accommodate the fish rolls, and warm your dinner plates.

Serving the fish. With a small metal spatula, remove the fish rolls one at a time and arrange them side by side on the heated platter. Let them rest a moment or two, then, using a bulb baster or a crumpled paper towel, remove the liquid that will have accumulated on the platter.

Spoon enough of the sauce of your choice over each rolled fillet to cover it completely and serve the fish at once, presenting the remaining sauce in a separate bowl.

A Selection of Vegetables

Nutritionists have their own firm convictions about how to cook fresh vegetables, and not for a moment would I dispute their contention that nutrients are conserved when vegetables are cooked in as small an amount of water as possible. My own contention is that it does little good to preserve nutrients if the vegetables are unlikely to tempt a discriminating palate.

The French, who have raised the cooking of vegetables to a notable art, insist upon boiling almost all vegetables in large quantities of salted water. Ideally, I would prefer to steam almost every vegetable I cook. Steaming not only retains the highest possible percentage of the food value, but it intensifies the natural color of the vegetable. I have deliberately chosen to describe the steaming of only a few green vegetables, most of them delicate enough to require as little as 5 minutes and no more than 10 minutes of steaming. Other than cooking time, the basic procedure is the same for all steamed vegetables.

Unfortunately, steaming all vegetables—while it can be done—is impractical for the home cook. Certain vegetables (large artichokes or potatoes, for example), because of their size or density, would require either too long a steaming time or the use of restaurant-size steaming equipment.

Therefore, you will find in the following recipes that I bow to the French preference by boiling some vegetables and to my own preference by steaming others.

Preparing vegetables. Because in boiling, and especially in steaming, the quality and freshness of the vegetable are of paramount importance if you are to achieve perfection, I have included explicit directions for purchasing and preparing each kind of vegetable.

Preventing discoloration of vegetables. If you add a teaspoonful of lemon juice to each quart of water—this is called acidulating the water—for potatoes, cauliflower, or rice, discoloration will be prevented. Don't add lemon, however, when cooking green vegetables; the acid will turn them an unappetizing brown.

Intensifying the color of vegetables. Many inferior restaurants intensify the color of vegetables by adding bicarbonate of soda to the boiling water—and it does make green vegetables greener. This is an unfortunate practice at best—however advantageous it may be to a restaurant—because valuable nutritional elements are lost.

Bicarbonate of soda is entirely unnecessary for the green vegetables in this book. Properly boiled or steamed, after being prepared by the techniques described in each recipe, your green vegetables will be greener than you might expect.

Serving vegetables. Unless you intend serving at room temperature or chilled, boiled or steamed vegetables should be served immediately after they are done because there is no effective way to keep them warm without losing their characteristic texture and flavor. Furthermore, no boiled vegetable should be allowed to remain in its cooking water, or a steamed vegetable over hot water, once it is cooked to your taste. Any effort to keep vegetables hot in this fashion will result in their being soggy and overcooked.

Nor should you reheat vegetables by boiling or steaming them again. You can reheat them more creatively by adding them to soups, as described in "The Soup Pot" (page 34).

Alternatively, serve the vegetables cold or at room temperature, cut up and tossed with freshly made mayonnaise. In fact, a combination of many vegetables treated in this way has been named *salade à la Russe* by the French.

Boiled Vegetables

ARTICHOKES

Except in July and August, fresh artichokes are available throughout the year. When you buy them, search for those with tightly clustered fleshy leaves. Ideally, artichokes should be a uniform green, but those with a few brown outer leaves here and there are also acceptable, provided the base of the artichoke is firm and not pulpy and the vegetable is heavy for its size.

Artichokes are one of the most delectable of vegetables, and to my mind, boiling them is not only the simplest but the most satisfactory way to cook them. Furthermore, I firmly believe they need

nothing more than hot clarified butter and wedges of lemon to under-
line their subtle flavor. However, if you prefer a richer accompaniment, by all means substitute either Hollandaise (page 430), or
Béarnaise sauce (page 432).

Artichokes may also be served cold or at room temperature, as
you doubtlessly know. Again, they are at their best with the
simplest of dressings. The most traditional one is Vinaigrette Sauce.

There are two ways to prepare artichokes for cooking. The
first is the simplest, because the hairy choke of the artichoke is left
intact. The second way, described in detail below, involves removing
the choke. This is more time-consuming but cuts the cooking time
in half and eliminates the need for removing the choke at the table,
a complex maneuver at best.

Furthermore, the resulting hollow can hold clarified butter or
other dressings, making the vegetable itself a container for its
sauce. The same spectacular effect can be achieved with a cold artichoke by filling the center with an oil and vinegar dressing, or by
stuffing the hollow with small pieces of chopped shrimp or lobster,
mixed with a small amount of mayonnaise.

SERVES 4

The Artichokes:
4 firm artichokes weighing about 13 or 14 ounces each
½ lemon
5 quarts water
3 tablespoons salt

Accompaniments for Hot Artichokes:
Lemon wedges
½ pound (2 quarter-pound sticks) butter, clarified

Accompaniment for Cold Artichokes:
1 cup Vinaigrette Sauce (page 439)

Preparing the artichokes with choke intact. Soak the artichoke in
cold water for a half-hour or so to flush out any insect life. Then lay
each artichoke on its side and with a large sharp knife cut off the
stem flush with the base of the artichoke. Then grip the base of the
artichoke securely with one hand and, using a sawing motion of the
knife, cut about an inch off the top of the artichoke.

Snap off any small or discolored leaves. Then, with a small
pair of scissors, trim the artichoke further by cutting away the
sharp point of each remaining leaf. Rub all cut surfaces with the

lemon half to prevent the artichoke from discoloring. Position each artichoke on its base to make sure it stands upright securely; if it wobbles, trim the base as evenly as you can.

You may set the artichokes aside, unrefrigerated, for an hour or so, until you are ready to boil them.

Preparing the artichokes with choke removed. Prepare the artichokes for cooking as described above. Then, to remove the choke, proceed as follows: Spread the large leaves apart and firmly grasp the center core of small leaves with your fingers. Twist and turn the leaves until you are able to pull them out.

When the center of the artichoke has been uncovered, use a small teaspoon, or better still, a long-handled iced-tea spoon, to scrape out all the hairy choke. To make sure that no choke or small stray leaves remain, scrape the spoon around and around the bottom and sides of the hollow. Squirt a few drops of lemon juice into the opening of the artichoke, and firmly press it back into shape.

You may set the prepared artichokes aside, unrefrigerated, for an hour or two, until you are ready to boil them.

Boiling the artichokes. Pour 5 quarts of water into an 8-quart pot (any kind, except one made of aluminum), add the salt, and bring the water to a full boil over high heat.

Drop in the artichokes and, with a wooden spoon, push each one below the surface to flood their interiors with water. Even though they will bob around like corks in the water, try to keep their bases submerged as much as possible, because the base of an artichoke takes longer to cook than its top.

Let the artichokes boil uncovered for 30 to 40 minutes if whole, 15 to 20 minutes if the chokes have been removed, turning them over with a spoon every 10 minutes or so.

Start testing the artichokes for doneness after they have boiled for 15 minutes if the chokes are out, after 30 minutes if they are whole. Test by piercing the base of one artichoke with the tip of a small sharp knife. The artichoke is done when the knife meets only the slightest resistance.

Don't be dismayed by the color of the cooked artichoke; it inevitably and correctly will be a drab slightly grayish green.

Serving the artichokes hot. Remove the artichokes from the pot with tongs, or by spearing their bases with a long two-pronged fork. Place them upside down in a colander to drain for a minute or so.

Then set each artichoke upright on an individual serving plate and place a lemon quarter beside it.

Serve them at once with individual dishes of hot clarified butter, or with your choice of an accompanying sauce.

Serving the artichokes cold. Drain the artichokes as described above and let them cool to room temperature—my preference—before serving them with Vinaigrette Sauce.

You may, however, chill them for up to two days, covered securely with plastic wrap, if you like.

Eating an artichoke. The art of eating an artichoke is not universally known. With your fingers strip an outer leaf from the artichoke; it will come away easily. Holding the leaf by its top, dip the base in the butter or sauce, then draw the leaf through your teeth, concave side down, thus scraping off its delicious pulp. (Don't chew or swallow the rest of the fibrous leaf.)

Continue denuding and eating the artichoke in this fashion, laying the discarded leaves in neat overlapping circles on the plate. When you reach the choke, secure the base of the artichoke with your fork and scrape away the fibrous choke with the tip of a teaspoon. Then cut the base into bite-size pieces and dip each into the butter or sauce before eating it.

BROCCOLI

Today, most broccoli is sold in bunches. A bunch typically weighs about 2½ pounds, but the weight may vary from 1½ to 3 pounds. This bunching is a major disadvantage, for not all the tightly bunched stalks are likely to be equally firm and compact; and, even worse, a few may in fact have begun to flower. Moreover, the bottoms of some stalks may be hollow or overly fibrous. You must carefully examine each bunch of broccoli and choose the best of the lot.

Whole stalks of broccoli should never be served as an accompanying vegetable to a main dish of any kind. Broccoli is such an impressive and distinctively flavored vegetable that it has every right to stand on its own as a separate course, particularly when it is served with a sauce.

The Broccoli:

1 bunch broccoli (about 2½ pounds)

5 quarts water

2 tablespoons salt

The Accompaniments:

Lemon Sauce (page 434), or Hollandaise Sauce (page 430), or
Béarnaise Sauce (page 432), or hot clarified butter and
lemon wedges

Preparing the broccoli. With a small sharp knife, cut a ½-inch
slice off the bottom of each stalk of broccoli. Then, starting at the
base, cut into the fibrous layer about ¼ inch deep and in one continuous movement strip away the skin up to the beginning of the
stems of the flowerets. The cut at the base should be deep enough to
expose the pale-green flesh, but after you have peeled 2 or 3 inches
of the tough fibrous stalk, you will find that the skin comes off by
merely stripping, like the skin of an onion.

Continue to remove the fibrous covering from the stalk (including, if you are a perfectionist, even the skin of the stems con-
nected to the flowerets). The result will be a denuded section of
broccoli which will be deliciously edible, stalk and all.

Ideally, all the stalks in a bunch should be of about the same
thickness; and if there are any much thicker than the rest, cut them
in half lengthwise from the base straight through the floweret.

When the broccoli has been peeled, wash it thoroughly and
quickly under cold running water.

Boiling the broccoli. Pour the water into an 8-quart pot (any kind,
except one made of aluminum), add the salt, and bring the water to
a full boil over high heat.

Add the broccoli. It should be covered with water; if necessary,
rearrange the stalks with tongs until all of them are totally submerged. When the water returns to the boil, turn down the heat a
bit to prevent the water from churning too violently and bruising
the flowerets.

Boil the broccoli, undisturbed and uncovered, for about 8
minutes. Then test it for doneness by piercing the thick part of a
stalk with the tip of a small sharp knife, which should meet only
the barest resistance when the broccoli is done. Depending upon
the freshness and thickness of the broccoli, you may find it necessary to boil it a minute or two longer; but if in doubt, undercook
rather than overcook it for the most successful result.

During the last few minutes of cooking, warm a large serving platter.

Serving the broccoli. One at a time, remove the stalks of broccoli from the water by piercing them through the base with a long two-pronged fork or by grasping the base with tongs. Hold each stalk over the pot for a few seconds to drain, then place the broccoli on the heated platter. Some additional water will collect in the platter in a matter of seconds. Tip the platter slightly and siphon off the liquid with a bulb baster, or blot it up with a crumpled paper towel.

Serve the broccoli at once with any of the suggested sauces.

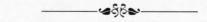

A REMOLDED HEAD OF CAULIFLOWER

Boiled cauliflower is not generally considered the most glamorous of vegetables, particularly as it is served in most American households today. Yet, when it is properly cooked and dramatically served, it can become a dish of considerable importance.

Contributing to the ignominious rank cauliflower occupies among our vegetables is the fact that it is generally cooked whole, with the consequence that the outside is almost always overdone while the inside of the head is too firm. Obviously, the way to avoid this is to separate the cauliflower into flowerets before cooking.

A great French cookbook writer of the late nineteenth century, Madame Saint-Ange, devised an ingenious method for remolding these flowerets after they are cooked so that the cauliflower looks almost precisely as it did in its original compact state. Among the many advantages of this extraordinary method is that the cauliflower may be cooked and left in its mold, ready to be reheated, hours before you plan to serve it.

Should you wish to serve the molded head of cauliflower cold —and it makes a most impressive display on a buffet—you may unmold it soon after it is cooked. Then refrigerate the cauliflower and serve it thoroughly chilled. It may at that point be moistened with Vinaigrette Sauce (page 439) to which you may add coarsely chopped pimientos; rinsed, drained, and dried capers; thinly sliced black olives; and a tablespoon or so of chopped parsley. Or, taking off from there, you may exercise your creative ingenuity to any extent you like.

As for the quality of the vegetable, buy only cauliflower of a uniform creamy color. The knobby head should be firm, with tightly clustered flowerets. The leaves at the base should be a good healthy green and have no perceptible odor.

SERVES 4 TO 6

1 large or 2 small heads cauliflower weighing 2 to 2½ pounds in all
5 quarts water
2 tablespoons salt (for the cooking water)
1½ cups milk or 2 tablespoons fresh lemon juice (optional)
½ teaspoon salt (for the cooked cauliflower)
¼ pound (1 stick) hot melted butter, preferably clarified

Preparing the cauliflower. With a small sharp knife, trim away the green leaves from the base of the cauliflower. Then cut off the stem at the base of the head. Break the cauliflower into clusters, more or less the same size, leaving the short stems attached, and quickly rinse the flowerets in a colander set under cold running water.

Boiling the cauliflower. Pour the water into a 7-quart enameled cast-iron casserole and add 2 tablespoons of salt. If you want the cooked cauliflower to be dazzlingly white, add either the milk or the lemon juice to the water. Bring to a full boil over high heat.

Drop in all the cauliflower and, when the water returns to the boil, cook it, uncovered, for 8 to 10 minutes, or until a stem, when pierced with the tip of a small sharp knife, offers only the barest resistance.

Serving the cauliflower. When the cauliflower is done, drain it immediately in a large colander. Spread the flowerets out on a kitchen towel or on two or three layers of paper towels to drain further, then sprinkle them evenly with ½ teaspoon of salt.

There are two ways you can serve the cauliflower:

THE SIMPLE METHOD. After the cauliflower has been seasoned, serve it at once in a heated deep serving bowl, tossing it gently with as much hot melted butter as you like.

THE MOLDED METHOD. Place the largest floweret, stem up, in the center of a warmed, curved-sided 1-quart glass bowl. Place the other large flowerets around it, stems up, as close together as possible, saving the smallest pieces. When the bowl has been lined with flowerets, fill the bowl to slightly above its rim with the remaining pieces, stems downward, so that the cauliflower has a reasonably level surface.

Over the cauliflower immediately invert a heated round serving platter that is 2 inches larger in diameter than the bowl. Using both hands, press firmly on the platter to force the cauliflower into a compact mass in the bowl. Then, grasping bowl and platter together, carefully invert them. Insert the tip of a small knife between the rim of the bowl and the platter and gently raise the bowl until you can put your fingers beneath it. Then, ever so gently, remove the bowl, leaving the seemingly intact head of cauliflower on the plate.

Pour as much of the hot butter as you like over the cauliflower and serve it at once, either alone in its glory or as the accompaniment to any main dish.

Reheating a molded head of cauliflower. You may, if you like, cook and mold the cauliflower as much as 6 hours before serving it and then reheat it, but in this case you must use a heatproof glass bowl.

Proceed as directed above until the bowl has been filled. Then allow the cauliflower to cool. Cover the bowl securely with aluminum foil and set it aside, unrefrigerated, for up to 6 hours.

About 10 minutes before you plan to serve the cauliflower, set the foil-covered bowl in a 5-quart enameled cast-iron casserole and pour enough boiling water around it to come halfway up the sides of the bowl. Cover the casserole tightly and, over moderate heat, simmer for about 10 minutes, or until the cauliflower is heated through. Remove the bowl from the water, wipe it dry, then unmold the cauliflower as described above.

BOILED NEW POTATOES

New potatoes—not a specific type, as you might suppose, but any variety of potato harvested when young—are comparatively low in starch content and are easily identifiable by their size. They usually range from 1 to 3 inches in diameter. Because they remain intact after cooking, they are my preference for serving whenever boiled potatoes are appropriate with any of the main-course dishes in this section. They are superb served in ther jackets, glistening with butter and sprinkled with coarse salt.

SERVES 4

3 quarts water

1 tablespoon salt

12 new potatoes and 1 extra for testing, all about 2 to 2½ inches in diameter, thoroughly scrubbed with a stiff brush under running water

Boiling the potatoes. Pour the water into a 4-quart saucepan, add the salt, and bring it to a full boil over high heat.

Drop in the scrubbed potatoes. When the water returns to the boil, lower the heat a bit so that the water continues to boil actively, yet not so vigorously as to buffet the potatoes about.

Depending upon the size of the potatoes, they should be fully cooked in 15 to 20 minutes. Test for doneness after 15 minutes by piercing the center of one potato with a thin skewer. Should the skewer meet decided resistance, boil the potatoes longer.

When you are reasonably sure the potatoes are done, remove the expendable testing potato with a slotted spoon and cut it open. It should be a uniform texture throughout, neither too firm nor too soft.

Serving the potatoes. Drain the potatoes immediately in a colander. Their skins will dry in seconds. Serve them at once as they are; or you may, as I often do, toss them with hot melted butter and coarse salt, using as much of each as you like.

I never consider peeling tiny new potatoes either before or after cooking them. Not only do I enjoy the flavor and texture of the delicate young skin, but the skin helps to keep the potatoes hot.

MASHED POTATOES

Potatoes to be mashed should be of the "baking" type; fortunately, they can be of any size or shape. Baking varieties are fairly easy to select, because they are identified as such in most supermarkets. The high starch content of baking potatoes ensures that they will have a moist, silky sheen after they are mashed with butter, milk, and cream as my recipe directs.

The Potatoes:

2 pounds baking potatoes (about 5 medium potatoes), all about
the same size, scrubbed with a stiff brush under running
water

3 quarts water

1 tablespoon salt (for the cooking water)

4 tablespoons butter, softened at room temperature

½ cup hot milk

4 to 6 tablespoons heavy cream, heated to lukewarm

Salt (for the cooked potatoes)

The Garnish (optional):

1 tablespoon finely cut fresh dill, chives, or parsley

Preparing the potatoes. If you are going to mash the potatoes with
a food mill, a potato masher, a fork, or an electric beater, you must
peel them before cooking. If you use a potato ricer, however, there is
no need to peel the potatoes because during the ricing the skins of
the potatoes are entrapped within the ricer itself, and only the
pulp of the potato is forced through as a smooth purée.

Boiling the potatoes. Pour the water into a 4-quart saucepan, add 1
tablespoon of salt, and bring to a full boil over high heat.

Drop in the scrubbed potatoes and boil them for 20 to 30
minutes, the exact time depending upon their size. At the end of
20 minutes, test them for doneness by piercing the center of a
potato with a long skewer. If it meets any resistance, boil the potatoes until the point of the skewer goes through easily.

Immediately pour the potatoes and their cooking water into a
colander set over a large mixing bowl. Remove the colander and
quickly drain and dry the now heated mixing bowl; and just as
quickly, cut the potatoes into quarters on a cutting board.

Warm a serving bowl.

Mashing the potatoes. Fill the ricer with as many potato quarters
as it will hold and force the pulp into the hot bowl. Then, with a
spoon, remove the peel adhering to the interior of the ricer and
purée the remaining potatoes. Or, lacking a ricer, mash the potato
quarters in the mixing bowl with a potato masher, a fork, or an
electric beater, or force them through a food mill into the mixing
bowl.

With a large wooden spoon, beat the butter into the potatoes.
Still beating vigorously, pour in the hot milk in a slow thin stream.

Beat in the cream a tablespoonful at a time, using as much as you need to give the potatoes the consistency you like. Taste for seasoning; the potatoes will probably need more salt.

Serving the potatoes. Transfer the potatoes to the heated serving bowl and serve them at once.

You may, if you like, sprinkle the potatoes with any finely chopped herb. Fresh dill and chives are among the ones I prefer.

Steamed Vegetables

ASPARAGUS

The thickness of asparagus spears varies enormously, and to ensure uniform steaming, all the spears should be of approximately the same diameter at the base. For that reason alone, don't be seduced into buying neat bundles of tied asparagus; the variations in size are usually too great. Furthermore, although many of the tips will be tightly closed, as they should be, often others will be undesirably open. Therefore, I suggest that you buy asparagus by the pound, choosing the spears individually.

SERVES 4

The Asparagus:
2½ to 3 pounds asparagus of uniform thickness
(about ½ to ¾ inch thick at the base)
1 teaspoon salt
2 cups water

The Accompaniments:
4 to 8 tablespoons hot melted butter and lemon quarters, or Hollandaise Sauce (page 430), or Béarnaise Sauce (page 432), or Lemon Sauce (page 434)

Preparing the asparagus. Lay the asparagus on a chopping board and, using a very sharp knife, cut off the bases so that each spear is about 6 inches long. Then, with a swivel-bladed vegetable peeler, peel the asparagus as deeply as you can, starting the peeling just below the tip and continuing down the length of the stalk. When you have finished, each stalk should be denuded, its pale-green color contrasting with the untouched tip of darker green.

Wash the asparagus under cold running water to rid the tips of any hidden sand. Then sprinkle them evenly with the salt.

Steaming the asparagus. Pour the water into a round 5-quart enameled cast-iron casserole and set your steamer in the pot. Bring the water to a full boil.

Arrange the asparagus in the steamer in layers. Cover the casserole, lower the heat to moderate, and steam the spears for 10 minutes.

Then test the asparagus for the doneness you prefer by piercing the base of a spear with the tip of a small sharp knife. Ideally, the knife should meet only the barest resistance; if the base seems too firm, re-cover the pot and steam the asparagus 1 or 2 minutes longer, or until it is as well cooked as you like.

Shortly before the end of cooking, warm a serving platter.

Serving the asparagus. With tongs, transfer the asparagus to the heated platter. Pour as much of the melted butter as you like over the asparagus and garnish the platter with lemon wedges. Alternatively, you may serve any of the suggested sauces in a separate bowl.

BUTTERED BRUSSELS SPROUTS

Buy only sprouts that are fully green, compact, unblemished, and of uniform size. If they are not uniform in size, the small sprouts will be done sooner than the larger ones and will, consequently, be overcooked.

SERVES 4

1 pound Brussels sprouts
½ teaspoon salt
2 cups water
4 tablespoons hot melted butter

Preparing the Brussels sprouts. With a small sharp knife, cut a thin slice from the base of each sprout and remove any wayward leaves that are not firmly attached to the sprout. To ensure even steaming, make a small, deep cross in the fibrous core of each sprout.

Drop the sprouts into a colander, run cold water over them, then let them drain.

Transfer the sprouts to a bowl, add the salt, and toss them about to season them evenly.

Steaming the Brussels sprouts. Pour the water into a 5-quart enameled cast-iron casserole and set your steamer in the pot. Bring the water to a full boil.

Distribute the sprouts evenly in the steamer, cover the casserole tightly, and lower the heat to moderate. Steam the sprouts for 8 minutes, then test them for doneness by piercing one with the tip of a small sharp knife. Steam them a moment or two longer if the sprout seems too firm. Ideally, however, they should be steamed only to the point where they retain more than a hint of their original firmness. Oversteaming will dull their brilliant green color, to say nothing of producing an unpleasant odor like that of overcooked cabbage.

Shortly before the steaming is finished, warm a deep serving bowl.

Serving the sprouts. With a slotted spoon, transfer the sprouts to the warmed serving bowl, pour the hot butter over them, and toss the sprouts lightly and gently about with the spoon until each sprout is thoroughly coated. Serve at once.

CABBAGE QUARTERS WITH SOUR CREAM AND NUTMEG

Choose a crisp, firm, compact head of cabbage, avoiding any heads that show even a hint of yellow discoloraion.

SERVES 4

The Cabbage:
2-pound head green cabbage
1 teaspoon salt
2 cups water

The Accompaniments:
½ pint sour cream
¼ teaspoon nutmeg, preferably freshly grated

Preparing the cabbage. Remove and discard all loose or coarse outer leaves of the cabbage and, with a sharp knife, cut off the stem flush with the base of the head. Cut the cabbage vertically in half. Lay each half, cut side down, on a chopping board, then cut the halves lengthwise to make 4 quarters. Carefully slice off most of the hard core from each quarter, leaving only enough core to hold the leaves together.

Place the cabbage in a colander and briefly run cold water over the quarters to moisten them lightly; this extra moisture is desirable for steaming cabbage in large wedges. Sprinkle the quarters with the salt.

Steaming the cabbage. Pour the water into a round 5-quart enameled cast-iron casserole and set your steamer in the pot. Bring the water to a full boil.

Arrange the cabbage quarters, cut side up, in the steamer, cover the casserole, and lower the heat to moderate. Steam the cabbage for 5 minutes, or until it seems somewhat tender but still shows some resistance when pierced with the tip of a small sharp knife. It is important not to oversteam the cabbage, lest it lose its glistening green color and turn gray and unattractive. Moreover, oversteaming will produce an unpleasant odor, while properly steamed cabbage will smell green and fresh.

While the cabbage steams, warm a serving platter.

Serving the cabbage. With tongs, transfer the cabbage quarters to the heated platter. Drop 2 tablespoons of the sour cream onto each cabbage quarter, then sprinkle the cream with nutmeg.

SPINACH WITH PINE NUTS

Most spinach today is sold packed in cellophane bags. Although it has presumably been washed before packing, I have never found it to be totally free of sand. If you can find loose young spinach—that is, spinach with small delicate leaves rather than coarse large ones—buy it by all means.

The Spinach:
1 pound fresh spinach
1/2 teaspoon salt
2 cups water

The Sauce:
4 tablespoons butter, softened at room temperature
2 tablespoons pine nuts (*pignoli*)

Preparing the spinach. A quick and easy way to stem spinach is to lay a few spinach leaves in one hand with the undersides up, then fold the leaves over. Holding the folded spinach leaves firmly, grasp the stems with the other hand and, with a short, quick jerk, pull the stems out; or use a small sharp knife to cut off any knobby ends and overly thick stems. Then fill your largest mixing bowl—or better yet, a sink basin or dishpan—with cold water and drop in the spinach. Stir the leaves gently in the water to dislodge any sand. When you are certain the spinach is thoroughly clean, drain it in a colander. Sprinkle it with the salt, tossing the leaves about with your hands to season them evenly.

Steaming the spinach. Pour the water into a round 5-quart enameled cast-iron casserole and set your steamer in the pot. Bring the water to a boil.

Transfer the spinach to the steamer; if it rises above the top of the pot, simply press down hard on the pot cover to prevent any steam from escaping. The spinach will wilt and reduce in volume as it begins to steam.

Lower the heat to moderate and steam the spinach, covered, for 7 minutes, then test it for doneness by tasting a leaf. I prefer my spinach somewhat underdone and slightly resistant to the bite. You may, however, steam it a minute or two longer if you prefer.

Just before the spinach is done to your taste, warm a serving dish.

Serving the spinach. With tongs, transfer the spinach to the warmed serving bowl and cover it.

Quickly melt the softened butter in an 8-inch frying pan set over moderate heat. When it has melted, add the pine nuts and fry them for 10 seconds or so in the sizzling butter, stirring constantly.

Pour the butter and nuts over the spinach. Lift the spinach up and over the butter and nuts repeatedly until they are well combined and the nuts and butter are distributed evenly. Serve at once.

Two Dramatic Poached Desserts

The word "dessert" can conjure up many things to many people, and the passion of one's response often depends upon national origin, nostalgic memories of childhood, and, finally, upon a love of sweets in general. To some, desserts are unthinkable without mounds of whipped cream, while others dream only of rich moist tortes, or tier upon tier of layered and frosted cakes, or even of the inevitable strawberry shortcake or homely apple pie.

For some inexplicable reason, many important desserts are associated only with baking, and sadly neglected are desserts that are poached. Yet poaching, which by definition implies delicacy and refinement, has in fact produced some of the greatest desserts in the world. Of the innumerable examples I might have chosen to illustrate this point, the two desserts which follow are among the most magnificent I know.

FLOATING ISLAND

In old French cooking a favorite dessert consisted of alternating layers of liqueur-moistened cake and puréed fruit, all surrounded by a custard sauce, the classic *crème à l'Anglaise*. The French called this elaborate construction *île flottante*—floating island—because the cake did indeed resemble an island. But the dessert we now call Floating Island is of an entirely different character. Instead of a cake that is anchored to the plate, delicate meringues truly float, islandlike, on a sea of custard. Small wonder that this gossamer dessert has become so popular in many other countries, including our own, as well as in France, where it has the delightful name *oeufs à la neige*, snow eggs.

Practically speaking, my version of Floating Island must be

made at least 3 hours in advance and then refrigerated until time to serve. And you may be pleased to learn that it may be made as much as 8 hours in advance. The meringues, instead of disintegrating in the sauce as you might expect, will, surprisingly, continue to hold their shape during such prolonged chilling.

SERVES 4 TO 6

The Meringues:
4 egg whites
⅓ cup sugar

The Poaching Liquid:
3 cups milk
1 teaspoon vanilla

The Vanilla Custard Sauce:
1½ cups milk from the poaching liquid
4 egg yolks
¼ cup sugar
1 teaspoon cornstarch
1 teaspoon vanilla

Preparing the meringues. Place the egg whites in the bowl of your electric mixer, or in any other glass or stainless steel bowl if you want to use a rotary beater or a hand-held electric beater.

Beat vigorously for a minute or so, until the whites begin to froth. Then, if you are using an electric mixer or beater, pour ⅓ cup of sugar slowly into the whites as you continue to beat. If you are using a rotary beater, add the sugar a tablespoon at a time at intervals, resuming the beating after each addition.

After all the sugar has been added, beat the meringue uninterruptedly for 5 minutes. It should then be dense enough to stand in firm peaks in the bowl after the beater is removed. If in doubt, beat a longer rather than a shorter time; it is virtually impossible to overbeat a meringue.

Poaching the meringues. Pour 3 cups of milk and 1 teaspoon vanilla into a 12-inch frying pan. Bring the mixture to a simmer over moderate heat, but don't let it even approach the boiling point, lest it froth up and overflow the pan.

Meanwhile, line a shallow pan with a double layer of paper towels and set it at hand near the stove.

Then, with a rubber spatula, mound an ordinary tablespoon with the meringue. Don't be concerned with shaping it too meticulously on the spoon; irregularity will give the "islands" a free-form charm.

With the aid of your spatula, gently slide the meringue from the spoon into the simmering milk. Shape and add to the pan as many meringues as it will hold, allowing about 2 inches of space between them so they will not cling together as they poach.

Simmer the meringues undisturbed for about 2 minutes, then turn each one over gently with a slotted spoon. Poach for 1 to 2 minutes longer, but be careful not to allow the meringues to over-cook or to let the milk heat beyond the simmering point. If you are careless in the least about these crucial points, the meringues may disintegrate.

One at a time, lift the meringues from the milk with a slotted spoon and transfer them to the paper-lined pan to drain.

Then, without wasting a moment, shape and poach more meringues, cooking them in three batches if necessary. You should have a total of 12 to 15 meringues. When all the meringues are done, reserve the poaching liquid.

Let the last batch of meringues cool for about 10 minutes. Then, using a small metal spatula, carefully transfer all of them to a large platter. Cover the platter loosely with plastic wrap and set it aside while you make the sauce. You may refrigerate the meringues of you like, but it is not necessary.

Making the vanilla custard sauce. Place a small, fine-meshed sieve over a 2-cup glass measuring cup and strain enough of the reserved poaching milk into it to reach the 1½-cup mark. Pour the measured milk into a 2-quart enameled or stainless steel saucepan and set it aside.

Then, using an electric mixer or beater, or a bowl and a rotary beater, vigorously beat together the egg yolks, ¼ cup of sugar, and the cornstarch for 4 to 5 minutes, or until the mixture is a little thicker than heavy cream.

Set the saucepan of milk over moderate heat and bring the milk to a simmer, watching it constantly lest it boil. Remove and slowly pour the milk into the beaten egg mixture, stirring with a whisk as you pour.

Pour the contents of the bowl back into the saucepan and set the pan over low heat. Immediately begin stirring the custard mix-ture with a rubber spatula, running it not only across the bottom but also around the sides and the crease of the pan, where the custard is likely to coagulate.

Stirring constantly and never allowing it to come even to a

simmer, cook the custard for 4 to 5 minutes, or until it thickens enough to coat the spatula lightly. If the heat is too high at any point during this period, the custard is likely to curdle. Professionals never take chances in this respect; they lift the pan off the heat for an instant every minute or so while the custard is cooking. If you use this procedure, you may discover that you will have to increase the cooking time by several minutes.

Immediately pour the custard into a small stainless steel or glass bowl, stir in 1 teaspoon of vanilla, and let the custard cool to room temperature, stirring it from time to time to prevent a skin from forming on the top. Then cover the bowl with plastic wrap and refrigerate it until the custard is thoroughly chilled.

Assembling and serving the Floating Island. Pour the custard into an attractive shallow serving dish large enough to hold all the poached meringues without crowding. Then float the "islands" on the surface of the custard.

Either serve the dessert at once or refrigerate it, uncovered, for up to 3 hours, if necessary.

PÊCHES MELBA

In France it has long been the custom for chefs to create dishes in honor of illustrious personages of their time. Often the dishes pass into oblivion together with the personages for whom they were named. But Pêches Melba, a tribute to the famous Australian soprano Nellie Melba, has not only survived but has become a classic of the French and international cuisines.

This masterpiece requires poached peaches, ice cream, whipped cream, and a cooked and cooled purée of fresh raspberries.

Because fresh raspberries are exceedingly expensive during their brief season, and even then often difficult to find, I have devised a liqueur-flavored sauce that uses the now readily available frozen raspberries and requires no cooking at all. For good texture, purée the berries in a sieve; do not use a blender or food processor.

The Peaches:
4 medium fresh peaches
8 cups water
2 tablespoons fresh lemon juice

The Poaching Syrup:
3 cups water
1½ cups granulated sugar
1 teaspoon vanilla
1 teaspoon fresh lemon juice

The Ice Cream:
1 quart vanilla ice cream

The Raspberry Sauce:
2 packages (10 ounces each) frozen raspberries, completely
   defrosted and drained
2 tablespoons confectioners' sugar
2 teaspoons Kirsch

The Cream:
½ cup chilled heavy cream

Preparing the peaches. Choose firm, unblemished peaches that are ripe but definitely not overripe.

Pour 4 cups of the water into a 2-quart enameled cast-iron or stainless steel saucepan and bring to a full boil over high heat. Drop the peaches into the boiling water and, turning them over once or twice with a spoon, let them boil for no more than 1 minute. Immediately transfer the peaches to a sieve and run cold water over them until they are cool enough to handle.

Meanwhile, pour the remaining 4 cups of water into a large glass or stainless steel bowl and stir in 2 tablespoons of lemon juice.

With a small sharp paring knife, strip away the skin of each peach as if you were peeling an onion. If you find it impossible to remove the skin in this fashion, you may have to pare the peaches with the knife. Drop each peeled peach into the acidulated water to prevent the flesh from discoloring.

Poaching the peaches. Into a 2-quart saucepan pour 3 cups of water, the granulated sugar, vanilla, and 1 teaspoon of lemon juice. Set the pan over high heat and bring the mixture to a boil, stirring until the sugar has dissolved. Let the liquid boil uninterruptedly for about 5 minutes. Then, one at a time, using a slotted spoon, lower the peaches into the syrup. Reduce the heat to low.

Poach the peaches in the simmering syrup, turning them every 5 minutes or so as they float and cook. Depending upon the variety and ripeness of the peaches, they will take 15 to 30 minutes to poach. Begin to test them for doneness after 15 minutes of poaching. When a small skewer inserted deeply into a peach meets only the barest resistance, the peaches are fully poached.

Remove the pan from the heat and let the peaches cool in their syrup at room temperature. Then, one at a time, carefully cut each peach in half lengthwise, discard the pit, and place the halves in a glass or stainless steel bowl. Pour the syrup over them, cover the bowl with plastic wrap, and refrigerate it until you are ready to assemble the dessert.

Preparing the ice cream. Working quickly and using an ice cream scoop if you have one, shape the ice cream into 8 individual servings in attractive dessert dishes, sherbet glasses, or long-stemmed goblets. Then, with the back of a teaspoon, press the top of each serving of ice cream to form a smooth deep depression just large enough so that, when you come to assemble the dessert, it will hold half a peach, curved side up. Immediately place the dishes in your freezer to firm up the ice cream while you prepare the raspberry sauce.

Making the raspberry sauce. Place the drained raspberries in a fine-meshed sieve set over a bowl. With the back of a large metal spoon, rub the raspberries into the bowl, occasionally lifting up the sieve as you proceed so that you can scrape into the bowl the thick purée that will cling to the outside of the sieve. When you have finished, you should have about ⅓ cup of thick, smooth, seedless purée.

With a small whisk, beat the confectioners' sugar into the raspberry purée, whisking until the sugar is completely absorbed. Then stir in the Kirsch, cover the bowl with plastic wrap, and refrigerate it until you are ready to use it.

Whipping the cream. With a whisk or a rotary or electric beater, beat the cream in a chilled glass or stainless steel bowl until it thickens enough to hold its shape on the beater when it is lifted. Be careful not to overbeat, lest the cream turn to butter.

Cover the bowl securely with plastic wrap and refrigerate it —but for no more than 10 to 15 minutes—while you assemble the dessert.

Assembling the Pêches Melba. Just before serving time, remove the peach halves from the syrup with a slotted spoon and place a peach half, curved side up, in the hollow of each scoop of ice cream. Pour a spoonful of the raspberry purée over each peach half, masking it completely. Then cover the exposed part of the ice cream with swirls of whipped cream or pipe it through a pastry bag fitted with a No. 6 decorative tip. Serve at once.

Frying, Deep Frying, and Sautéing

*P*robably every edible substance has been fried, deep fried, or sautéed in some place or at some time by an adventurous cook, for one form or another of these quick-cooking methods can be used for almost any meat, chicken, fish, shellfish, vegetable, fruit, and even for pastry and desserts—in fact, for any foods that don't require long slow cooking and/or moisture to break down their resistant tissues.

Most people, I am convinced, secretly adore fried, deep-fried, and sautéed foods as much as I do. But the very thought of these may conjure up ominous gastronomic visions: indigestible fats, excess calories, not to mention greasy fried pork chops, soggy croquettes, and limp, gray scaloppines. Let me assure you that when you pan fry foods properly, deep fry correctly, and make well-sauced sautées, the resulting dishes can be as easily digested and are almost as low in calories as foods prepared in other ways, for one of the basic rules for all fried, deep-fried, and sautéed foods is that when finished, they must be both internally and externally as free of fat as possible.

Frying, deep frying, and sautéing—often erroneously categorized under the catchall word "frying"—are quite distinct and different processes.

Frying. This is an operation in which the entire cooking is carried out in one pan, and no sauce is based on the fat left in the pan. There are three types of frying:

Shallow frying, in which coated or uncoated food is fried in a shallow skillet in about an inch of fat;

Pan frying, similar to shallow frying but using considerably less fat;

Stir frying, not often employed by Americans, which departs entirely from shallow and pan frying. Only enough fat is used to film the pan, and, for the most part, stir frying requires the addition of a liquid, usually lightly thickened at the end, to complete the cooking.

Deep-fat frying. This is a procedure in which foods are completely immersed in very hot fat in a deep-frying pan or large pot and cooked until done.

Sautéing. This term is often used synonymously for frying; the truth of the matter is that, classically, it is the name of a whole method of preparation, a shorthand description of a cooking process which does, indeed, include a preliminary frying. The food, which can be lightly coated or not coated at all, is first fried in a small amount of fat, then removed, and the drippings, or glaze, left in the pan are used as a base for the sauce.

Frying, deep frying, and sautéing have one great advantage over other methods of cooking: with few exceptions, the food is cooked uncovered and is constantly in full view. You are able to poke, peer, and pry to your heart's content, secure in the knowledge that the dish you are cooking is constantly under your control and that predictable results are assured.

Fats for Frying, Deep Frying, and Sautéing

Every country in the world follows its national traditions in choosing a fat to give its fried, deep-fried, or sautéed dishes a special flavor—or lack of flavor, as the case may be. We think of butter as being used in France, peanut oil in China, lard in Austria, goose fat in Germany, olive oil in Italy, and vegetable oil, shortening, or bacon fat in our own country.

From my point of view, flavor itself is not the primary consideration in choosing a fat. Scientifically speaking, fats are cooking agents used to achieve a special effect. In frying and deep frying, the fat serves the purpose of first sealing the surface of the food and then browning it to the point of crackling crispness. It is only in sautéing, when crispness is never a consideration, that the fat contributes a special flavor during the browning and later becomes the base of the sauce of the classic sauté.

The most important consideration in choosing a fat is how much heat it can tolerate before beginning to burn; any fat heated beyond its smoking point can catch fire. It is therefore necessary to understand the heat tolerance of each fat you cook with, flavor aside, and why one fat is preferable to another for each of the recipes in this book.

Vegetable oils. The vegetable oils most commonly used in frying and deep frying are extracted from corn, cottonseed, peanuts, safflower seed, or soybeans. Certain brands contain a combination of oils.

Oils are, in effect, interchangeable not only with each other but also with solid vegetable shortenings. The oils tend to be more or less flavorless, but some have detectable flavor characteristics. All vegetable oils have an extraordinarily high tolerance for heat. They are ready for frying when the surface looks watery and shows ripples.

The keeping time of oils varies from one type to another and depends somewhat on storage conditions; cap oils tightly and keep them in a cool kitchen cabinet, not a refrigerator. Any oil, once opened, will eventually turn rancid. To be on the safe side, always smell it before using it; if the odor is perceptible, discard the oil. Rancid oil will unpleasantly affect the flavor of any food cooked in it.

Vegetable shortenings. Solid vegetable shortenings are creamy-textured white or ivory-colored substances made by solidifying vegetable oils. They are sold under a variety of brand names. Whatever flavor they have is scarcely detectable.

Shortening can be heated to as high a temperature as 400° F. before it smokes. Vegetable oils and shortenings are, therefore, especially useful for deep-fat frying, in which the fat, if it is to serve its purpose, must usually be heated to 375° F. or above. Many other fats would either smoke or literally burst into flame at that temperature. Beyond the danger of fire, when a fat is hot enough to smoke, it is beginning to break down; cooking in it, you risk not only burning your food but also giving it an acrid, "off" flavor and an indigestible character.

Solid vegetable shortenings in opened containers keep well— almost indefinitely, in fact. They may be refrigerated, if you like, but do not require it; however, it is wise to keep shortenings tightly covered and in a cool place.

One pound of solid shortening, when melted, yields 2 cups.

Butter. Butter is used in frying and sautéing primarily for the richness and flavor it contributes to the food or to its sauce. Because unclarified butter cannot be heated beyond a rather low temperature without burning, sensible cooks never use it alone for frying and sautéing; and for the same reason, of course, it is out of the question for deep frying.

On the other hand, when butter is combined with vegetable oil, as you will see in my recipes, the oil will support the butter and the combination may be heated to a higher temperature than would be possible if butter alone were used. A combination of butter and oil, or butter and vegetable shortening, is at the correct temperature for frying when it begins to have a nutty odor and turns faintly brown.

Butter for frying or sautéing need not be of the absolutely highest quality (that is, graded AA or A), and it matters not at all if it is salted or sweet.

Olive oil. Olive oil has perhaps the most distinctive flavor of all oils. I use it only in dishes such as Breaded Veal Cutlets Milanese and Sautéed Shrimp, for it would be inconceivable to fry these most Italian of dishes in anything else. However, olive oil will not do at all for deep frying, even if the food to be deep fried is Italian in origin; it tends to smoke and burn at a relatively low temperature when compared with vegetable oils. When used for frying and sautéing, olive oil is ready when its surface looks watery and shows ripples.

Olive oil keeps best out of the light, preferably in a cool cupboard, and tightly covered.

Lard. Because lard has a very definite flavor—and one that is not to everyone's taste—it must be used with discretion for frying. But those who like the flavor of lard, as I do, will be pleased to know that this fat can be heated to almost as high a temperature as vegetable oils and shortenings before it is in danger of smoking. Consequently, you can use it not only for pan frying but for deep frying too. For pan frying, lard may be combined with butter, which makes for an interesting flavor.

Lard keeps almost indefinitely if stored, closely wrapped, in the refrigerator. One pound, when melted, yields 2 cups. When it is ready to use for frying, its surface will show watery ripples, and a keen eye can detect a faint haze.

Bacon fat. The flavor of bacon fat is unmistakable, pervasive, and distinctively American. Bacon in other countries is generally not cured and smoked in the way ours is and therefore has an entirely different taste.

Dishes fried in bacon fat are typical of certain American regions. Many Southerners, for example, use bacon fat for frying chicken; trout fishermen often fry their fish in it; and a Midwesterner might well use it to fry fresh corn fritters or thickly sliced ripe or green tomatoes.

Like olive oil, however, bacon fat has too assertive a flavor for dishes as delicate as most classic sautés, and because it burns at a fairly low temperature it should never be used for deep frying.

Margarine. Margarine has all the disadvantages of butter in its response to heat and none of its advantages. Apart from its unpleasant flavor, it burns easily. Therefore, it should never be considered for frying of any kind.

The Matter of Seasonings

When and how to season the foods in this section is covered in detail in my individual recipes. It is my firm contention that any coated food should be seasoned *before* it is coated, for the obvious reason that seasoning the coating alone would have little effect on the food itself.

On the other hand, if you are pan frying a steak that you want to be beautifully brown, do not salt the meat before cooking it; salt will impede the browning by drawing moisture to the surface. Salt and pepper your pan-fried steaks *after* they are cooked.

Meat or poultry for sautés is almost always seasoned before it is cooked because browning is not your primary aim, as it is in pan frying a steak.

When you are deep frying uncoated foods such as potatoes, it would obviously be useless to salt them before frying; the salt would simply fall off into the fat. Salt will adhere best to deep-fried food if it is sprinkled on after cooking, while the food is still very hot.

The Crucial Importance of Proper Coating

Coating or not coating foods is determined by tradition, by the foods themselves, or by the effect on foods that you want to achieve.

Uncoated foods will produce a natural brown crust of their own—examples are pan-fried steaks and French-fried potatoes. A coating of flour alone will intensify the browning and produce a delicate crust, superimposed on the food itself. The most protective coating of all—which uses flour, eggs, and bread crumbs and which I call a "trio coating"—not only creates the crispest of crusts on fried or deep-fried foods but adds definite textural interest to the food itself. Descriptions of each coating method follow.

Three flour-coating methods. The only flour I use for coating is all-purpose flour. Unless it has been stored for some time and has become too settled and dense, there is no reason whatsoever to sift it.

There are three ways to coat food with flour, and whichever you choose, it is imperative that you flour the food just before frying it. If floured food is allowed to stand more than a minute or so, the moisture of the food will inevitably seep through the flour and turn it gummy.

THE WAX PAPER METHOD. This method is useful for coating large pieces of food—liver, for example. Arrange two long sheets of wax paper alongside each other, then spread the required amount of flour on one sheet and leave the other free to receive the coated food. Pat the food to be coated completely dry with paper towels, then dip each side in turn into flour. Shake each piece vigorously to remove the excess flour. Place the floured pieces on the second sheet of wax paper, then cook them at once.

THE PAPER BAG OR PLASTIC BAG METHOD. This is an easy way to coat sturdy foods, such as chicken parts. Dump the required amount of flour into a strong paper or plastic bag and then drop in the thoroughly dried and seasoned pieces of food. Twist the open end of the bag tightly and shake the bag vigorously until each piece of food is completely coated. Then remove and shake each piece vigorously over the bag to remove all excess flour before dropping it into the pan.

THE BAG-AND-SIEVE METHOD. This method is particularly useful for coating small pieces of food with a very fine film of flour. Follow the bag method above, but instead of shaking each piece individually, pour the well-coated contents of the bag into a large sieve and shake gently from side to side (over a sheet of wax paper for easy cleanup) to free the food of all excess flour.

Trio coating. In this method, the flour is used as a preliminary coating. It is followed by two more layers: first a coating of egg, then one of bread crumbs.

The function of egg, when applied to the flour-coated food, is to provide a moist, sticky base to which bread crumbs will adhere. In recipes requiring the trio method, you will notice that the eggs are always beaten with either vegetable oil or water, and the proportions are 2 teaspoons of liquid to 1 egg. Water is added to the egg when the food to be coated is a fairly fatty one, pork chops, for example; oil is added when the food contains little or no fat, scallops or liver, for example. The eggs and the liquid should be beaten with a fork or whisk only long enough to combine them. If the mixture is beaten to the foamy stage its holding power will weaken and the bread crumbs, when you apply them, may not adhere.

The trio procedure calls for placing a wire cake rack over, or in, a flat, shallow pan and set within easy reach. Then two long sheets of wax paper are laid side by side, one spread with flour, the other with bread crumbs. With a fork or small whisk, the egg and the liquid are combined in a large shallow bowl. When all of this is ready, the coating can begin.

One piece at a time, lay the food to be coated on the flour, turning it to cover all sides. Shake it vigorously to remove the excess flour and drop it gently into the egg mixture. Turn with fingers or tongs. When it has been thoroughly moistened on all sides, lift it and allow excess egg to flow off. Finally, lay the food in the bread crumbs, turn it to coat all surfaces, and, with your fingers, pat the bread crumbs firmly into the surface, making sure all crevices are filled. The food should be thoroughly, but not thickly, blanketed with crumbs. As you coat each piece of food, place it on the rack.

Refrigerate the rack of food for at least 20 minutes, but for no longer than 1 hour. Or place it in your freezer for 5 to 10 minutes if you are pressed for time. It is perilous to fry the food without chilling, because you risk having the coating fall away in the fat.

Frying: A Lively Art

Frying is perhaps the most demanding of the three culinary techniques in this section. It requires constant attention and, unlike sautéing, is a last-minute operation that must not be interrupted.

Foods to be fried are generally in larger pieces than those to be sautéed or deep fried. And whether they are cooked in a frying pan or, to use an old-fashioned word, a skillet—or an even older word, a spider (a pan with small feet)—they require a comparatively longer cooking period than sautéed or deep-fried foods.

In most frying operations the food is never totally immersed in fat, and the pan is not usually covered. As a consequence, the upper part of the food, which is exposed to air, cooks at a much slower rate than the underside that is sizzling away in the fat. If you are careless or inattentive, or turn the food over at the wrong time, you may end up with one side overcooked or overbrowned, and the other undercooked and possibly pallid. Then there is also the danger of frying at too low or too high a temperature.

Techniques for Frying

The frying pan. Use a pan of heavy cast aluminum, preferably with a nonstick lining, which will retain heat consistently and evenly. Lighter-weight pans—admittedly easier to lift—heat too quickly and sometimes unevenly; moreover, they don't retain heat well. Consequently, when you fry your food at high heat, as ideally you should, there is the ever-present danger of its burning if the pan is too light.

Use a pan that is just large enough to fry the food in one batch without crowding the pan. Most of the following meat recipes call for a 12-inch frying pan for that reason. If you use an 8- or 10-inch frying pan and don't halve the recipe, you will have to fry in two pans at once or fry in two batches and keep the finished food warm while you fry the rest.

Don't preheat the pan. Preheating the frying pan before adding the fat not only damages the pan but causes the fat—especially butter—to burn. Simply put whatever fat you are using into a cold pan, then set it over the heat until the fat reaches its correct frying temperature.

Heat control. Only when each fat has reached its correct temperature will it be able to "seize" the food (as professional cooks call this process) or, more colloquially, to seal the surface instantly and prevent the near-disastrous consequences of too-slow cooking: sogginess, greasiness, or having the coating fall off the food. In the case of uncoated foods such as hamburgers and steaks, the high heat sears the surface and prevents the juices from escaping.

In most cases, the heat is lowered from high to moderate immediately after the seizing or searing has been completed. This prevents the outside from burning while the interior is cooking to the desired state of doneness.

Turning food. To turn fragile foods like hamburgers and fish or those with easily dislodged coatings, like breaded pork chops, use a wide spatula. Never grip such foods with tongs; the clamps will break the surface or the coating. However, a pair of tongs or a long-pronged fork is preferable for turning chicken and steak. When turning steak, insert the tines of the fork alongside the bone or into the rim of fat to prevent any juices from escaping.

Draining food. Thoroughly drain fried foods, particularly those that have been coated and then fried in oil. Turn them onto a shallow pan or heatproof platter that has been lined with a double layer of paper towels. Pat the upper surfaces with additional paper towels to make the food as fat-free as possible.

Keeping fried food warm. You can keep the drained food warm by placing the pan in an oven preheated to its lowest possible setting, keeping it there until you are ready to serve the food or while you fry another batch. Never cover any fried food being kept warm; to do so would soften the crisp crust you have labored so hard to achieve.

Ideally, all fried foods should be presented on preheated platters and served on preheated plates.

WIENER SCHNITZEL

The name of this dish, literally translated, means "Viennese cutlet." The cutlet, always of veal, is breaded and fried and is served, in Vienna at least, either plain or with one of a variety of garnishes that can range from anchovies to capers and even to a fried egg. Purists insist that the perfect garnish is simply a wedge of lemon, and I, for one, agree.

Buy the best-quality veal you can afford. It should be the lightest pink in color and free of gristle and external fat. After your butcher has cut the veal into slices ½ inch thick (the number of slices will vary according to the area from which the veal is cut), ask him to pound each slice between pieces of wax paper until it is about ⅜ inch thick.

SERVES 4

The Veal:
1½ to 2 pounds boneless veal cutlets, cut from the leg or rump, in slices ½ inch thick
2 teaspoons salt
Freshly ground black pepper

The Trio Coating:
¼ cup unsifted flour
1 egg, beaten with 2 teaspoons water
1 cup fine dry bread crumbs

For Frying:
1½ cups lard

The Garnish :
Lemon quarters

Preparing the veal. Pat the cutlets thoroughly dry with paper towels and sprinkle them on both sides with salt, using the entire 2 teaspoons or a little less, if you prefer. Grind as much black pepper as you like over each cutlet. Then, using as much as you need of the flour, the egg beaten with water, and the bread crumbs, follow the trio coating method (page 79) to coat the cutlets. Refrigerate the coated cutlets on the rack for at least 20 minutes, but for no more than 1 hour, before frying them.

Line a shallow pan or heatproof platter with a double layer of paper towels.

Before beginning to cook the veal, preheat the oven to its lowest setting. Place a large heatproof serving platter and your dinner plates in the oven to warm.

Frying the cutlets. In a 10-inch sauté pan or a 12-inch frying pan melt half the lard (¾ cup) over high heat, watching it closely. When the lard has almost, but not quite, reached the smoking point

—it will show faint watery ripples on its surface and give off a very light haze—add half the cutlets.

Fry the cutlets for about 4 minutes on the first side, then turn them over with a spatula and fry the second side for about the same amount of time; both sides should be light golden brown. If at any point during the frying the coating seems to be browning too rapidly, lower the heat for a moment or so to prevent it from burning; then return the heat to high so that the cutlets reach a light golden brown within the specified cooking time.

Transfer the finished cutlets to the paper-lined pan or platter and quickly pat the top surfaces with additional paper towels to free them of surface fat. Set the pan of cutlets in the preheated oven.

Quickly pour off all the cooking fat, wipe the pan clean with a paper towel, and add the remaining ¾ cup of lard. Heat the lard as before, almost to the smoking point, and fry and drain the remaining cutlets.

Serving the Wiener Schnitzel. Transfer the cutlets to the heated platter, garnish them with lemon quarters, and serve them at once on the heated plates.

VARIATION: BREADED VEAL CUTLETS MILANESE

Here is the Italian variation on the same theme. The quantities of ingredients are the same as for Wiener Schnitzel, but instead of using plain bread crumbs, coat the cutlets with ¾ cup of fine dry bread crumbs mixed with ¼ cup of freshly grated imported Parmesan cheese. Fry and drain the cutlets precisely as for the Wiener Schnitzel, but use 1½ cups of olive oil instead of lard. When the oil is hot enough for frying, it will show a rippled pattern and appear somewhat watery, with a very faint haze over its surface.

FRIED CALF'S LIVER

Without a doubt, calf's liver has the most delicate flavor and texture of all livers, and it is easy to understand why, despite its exorbitant price, it is the most popular. However, it is unfortunate that many Americans are unaware of the excellence (and nutritional value) of other livers: lamb, pork, and beef.

Although pork and lamb's liver are difficult to find, beef liver is readily available and relatively inexpensive. On all counts, you might find it rewarding, in this recipe at least, to substitute beef liver for calf's, but you must, of course, fry it precisely as described below.

Firmly insist that your butcher slice the liver to order in even ½-inch slices, and refuse to accept slices that taper off in thickness at the ends. Such tapered slices cook unevenly, with the result that the thinner ends will be dry and tough. Calf's liver is exceedingly expensive, and you are entitled to get what you pay for.

SERVES 4

The Liver:
1¼ to 1½ pounds calf's liver, cut ½ inch thick
1 teaspoon salt
Freshly ground black pepper

The Coating:
2 cups soft fresh bread crumbs

For Frying:
3 to 5 tablespoons vegetable oil
2 or 3 tablespoons butter

The Garnish:
Lemon quarters

Preparing the liver. With a small sharp knife, remove the membrane from the edge of each slice of liver; insert the knife under the thin membrane and strip it away as if you were peeling an onion. This will prevent the slices from curling when they are immersed in the fat.

Do not wash the liver; simply pat it dry with paper towels. Then lay the slices side by side on a sheet of wax paper and sprinkle them on one side with ½ teaspoon of the salt, distributing the salt evenly by rubbing it lightly with your fingers, and with freshly ground black pepper. Turn the slices and season the other side.

Line a shallow pan or heatproof platter with a double layer of paper towels.

A few minutes before you are ready to fry the liver, preheat the oven to its lowest setting and place a large serving platter and your dinner plates in it.

Coating the liver. Because liver is so moist, it does not require the addition of eggs to get the coating to adhere. Yet, just because it is so moist, it must be cooked immediately after breading. If you allow too much time to elapse, the coating will pick up too much moisture from the liver and will not have a desirable crispness after it is fried. Sprinkle 1 cup of the bread crumbs on the liver, pressing the crumbs into each slice with your fingers to make them adhere. Turn the slices over and coat the other side with the remaining bread crumbs, again pressing them into the liver. The liver should be heavily coated; do not shake off any excess crumbs. Immediately prepare the pan for frying.

Frying the liver. Combine 3 tablespoons of vegetable oil and 2 tablespoons of butter in a heavy 12-inch frying pan. Set the pan over high heat. When the butter has dissolved in the oil and begins to turn slightly brown, add as many slices of liver as you can without crowding the pan.

Lower the heat to moderate and fry the liver for about 2 minutes; then, with a wide spatula, carefully turn the slices over and fry for about 2 minutes more. Test the liver for doneness by cutting into a slice with the tip of a small sharp knife. It should be somewhat pink. Fried beyond that stage, the liver may become tough.

Transfer the liver to the paper-lined pan or platter and keep it warm in the preheated oven while you fry and drain the remaining slices, adding the remaining oil and butter to the pan if necessary.

Serving the liver. Arrange the liver on the warmed platter, slightly overlapping the slices if you like. Garnish with lemon quarters, and serve the liver at once on heated plates.

PAN-FRIED STEAK

Most Americans broil rather than fry their steaks, yet pan frying a steak is a long-established practice in France and other countries where broilers are not standard equipment in many household kitchens.

Pan frying a steak has many advantages; and when you know how to do it properly, it produces superior results. Moreover, it is the most practical way to cook any steak that is less than an inch thick. Should you attempt to broil such a thin steak in even the most modern of household broilers, it would be almost impossible to achieve sufficient browning without overcooking the interior of the meat. The technique I have devised not only seals in the juices of the steak, but also, because of the frequent turnings, prevents the formation of an undesirable thick, hard crust.

Any tender bone-in steak—a porterhouse, for example—can be fried in the fashion described in this recipe. If you find the steak you have purchased is too large for your pan, it is a simple matter to remove the bone with a thin-bladed sharp knife and insert a small metal skewer into the meat to reshape the steak. Alternatively, you may use any trimmed boneless steak or individual boneless steaks cut ¾ inch thick, allowing about ½ pound per person.

SERVES 4

3 to 3½ pounds sirloin steak or other cut of your choice, cut no more than ¾ inch thick, trimmed of all but ¼ inch of outside fat
2 tablespoons vegetable oil
1 tablespoon butter
Salt
Freshly ground black pepper

Preparing the steak. With a small sharp knife, notch the outside fat every inch or two to prevent the steak from curling unattractively as it fries. Pat the steak thoroughly dry with paper towels. The meat will not brown well if it is the slightest bit moist. For the same reason, do not season the steak with salt before frying; salt draws moisture to the surface of the steak as it fries.

Just before you fry the steak, preheat your oven to its lowest setting and set in it your dinner plates and a serving platter (if you are not serving the steak on a carving board).

Frying the steak. Combine the oil and butter in a 10-inch sauté pan or a 12-inch frying pan, and set the pan over high heat. When the combined fats are as hot as they can get without smoking (the butter will begin to brown very faintly), add the steak.

Immediately lower the heat to moderate and fry the steak for 1 minute. Then turn the steak over with tongs, or with a fork inserted close to the bone or into the rim of fat. Fry the other side for 1 minute, then turn the steak again. Continue cooking and turning the steak every minute or two for a total cooking time of 6 minutes if you prefer your steak rare. Should you prefer the steak on the medium-rare side, fry it for a minute or two longer.

A minute or two before you think the steak is cooked to your taste, you might do well to test it for doneness, employing the touch technique used by professional cooks: poke the center of the steak firmly with your forefinger—if the meat is fairly soft and yielding the steak will be rare; if it is slightly resistant, medium-rare; and if it is quite firm to your touch you will, unfortunately (in my view, at least), have a well-done steak on your hands.

Another method of testing, which does not have my entire approval because it allows the juice of the steak to escape, is to cut into the meat close to the bone or at the edge of the fat with a small sharp knife. After spreading the cut open, you will know whether to fry the steak longer or not.

Serving the steak. Immediately transfer the steak to a carving board or a heated platter. Sprinkle it on both sides with salt and freshly ground pepper to your taste. Slice the steak and serve it at once on the heated plates.

FRIED PORK CHOPS

My recommendation in this recipe that you use pork chops from the loin or rib is deliberate. Less expensive chops cut from the end of the loin of pork, called shoulder or blade chops, do not lend themselves to frying. They contain much too much fat, which does not break down during the comparatively short frying time for this recipe.

Because pork is so rich, a cooked fruit accompaniment of some kind has become almost traditional. In America, at least, fried pork chops are usually served with applesauce, and you might give the sauce more interest by spiking it with some horseradish.

Insist that your butcher cut your chops precisely and uniformly ¾ inch thick, and have him trim away all but ⅛ inch of the rim of fat on each one. Don't settle for precut chops unless you must; too often they will be carelessly cut and uneven in thickness, and you will find that the thin ends will be dry and overcooked.

The Pork Chops:
6 to 8 pork chops, preferably from the loin, cut ¾ inch thick
2 teaspoons salt
Freshly ground black pepper

The Trio Coating:
½ cup unsifted flour
2 eggs, beaten with 4 teaspoons cold water
2 cups fine dry bread crumbs

For Frying:
3 to 5 tablespoons vegetable oil
2 tablespoons butter, cut into bits

The Garnish:
Lemon wedges

Preparing the chops. Pat the chops thoroughly dry with paper towels. Sprinkle them on both sides with the salt, then grind as much pepper as you like onto both sides of the chops.

Using as much as you need of the flour, the eggs beaten with water, and the bread crumbs, follow the trio coating method (page 79) to coat the chops. Refrigerate them on their rack for at least 20 minutes, but no more than 1 hour.

Line a shallow pan or platter with a double layer of paper towels.

Turn your oven to its lowest setting and in it warm a serving platter and the dinner plates.

Frying the chops. Combine 3 tablespoons of the vegetable oil and all the butter in a heavy 12-inch frying pan, and set the pan over high heat. When the butter has barely begun to turn faintly brown, add the chops. Don't crowd them, or you will have difficulty turning them over without dislodging the coating.

Lower the heat to moderate, and fry the chops, uncovered, for about 8 minutes, lifting them up with a wide spatula and peeking under them every now and then to make sure they are not browning too rapidly. If they are, reduce the heat.

Carefully turn the chops over with a long-pronged fork inserted close to the bone or fat, adding a tablespoon or more of the remaining oil to the pan if its surface is not entirely covered with fat.

Fry the second side of the chops for about 8 minutes. After a total of 15 or 16 minutes, the chops should be golden brown and fully cooked. If you are the least bit doubtful about the doneness of the pork—and it *must* be fully cooked—cut into one of the chops close to the bone with a small sharp knife and spread the cut slightly apart. If the meat appears even slightly pink, lower the heat and fry the chops for a minute or two longer.

Transfer the chops to the paper-lined pan or platter and, with another paper towel, lightly pat their top surface to remove any excess fat.

Serving the chops. Arrange the chops attractively on the heated platter, garnish with the lemon wedges, and serve at once.

SOUTHERN FRIED CHICKEN

By covering Southern Fried Chicken as it fries, I violate my own precept that food being fried should never be covered. Still, some of the best Southern cooks I know always fry their chicken in this fashion; and because it is so successful, I see no reason to tamper with the custom.

And some Southerners, you might like to know, serve fried chicken at room temperature rather than hot, straight from the pan. Although it is not as crisp as freshly fried chicken, it has an attractive quality all its own.

SERVES 4

The Chicken:
A 2½- to 3-pound chicken, usually called a broiler-fryer
1 lemon, cut in half crosswise
Salt
Freshly ground black pepper (optional)

The Coating:
1 cup unsifted flour

For Frying:
1 cup vegetable shortening
8 tablespoons butter (a quarter-pound stick), cut into bits

The Garnish:
Crisp watercress

Preparing the chicken. Have the butcher divide the chicken into 10 serving pieces and ask him to use a knife, not a cleaver, which may leave bone splinters lodged in the chicken. The pieces should consist of the two thighs separated from the legs, the two wings, and the two sides of the breast divided lengthwise, then each cut crosswise in half.

With paper towels, pat the chicken pieces thoroughly dry, then rub all their surfaces with the cut sides of the lemon halves. Sprinkle the pieces liberally on both sides with salt and, more discreetly, with freshly ground black pepper, if you like the flavor.

Dump the flour into a sturdy paper or plastic bag and drop in all the chicken pieces. Twist the open end of the bag tightly and shake it vigorously until each piece of chicken is completely coated.

Line a shallow pan or platter with a double layer of paper towels.

Frying the chicken. Combine the shortening and butter in a 10-inch sauté pan or a 12-inch frying pan. The pan must have a tight-fitting cover. Set the pan, uncovered, over high heat. When the butter and shortening have melted and the butter has barely begun to show a faint tinge of brown, add the chicken in the following fashion: Holding the bag close to the pan, lift up a piece of chicken and shake it vigorously over the bag to remove any excess flour. Immediately lay the piece, skin side down, in the hot fat. Repeat this procedure until all the pieces of chicken are in the pan.

Cover the pan tightly, reduce the heat to moderate, and fry the chicken for about 15 minutes, lifting the lid once or twice and checking to make sure the skin side is not browning too rapidly. If it is, lower the heat a bit. When the skin is crisp and golden brown, turn the chicken over with tongs, re-cover the pan, and fry the other side for 10 minutes or so. (The flesh side of the chicken always requires a shorter frying time than the skin side.)

After 25 minutes of cooking, the chicken should be a deep golden brown and cooked throughout. If you have any doubt about its doneness, cut into the fleshy part of a thigh with a small sharp knife and spread the cut slightly apart. If the flesh is still slightly pink, re-cover the pan and fry the chicken 2 or 3 minutes longer. Then drain the chicken in the paper-lined pan or platter.

Serving the chicken. If you are serving the chicken hot, arrange it, skin side up, on a heated platter, surround it with watercress, and serve it at once. If it is to be served at room temperature, it can rest, uncovered, for as long as 4 hours.

————— ❧❦❧ —————

PAN-FRIED WHOLE FISH

Any small fish—brook trout, perch, sea bass, porgies, mackerel, or other regional fish—are suitable for pan frying. The fish should be as fresh as possible, and, after being scaled and eviscerated, it should be left whole—that is, with head and tail intact. Many Americans take a dim view of fish served in this fashion, but I have discovered that if, after the fish is fried, I remove the eyes with the point of a small sharp knife and insert a slice of black or green olive into the openings, my guests' dismay at the sight of the head is somewhat diminished. The fact is, whole fish have far more flavor than headless fish. Leaving the head on helps keep the flesh moist by reducing the cut surface. You can, however, have the heads removed if you wish.

A 1-pound fish, particularly if its head and tail are intact, occupies so much room on a plate that I like to serve it with nothing more than a baked potato. Often I begin the dinner with a vegetable course.

SERVES 4

The Fish:
4 whole fish, each weighing about 1 pound before cleaning
2 teaspoons salt

The Trio Coating:
⅓ cup unsifted flour
2 eggs, beaten with 4 teaspoons vegetable oil
1 cup fine dry bread crumbs

For Frying:
1 cup vegetable oil
6 tablespoons butter, cut into bits

The Garnish:
Lemon quarters
Parsley sprigs

Preparing and coating the fish. Have your fishman scale, eviscerate, and prepare the fish in whatever way you prefer. Wash the fish thoroughly under cold running water, then dry the cavity and skin with paper towels and sprinkle the fish inside and out with the salt, dividing it equally among them.

Using as much as you need of the flour, the eggs beaten with 4 teaspoons of vegetable oil, and the bread crumbs, follow the trio coating method (page 79) to coat the fish. Then refrigerate the fish for about 20 minutes, or up to an hour if you must, before frying them.

Line a shallow pan or platter with a double layer of paper towels.

Preheat your oven to its lowest setting. Place a serving platter and dinner plates in it to warm.

Frying the fish. Combine the 1 cup of vegetable oil and the butter in a heavy 12-inch frying pan. Set the pan over high heat and, when the butter has begun to turn very lightly brown, add the fish. (If the pan won't hold all 4 fish comfortably, fry them in two batches, using more oil and butter, if necessary, for the second batch. Keep the first batch of fish warm in the preheated oven.)

Lower the heat to moderate, and fry the fish for about 3 minutes. If at any point the fish appear to be burning, lower the heat. Then, with a wide spatula and with your forefinger placed on top of the fish to steady it, carefully turn each fish over. Fry the fish on the other side for 3 minutes. If you have any doubt that the fish are thoroughly cooked, insert the tip of a small sharp knife into the cavity of one of the fish and spread the flaps gently apart. If the area close to the spine seems the slightest bit glossy (it should be opaque), fry the fish a minute or two longer.

Remove the fish from the pan with the spatula and place them on the paper-lined pan or platter to drain. Pat each fish gently with another paper towel to remove any excess fat.

Serving the fish. Arrange the fish side by side on the heated platter, garnish with the lemon quarters and parsley, and serve them at once on the warmed plates.

A CRISP BROWN POTATO CAKE

One might, at first glance, think of this potato dish as ordinary hash-browned potatoes. But it is nothing of the kind. Unlike typical American "hash browns," which are made of cold, previously cooked potatoes, my version calls for potatoes fried in their raw state. Cooking them in this fashion not only retains their natural flavor, but the starch in the raw potatoes makes the finely chopped potatoes adhere closely as they fry—thus, in effect, creating a moist compact cake, deeply and crisply browned on both sides. It makes an excellent accompaniment to any of the sautés in this section.

SERVES 4

The Potatoes:
2 to 3 pounds baking potatoes (enough to make 4 cups potatoes when cut into ¼-inch cubes)
⅓ cup finely chopped scallions, including about 2 inches of green tops
1 teaspoon salt
Freshly ground black pepper

For Frying:
4 tablespoons butter, cut into bits
2 tablespoons vegetable oil

The Garnish:
1 tablespoon finely chopped fresh parsley

Preparing the potatoes. With a large sharp chef's knife, chop the cubed potatoes into the finest possible bits, then spread them out on a double sheet of paper towels and pat them thoroughly dry with more towels. Working quickly—the potatoes will darken if they are allowed to stand for more than 2 minutes or so—place them in a medium-size mixing bowl. Add the scallions, salt, and as much freshly ground black pepper as you like. With a large wooden spoon or your hands, toss all the ingredients together; and, if you are not averse to the taste of raw potatoes (there is no reason why you should be), taste the mixture for seasoning.

Frying the potatoes in a nonstick pan. Combine the butter and oil in a heavy 8-inch frying pan with a nonstick surface. Set the pan over high heat, and when the butter has begun to turn very lightly brown, dump in the potato mixture. With a metal spatula, spread the potatoes out evenly and pat them down firmly.

By this time the potatoes will have begun to sizzle. Lower the heat to moderate, cover the pan, and fry the potatoes for about 8 minutes, from time to time inserting a spatula under them and looking to make sure the bottom is not browning too fast or burning. If it is, lower the heat even further. Now uncover the pan and fry the potatoes for about 4 minutes longer, or until the bottom is golden brown and the top layer is almost, but not quite, tender.

Turning the potato cake. The next operation is a fairly tricky one, but with courage you can execute it easily. Remove the pan from the heat, placing it so that its handle is turned directly away from you. Invert a round platter—ideally about 10 to 11 inches in diameter—directly over the pan. Then, with two potholders, grasp the pan and the plate firmly together and turn them over, leaving the potato cake, browned side up, on the plate. Remove the pan, set it right side up, and gently slide the potato cake off the platter back into the pan. It may crumble a bit, but all you need to do is pat the pieces back into place with your spatula.

Now fry the potatoes, uncovered, over moderate heat for about 8 minutes, again checking from time to time to make sure the bottom is not burning or browning too rapidly.

Frying the potatoes in an ordinary frying pan. Cooking these potatoes in any type of frying pan other than one with a nonstick surface is difficult, because the potatoes tend to stick as they fry. If you must use an ordinary pan, follow the cooking instructions above, and every now and then slide the pan back and forth on the range so that the potatoes move in one mass. If they don't move, you may be sure they are sticking. In that event, insert a long, narrow spatula under the potatoes to free them wherever they adhere to the pan, then resume frying. When you turn the potatoes over, add an extra tablespoon of vegetable oil to the pan before sliding the potatoes back into it. During the cooking of the second side, slide the pan back and forth and check for sticking as before.

Serving the potato cake. When the potato cake is as brown as you like, invert it onto the platter as before, sprinkle the top with the parsley, and serve it at once.

If for any reason the potatoes must wait, you may safely leave them in a preheated warm oven for up to 15 minutes.

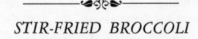

Stir Frying

Stir frying is a unique frying technique, one used primarily by the Chinese. Its most important difference from standard frying procedures is that the object is not to brown the food—the Chinese deep fry food when they want to brown it—but to cook it very quickly in a small amount of oil (usually peanut oil) in order to retain its natural crispness, color, and flavor. The following recipes for stir-fried vegetables are in the Chinese tradition. A light glaze is added at the last moment of cooking to coat the food so that it literally shimmers.

Because the stir-frying process takes only minutes, it is absolutely essential that you have all the ingredients prepared and close at hand before you start.

Any of the following stir-fried vegetables make excellent accompaniments for most of the main course dishes in this book. But a note of warning: plan to serve the vegetables with dishes that do not require last-minute preparation, or you will have your hands full indeed.

STIR-FRIED BROCCOLI

SERVES 4

    1 bunch fresh, firm broccoli (about 1½ pounds)
    2 teaspoons cornstarch
    2 tablespoons water
    1½ cups fresh or canned chicken broth
    2 tablespoons peanut oil (or other oil, if you must)
    1 teaspoon salt

Preparing the broccoli and glaze ingredients. With a small sharp knife, cut the broccoli flowerets, including about an inch of their thin stems, away from the heavy stalks. If the flowerets are very large, cut them lengthwise into halves or thirds, starting at the base of the stalk. Drop the flowerets into a mixing bowl and cover them with cold water while you prepare the large stalks.

Cut a slice about ½ inch thick off the bottom of each stalk; then, starting from the base, use a small sharp knife to strip away the fibrous layer of skin, peeling the stalk ruthlessly to its tender flesh. Cut the stalks on the diagonal into slices about ½ inch thick. Spread them on paper towels, pat them dry, and drop them into a small bowl.

Drain the flowerets, pat them dry with paper towels, and drop them into another bowl.

In still another small bowl or a cup, mix the cornstarch with the water.

Set all three bowls close at hand, near the stove.

In a small saucepan over high heat, bring the chicken broth to a turbulent boil. Then turn off the heat immediately, cover the pan, and set it aside.

Stir frying the broccoli. Pour the oil into a wok or 10-inch sauté pan or 12-inch frying pan and place the wok or pan over high heat. When the oil is as hot as it can get without smoking (there will be watery-looking ripples on its surface), tip the wok/pan from side to side to spread the oil over the entire surface. Drop in the sliced broccoli stalks, and, with a wooden spoon, turn and toss—in other words, stir fry—them for 30 seconds to 1 minute, until each piece is coated with the oil. Then, without losing a moment, add the broccoli flowerets and continue to stir fry for another 30 to 60 seconds.

Quickly pour the hot chicken broth over the broccoli and, stirring constantly, add the salt. Cover the wok/pan and continue to cook the broccoli over moderate heat.

After 4 or 5 minutes, taste the broccoli; it should feel quite firm to the bite. If it is too firm for your taste, cook it uncovered for another minute or two, stirring it once or twice and tasting to make sure you are not overcooking it.

Stir the cornstarch and water rapidly to make sure they are well combined, then pour the mixture into the pan, stirring continuously until the liquid thickens and coats the vegetable pieces with a shimmering glaze.

Serving the broccoli. With a spatula, transfer the broccoli to a deep dish and serve it at once.

STIR-FRIED ASPARAGUS

SERVES 4

1½ pounds fresh, firm asparagus
2 teaspoons cornstarch
2 tablespoons water
1 cup fresh or canned chicken broth
2 tablespoons peanut oil (or other oil, if you must)
1 teaspoon salt

Preparing the asparagus and the glaze ingredients. Cut off and discard the tough white ends of the asparagus; then cut off the asparagus tips and drop them into a bowl of cold water while you prepare the stalks. Lay the asparagus stalks on a flat surface and, one at a time, with a swivel-bladed vegetable peeler, strip away the outer layer of tough skin on each stalk. Slice the stalks on the diagonal into pieces about ¼ inch thick. Spread the slices on paper towels, pat them dry, and drop them into a small bowl.

Drain the asparagus tips, pat them dry with paper towels, and drop them into another bowl.

In still another small bowl or a cup, mix the cornstarch and water.

Set all three bowls close at hand near the stove.

In a small saucepan bring the chicken broth to a turbulent boil over high heat. Then turn off the heat immediately, cover the pan, and set it aside.

Stir frying the asparagus. Pour the oil into a wok or 10-inch sauté pan or 12-inch frying pan and place the wok or pan over high heat. When the oil is as hot as it can get without smoking (there will be watery-looking ripples on its surface), tip the wok/pan from side to side to spread it over the entire surface. Drop in the sliced asparagus stalks and, turning and tossing them gently with a wooden spoon, stir fry them for 30 seconds to 1 minute, or until each piece is coated with the oil. Then, without losing a moment, add the asparagus tips and continue to stir fry for another 30 to 60 seconds.

Quickly pour the hot chicken broth into the wok/pan and add the salt. Stirring gently and constantly, let the broth come to a boil, and continue to boil for 2 to 3 minutes. The asparagus is done when it is tender but still crisp to the bite.

With a spoon, give the cornstarch and water a few rapid stirs to make sure they are well combined. Pour the mixture into the wok/pan, stirring continuously until the liquid thickens and coats the asparagus pieces with a shimmering glaze.

Serving the asparagus. With the aid of a rubber spatula, transfer the asparagus to a deep dish and serve it at once.

VARIATION: STIR-FRIED GREEN BEANS

SERVES 4

Substitute 1 pound of fresh, young green beans for the broccoli in the preceding recipe. Trim the beans at each end and cut them crosswise, slightly on the diagonal, into pieces about 2 inches long. Wash the beans, pat them dry with paper towels, and set them aside in a bowl. Prepare the cornstarch mixture and chicken broth as in the preceding broccoli recipe and follow the same stir-frying procedures to cook the beans.

STIR-FRIED CUCUMBERS AND SCALLIONS

SERVES 4

2 large firm cucumbers
1 teaspoon salt
4 medium scallions
2 teaspoons cornstarch
2 tablespoons water
1 cup fresh or canned chicken broth
2 tablespoons peanut oil (or other oil, if you must)

Preparing the vegetables and the glaze ingredients. Peel the cucumbers, cut them in half lengthwise, and, with the tip of a teaspoon, scrape out the seeds. Then cut each half of cucumber lengthwise in half again and slice the strips crosswise into pieces about ½ inch thick.

Place the pieces in a small bowl, sprinkle them with ½ teaspoon of the salt, and toss them well with a wooden spoon. Set the cucumbers aside for 30 minutes. The salting will draw out the excess juice and any bitterness.

Wash the cucumbers under cold running water to rid them of the salt, drain them, and then dry them thoroughly with paper towels. Dry the bowl and return the cucumbers to it.

Trim the roots from the scallions and wash them under cold running water. Cut the white parts crosswise into 1-inch pieces and drop them into the bowl with the cucumbers. Slice all the fresh green part of the stems and the tops into ¼-inch rounds and place them in another small bowl.

In still another small bowl or cup, mix the cornstarch with the water.

Set all three bowls at hand, as close to the stove as possible.

In a small saucepan, bring the chicken broth to a turbulent boil over high heat. Immediately turn off the heat, cover the pan, and set it aside.

Stir frying the vegetables. Pour the oil into a wok or 10-inch sauté pan or 12-inch frying pan and place the wok or pan over high heat. When the oil is as hot as it can get without smoking (there will be watery-looking ripples on its surface), tip the wok/pan from side to side to spread the oil over the entire surface. Drop in the cucumbers and the white parts of the scallions and stir and toss them with a wooden spoon for 30 to 60 seconds, stir frying to coat them with the oil.

Quickly pour the hot broth over the vegetables, and add the remaining ½ teaspoon of salt. Stirring constantly over high heat, cook the vegetables for a minute or two. Cooked any longer, they will lose their crispness; if in doubt, undercook rather than overcook them.

With a spoon, give the cornstarch and water a few rapid stirs to make sure they are well combined, then pour the mixture into the wok/pan, stirring continuously until the liquid thickens and coats the vegetables with a shimmering glaze.

Serving the vegetables. With the aid of a rubber spatula, transfer the vegetables to a deep dish, scatter the sliced scallion greens over the top, and serve at once.

Deep Frying: Simple and Quick

Temperature and timing are the crucial elements in all deep frying, which is the simplest and quickest of all frying techniques. Results are almost always predictable, because a deep-frying thermometer —a magic wand, as it were—allows you to keep your frying fat at precisely the temperature you want. In addition, I have carefully spelled out precise cooking times so that nothing is left to chance.

Succinctly stated, the deep-frying process consists of dropping small pieces of food, coated or uncoated, into fat that has been heated to a prescribed temperature, usually 375° F., and cooking them until they are done. In properly done deep-fat frying, the hot fat instantly "seizes" and seals the surface of the food, thus providing a shield which the fat cannot penetrate. At the same time the sealed surface traps the steam inside the food so that it cooks through thoroughly. Obviously, if the fat is too hot, the coating will burn before the food has a chance to cook; conversely, fat at a too-low temperature cannot create a seal quickly enough to prevent the fat from seeping into the food. For these reasons I consider a deep-fat thermometer absolutely indispensable for successful deep-fat frying.

For this section on deep frying I have devised recipes for croquettes, pastry of various sorts, vegetables and seafoods in batters, and potatoes that are innocent of any covering but their own crispness.

Techniques for Deep Frying

The deep fryer. Use a deep fryer or frying kettle with a capacity of at least 4 or 5 quarts. A smaller pot does not have the necessary headroom to accommodate the bubbling up or foaming that frequently occurs when cold food is immersed in hot fat.

Fats for deep frying. In the discussion of frying fats (pages 74–77)

I indicate that some recipes specify a particular fat because of its flavor and others specify a fat because it is without any flavor. In my recipes for deep-fried foods, I name the type of fat to be used when one kind is preferable to others. You may, however, choose any vegetable oil, vegetable shortening, or lard according to its availability or your own taste.

I know it is an extravagance, but I never reuse fat which I have used for any appreciable amount of deep frying. The fat tends to wear out, or "break," as professionals say, with successive use. If you are economy-minded and want to reuse the fat, strain it into a clean, dry container through a fine sieve lined with a double layer of cheesecloth. Store the container, tightly covered, in a cool place.

Fat or oil used for deep frying will pick up the flavor of the food that has been fried in it; if possible, then, fry similarly flavored foods in fat that is being reused. And never use fat in which fish has been fried for anything but fish.

To determine the amount of oil or fat you will need, pour water into the deep fryer to a depth of at least 3 inches, then measure the water. Since oils are bottled by the pint, quart, half-gallon, or gallon, you can easily determine how much to buy. Solid shortening is sold in 1- and 3-pound cans, lard usually by the pound; a pound of either of these fats will yield 2 cups when melted.

Heating the fat. If cooking in fat that is not hot enough to seal the food and protect it from sogginess is the major culinary crime in deep-fat frying, the second worst crime is cooking in fat that has been allowed to overheat until it literally smokes.

As you will note from the recipes, there is an optimum temperature for cooking each deep-fried food. Using a deep-fat frying thermometer is the only way you can be absolutely sure that your fat reaches and maintains the correct temperature when you deep fry over direct heat in a heavy pot or saucepan. You would be wise to use a thermometer even if you have a thermostatically controlled electric deep fryer; the thermometer will give you a double check on its performance. In either case, be sure that you clamp the thermometer securely to the side of the pan, even if it is awkward to do so.

Using the frying basket. A frying basket is by no means essential; you can just as successfully let the food float free in the fat and then remove it with a slotted spoon when it is done. A basket is useful, however, when the pieces you are frying are small or numerous, as is the case with batter-fried seafood or French-fried potatoes.

When you use a basket, set it into the deep fryer after filling the kettle with fat, and let the basket remain there while the fat heats to the proper temperature. Then lift the basket above the surface to receive the food to be fried. Immersing a cold basket in hot fat not only increases the possibility of spattering but reduces the temperature of the fat.

Heat control. It is a good idea to lower a basket of food slowly into the fat; when the food contains much moisture or when it is quite cold, a great deal of bubbling is to be expected. If the bubbles threaten to rise to the brim, simply lift the basket for a moment, hold it above the surface until the turbulence subsides, then lower it into the fat again.

Immersing cold food in hot fat will also cause the temperature of the fat to drop, and the more food you attempt to fry at one time, the greater the drop in temperature. Therefore, never crowd the deep fryer; each piece of food should swim free, as it were, and have ample space for turning.

To cope with any drop in temperature when deep frying on top of the stove, immediately raise the heat until the thermometer returns to the original temperature required by your recipe.

An electric deep fryer must be manipulated in another way. When you add the food, turn the control to a setting 5 or 10 degrees above your frying temperature and leave it there for 2 or 3 minutes; then return it to the setting with which you began. If you are also using a thermometer with your electric deep fryer, you will be able to see when the recommended temperature is reached, so that you can reset the control.

Turning food. After foods have been placed in properly heated deep fat, they usually return to the surface in a moment or two. I can't stress strongly enough the importance of turning the pieces of food almost constantly as they float and cook. If you don't, the underpart will be cooked and done before the upper part has even begun to color because the frying process is so rapid.

While deep frying small pieces of food, an occasional up-and-down jiggling of the frying basket will prevent the food from sticking together or to the sides or bottom of the basket. When cooking larger pieces of food, use a slotted spoon or tongs to turn the food at frequent intervals.

Draining food. Because deep-fried foods have been totally immersed in fat, it is absolutely necessary that you drain them thoroughly. The most effective way to do this is to line a cookie sheet or any shallow pan with a double or triple layer of paper towels and have it ready to receive the deep-fried foods. Then gently pat the upper surface with additional paper towels to free the food of as much fat as possible.

Keeping food warm. The advantage of using a baking pan for draining is that the food can be kept warm in a preheated oven. And a further advantage, if you are deep frying food in two or more batches, is that you can keep the first batch warm while you fry the rest. However, never cover deep-fried food while you are keeping it warm, or it will become soggy.

A Note on Safety

It is good sense to bear in mind that any fat heated beyond its smoking point can catch fire. This will not happen if you understand the smoking-point characteristics of each fat and always use a deep-frying thermometer.

There are other safety precautions you should take. Never deep fry on a front burner of your stove, or with the handle of the pot pointing toward you. The danger that the pot will tip is lessened on a back burner, and if it should tip, the fat would splash on the stove rather than on you.

If, in spite of all your precautions, a flare-up should occur, don't panic. If the flames are within the kettle itself, cover it closely with a lid, thus putting out the fire by cutting off the supply of oxygen. If the flames are outside the pot as the result of spillage, turn off the heat immediately and throw a handful of baking soda or salt over the flames. Never, never pour water over flaming fat or oil: it will only cause the flames to spread.

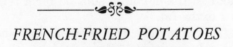

FRENCH-FRIED POTATOES

The boiling potatoes that I recommend produce a crisp, golden-brown French fry with sufficient interior moisture to give the potatoes a texture I like. You may, however, prefer to use baking potatoes. They contain more starch than the boiling varieties and produce a French fry which has a more mealy interior.

Not only are there two types of potatoes from which you can choose, but also two methods of frying them. The first involves only one frying, but it produces, for my taste, an overly thick crust. The second, or two-frying, method has definite advantages: you can prefry the potatoes and let them stand; then, a few minutes before serving, you can quickly complete the frying. I prefer this method because the potatoes, when cooked, have a thinner and more delicate crust.

SERVES 4

4 or 5 medium potatoes, preferably the boiling type, peeled and cut into strips ⅜ inch wide, ⅜ inch thick, and 2 inches long (about 4 cups)

Vegetable oil (or any other deep-frying fat you prefer) to fill a deep fryer to a depth of at least 3 inches

Salt

Preparing the potatoes. Ideally, the potatoes should be peeled and cut into strips immediately before they are fried. If you must prepare them earlier, drop the strips into a bowl of cold water to prevent them from discoloring. In either case, immediately before frying them, spread the potatoes out on a double layer of paper towels and pat them completely dry with more paper towels.

Line a shallow pan with a double or triple layer of paper towels.

Preheat the oven to its lowest setting for keeping the first batches of potatoes warm after they are fried.

The one-frying method. Heat the oil or fat until it reaches a temperature of 375° F. Set the frying basket in place to preheat.

Raise the basket, drop a large handful of the potatoes into it, and lower it slowly into the pot. The fat will instantly bubble up and possibly foam; if it comes too near the brim, lift the basket out of the pan and let the bubbling subside for a few seconds. Then return the basket to the fat.

Watch the thermometer. The temperature should return to 375° F. within a minute or so. If not, increase the heat until you obtain that reading, then lower the heat again to maintain that temperature.

To prevent the potatoes from sticking to the basket or to each other, every now and then lift the basket partially out of the fat and shake it gently. The potatoes should be golden brown and crisp in 8 to 10 minutes. If you feel they have reached the color you like in less time, taste one to make sure it is done. If it is too firm to your bite, lower the heat a bit and continue deep frying for a minute or two longer.

Immediately remove the basket from the fat and turn the

potatoes out onto the paper-lined pan to drain. Set the pan in your preheated oven. Batch by batch, fry and drain the remaining potatoes as before. Sprinkle them liberally with salt and serve at once.

The two-frying method. For the first frying of the potatoes, heat the fat to a temperature of 325° F. Set the frying basket in place to preheat. Fry the potatoes, batch by batch, for only about 6 minutes per batch, or until they have just begun to color, draining them on the paper towels as you proceed. The potatoes may be flabby and unattractive, but don't be concerned. They can now be set aside at room temperature for anywhere from 5 minutes to an hour before the second frying.

A few minutes before you intend to serve the potatoes, reheat the fat to a temperature of 375° F. and preheat the frying basket in the fat. Then, handful by handful as before, deep fry the potatoes for about 2 minutes, or until they are golden brown and crisp, adjusting the heat as described above if it drops too much. Drain and salt the potatoes and serve them at once.

HAM CROQUETTES

You needn't be limited to ham when you make these croquettes. You can use any number of leftovers you might have on hand: lamb, pork, tongue, chicken, or turkey would make respectable substitutes. The meat must, of course, be ground and used in the same amount as the ham. Depending upon the meat you choose, you may want to change the seasonings to your taste.

Instead of shaping the croquettes into the balls I suggest in the recipe, you can, if you like, roll the mixture into cones or cylinders, forms that are in a sense more traditional than the more easily made balls. But whatever their shape, croquettes can be served as a luncheon or dinner dish and accompanied by almost any vegetable, and small croquettes make delectable accompaniments for drinks of any kind. If you shape them into small balls about 1 inch in diameter, somewhat reduce the frying time given in this recipe.

Croquettes may be kept warm for 10 minutes or so in a low oven without harm.

The Croquette Mixture:

3 tablespoons butter, cut into bits
3 tablespoons finely chopped onions
3 tablespoons flour
¾ cup warm fresh or canned chicken broth
2 egg yolks
1 pound baked or boiled ham, trimmed of all fat and finely
    ground (about 2 cups, firmly packed)
2 tablespoons finely chopped fresh parsley
1 teaspoon prepared mustard
Freshly ground black pepper
½ teaspoon strained fresh lemon juice

The Trio Coating:

½ cup unsifted flour
2 eggs, beaten with 4 teaspoons cold water
1½ cups fine dry bread crumbs

For Frying:

Vegetable shortening (or any other deep-frying fat or oil you
    prefer) to fill your deep fryer to a depth of at least 3 inches

The Garnish:

Lemon wedges
Parsley sprigs

Making the croquette mixture. Drop the butter bits into a 2-quart
saucepan and set it over moderate heat. When the butter has
melted but not yet begun to brown, add the onions. Stirring occasionally with a wooden spoon, cook the onions for about 5 minutes,
or until they are translucent and soft. Don't let them brown; if at
any point they begin to color, lower the heat.

Add the 3 tablespoons of flour, stirring it into the butter and
onions, and continue to stir until a fairly smooth mixture is formed.
Pour in the warm chicken broth and, using a whisk, stir the mixture
until it comes to a slow boil and thickens into a smooth sauce. Then
reduce the heat to low and cook the sauce slowly for a minute or
two to remove any taste of raw flour.

Remove the pan from the heat and, one at a time, beat in the
egg yolks, whisking until they have been completely absorbed.

With a wooden spoon, stir into the sauce the ground ham,
parsley, mustard, a few grindings of pepper, and lemon juice; taste
for seasoning. Because the ham is salty, it is unlikely that the
croquette mixture will require any more salt.

With a rubber spatula, spread the mixture in a 2-inch layer on a large platter. Cover the platter with plastic wrap and refrigerate it for 2 or 3 hours, or until the mixture is firm enough to shape into croquettes.

Forming and coating the croquettes. With your hands or a large wooden spoon, scoop up enough of the mixture to make a compact ball 2 to $2\frac{1}{2}$ inches in diameter, then roll the mixture around between your palms. To make a cylinder, shape a ball, then roll it back and forth on the work surface under gentle pressure. To make a cone shape, begin with a ball, then mold it to a peak with the fingers. Shape the remaining mixture similarly. When you finish, you should have 8 to 10 croquettes of whatever shape you are making.

Then, following the trio coating method (page 79), coat the croquettes with as much as you need of the flour, the eggs beaten with water, and the bread crumbs. Make sure that each croquette is thoroughly blanketed with the crumbs; if it is not, the creamy inside may break through the crust when it is deep fried.

Although you may deep fry the croquettes at once, the result will be more predictable if you chill them on a cake rack for about an hour, or until the coating has set.

Line a shallow pan with a double layer of paper towels.

Just before you begin the frying, preheat your oven at its lowest setting, and warm a serving platter and the dinner plates in it.

Deep frying the croquettes. Heat the fat in your frying kettle or electric deep fryer to 375° F. If you are using a frying basket, set it in place to preheat. Depending on the size of your deep fryer, lower 4 to 6 croquettes into the fat, using a slotted spoon if you have no frying basket.

Fry the croquettes for 4 to 6 minutes, turning them gently about from time to time until they are a deep golden brown. Remove them from the fat with the spoon or basket and drain them on the paper-lined pan. Pat them gently with more paper towels. Place uncovered in the preheated oven. Then fry and drain the remaining croquettes in precisely the same way.

Serving the croquettes. You may keep the finished croquettes in the preheated oven for up to 10 minutes or so without their coming to harm; or you can serve them at once. In either case, present them on a large warmed platter, surrounded with lemon wedges and parsley sprigs, and serve them on heated plates.

------~§⅜~------

DEEP-FRIED SHELLFISH: OYSTERS, SHRIMP, CLAMS, OR MUSSELS

The function of beer in batters is generally misunderstood. Contrary to what you might expect, it is not the yeast in the beer (present in many European beers, but scarcely ever in American types) that lightens the batter; rather it is the small alcoholic content of the beer that has a tenderizing effect on the flour. In this recipe, the beer and eggs enrich yet lighten the batter; and the combination makes for a delicate, crisp coating appropriate to the subtle flavor of the shellfish.

SERVES 4

The Batter:
1½ cups sifted all-purpose flour
¾ teaspoon salt
1 cup beer, preferably flat; if freshly opened, pour it into
    a bowl and let it rest for 10 minutes or so to allow
    foam to subside
¼ cup vegetable oil
2 egg yolks
1 egg white

The Shellfish:
Your choice of:
    3 dozen large oysters, freshly shucked, or about 1 pound of
        fresh oysters in a sealed container; or
    1½ pounds medium shrimp, shelled and deveined as described
        in the recipe for Sautéed Shrimp (page 137); or
    4 dozen clams, preferably littlenecks or cherrystones,
        freshly shucked; or
    3 dozen large or 4 dozen medium mussels, shucked

For Frying:
Vegetable oil (or any deep-frying fat you prefer) to fill your
    deep fryer to a depth of at least 3 inches

The Garnish:
Lemon quarters
Deep-Fried Parsley (optional; page 110)

Making the batter. Combine the sifted flour and salt and sift them together into a 2-quart mixing bowl. Pour in the beer and, with a wire whisk, stir the ingredients together only long enough to combine them. Then whisk in the vegetable oil and egg yolks. When the eggs have been thoroughly absorbed, set the batter aside. Let it rest, uncovered, for 1 hour at room temperature.

A few minutes before you intend to deep fry the shellfish, beat the egg white in a small glass or stainless steel bowl with a rotary beater or a whisk until it forms firm, unwavering peaks on the lifted beater.

With a rubber spatula, fold the beaten egg white into the batter, cutting down with the spatula and lifting the heavier batter over the lighter egg white. Continue this process until only a streak or two of the white shows. Do not overmix; the batter should be light.

Line a shallow pan with a double layer of paper towels.

To keep the first batch of shellfish warm while you fry the rest, preheat your oven at its lowest setting. Place a heatproof serving platter and the dinner plates in the oven to warm.

Deep frying the shellfish. Heat the fat in your frying kettle or electric deep fryer to 375° F. If you are using a frying basket, set it in place to preheat. Then quickly proceed to coat and deep fry the shellfish you have chosen.

With only minor variations, the procedure is the same for all of the shellfish suggested in this recipe. For oysters, place them in a sieve and shake the sieve to drain them thoroughly. For shrimp, wash them under cold running water and drain them in a sieve. For clams or mussels, if they seem at all sandy, drop them into a sieve and wash them briefly under cold running water, even at the expense of a loss of flavor.

Then spread the shellfish out on a double layer of paper towels and pat them dry with more towels. Drop them into the batter and stir them about with a wooden spoon only long enough to separate them and coat each one with the batter.

Set the bowl of shellfish as close to the deep fryer as possible. Pick up an oyster, shrimp, clam, or mussel with tongs, hold it above the bowl to allow excess batter to drain off, then drop it into the fat. Follow this procedure rapidly with about 8 to 12 pieces; the number will depend on the size of your fryer. Don't crowd them; it is always better to fry fewer pieces at a time rather than more.

Let the shellfish fry undisturbed for a few seconds, then carefully turn them, using a slotted spoon. Cook the oysters for a minute or so, until they are golden brown. For shrimp, let fry for a minute or so before turning, then cook for 2 to 3 minutes, until golden brown. Cook the clams and mussels for about 2 minutes in all, until they are a deep golden brown. In all cases, turn them constantly while they are cooking.

Remove the shellfish from the fryer, using the basket or a slotted spoon, and scatter them on the paper-lined pan to drain. Place the pan in your preheated oven.

Before adding a fresh batch to the fryer, remove any floating bits of batter from the fat, using a slotted spoon. Then, working quickly, fry and drain the remaining shellfish in batches of the same size as the first.

Arrange the shellfish on a warmed serving platter, and garnish them with the lemon quarters and the fried parsley, if you like. Serve them at once on heated plates.

DEEP-FRIED PARSLEY FOR GARNISHING

With Deep-Fried Shellfish—or, for that matter, any other fried food—Deep-Fried Parsley makes a garnish that is both delicious and attractive.

Simply drop sprigs of parsley, which must be free of any trace of dampness, into the hot fat for a second or two. Remove them with a slotted spoon as soon as they turn crisp, which will happen almost instantly. Drain the parsley on paper towels and serve it at once.

DEEP-FRIED SAVORY TURNOVERS

Instead of making the large turnovers suggested in this recipe, which would be served as a first or main course, you may wish to make cocktail-size turnovers. If so, cut the pastry into 3-inch rounds and reduce the quantity of filling for each to a tablespoon or less. The frying time will be shorter than that given for large turnovers. The golden color of the pastry will indicate when the cocktail turnovers are done. As you will notice, the turnover filling, except for the cream, is precisely the same as the preceding Ham

Croquette mixture. As in the croquette recipe, you may substitute for the ground ham any number of leftovers you may have on hand: ground lamb, pork, tongue, chicken, or turkey; and, depending on the meat you choose, you may wish to change the seasonings as well.

MAKES 8 LARGE TURNOVERS

The Pastry:
2 cups sifted all-purpose flour
½ teaspoon salt
8 tablespoons butter (a quarter-pound stick), cut into ¼-inch cubes and thoroughly chilled
3 tablespoons shortening, thoroughly chilled
⅓ cup ice-cold water
¼ cup unsifted flour

The Filling:
3 tablespoons butter, cut into bits
3 tablespoons finely chopped onions
3 tablespoons flour
¾ cup warm fresh or canned chicken broth
2 egg yolks
1 pound baked or boiled ham, trimmed of all fat and finely ground (about 2 cups, firmly packed)
2 tablespoons finely chopped fresh parsley
1 teaspoon prepared mustard
Freshly ground black pepper
½ teaspoon strained fresh lemon juice
2 tablespoons heavy cream

For Frying:
Vegetable oil (or any other deep-frying fat you prefer) to fill your deep fryer to a depth of at least 3 inches

Making the pastry. To 2 cups of sifted flour add the salt and sift them together into a large mixing bowl. Add 8 tablespoons of cubed butter and the shortening, and toss the ingredients together with your hands to coat the butter and shortening with flour. Then rub the flour and fats together, using the thumbs and first two fingers of each hand in a sliding motion, as if you were counting out money. Do not squeeze or press the dough.

After a moment or two, rub a handful of the mixture between both hands with a sliding motion, letting the flakes fall into the bowl. Then return to the thumb-and-finger operation. Continue until the fats and flour are fairly well integrated in comparatively dry flakes. Don't attempt to make the blend too uniform; there should be occasional small nuggets of flour-coated fat among the flakes.

Immediately pour the ice-cold water over the mixture and toss it with your hands until you are able to gather the dough into a compact ball. If it seems crumbly (most unlikely), sprinkle in an additional teaspoonful—no more—of cold water. You should then have no difficulty in patting the dough into a ball.

Hold the ball in one hand and, with the other, lightly and evenly sprinkle it with the ¼ cup of unsifted flour.

Pack the dough in plastic wrap or a plastic bag and refrigerate it for at least 3 hours—or, better yet, for a day or overnight. The pastry must be thoroughly chilled before it is used.

Making the filling. Drop the 3 tablespoons of butter bits into a 2-quart saucepan and set it over moderate heat. When the butter has melted but not yet begun to brown, add the onions. Stirring occasionally with a wooden spoon, cook the onions for about 5 minutes, or until they are translucent and soft. Don't let them brown; if at any point they begin to color, lower the heat.

Add 3 tablespoons of flour, stir it into the butter and onions, and continue to stir until a fairly smooth mixture is formed. Pour in the warm chicken broth and, using a whisk, stir the mixture until it comes to a slow boil and thickens into a smooth sauce. Then reduce the heat to low and cook the sauce slowly for a minute or two to remove any taste of raw flour.

Remove the pan from the heat and, one at a time, beat in the egg yolks, whisking until they have been completely absorbed.

With a wooden spoon, stir in the ground ham, parsley, mustard, a few grindings of pepper, lemon juice, and heavy cream; taste for seasoning. It is unlikely that the croquette mixture will require any more salt because of the saltiness of the ham.

You may refrigerate the mixture if you like, but it is not essential. However, the filling must be cooled completely before it is used.

Rolling the dough. Remove the dough from the refrigerator, unwrap it, and let it rest at room temperature until it softens just enough for you to press your forefinger into it fairly easily. Don't let the dough get too soft.

Place the ball of dough on a floured pastry cloth and pat it into a circle about 4 inches in diameter.

Position your rolling pin, encased in its floured sleeve, across the center of the dough and roll it away from you in one firm continuous stroke, lifting the pin as you near the edge of the dough.

Shifting your direction slightly to the right, return the pin to the center of the dough, and again roll it away from you precisely as before.

Continue this rolling procedure all around the circle of dough, each time overlapping the last stroke by about 1 inch. Your strokes will circle the pastry like a hand around the face of a clock. When you reach the point where you began, your pastry circle should be about ⅛ inch thick and 13 inches in diameter.

Using a saucer or dish of 6-inch diameter as a guide, cut the pastry into rounds with a small sharp knife or a pastry wheel. When you have made as many rounds as you can, gather the scraps of dough together into a ball and reroll the dough. Again cut out as many 6-inch rounds as you can. If you do not yet have a total of 8 rounds, reroll and cut the remaining scraps of dough.

Making the turnovers. Lay the pastry rounds on a sheet of wax paper and drop 2 tablespoons or more of the croquette mixture onto the center of each. With a pastry brush, moisten the edges of the rounds with a little cold water and fold the pastry over the filling to make half-moon shapes. Press the prongs of a table fork all round the curved edges to seal the pastry securely. The turnovers may now be covered with plastic wrap and refrigerated for anywhere up to 6 or 8 hours; or they can be deep fried at once.

Line a shallow pan with a double layer of paper towels.

Just before you begin the frying, preheat your oven at its lowest setting, and warm a serving platter in it. If you are serving the turnovers as a first or main course, also warm the dinner plates at the same time.

Deep frying the turnovers. Heat the fat in your frying kettle or electric deep fryer to 375° F. If you are using a frying basket, set it in place to preheat. Depending on the size of your deep fryer, lower 2 or 3 turnovers into the fat, using a slotted spoon if you have no basket.

Fry the turnovers for 6 to 8 minutes, turning them over gently with a slotted spoon from time to time so they brown evenly. When the turnovers are a deep golden brown, lift them from the fat and drain them on the paper-layered pan. Pat off any excess fat with other paper towels. Place uncovered in the preheated oven. Fry and drain the remaining turnovers in similar batches. Serve them immediately when all are done.

APPLE FRITTERS

In this recipe for deep-fried fruit in batter, which is Dutch in origin, the beer serves the same tenderizing functions as it does in the batter for shellfish (page 108). But because this batter contains no eggs, it produces a different type of coating. It is much like a crisp pastry, and it is dense enough to enclose the moist fruit securely.

These substantial fritters may be served as a dessert after a fairly simple main course, but they are equally effective accompanied by crisp bacon or a slice of grilled ham for breakfast or luncheon.

SERVES 4

The Batter:
1¾ cups sifted all-purpose flour
1½ cups beer (a 12-ounce can), preferably flat; if freshly
   opened, pour it into a bowl and let it rest for 10 minutes
   or so to allow foam to subside

The Fruit:
½ cup granulated sugar
½ teaspoon cinnamon
4 medium apples, preferably Greenings (about 2 pounds),
   peeled, cored, and cut crosswise into ½-inch slices

For Frying:
Vegetable oil (or any vegetable shortening you prefer) to fill
   your deep fryer to a depth of at least 3 inches

For Dusting the Fritters:
Confectioners' sugar

Making the batter. Pour the sifted flour into a 2-quart mixing bowl and add the beer. Then, using a wire whisk, stir—don't beat—the two together for about 2 minutes, or until the mixture is quite smooth. The batter may be used at once, but it will have a far better texture if it is allowed to rest, uncovered and at room temperature, for 2 hours.

Preparing the fruit. In a small bowl, mix together the granulated sugar and the cinnamon. Dip each slice of apple into the mixture, coating both sides. Place the slices on a cake rack set over a sheet of wax paper and let them rest for 30 minutes, but no longer.

Line a shallow pan with a double layer of paper towels.

Just before you fry the fritters, preheat your oven at its lowest setting and place a serving platter and the plates in it to warm.

Deep frying the fritters. Heat the fat in your frying kettle or electric deep fryer to 375° F. If your fryer has a basket, set it in place to preheat. Then quickly proceed to coat and deep fry the apples.

Set the bowl of batter and the rack of apple slices close to the deep fryer. With tongs, pick up a slice of apple, dip it into the batter, then hold it above the bowl to allow the excess batter to drain off. Gently drop it into the hot fat.

Repeat this procedure rapidly with 3 or 4 more slices; remember not to overcrowd the frying kettle. Let the fritters fry undisturbed for a minute or two, then turn them carefully with tongs. As they continue to fry, turn the fritters every minute or so until they are golden brown and crusty. They should take about 5 minutes in all to cook through.

Remove the finished fritters from the pot with tongs and drain them on the paper-lined pan. Gently pat them with more paper towels to remove any excess fat. Set the pan in the preheated oven. Then quickly fry and drain the remaining apple slices in batches of the same size as the first one.

Serving the fritters. Transfer the fritters to the warmed platter, dust each one with a little confectioners' sugar, and serve them at once on warmed plates.

VARIATION: PINEAPPLE FRITTERS

You may make Pineapple Fritters by substituting a can of sliced pineapple (1-pound 4-ounce size) for the apples. Omit the sugar and cinnamon coating, but drain the pineapple and pat the slices dry before coating and frying them in precisely the same way as the apple slices.

Dust the finished fritters with confectioners' sugar and serve them at once.

————— ·❧§❧· —————

BATTER-FRIED VEGETABLES:
ARTICHOKE HEARTS, SQUASH, OR EGGPLANT

The exceedingly simple batter for the vegetables in this recipe was undoubtedly first devised by the Italians. They use it for the most part to make their famous *fritto misto,* or mixed fry. The batter produces a lacy-edged, crisp coating that is eminently suitable for vegetables because it in no way masks the pristine flavor of the vegetables themselves.

You might want to experiment on your own with vegetables other than the ones I suggest. Be careful to choose only those— such as mushrooms and zucchini—that require a minimum amount of cooking, or you will find that the batter will be crisp but the enclosed vegetables underdone.

I prefer to serve Batter-Fried Vegetables the way the Italians do—as a separate course. I combine as many suitable seasonal vegetables as I can find and present them in a magnificent heap on a large platter garnished with lemon wedges and parsley or watercress.

SERVES 4

The Batter:
1½ cups sifted all-purpose flour
¾ teaspoon salt
1 cup tepid water
¼ cup olive oil
2 egg whites

The Vegetables:
Your choice of:
    1 package (9 ounces) frozen artichoke hearts,
      completely defrosted; or
    1½ pounds tender yellow summer squash; or
    1 or 2 eggplants (about 1½ pounds)
Salt
Freshly ground black pepper

For Frying:
Vegetable oil (or any deep-frying fat you prefer) to fill
    your deep fryer to a depth of at least 3 inches

Making the batter. Pour the flour, ¾ teaspoon salt, and water into a 2-quart mixing bowl. With a wire whisk, stir the ingredients together only long enough to combine them. Whisk in the olive oil, and continue to whisk until the batter is smooth.

The batter may be used at once, but ideally it should stand uncovered at room temperature for at least 30 minutes before it is used.

A few minutes before you intend to deep fry the vegetables, beat the egg whites with a rotary beater in a small glass or stainless steel bowl—or, for more volume, use a copper bowl and a balloon whisk—until they form firm, unwavering peaks on the lifted beater.

With a rubber spatula, fold the beaten egg whites into the bowl of batter, cutting down with the spatula and lifting the heavier batter over the lighter egg whites. Continue this process until you can see only a streak or two of the whites. Do not overfold.

Line a shallow pan with a double layer of paper towels.

Just before you fry the vegetables, preheat your oven at its lowest setting, and place a heatproof serving platter and the plates in it to warm.

Preparing the vegetables: artichoke hearts. Spread the defrosted artichoke hearts on a double layer of paper towels and dry them completely with more towels. Because artichokes vary in size and you want uniform pieces for deep frying, cut any large hearts in half. Sprinkle the artichokes lightly with salt and, if you like, with a liberal grinding of black pepper.

Preparing the vegetables: yellow summer squash. Trim the squash, but don't peel them, and slice into rounds about ¼ inch thick. Sprinkle the slices lightly with salt and, if you like, more liberally with black pepper.

Preparing the vegetables: eggplant. With a swivel-bladed vegetable peeler, peel the eggplant; trim away about ½ inch from each end. Then cut the eggplant into quarters lengthwise. Lay each quarter on one of its flat sides and cut it crosswise into slices about ¼ inch thick. This will make about 3 to 4 cups of triangular eggplant pieces.

Drop the pieces into a 2-quart glass or stainless steel bowl, sprinkle them with 1 teaspoon of salt, and toss them about with a wooden spoon to distribute the salt evenly. Let the eggplant rest for an hour to remove any bitterness and excess moisture. Then drain the eggplant in a sieve, spread the pieces out on a double layer of paper towels, and pat them dry with more paper towels.

Deep frying the vegetables. Heat the fat in your frying kettle or electric deep fryer to 375° F. If you are using a frying basket, set it in place to preheat. Then quickly proceed to coat and deep fry the vegetables as follows.

Drop the vegetable pieces into the batter and stir them about gently with a wooden spoon only long enough to separate them and coat each one with batter.

Set the bowl of vegetables as close to the deep fryer as possible. With tongs, pick a piece out of the batter and hold it above the bowl to allow the excess batter to drain off, then drop it into the hot fat. Repeat this procedure rapidly until you have filled the deep fryer with 6 to 8 pieces of artichoke hearts or about a third to a half of the squash or eggplant; the number of pieces will depend on the size of your fryer. Don't overcrowd the pot.

Let the squash fry undisturbed for a few seconds, the artichoke hearts and eggplant for about a minute, then turn the pieces carefully with a slotted spoon and let them fry for another minute or so longer, turning them often, until they are golden brown.

Lift the vegetables from the fat, using the basket or a slotted spoon, and transfer them to the paper-lined pan to drain. Set the pan in the preheated oven. Fry and drain the remaining pieces in batches of the same size as the first one. When all are done, serve them at once.

PARMESAN CHEESE FRITTERS

Chou paste, or *pâte à choux* as the French call it, most frequently used to make cream puffs and other baked pastries, takes on another dimension entirely when it is deep fried. It explodes into fritters of the most fanciful shapes. Either dusted with powdered sugar or served with a fruit sauce such as apricot-peach sauce (page 120), they make a spectacular dessert. And such is the versatility of chou paste that, with the addition of cheese, as in this recipe, or of other seasonings, fritters made from it become a perfect savory accompaniment for drinks.

Do not attempt to double or halve these recipes, or the results may be unpredictable. If you need more than the 2 cups of paste my recipe yields, make two separate batches. If you need half the amount, make the full amount and wrap the surplus in foil and refrigerate it for another use, such as for cream puffs (page 421) or savory puffs (pages 418 and 420).

MAKES 25 TO 30 FRITTERS

The Pastry:
Chou Paste (page 414)
1 teaspoon prepared mustard
1½ cups freshly grated imported Parmesan cheese

For Frying:
Vegetable oil (or any deep-frying fat you prefer) to fill your
deep fryer to a depth of at least 3 inches

Making the pastry. Follow the instructions for making Chou Paste. To the paste, add the prepared mustard and 1 cup of the grated Parmesan cheese. Using a wooden spoon, beat the paste vigorously for 1 to 2 minutes. Taste the mixture for seasoning and add more mustard and some salt if you like.

Allow the paste to cool to lukewarm, then deep fry the fritters at once. Or, if you prefer, you can cool the paste to room temperature, then cover it with plastic wrap and set it aside, unrefrigerated, for as long as a day.

Deep frying the fritters. Line a shallow pan with a double layer of paper towels.

Preheat the oven at its lowest setting and warm a serving platter in it.

Heat the frying fat until it reaches a temperature of 375° F. If you are using a frying basket, set it in place in the kettle to preheat.

Pick up a heaping teaspoonful of the pastry and push it off into the fat with the back of another teaspoon. Repeat this procedure until you have made about 8 fritters, the number depending upon the size of your deep fryer. They will begin to puff up in a minute or two, so don't crowd the kettle.

Theoretically at least, the fritters should turn over on their own accord as they fry, but don't count on it. You will be on the safe side if you turn the fritters over every minute or so with a slotted spoon. They should be well puffed and a deep golden brown in about 4 to 5 minutes. Remove the fritters at once from the fat and drain them on the paper-lined pan. Place this in the preheated oven.

Fry and drain the remaining pastry in similar batches. You

may serve the fritters at once, or keep them warm in your preheated oven for anywhere from 5 to 10 minutes without their coming to any harm.

Serving the fritters. Arrange the fritters attractively on a warmed platter and sprinkle them with the remaining ½ cup of grated Parmesan cheese.

VARIATION: DESSERT FRITTERS WITH APRICOT-PEACH SAUCE

SERVES 6

The Sauce:
1 medium can (about 1 pound) apricots, preferably pitted
1 medium can (about 1 pound) sliced peaches, preferably
   the Elberta variety
2 cups granulated sugar
¼ cup Grand Marnier or any other orange-flavored liqueur
   (Curaçao, Cointreau, or Triple Sec, for example)

The Pastry:
Chou Paste (page 414)
1 tablespoon granulated sugar (optional)
1 teaspoon vanilla (optional)

For Frying:
Vegetable oil (or any vegetable shortening you prefer) to fill
   your deep fryer to a depth of at least 3 inches

For Dusting:
Confectioners' sugar

Making the sauce. Combine the apricots (pitting them first, if necessary), the peaches, and the syrup of both in the container of an electric blender or food processor. Blend until the fruits are thoroughly puréed (at high speed for a minute or so in a blender; or by turning the food processor on and off 4 or 5 times). If you must do this by hand, simply drain the fruit juices into a large bowl, then force the fruit through a food mill into the bowl of juices; or rub it through a medium-meshed sieve with the back of a large metal spoon. Discard any skins or coarse pulp remaining in the food mill or sieve.

Pour the purée into a heavy 2-quart saucepan, add the granulated sugar, and stir thoroughly with a large wooden spoon. Set the pan over moderate heat and, stirring constantly, bring the purée to a boil. Immediately reduce the heat to low and simmer the mixture, uncovered, until it thickens into a heavy but still fairly fluid sauce. This may take anywhere from 1 to 1½ hours. During this period, stir it from time to time, especially around the crease of the pan, to prevent it from scorching or sticking.

When the sauce is finished, stir in the liqueur, pour the mixture into a serving bowl, and cool it to room temperature before serving. Or refrigerate it, securely covered with plastic wrap. The sauce may be safely refrigerated for several days or even a week.

Making the pastry. Follow the instructions for making Chou Paste. While it is still warm, you may stir into the paste the optional tablespoon of granulated sugar and the vanilla. Because the fritters will be dusted with confectioners' sugar and served with a sweet sauce, I think the sugar and vanilla unnecessary; but if you like your desserts very sweet, by all means include them.

Deep frying the fritters. Follow the preceding recipe precisely as you deep fry and drain the fritters. You may, if you wish, keep the succeeding batches warm in an oven preheated at its lowest setting while you finish the frying.

Serving the fritters. Arrange the fritters on a large warmed platter or on warmed individual serving plates and dust them with confectioners' sugar. Serve the bowl of apricot-peach sauce separately.

Or omit the dusting of confectioners' sugar and pour a spoonful or so of the sauce around each serving. Present the remaining sauce in a bowl. (Any leftover sauce can be used as a topping for ice cream or other desserts.)

Sautéing: Gentle Browning, Subtle Saucing

The French term *sauté* implies rapidity: it comes from the word *sauter*, meaning "to jump." Its use derives from the fact that French professional chefs toss pieces of food around like beanbags in a sauté pan (*sautoir*), making them jump in order to brown them rapidly and evenly. You will doubtless be relieved to know that these calisthenics are entirely unnecessary. The same rapid and uniform browning can be achieved calmly, if less spectacularly, by turning the food over in the pan with a spatula or tongs.

Your object in making a true sauté is not the crispness achieved by frying, a term often used synonymously for sautéing, but the light browning of a food that will be bathed in a sauce. The sauce is not made entirely apart from the sauté; it is prepared directly in the sauté pan and based on the drippings, or glaze, left behind when the browned food is removed.

You will note that there are no fish sauté recipes in this section, a deliberate omission on my part. The drippings of browned fish can be unpleasant in flavor, and no really sensitive cook would ever consider them as a base for a sauce. The recipe for Filets de Soles à la Meunière clearly illustrates this point. The dish might almost be called a sauté except for the fact that, after the fish has been fried, the drippings are discarded entirely, the pan is wiped clean, and a simple brown-butter sauce is quickly made in the same pan. Apart from this one culinary ambiguity, the sautéing process in all the other recipes is clearly defined.

Techniques for Sautéing

The sauté pan. Ideally, all sautéed dishes should be made in *sautoirs*, heavy sauté pans. I recommend a 10-inch aluminum one because it can be considered an all-purpose sauté pan for the recipes in this section. Heavy 12-inch sauté pans are also available, but they are exceedingly expensive and take considerable strength to lift. In specific recipes, wherever possible, I offer the alternative of using a 12-inch frying pan—it has a 10-inch bottom—when the substitution will not affect the results.

For a sauté containing wine, lemon juice, or egg yolks, never use a black iron skillet. The iron will discolor such sauces and give them a metallic taste. Any other heavy frying pan—one of stainless steel, for example—will do in a pinch.

Sautéing the food. Because your object in sautéing, unlike that in pan frying and deep frying, is not to brown foods deeply or to create and maintain a crisp coat, it is important that you exercise extreme care to prevent too deep a browning during the initial, or frying, step of preparing a sauté. Nor should you allow the brown sediment of drippings that forms on the bottom of the pan to burn; this glaze is the basis of the sauce after the lightly browned food is removed.

The glaze. As you will see in some of the following recipes, the fatty part of the drippings is often discarded, except for a filmy layer left in the pan. This layer contains the beautiful brown particles—the concentrated essences—which, when dissolved in the appropriate liquid over high heat, give body and flavor to the sauce. The small amount of fat remaining in the pan with the glaze contributes its flavor to the sauce as well. In the unfortunate event that the glaze should burn during the initial browning, wipe the pan clean with a paper towel and in place of the glaze use 2 tablespoons of melted butter as a base for the sauce.

Liquids for the sauce. The most commonly used liquids for combining with the glaze are chicken or beef stock and wine. Chicken or beef stock is best freshly made, but a good canned brand—always called broth, incidentally, on the can—will serve almost as well. If the canned broth is a condensed type, follow the directions on the can for diluting it with water. There are, however, other brands of chicken and beef broth that do not call for any dilution. I think these, for the most part, are superior to the condensed broths. Don't use canned consommé, either chicken or beef, as a substitute for broth; it is generally too sweet in flavor and may contain added gelatin.

When wine is called for, make certain it is dry and not sweet wine. Any good domestic white wine, such as a Mountain White or a Chablis, will do. If you buy a wine for use in a recipe, you might —as discriminating diners do—drink the remainder of the bottle with the sautéed fish. Under no circumstances use a so-called cooking wine or a wine that you wouldn't drink; it will taste just as bad in the sauce as it would in a glass.

Reducing the sauce. All sauces for sautés require the culinary process known as "reduction." It consists of boiling liquids and glaze together, uncovered, so that half of the sauce, more or less, evaporates, thus concentrating and intensifying its flavor.

Reheating sautés. Except for those made with liver, beef, or shrimp, the sautés in this section may be prepared ahead of time and reheated before serving. Reheat them gently, and make certain that the sauce does not come to a boil. Your object is to heat the food and sauce through without any further cooking.

Serving sautés. It is even more important than for fried foods that all sautéed dishes be served on preheated platters and plates. Therefore, 15 minutes before serving any sauté dish, place a heatproof platter and your dinner plates in the oven, then turn on the oven to its lowest possible setting.

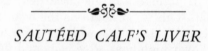

SAUTÉED CALF'S LIVER

For this sauté recipe I definitely prefer the delicate flavor and texture of calf's liver to other livers. You may, of course, experiment with beef liver if you like.

SERVES 4

1 to 1½ pounds calf's liver, cut into slices ¼ inch thick
1 teaspoon salt
Freshly ground black pepper
⅓ cup unsifted flour
5 tablespoons butter, cut into bits
1 tablespoon vegetable oil
1 cup fresh or canned chicken broth
¼ teaspoon fresh lemon juice
2 tablespoons finely chopped fresh parsley

Preparing the liver. With a small sharp knife, remove the membrane from the edge of each slice of liver; insert the knife under the thin membrane, and strip it away as if you were peeling an onion. This will prevent the slices from curling unattractively when they are placed in the hot fat.

Do not wash the liver; simply pat it dry with paper towels. Then lay the slices on a sheet of wax paper and sprinkle them with

½ teaspoon of the salt, distributing the salt evenly by rubbing it lightly with your fingers over each slice. Season with as much pepper as you like, then turn the slices over and season on the other side with the remaining salt and with pepper to your taste.

Just before beginning the sauté, turn your oven on at its lowest temperature and warm a serving platter and plates in it.

Frying the liver. Spread the flour on a strip of wax paper. Using the wax paper method (page 78), flour the liver. When all the slices have been floured with a powdery-thin layer, sauté them at once; any delay will cause the moisture to seep through the coating and turn it gummy.

Combine 4 tablespoons of the butter bits with the vegetable oil in a heavy 12-inch frying pan with a nonstick surface. Set the pan over high heat. When the butter begins to brown very lightly, add the liver, one slice at a time. Each slice will instantly contract and thus make space for the remaining ones.

When all the liver is in the pan, lower the heat to moderate. Fry the slices for no more than 2 minutes, or until small spots of blood begin to appear here and there on the surface. Then, with a spatula or tongs, quickly turn the liver over and brown the other side as you did the first. When small blood spots appear on the already browned side, the liver (for my taste at least) is done. It should be medium-rare.

If you are doubtful about this, cut into one of the slices with the point of a small sharp knife. If the liver is too rare for your taste, fry the slices for about a minute longer. Do not, however, overcook the liver, or it may toughen.

Immediately remove the pan from the heat and lay the liver slices in an overlapping row down the center of the heated platter. Cover the platter loosely with a sheet of foil to keep the liver warm while you quickly make the sauce.

Making the sauce and serving the sauté. Pour the chicken broth into the drippings remaining in the pan and set it over high heat. As the broth comes to a boil, scrape and stir constantly with a wooden spoon to dissolve the glaze. Then continue to boil the sauce for about 3 minutes, or until it has reduced to about half the original amount. Stir in the lemon juice and parsley.

Remove the pan from the heat and add the remaining butter bits, tipping the pan back and forth until they melt. Immediately pour the sauce over the liver and serve it at once on the heated platter.

———————— ❧❧❧ ————————

CHICKEN SAUTÉ PAPRIKA

Chicken Sauté Paprika must not be confused with Hungarian chicken *paprikash*, which is usually made by poaching or braising a chicken with onions and paprika and thickening the sauce with sour cream.

This recipe is frankly an invention of my own and, although Hungarian in its orientation, is based on the classic French chicken sauté. But it is still Hungarian enough in essence to call for a Middle European accompaniment; and the most suitable one I can think of would be buttered noodles, tossed with caraway seeds.

SERVES 4

A 2½- to 3-pound chicken (a broiler-fryer)
2 teaspoons salt
3 tablespoons lard
1 cup finely chopped onions
1 teaspoon finely chopped garlic
2 tablespoons flour
2 tablespoons sweet Hungarian paprika
1 teaspoon finely cut fresh dill leaves or ½ teaspoon
    dried dill weed
1½ cups fresh or canned chicken broth
½ cup sour cream
⅛ teaspoon fresh lemon juice
1 tablespoon finely cut fresh dill leaves or
    finely chopped fresh parsley

Preparing the chicken. For this sauté, don't buy the quartered chickens sold prepackaged in most supermarkets unless you have no choice. Hacked with a cleaver more often than not, they look unattractive and may contain bone splinters as well.

Following the instructions on page 174, quarter a chicken or, if you prefer, have your butcher cut up the chicken in the manner indicated. Chicken cut up in this fashion will not shrink unduly as it cooks. Moreover, it will retain its natural juices as a properly sautéed chicken should. Just before serving you may, if you wish, divide each quarter into two pieces as described below.

Pat the chicken quarters thoroughly dry with paper towels; they won't brown well if they are the least bit damp. Lay the pieces on a sheet of wax paper and sprinkle them evenly on one side with 1 teaspoon of the salt. Turn the quarters over and season the other side with the remaining salt.

Just before beginning the sauté, turn your oven on at its lowest temperature and warm a serving platter and dinner plates.

Frying the chicken. In a 10-inch sauté pan, melt the lard over high heat. When the lard almost, but not quite, reaches the smoking point —it will show faint watery ripples on its surface and give off a light haze—add the chicken pieces, skin side down.

Brown the chicken as quickly as you can, regulating the heat so that the skin turns golden brown after 6 to 7 minutes of frying. Every now and then lift the chicken pieces with tongs, checking to make sure they are not browning too rapidly. Then turn the pieces with the tongs and brown the flesh side for 3 or 4 minutes. This side of the bird takes less time to brown than the skin side.

Now cover the pan tightly, reduce the heat to low, and simmer the chicken for about 15 to 20 minutes. Two or three times during the cooking period, baste the chicken with the pan juices, using a bulb baster, and re-cover the pan tightly each time.

At the end of 15 minutes' simmering, test the chicken for doneness by piercing the fleshy part of the thigh with the point of a small sharp knife. You may have to poke around a bit, but you will soon discover a spot in the thigh which will give off a thin trickle of juice. If the juice is a faint yellow color, the chicken is done; if it is tinged with pink, re-cover the pan and simmer the chicken a little longer.

Transfer the chicken to a large plate and cover it loosely with foil to keep warm while you make the sauce.

Making the sauce. Leaving behind in the pan any dark-brown bits (the glaze), pour all the fat into a small dish, then return 3 tablespoons of the fat to the pan, discarding the rest. Add the chopped onions and garlic and cook over low heat for about 8 minutes, stirring occasionally with a wooden spoon until the vegetables have softened and colored very lightly.

Meanwhile, in a small bowl, combine the flour, paprika, and 1 teaspoon of fresh dill or ½ teaspoon of dried dill weed.

Stir the mixture into the simmering onions; dark-red clumps will form almost instantly. Still over low heat, stir the mixture into a paste with a whisk, then pour in the chicken broth. Raise the heat to high and bring the sauce to a boil, whisking constantly. Immediately lower the heat, and still whisking, simmer the sauce for 2 or 3 minutes, or until it is very thick and smooth.

Now, using your whisk as if it were a spoon, dip it into the sour cream and stir the cream clinging to the wires into the simmering sauce; don't let the sauce boil from this point on. Repeat this process until all the sour cream has been added. Then add the lemon juice and taste the sauce for seasoning; it will probably need some salt. Don't be timid about this; the sauce should have a definite, assertive flavor.

If you prefer to serve the chicken in 8 pieces rather than in quarters, separate the thighs from the drumsticks and cut each breast in half diagonally.

With your tongs, return the chicken to the pan, together with any juices that may have collected around it. Turn the chicken over in the sauce until every part of it is coated. Then cover the pan and simmer the chicken for 2 or 3 minutes, or long enough to heat it through.

Once the sauté has been completed, it may be set aside in its pan, unrefrigerated and loosely covered, for anywhere up to 2 hours. Before serving, cover the pan and reheat the chicken over moderate heat for 5 minutes or so, turning and basting it with the sauce, until it is heated through. Don't, however, allow the sauce to come to a boil; it may become too thin, or possibly curdle.

Serving the sauté. Lift the chicken out of the pan with tongs and arrange the pieces, skin side up, on a heated serving platter. Pour the sauce over the chicken, using a rubber spatula to remove all of it from the pan. Sprinkle the top with the tablespoon of dill or parsley and serve at once on heated plates.

SAUTÉED STEAK STRIPS IN A CHINESE SAUCE

You will never find this dish in either a Chinese cookbook or a Chinese restaurant, but its overtones are unmistakably Chinese. Although I have included it in this section because I follow my sauté techniques in making it, it could just as easily have been placed in the stir-frying section, since the meat is stir-fried before being sauced.

Authentically Chinese or not, Sautéed Steak Strips should be accompanied by hot boiled rice; you might even serve the steak and its sauce over the rice.

SERVES 4

2 pounds boneless sirloin, strip, or tenderloin steak,
   cut ½ inch thick
½ teaspoon salt
Freshly ground black pepper
1 tablespoon cornstarch
2 tablespoons cold water
3 tablespoons peanut oil
2 teaspoons finely chopped garlic
5-ounce can whole water chestnuts, drained and cut into
   ¼-inch matchstick strips (about ½ cup)
¾ cup fresh or canned chicken or beef broth
2 tablespoons soy sauce
½ cup coarsely chopped scallions, including about
   2 inches of green stems

Preparing the steak and the sauce ingredients. With a large sharp knife, trim the steak of all fat, then slice the meat into strips ¼ inch wide and 2 inches long. Place the strips in a medium-size mixing bowl and add the salt and a discreet grinding of pepper. With a wooden spoon or your hands, toss the meat about for a moment or two, until the strips are evenly seasoned.

In a small dish, stir the cornstarch and cold water together and set the dish aside.

Set your oven to its lowest setting and in it warm a serving platter and dinner plates. Because the sautéing and saucing of the meat are done so rapidly, it is imperative that you have a heated serving platter right next to you when you begin.

Making and serving the steak sauté. Pour the peanut oil into a wok or 10-inch sauté pan or a 12-inch frying pan and set it over high heat. Let the oil become as hot as it can get without smoking; test it by dipping the end of a steak strip into it—the oil should sizzle instantly.

Add the meat all at once, and, stirring constantly with a wooden spoon, fry the strips over high heat for no longer than 3 minutes, or only until no trace of redness remains. Immediately stir in the garlic and water chestnuts and continue to stir for a moment; then add the chicken or beef broth.

When the sauté comes to a boil, in a matter of seconds, give the cornstarch and water a couple of quick stirs to make certain the mixture is smooth, then stir it into the boiling sauce. The sauce will thicken and clear almost instantly. Mix in the soy sauce and taste for seasoning, adding a little more soy sauce if you like.

With the aid of a rubber spatula, transfer the contents of the wok/pan onto the heated platter and spread out the steak strips. Scatter the chopped scallions over the top and serve the sauté at once on the heated plates.

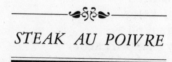

STEAK AU POIVRE

The amount of black pepper in this recipe may strike you as inordinate. Let me assure you that, rather than making the flavor of the sautéed shell steak fiery hot, the coarsely crushed peppercorns give it a tantalizing piquancy. The French, who may or may not have invented the dish, obviously adore it, because they serve it on every possible occasion. My version is somewhat different from theirs—and considerably easier to make—but the final result is equally effective.

SERVES 4

4 boneless shell steaks or strip steaks weighing
    about ¾ pound each, cut ¾ inch thick, trimmed of
    all but ¼ inch of outside fat
1½ teaspoons salt
1½ tablespoons black peppercorns, coarsely crushed
⅓ cup Cognac or any good domestic brandy
1 teaspoon arrowroot
1 tablespoon water
4 tablespoons butter, cut into bits
1 tablespoon vegetable oil
¾ cup fresh or canned beef broth
½ teaspoon fresh lemon juice
2 tablespoons finely cut fresh chives, or 3 tablespoons
    frozen chives

Preparing the steaks. Lay the steaks on a chopping board or a sheet of wax paper, and rub them on both sides with the salt. Then sprinkle half of the crushed peppercorns evenly over one side of the steaks. With the side of your clenched fist, pound the pepper as firmly into the meat as you can. Turn the steaks over, sprinkle on the remaining peppercorns, and again pound in the pepper as before. Naturally, the steaks will be thinner after pounding, probably about ½ inch thick.

Just before you cook the steaks, preheat the oven at its lowest setting and warm a serving platter and dinner plates.

Frying the steaks. Pour the Cognac or brandy into a small saucepan and set it aside. In a small dish, mix the arrowroot and water together and place nearby.

Combine 3 tablespoons of the butter bits with the oil in a 10-inch sauté pan or a 12-inch frying pan and set the pan over high heat. When the butter has begun to turn ever so lightly brown, add the steaks. Immediately, lower the heat to moderate and fry the steaks for 1 minute. Then, with tongs, or a fork inserted close to the rim of fat, turn the steaks over. Fry the other side for 1 minute, then turn the steaks again. Continue cooking and turning every minute or so for a total cooking time of 4 minutes if you prefer your steak rare. Should you prefer steaks on the medium-rare side, fry them a minute or two longer.

A minute or two before you think the steaks are cooked to your taste, you might do well to test one of them for doneness, employing the touch technique used by professional cooks: Poke the center of the steak firmly with your forefinger. If the meat is fairly soft and yielding, the steak will be rare; if it is slightly resistant, medium-rare. These steaks should *never* be cooked to the well-done stage.

Another, but less desirable, testing method for steaks is to cut into the meat close to the bone or at the edge of the fat with a small sharp knife. Peer into the cut; you will then know whether to cook the steaks longer or not.

Now remove the pan from the heat. Quickly heat the reserved saucepan of Cognac or brandy just to lukewarm (you can test it with your fingertip) and, holding the pan well away from you, touch the surface of the brandy with a lighted kitchen match. Slowly pour the flaming Cognac over the steaks, simultaneously sliding the pan back and forth sharply until the flames die out.

Immediately remove the steaks from the pan and arrange them attractively on the heated platter. Cover the platter loosely with foil to keep the steaks warm while you make the sauce.

Making the sauce and serving the steaks. Pour the beef broth into the sauté or frying pan and set it over high heat. As the broth comes to a boil, scrape and stir constantly with a wooden spoon to dissolve the dark glaze. Then continue to boil undisturbed for about 2 minutes.

Stir the arrowroot and water to make certain the mixture is

smooth, then stir it into the boiling sauce. It will thicken almost instantly.

Remove the pan from the heat, and add the lemon juice, chives, and remaining butter bits. Tip the pan back and forth until the butter has melted.

Immediately pour the sauce over the steaks, using a rubber spatula to remove all of it from the pan. Serve the steaks at once on the heated plates.

ÉMINCÉ DE VEAU

This very rich dish of sautéed veal strips in wine and cream sauce is a great classic of the Swiss cuisine, its native country, and is usually served with a shredded fried potato cake called *rösti*. Émincé de Veau really means "minced veal," and it is so popular in Switzerland that the Swiss have invented special machines for cutting the veal into strips.

The veal should be of the best quality you can afford, light pink in color and free of gristle and external fat.

SERVES 4

1½ pounds boneless veal from the leg or rump, cut into
    slices ½ inch thick
½ teaspoon salt
⅛ teaspoon white pepper
5 tablespoons butter, cut into bits
1 tablespoon vegetable oil
2 tablespoons finely chopped shallots or
    white parts of scallions
½ cup dry white wine
1 cup heavy cream
1 tablespoon finely chopped fresh parsley

Preparing the veal. After your butcher has cut the veal into ½-inch slices, ask him to pound the slices until they are ⅛ inch thick; then slice the pounded meat into strips about ¼ inch wide and 1 inch long.

Place the veal strips in a medium-size mixing bowl, add the salt and white pepper, and toss the meat with a wooden spoon or your hands until the strips are evenly seasoned.

Just before you fry the veal strips, turn on your oven at its lowest setting and warm a serving platter and dinner plates in it.

Frying the veal strips. Combine 3 tablespoons of the butter bits with the vegetable oil in a 10-inch sauté pan and set the pan over high heat. When the butter begins to brown very faintly, add the veal strips all at once. Stirring constantly over high heat with a wooden spoon, fry the veal for 2 or 3 minutes, or until all trace of pinkness has disappeared. Then pour the contents of the pan into a large sieve set over a mixing bowl and allow the veal to drain while you prepare the sauce.

Making the sauce. Return the pan to moderate heat and add the remaining butter bits. When they have melted but not yet begun to turn brown, add the shallots or scallions. Stirring with a wooden spoon, cook them gently for a minute or two, or until they are soft and translucent but not brown.

Immediately pour in the wine, raise the heat to high, and bring the sauce to a rapid boil. Let it boil turbulently for about a minute, then pour in the cream and all the juices that have collected in the bowl under the sieve. (You can then empty the veal into the bowl and set it aside.)

Again bring the sauce to a rapid boil, then lower the heat to moderate. Cook, stirring almost continuously, for 6 or 8 minutes, or until the sauce has reduced sufficiently to cling in a light film to your spoon. Reduce the heat to low and add the veal, tossing the meat lightly about for a minute or two while it heats through and becomes coated thoroughly with the sauce. Taste for seasoning.

You can prepare this dish 2 or 3 hours before you plan to serve it. Reheat it for 2 or 3 minutes, turning the meat gently in the sauce, or only until the meat and sauce are warmed through. Be careful not to heat it beyond that point, lest the veal become tough. The sauce, however, may now be too thick. In that event, thin it with 2 or 3 tablespoons of heavy cream, adding more salt if you think the sauce needs it.

Serving the sauté. With the aid of a rubber spatula, transfer the veal strips and sauce onto the heated platter. Sprinkle the top with chopped parsley. Serve the sauté at once on heated plates.

—◦§◦—

SCALOPPINE AL LIMONE

The Italians make veal scaloppine in innumerable ways—sometimes with wine, sometimes with mushrooms, other times with peppers or even cream. But of them all I prefer this version of scaloppine with lemon sauce, called Scaloppine al Limone in most Italian restaurants.

Don't be misled by its simplicity. When perfectly made, it is an exquisite dish; but it does demand the best quality of veal—veal the lightest pink in color and free of all external fat and all gristle. Often, veal for scaloppine sold in most supermarkets is pounded too thin, with the result that the veal cooks too quickly and there is no time for the necessary glaze to form in the pan.

Because veal is so expensive, you have a perfect right to insist that your butcher slice and pound the veal to your order. Strongly object to his "butterflying" any small pieces of veal—that is, cutting the piece lengthwise, but not all the way through, then pounding it to give it the appearance of a single slice of meat. "Butterflied" veal, when sautéed, will invariably retract at the seam and make your scaloppine unattractive. Try to persuade your butcher to pound the slices of veal to uniform thickness and to make them as symmetrical as possible.

SERVES 4

1½ pounds boneless veal from the leg or rump, sliced ⅜ inch
    thick and pounded until ¼ inch thick
½ teaspoon salt
½ cup flour
4 tablespoons butter, cut into bits
1 tablespoon olive oil
¾ cup fresh or canned chicken broth
1 teaspoon fresh lemon juice
8 to 10 very thin slices unpeeled lemon, seeds removed

Preparing and coating the veal. Sprinkle the veal lightly with salt on both sides. Then, using as much of the flour as you need, follow the wax paper flour-coating method (page 78) to coat the veal slices on both sides. Do this immediately before frying them.

Preheat the oven to its lowest setting and warm a large platter and dinner plates in it.

Frying the veal. Combine 3 tablespoons of the butter bits with the olive oil in a 10-inch sauté pan or a 12-inch frying pan and set the pan over high heat. When the butter begins to turn ever so lightly brown, quickly add the veal slices one at a time; each slice will instantly contract and thus make space for the remaining ones.

Fry the veal slices for 3 or 4 minutes on each side, using tongs to turn them. You can tell when the veal is fully cooked by pressing a piece with your finger. It should offer decided resistance to the touch. If the veal still feels soft, fry it for a moment longer, but be careful not to let it burn. The slices should be a delicate golden brown on both sides when they are done.

Remove the pan from the heat and immediately transfer the scaloppine to the heated platter, picking up the slices with tongs and arranging them in one or two overlapping rows down the length of the platter. Cover the platter loosely with a sheet of foil to keep the veal warm while you make the sauce.

You can prepare the sauté up to this point as much as 2 or 3 hours before serving time. Set the browned veal aside and cover it loosely with foil, leaving the drippings in the pan. Make the sauce just before serving.

Making the sauce and serving the veal. Pour off and discard all but the thinnest layer of fat from the pan and return the pan to high heat. Add the chicken broth and bring it to a boil, stirring and scraping constantly with a wooden spoon to dissolve the brown particles on the bottom of the pan. Continue to boil the sauce, uncovered, for 2 to 3 minutes, or until it has a slightly syrupy consistency. If in doubt, let it be thinner rather than thicker. Then stir in the lemon juice and taste the sauce for seasoning. Add the remaining butter bits, remove the pan from the heat, and tip it back and forth until the butter has melted. Immediately pour the sauce over the veal, top the dish with the lemon slices, and serve at once on heated plates.

If you have fried the veal ahead of time, make the sauce just before serving. When you have reduced the sauce to its proper consistency, lower the heat and return the veal to the pan. Basting constantly with sauce, heat the meat only until warmed through. Garnish and serve the dish as described above.

꒰⋅⋇⋅꒱

SAUTÉED CHICKEN LIVERS

This simple and quickly prepared sauté demands nothing more as accompaniments than buttered rice or noodles and Broiled Tomato Halves (page 193). Or you may, if you like, serve the sauté over triangles of hot buttered toast.

SERVES 4

1 pound chicken livers
1½ teaspoons salt
Freshly ground black pepper
⅓ cup unsifted flour
3 tablespoons butter, cut into bits
1 tablespoon vegetable oil
4 tablespoons finely chopped scallions, including about 1 inch of green stems
¼ cup fresh or canned chicken broth
½ teaspoon fresh lemon juice

Preparing the chicken livers. Fresh chicken livers are in every way preferable to frozen ones. If you must use frozen livers, defrost them completely. With a small sharp knife, trim the livers of all fat and any green-tinged bits, then cut each liver in half. Spread them out on a double layer of paper towels and pat them thoroughly dry with more towels. The livers won't brown well if they are even slightly damp.

Place the livers in a medium-size bowl and sprinkle them with the salt and as much pepper as you like. With a wooden spoon, gently toss the livers to season them evenly.

Dump the flour into a sturdy brown paper bag or a plastic bag and drop in the livers. Twist the open end of the bag tightly closed and shake the bag vigorously to coat each piece of liver completely with flour. Pour the contents of the bag into a large sieve and gently shake the sieve from side to side over a sheet of wax paper, leaving the livers coated with only the thinnest layer of flour.

Just before frying the livers, set a serving platter and dinner plates in your oven and turn it on to its lowest setting.

Frying the livers. Combine 2 tablespoons of the butter bits with the vegtable oil in a 10-inch sauté pan or a 12-inch frying pan. Set the pan over high heat. When the butter begins to turn a very light brown, add the livers, tossing them about constantly with a wooden spoon for about a minute. Then lower the heat to moderate and, tossing them only occasionally, fry the livers for about 3 to 4 minutes more. When done, they should still be pink inside. Test one of the liver halves by cutting into it with a small sharp knife. If it is too pink for your taste, fry the livers for a minute or two longer, but do not overcook them lest they toughen.

Immediately remove the pan from the heat and, with a slotted spoon, transfer the livers to the heated serving platter. Cover the platter loosely with foil to keep the livers warm while you make the sauce.

Making the sauce and serving the sauté. Immediately return the pan, with all its drippings, to moderate heat. Add the scallions and, stirring constantly with a wooden spoon, cook them for about 2 minutes, or until they are soft and lightly colored. Pour in the chicken broth, raise the heat to high, and bring the mixture to a rapid boil. Continue to boil the sauce for a moment or so, then stir in the lemon juice.

Remove the pan from the heat and drop in the remaining butter bits. Tip the pan back and forth while the butter melts. Pour the sauce over the waiting livers and serve them at once on the heated plates.

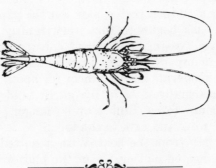

SAUTÉED SHRIMP

I would be inclined to serve this Italian-influenced sauté as a luncheon dish with no other accompaniment than the indispensable hot Italian or French bread with which to sop up the juices. It can, naturally, also serve as the main course at dinner.

Fresh shrimp, which are sometimes difficult to find, are preferable to frozen ones. If you must use frozen shrimp, make sure that they are uncooked, and defrost them completely.

SERVES 4

1½ pounds medium-size shrimp
4 tablespoons butter, cut into bits
1 tablespoon olive oil
1 to 2 teaspoons finely chopped garlic, according to taste
⅓ cup dry white wine
Salt
Freshly ground black pepper
2 tablespoons finely chopped fresh parsley
Lemon quarters

Preparing the shrimp. Shell the shrimp carefully; then, with a small sharp knife or a pair of small scissors, make a shallow incision all along the outer curve of each. With the point of a knife lift out the intestinal vein that is about ⅛ inch under the surface and runs the length of the shrimp's body. Depending on the type of shrimp, the veins will vary in color; they may be black, white, or yellow. Spread the shrimp in one layer on a double thickness of paper towels and pat them thoroughly dry with more paper towels.

Just before frying the shrimp, set a serving platter and the dinner plates in your oven and turn it on to its lowest setting.

Frying the shrimp. Combine the butter bits and olive oil in a 10-inch sauté pan or a 12-inch frying pan. Set the pan over high heat. When the butter has begun to turn very faintly brown, add the shrimp all at once. Tossing them about constantly with a wooden spoon, fry the shrimp over high heat for about a minute, then lower the heat to moderate and fry them for about 3 minutes more, tossing them occasionally. Stir in the garlic, and continue to toss and cook the shrimp for a minute or so longer. When done, the shrimp should be pink and firm to the touch.

Remove the pan from the heat. With a slotted spoon, transfer the shrimp to the heated platter. Cover the platter loosely with foil to keep the shrimp warm while you make the sauce.

Making the sauce and serving the sauté. Immediately return the pan, with all its drippings, to high heat. Pour in the wine and bring it to a rapid boil. Boil it briskly for about a minute, then remove the pan from the heat. With a rubber spatula, scrape up the sauce and pour it over the waiting shrimp, then sprinkle the shrimp lightly with salt and more liberally with freshly ground black pepper. Scatter the parsley over the top, garnish the dish with lemon quarters, and serve the shrimp at once on the heated plates.

—◆§§◆—

FILETS DE SOLES À LA MEUNIÈRE

The oft-used and perhaps perplexing name you have seen on countless menus—Filets de Soles à la Meunière—simply means sole sautéed in the style of the miller's wife. Because the sole is floured before being sautéed, the French, with their penchant for culinary whimsicality, can at least justify the use of the name; certainly a miller's wife would have, if nothing else, an ample supply of flour. But the dish is far more than floured and fried fish, which is surely the reason it has endured for so many years. It lends itself not only to fillets of any white-fleshed fish but also to countless variations, one of which I have included at the end of this recipe—Filets de Soles Amandine, or sautéed fillets of sole garnished with almonds.

SERVES 4

1½ pounds fillet of sole or fillets of any white-fleshed fish, cut
    about ¼ inch thick
1 teaspoon salt
⅓ cup unsifted flour
6 tablespoons butter, cut into bits
3 tablespoons vegetable oil
1 tablespoon finely chopped fresh parsley
1 teaspoon fresh lemon juice
Lemon quarters

Preparing the fish. Wash the fillets quickly under cold running water, spread them on a double thickness of paper towels, and pat them dry with more towels. With a large sharp knife, cut them crosswise into 4-inch serving pieces.

Sprinkle half the salt evenly over the fish, rubbing it into the pieces with your fingers. Turn the fish over and rub in the remaining salt.

Place a serving platter and the dinner plates in your oven and turn it on to its lowest setting.

Flouring the fish. Using the wax paper flour-coating method (page 78), flour the fish with as much of the flour as you need, leaving it with a powdery-thin layer of flour.

Fry the fish at once. Delay will allow the moisture in the fish to seep through the coating and turn it gummy.

Frying the fish. Combine 2 tablespoons of the butter bits with the oil in a 12-inch frying pan and set the pan over high heat. When the butter begins to turn very faintly brown, add the fish. Fry the fillets briskly for about a minute, or until the undersides are a light golden brown. Then, with a slotted spatula, gently turn the pieces over and fry them for a minute or so longer. Naturally, the frying time will depend upon the thickness of the fillets. You can be certain the fish is done when it feels firm to the touch and flakes easily when prodded gently with a fork.

With your spatula, transfer the fish to the heated serving platter, arranging the pieces down the center, overlapping them slightly. Without waiting a second, discard *all* the drippings in the frying pan and wipe the pan clean with a paper towel.

Making the sauce and serving the fish. Drop the remaining butter bits into the pan and set it over high heat. The butter should melt very quickly. When it begins to turn faintly brown and gives off a sweet nutty aroma, stir in the chopped parsley. Fry the parsley for about 10 seconds, then add the lemon juice. The butter will instantly froth and foam. While it is still foaming, pour it over the waiting fish, moistening each piece evenly. Surround the fish with the lemon quarters and serve it at once.

VARIATION: FILETS DE SOLES AMANDINE

This recipe calls for the same ingredients as Filets de Soles à la Meunière, with the addition of 10 to 15 blanched, slivered but untoasted almonds.

Preparing the fish, flouring the fish, and frying the fish. Follow the instructions in the preceding recipe for Filets de Soles à la Meunière.

Making the sauce and serving the fish. Drop the remaining butter bits into the pan and set it over high heat. Let the butter melt, but do not let it brown. Drop in the almonds and stir them about in the butter for 2 or 3 minutes, or until they are lightly browned. Then add the lemon juice and, when the butter foams, quickly pour the contents of the pan—butter, almonds, and all—over the waiting fish. Sprinkle the fish with the parsley, surround it with the lemon quarters, and serve it with the utmost dispatch on warmed plates.

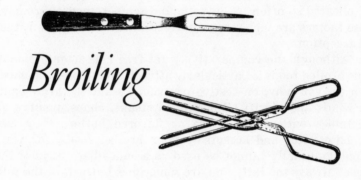

Broiling

*B*roiling is at once the simplest, quickest, and, paradoxically, the most demanding of culinary procedures. Present-day broiling—or grilling, as it is also called—has come a long way from the days when primitive man crudely charred his kill over an open wood fire and consumed it without further ado. Yet, despite the development of our advanced equipment and refined fuels, our basic broiling methods remain essentially the same: our meats, fowl, fish, or vegetables are exposed to the intense and radiant heat produced by glowing charcoal, wood coals, fiery gas jets, red-hot electric coils, ceramic material, or metal, and broiled on a grid, usually one side at a time, to a desired state of doneness.

The foods especially suitable for broiling are, first of all, the tender parts of beef, cut into steaks; several cuts of lamb; chickens in the broiler-fryer category; young and tender ducklings; almost any kind of fish; certain shellfish; vegetables with a fairly high moisture content; and some of the vaguely termed "variety meats,"

141

especially kidneys. I exclude veal and pork because of the essential dryness of these otherwise superb meats. I have also omitted any recipes for a method mistakenly called pan broiling. Despite the assurances of cookware manufacturers who produce ridged pans which presumably broil meats on top of the stove, the truth is that these pans fry your meat instead of broiling it.

My concern is with broiling in the accurate sense of the word, and by that I mean exposing a chosen food to intense heat and at the same time allowing air to circulate around it freely. This sounds simple—and it is—but there are nevertheless several factors involved: choosing suitable raw food for broiling and buying the right quantity, correct broiling temperatures and correct timing, complicated so often by quixotic and temperamental broilers. Once these factors are understood, perfection can be the rule rather than the exception.

Although the comparatively fat-free character of many delicious broiled foods is particularly attractive to those who must count calories, you may, on festive occasions, want to throw caution to the winds and glorify your broiled steaks, chops, poultry, fish, or vegetables with a fine sauce or flavored butter. They can lend exquisite notes and accents to your broiled foods, for which the drippings usually cannot be used as a sauce base because they are almost always too fatty and are sometimes burned. In the following recipes for broiled foods, I frequently suggest compatible sauces and flavored butters, the recipes for which will be found under "A Few Versatile Sauces."

Techniques for Broiling

Preheat your broiler. Successful broiling depends on highly intense radiant heat, so whatever the type or make of your broiler, preheat it at its highest setting for the length of time the manufacturer recommends, or for at least 15 minutes. Remember that the higher the overall heat you build, the more successful your broiling will be. My recipes are based on a broiling compartment temperature of 550° F., which is about as high a temperature as a household broiler compartment can reach.

Start with a cold grid for meats and poultry. Meats and poultry—unless they are thoroughly greased—will stick to a preheated grid. But more important, if your grid has been preheated, food placed on it will begin to cook simultaneously on both sides. Therefore, it is imperative that you begin with a cold grid and broil your meats and poultry first on one side, then on the other, to achieve perfectly controlled browning. Before you turn on your broiler, remove the broiler grid from its pan, then set the pan at the level indicated in each recipe and preheat the pan at the same time you preheat the broiler.

Start with a preheated grid for fish. Because, compared with meats and birds, most fish takes so short a time to broil, I find it advisable to cook fish on a preheated grid so that both sides will begin cooking at the start of the broiling.

Another important reason for preheating the grid is that fish —fillets, for example—are broiled on one side only, and the hot grid will help cook the underside while the top is becoming golden brown. Therefore, before preheating the broiler, set the pan, with its grid in place, at the level indicated in the recipe. As for the danger of the fish sticking to the hot grid, fish of any kind that is to be broiled is always first greased or buttered, and the grid itself is brushed with oil.

Temperature of foods before broiling. Steaks need not be brought to room temperature before being broiled; you may broil them immediately after removing them from the refrigerator. And the same holds true for lamb, poultry, seafood, and vegetables. Thermometer tests indicate that there is not the slightest difference in the total broiling time required by a steak taken directly from the refrigerator and the time needed by a corresponding cut that has been left to languish at room temperature for two hours or more. The warmer steak reaches an *intermediate* internal temperature before a cold steak does, but both arrive at any given stage of doneness— except extremely rare—at precisely the same time. The only exception to this rule is for a steak broiled to the so-called blue, or very rare, stage; I think steak cooked in this fashion something of a culinary barbarity—I would just as soon eat it raw—but for those of you who like it, let the steak come to room temperature before broiling it.

Broiling frozen foods. For the most part I avoid using frozen foods for broiling, but I realize that there are times and places where your choice may be limited to frozen meat, poultry, or seafood. Accordingly, I have included information that should be helpful. In general, beef and lamb may be broiled while still frozen. Chickens and ducklings, on the other hand, must be thoroughly thawed. Frozen fish should be barely defrosted. Shrimp, obviously, must be thawed before they can be separated and prepared for cooking.

Dry food before broiling. Because moisture turns to steam when exposed to dry heat, almost all foods to be broiled should be patted thoroughly dry with paper towels before being subjected to the heat of the broiler. If such foods were to be left moist, they would not begin to brown until the surface moisture had evaporated completely. However, as you will see in the recipes for shashlik and shish kebab, there are occasional exceptions to this rule.

Turning food during broiling. Food should be turned only once during broiling unless, as for fish fillets, it is not turned at all. If you follow the recipes precisely and adjust the heat or the distance from the heat as I suggest when food browns faster or more slowly than it should, one turning will be all that is necessary.

The utensils for turning a food during broiling vary with the food, and are usually specified in the recipes. A long-handled fork may be used for turning steaks and chops, but the tines of the fork should never pierce the meat; they should be inserted into the rim of fat to prevent loss of juices. Tongs, especially long-handled ones with fairly large clamps, are useful for firm-textured foods like steaks, chops, chicken, and shrimp.

Because of its delicate texture, fish presents special problems in turning. You will find on page 188 my technique for using two cake racks to turn a whole fish without breaking it. Fish fillets are broiled without turning, but you will need a broad spatula—or even two of them—to lift fillets safely from grid to platter.

Serving broiled foods. With the possible exception of a thick steak, which can rest without harm for as long as 5 minutes or so, all broiled foods should be served at once on heated platters and plates.

If your broiler is completely separate from your oven, turn the oven on at its lowest setting and warm the platter and plates in it while the food is broiling. If the broiling unit is in the main oven compartment, you may find you can warm your dishes in the space beneath the broiler pan, where they will be protected from the full heat of the broiling unit. A third possibility is to use the heating element of your dishwasher for a few moments. Set the control to "plate warming," or simply set it at a point near the end of the "dry" cycle.

A Note on Safety

Today's slotted broiler grids correctly allow hot air to circulate around food as it broils, but their slots are deliberately narrow to prevent any fat, as it collects in the pan, from catching fire.

In the unlikely event that the fat in the pan should flame up while broiling, don't panic. Calmly pull the shelf holding the broiler pan away from the source of heat and transfer the food to a platter. Then pour a cupful or so of cold milk—and I mean milk, not water, which would be disastrous—over the flames. The flames will expire instantly. Or, if you prefer a more standard procedure, throw a handful of baking soda over the flames to extinguish them. In either case, quickly pour off the accumulated fat from the broiler pan, rinse and dry the grid, and resume the broiling, taking into account any broiling time you may have lost.

Beefsteaks: The American Favorite

The steer is the largest of our domestic meat-producing animals, but of all of its hundreds of pounds of edible meat, only the steaks are tender enough to be broiled.

How to Choose a Steak

If you want to get the best steaks for your money, whatever the cut—and they are all relatively expensive—I would suggest that you learn the precise meaning of three key terms: aging, marbling, and grading.

Aging. Aged meat—that is, meat that has been held under controlled conditions of temperature and humidity for the purpose of tenderizing it and developing a special flavor—is difficult to find in most retail stores. Wholesalers age only the rib and loin sections, and then sell them mainly to restaurants.

The slightly gamy flavor characteristic of well-aged beef is not to everyone's taste. It is good to know, however, that from the time the steer is butchered until the meat reaches you, there is time for considerable natural tenderizing to take place.

If you like aged meat, make a determined effort to find it, but don't attempt to age meat in your own refrigerator. More likely than not, your beef will spoil.

Marbling. This is the term used to describe the small white flecks and short streaks of firm white fat scattered throughout the lean of a steak. When marbling is present in appreciable amounts, your steak is most likely to be juicy, well flavored, and tender.

Federal grading. A fairly good but not always reliable yardstick by which to measure the quality of a steak is the grade given to the carcass or the wholesale cut by a federal inspector. Although federal grading is not mandatory, most good steaks carry the shield-shaped grade mark stamped with a harmless purple dye on the fatty outside of the meat.

Don't confuse the grade mark, however, with the circular stamp which attests only to the mandatory inspection of meat shipped between states. The inspection stamp indicates that the meat is wholesome; the grade stamp, if present, indicates its quality.

Of the four grades available to you in your butcher shop or supermarket, only Prime and Choice need concern you; the other, lower grades of steaks are usually too tough to be broiled. And if the truth be known, there is little, if any, significant difference between superior steaks stamped Prime or Choice.

Steaks for Broiling

From the loin. There are various loin cuts available.

Club steak is the smallest bone-in steak from the loin.

Porterhouse steak includes a large section of top loin and a smaller one of tenderloin.

T-bone steak is much smaller than a porterhouse steak but is the same in structure.

Other steaks from the top loin strip are strip, shell (which are strip steaks with finger and feather bones), New York cut, or Kansas City cut. They are firm-textured and exceedingly expensive.

Filet mignon from the tenderloin is most tender of all steaks, but lacks flavor.

From the sirloin. Sirloin cuts are all pretty much the same except for the shape and placement of their bones. Tender but firm-textured, they are among the most flavorful of all beefsteaks.

A wedge-bone sirloin with a triangular bone is cut closest to the round.

A flat-bone sirloin has a narrow bone lying along one side.

A pin-bone sirloin contains a section of hipbone and part of the backbone.

Boneless sirloin can be any of the above three with the bone and tenderloin removed.

Top sirloin or sirloin tip, from the part of the primal sirloin cut lying next to the round, is also boneless and of good flavor, and is recommended for London broil.

From the ribs. Rib steak, a bone-in steak that tends to be soft-textured, is identical with a slice from a rib roast. Rib eye, or Delmonico, steak is the boneless tender heart of a rib steak.

From various other cuts. Some of the other beef cuts available are flank, top round, and chuck steaks.

Flank steak is a thin, sheetlike steak of lengthwise fibers and fine flavor; for London broil.

Top round steak has good flavor and is more tender than flank; for London broil.

Chuck steaks are various boneless cuts, including shoulder steak, with good flavor; for London broil.

Ground beef: Any cut of beef of good flavor may be ground for broiling; it needn't be a tender cut. Chuck, round, and shin, and steak or roast trimmings, are all usable and good.

Preparing Steaks for Broiling

Trimming the meat. Trim most steaks of all but a ½-inch collar of their surrounding fat to minimize the accumulation of fat in the broiling pan. If the butcher hasn't already done so, notch the fat at 1- or 2-inch intervals, cutting just to the edge of the meat to prevent the steak from curling as it broils.

Seasoning. Don't salt steaks before broiling them; it is not only unnecessary but harmful. Salt will inevitably draw moisture to the surface and inhibit the quick browning that gives steaks their mahogany color. Moreover, actual penetration of the salt—and for that matter, other seasonings as well—during the broiling process is minimal. Salt and pepper a steak just before serving it.

Marinating beef. Marinades should be approached warily. They do indeed contribute their flavor to beef, but their primary function is a tenderizing one. The acid—lemon or lime juice, wine, or vinegar —in any good marinade will, if it is allowed sufficient time to do its job, break down the tissues of meat and make them more tractable.

Only comparatively tough steaks—those in the London broil category, for example—should be marinated if you intend to broil them. But even many of these meats, if they are of the best quality, can be broiled successfully in their natural state. And as for marinating a steak of the first rank, why bother tenderizing it when it is a tender cut to begin with? The flavor contributed by a marinade is, of course, a matter of taste. But comparable and, in fact, more interesting flavors can easily and subtly be introduced with a sauce or a flavored butter.

On the other hand, if a tougher cut of beef you want to broil needs tenderizing, use a marinade, not commercial tenderizers; the action of their enzymes is too violent. Tenderizers not only make the texture of the meat pulpy, but they often destroy whatever character the meat might have were it cooked in more suitable ways.

A Word About Steak Broiling Time

Broiling times given in the Steak Broiling Chart (see pages 150–51) are for fresh or defrosted steaks and for broilers preheated to 550° F.

Broil a frozen steak almost twice as long as a fresh or defrosted steak of the same thickness, and place it at least twice as far from the heat.

Servings per steak are based on estimates of about ½ pound per serving of boneless meat and ¾ pound per serving of bone-in steaks.

Techniques for Broiling Steaks

From the recipes or from the Steak Broiling Chart, note the estimated broiling time that will be required for the steak to reach the point of doneness you prefer.

Place the steak on the cold grid over the preheated broiling pan and slide the pan, with its cargo of steak, into the preheated broiler. Recheck the distance between the surface of the meat and the heat, and begin timing.

Adjusting the broiling time and/or heat. As the steak broils, check it every few minutes so that you can make any necessary adjustments in broiling time or distance from the heat. If your steak is not browning at the rate at which you think it should, at about the midpoint of broiling each side raise or lower the rack, or increase or decrease the heat.

For example, if the total estimated broiling time for a steak is 10 minutes—or 5 minutes per side—and the steak has barely begun to brown after 3 minutes, move the broiler pan closer to the source of heat. And if your steak obstinately remains the same color, subtract a minute or so from the time reserved for the other side and broil the first side that much longer, until you think it is as brown as it should be. Then turn the steak over, replace the pan at its original distance from the heat, and broil the second side, subtracting the time you stole for broiling the first side to the desired shade of brown.

If, on the other hand, your steak seems to be too brown at the midpoint of broiling the first side, it is likely to be burned when the cooking time is up. Depending on your type of broiler, either reduce the heat or lower the rack for the time remaining for that side. When you turn the steak, return the heat or the pan to its original level. Finish broiling the steak, applying the same judgments as for the first side.

Testing for doneness. About 2 minutes before you expect the steak to be done, test it for doneness in one of the following three ways:

THERMOMETER METHOD. The only foolproof method for making certain your steak is rare, medium, or well done is to get an almost instantaneous reading with a "spot-check" thermometer. Pull out the broiler pan and insert the thermometer at least 2 inches deep into the side—not the top—of the steak at a point midway between its surfaces. Make sure the tip doesn't touch any fat or bone, or the thermometer won't function properly; about 2 inches of the stem above the tip contains the sensor, and this must be in contact with the meat itself.

Despite the higher readings which you may find printed on the dials of conventional thermometers, the following internal temperatures are those I consider correct for steaks: rare, 130° to 135° F.; medium, 140° to 145° F.; well done, 160° F.

THE TOUCH METHOD. All raw meat is comparatively soft to the touch. Exposed to heat, it becomes progressively firmer. By poking the center of the broiling steak periodically and sharply with a forefinger, as professionals do, you should soon be able to judge, by its increasing resistance to your touch, the point of doneness the meat has reached. If the meat is fairly soft and yielding, the steak will be rare; if slightly resistant, medium; if quite firm, well done.

Of course, there are variables in this system. A raw sirloin steak, for example, is considerably firmer to the touch than a raw filet mignon. But if you practice the touch method with your favorite steak often enough (backed up by the chart timing and, if possible, a "spot-check" thermometer as well), you can develop enough skill to trust this technique alone.

IF ALL ELSE FAILS . . . THE CUTTING METHOD. Perhaps because of a temperamental broiler or a faulty thermometer, or because of inexperience, you may find yourself still doubtful about whether your steak is done as you prefer. Then—and only then—should you cut into the meat close to the bone or the rim of fat with a small sharp knife and look at the meat quickly. If it does not appear to be the color you like, broil the steak for a moment or two longer.

STEAK BROILING CHART

NAME OF RETAIL CUT	THICKNESS	TYPICAL WEIGHT, TRIMMED
RIB STEAK (bone in and marinated)	1 inch	1 lb.
CLUB STEAK	1 inch	¾–1 lb.
	1½ inches	1–1½ lbs.
	2 inches	1½–2 lbs.
T-BONE STEAK	1 inch	1½–2 lbs.
	1½ inches	2¼–3 lbs.
	2 inches	2¾–3½ lbs.
PORTERHOUSE STEAK	1 inch	2–2½ lbs.
	1½ inches	3–3¾ lbs.
	2 inches	4–5 lbs.
OTHER STEAKS FROM THE LOIN STRIP (Shell Steak, etc.)	1 inch	¾–1 lb.
	1½ inches	1–1½ lbs.
	2 inches	1½–2 lbs.
FILET MIGNON	1½ inches	7–10 oz.
SIRLOIN STEAKS: Pin-Bone, Wedge-Bone, Flat-Bone	1 inch	3–3½ lbs.
	1½ inches	4–5 lbs.
	2 inches	6–7 lbs.
BONELESS SIRLOIN	1 inch	½–¾ lb.
	1½ inches	¾–1 lb.
	2 inches	1–1½ lbs.
LONDON BROIL CUTS (marinated or plain) Flank Steak	½-¾ inch	1½–2 lbs.
Top Round	1 inch	1½–2 lbs.
	1½ inches	2–3 lbs.
	2 inches	3–4 lbs.
Chuck (Shoulder)	1 inch	¾–1¼ lbs.
	1½ inches	1½–1¾ lbs.
	2 inches	1½–2½ lbs.
Top Sirloin	1 inch	¾–2 lbs.
	1½ inches	1–3 lbs.
	2 inches	1½–4 lbs.
GROUND BEEF STEAKS	2 inches	½ lb.

NUMBER OF SERVINGS	DISTANCE FROM STEAK SURFACE TO SOURCE OF HEAT	BROILING TIME—MINUTES PER SIDE		
		Rare 130°–135° F	*Medium* 140°–145° F	*Well Done* 160° F
1	1 inch		3–4	
1	2 inches	4–5	6–7	8–9
1 or 2	3 inches	5–6	7–8	9–10
2 or 3	4 inches	6–7	8–9	10–11
2	2 inches	4–5	6–7	8–9
3 or 4	3 inches	5–6	7–8	9–10
3 to 5	4 inches	6–7	8–9	10–11
2 or 3	2 inches	4–5	6–7	8–9
4 or 5	3 inches	5–6	7–8	9–10
5 to 7	4 inches	6–7	8–9	10–11
1 or 2	2 inches	4–5	6–7	8–9
2 or 3	3 inches	5–6	7–8	9–10
3 or 4	4 inches	6–7	8–9	10–11
1	2 inches	3–4	5–6	7–8
3 or 4	2 inches	4–5	6–7	8–9
4 to 6	3 inches	5–6	7–8	9–10
6 to 8	4 inches	6–7	8–9	10–11
1	2 inches	4–5	6–7	8–9
1 or 2	3 inches	5–6	7–8	9–10
2 or 3	4 inches	6–7	8–9	10–11
4	1 inch	3–4	4–5	
3 or 4	2 inches	4–5	6–7	
4 to 6	3 inches	5–6	7–8	
6 to 8	4 inches	6–7	8–9	
2 or 3	2 inches	4–5	6–7	
3 or 4	3 inches	5–6	7–8	
4 or 5	4 inches	6–7	8–9	
2 to 4	2 inches	4–5	6–7	
2 to 6	3 inches	5–6	7–8	
3 to 8	4 inches	6–7	7–8	
1	2 inches	4–5	6–7	8–9

BROILED SIRLOIN OR PORTERHOUSE STEAK

If you purchase a porterhouse steak, don't have the tail meat ground and reassembled into its original shape as is often done. At best, this is an unfortunate practice. The ground meat takes less time to broil than the steak to which it belongs, and therefore it overcooks to an almost inedible degree, especially if you prefer the steak medium or well done. You would be wiser to leave the tail attached to the steak, or to remove it and use it at another time as part of the beef for Broiled Ground Beef Steaks (page 157).

What to serve with a sirloin or porterhouse steak is not much of a problem. Parsley Butter or Marchand de Vins Sauce is an enlivening addition. If you are planning to broil a steak larger than the ones described, double or triple the sauce recipes.

SERVES ABOUT 4

The Steak:
4- to 5-pound bone-in sirloin steak, or 3- to 3¾-pound
   porterhouse steak, cut 1½ inches thick
Salt
Freshly ground black pepper

The Accompaniment:
Marchand de Vins Sauce (page 438) or Parsley Butter (page
   439)

Preheating the broiler. Remove the grid from your broiling pan and set the pan in the broiler about 4½ inches from the source of heat. Then turn on the broiler at its highest setting and let it preheat for 15 minutes.

Broiling the steak. Plan on broiling the steak for 5 to 6 minutes per side for rare (130° to 135° F.), 7 to 8 minutes per side for medium (140° to 145° F.), or 9 to 10 minutes per side for well done (160° F.). If your steak is thicker or thinner, choose your broiling time from the chart on pages 150–51.

Set the steak on the cold grid. When the grid is placed in the broiling pan, the surface of the steak should be about 3 inches from the source of heat.

Broil the steak on each side for the time indicated, turning it over with tongs or a long-handled fork inserted close to the bone or into the rim of fat. Two or 3 minutes before the broiling time is up, test the steak for doneness with a thermometer or by the touch or cutting methods described on page 149. Extend the broiling time if necessary.

Serving the steak. Transfer the finished steak to a large preheated platter and sprinkle it lightly with salt and pepper.

If you are serving Parsley Butter, spread it over the steak.

If you are serving Marchand de Vins Sauce, immediately set a pan of sauce over high heat and, stirring it constantly with a wooden spoon, bring it almost, but not quite, to the boil. This should take no longer than a minute or two, and the steak will be none the worse for resting.

Pour the sauce into a sauceboat and take the steak and sauce to the table.

Transfer the steak to a carving board. With a small sharp knife, or the tip of your carving knife, cut closely around the bone, then remove it. Then slice the steak crosswise into half-inch strips.

FILETS MIGNONS WITH MOCK HOLLANDAISE SAUCE

Filets mignons as sold in American markets are the very tender, boneless cuts from the narrow end of the tenderloin, usually sliced 1 to 1½ inches thick. Were you to pan fry the filets as the French do, the thinner steak would be preferable to the thicker one. But broiling an inch-thick filet will tend to dry it out quickly, because this cut of beef has little interior fat. That is why I recommend that you have your filets cut 1½ inches thick and, moreover, that you baste them with butter as they broil—a departure from the treatment of other steaks.

To give greater elegance and substance to these broiled filets on toast, you may, if you like, broil 4 large mushrooms (as described on page 195), timing them so that they will be done at the same time as the filets. When you serve the filets, top each one with a mushroom before moistening it with the sauce and garnishing it with crisp watercress bouquets.

The Steaks:
4 filets mignons cut about 1½ inches thick and weighing about
    ½ pound each
4 tablespoons butter, melted, then cooled
4 slices homemade-type white bread, cut into circles
    approximately the diameter of the steaks, toasted, and
    buttered
Salt
Freshly ground black pepper

The Accompaniment and Garnish:
Mock Hollandaise Sauce (page 433)
Watercress

Preheating the broiler. Remove the grid from your broiling pan and
set the pan in the broiler about 3½ inches from the source of the
heat. Then turn on the broiler at its highest setting and let it preheat for 15 minutes.

Broiling the filets. Plan on broiling the filets mignons for 3 to 4
minutes per side for rare (130° to 135° F.), 5 to 6 minutes per side
for medium (140° to 145° F.), or 7 to 8 minutes per side for well
done (160° F.).

With a pastry brush, coat the filets thoroughly on all sides
with about half the butter. Arrange the filets on the cold grid and
set the grid in the broiling pan. The surface of the meat should be
about 2 inches from the source of heat when you place the grid in
the pan.

Broil the filets on each side for the time you have chosen, turning them over with tongs. Brush the meat with the remaining
butter at the midpoint of the broiling time for each side. One or 2
minutes before the broiling time is up, test the filets for doneness
by your choice of the methods described on page 149.

Heating the sauce. Set a pan of Mock Hollandaise Sauce over moderate heat and stir the sauce with a whisk until it almost but not
quite comes to a boil. If it is too thick for your taste, thin it with a
tablespoonful or more of cream.

Serving the filets. Arrange each round of buttered toast in the
center of a heated plate. Place a filet mignon on each round and
sprinkle it liberally with salt and a few grindings of pepper. Spoon
a tablespoonful of the warm sauce over each filet. Garnish each

plate with 2 or 3 sprigs of crisp watercress and serve at once. Pass the remaining sauce separately in a small bowl or sauceboat.

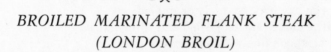

BROILED MARINATED FLANK STEAK (LONDON BROIL)

A flank steak of superior quality—it has a special and delicious flavor all its own—can be successfully broiled without marination, but generally the beef is not notable for its tenderness and is often improved by marination. Whether you marinate your flank steak or not—and this will not affect the broiling time—it must be served very rare, or at the most at the medium stage, if it is not to be too chewy; and it must be carved into thin, diagonal slices.

Steaks from other parts of the steer are also used for London Broil. They may be marinated in precisely the same fashion as a flank steak, or not marinated at all, and they are broiled and carved in the same manner. Use the following recipe for the other London Broil cuts of various thicknesses: simply make the adjustments in broiling time and distance from the heat that are indicated in the chart on pages 150–51. The London Broil cuts available are:

From the round. Top round steak used for London Broil is usually cut from 1 to 2 inches thick. The round has far less fat than the flank and tends, on the whole, toward greater tenderness and evenness of texture.

From the chuck. Superior-quality boneless chuck (shoulder clod) of various cuts, including boneless, chuck steak, or shoulder steak, has excellent flavor and is comparatively inexpensive. All chuck steaks should be tenderized by marination, because for the most part they are among the toughest of broilable steaks. You will discover that whatever part of the chuck you choose, the seams of meat often separate. This is easily remedied by having your butcher sew or skewer the openings together.

From the sirloin. The boneless steak called top sirloin or sirloin tip is usually cut about 1 to 1½ inches thick. Because it is usually tender, it need not be marinated unless you feel dubious about its quality.

The Marinade:
½ cup vegetable oil
4 tablespoons red wine vinegar
½ teaspoon salt
½ teaspoon very coarsely ground black pepper
1 large bay leaf, coarsely crumbled
2 large cloves garlic, peeled and thinly sliced
1 tablespoon finely chopped fresh parsley

The Steak:
1½- to 2-pound flank steak
Salt
A few grindings of black pepper
4 tablespoons butter, cut into bits

Making the marinade. Pour oil, vinegar, and ½ teaspoon of salt into a small bowl, and beat them together vigorously with a whisk until the vinegar and oil are thoroughly combined. Stir in ½ teaspoon of coarsely ground pepper, bay leaf, garlic, and parsley, and pour the entire mixture into a shallow glass or stainless steel baking dish just large enough to hold the steak snugly.

Dip the steak into the marinade, turning it over two or three times to moisten both sides thoroughly. Then lay it flat, spoon some of the marinade over it, and cover the dish with plastic wrap. Refrigerate for 6 to 8 hours, turning the steak over every few hours, or whenever you think of it.

Preheating the broiler. When you are ready to broil the steak, remove the grid from the broiling pan and set the pan in the broiler about 1½ to 2 inches from the source of heat. Then turn on the broiler at its highest setting and let it preheat for 15 minutes.

Broiling the steak. Plan on broiling the steak for 3 to 4 minutes per side for rare, 4 to 5 minutes per side for medium.

Remove the steak from the marinade and pat it dry with paper towels. Set the steak on the cold grid. When you return the grid to the broiling pan, the surface of the steak should be about 1 inch from the source of heat.

Broil the steak on each side for the time you have chosen, turning it over with tongs. A minute or so before the broiling time is up, test the steak for doneness, using the touch or cutting method (described on page 149) a flank steak is too thin for a reliable thermometer reading.

Carving and serving the steak. Transfer the steak to a heated platter, sprinkle it with salt and freshly ground pepper, and dot it with the butter bits.

At the table, place the steak on a carving board and carve it as follows: Use a long, very sharp carving knife. Place your carving fork firmly in the meat well back from the end where carving will begin. Hold the knife at as flat an angle as possible in relation to the steak in order to cut slices with large surfaces, and slice the meat across the grain as thinly as you can.

As you will note, conventional carving procedures will not do at all for any of the London Broil cuts; the very thin slices will make the meat seem considerably more tender than it may actually be.

Arrange the slices of steak on heated serving plates, then over each serving spoon a few tablespoons of the buttery juices which will have collected in the well of the carving board.

BROILED GROUND BEEF STEAKS

Contrary to some snobbish notions, a ground beef steak need not be made wholly from tender and expensive cuts of beef. In fact, I think a ground beef steak has flavor when cuts such as sirloin are combined with chuck, round, or shin, or with the tails of porterhouse steaks.

Grinding is in itself a tenderizing process, so you need not be concerned with the tenderness of the cuts. But whatever you use, insist that it be ground to order and in full view. Or better still, do it yourself—a simple matter if you have a grinding attachment for an electric mixer, a hand grinder, or a food processor.

And if you would have your ground beef steak moist and succulent, include 1 to 1½ ounces of fat for every pound of meat. The added fat can be ground suet (beef fat), chopped marrow, or soft butter mixed lightly into the meat. Or you may enclose a tablespoonful of butter, plain or herb-flavored, in the center of each of the steaks before broiling them, as I do in this recipe.

I must caution you, however, not to broil ground beef unless it is shaped into patties 1½ to 2 inches thick. Thinner patties—hamburgers—should be pan fried.

Serve ground beef steaks as you would a steak, either plain or, if you have omitted the herb-flavored butter, with Parsley Butter (page 439), Mock Hollandaise Sauce (page 433), or Marchand de Vins Sauce (page 438).

SERVES 4

2 pounds lean ground beef
1 teaspoon salt
Freshly ground black pepper
4 tablespoons butter, cut into 4 equal parts; or ¼ cup
   herb-flavored butter of your choice (pages 439–41)

Preheating the broiler. Remove the grid from your broiling pan and set the pan in the broiler about 4 inches from the source of heat. Then turn on the broiler at its highest setting to heat for 15 minutes.

Preparing the meat. Drop the ground meat into a bowl and, with your hands, toss it lightly with the salt and a few grindings of pepper. Divide the beef into 8 equal parts, flattening them a trifle but still handling the meat lightly; you don't want to compress it too much. Place 1 tablespoon of the butter on each of 4 portions, then top the butter with one of the remaining 4 portions of meat. With your hands slightly moistened with cold water, gently pat the "sandwiches" into ovals about 2 inches thick, making sure that the butter in each is securely enclosed.

Broiling the ground beef steaks. Plan on broiling the ground beef steaks for 4 to 5 minutes per side for rare (130° to 135° F.), 6 to 7 minutes per side for medium (140° to 145° F.), and 8 to 9 minutes per side for well done (160° F.).

Place the steaks on the cold grid. When the grid is placed in the broiling pan, the surface of the steaks should be about 2 inches from the source of heat.

Broil the ground beef steaks on each side for the time indicated, turning them carefully with a spatula. Two or 3 minutes before the broiling time is up, test them for doneness by any of the methods described on page 149. Serve the ground beef steaks at once on a large heated platter.

RIB STEAKS FLORENTINE

Because of their characteristically soft texture, rib steaks were never a favorite of mine. I'd always felt that ribs of beef should be left in their majestic glory and roasted rather than cut into steaks. But that was before I tasted the superb Florentine beef, from the breed called Chianina, which the Italians broil as steaks. I was determined to duplicate their meltingly tender texture with American beef.

After experimenting with every standard cut, I found that I preferred a steak that is also a Florentine favorite. It is a rib steak cut 1 inch thick, marinated in olive oil and fresh lemon juice, then broiled—not to rare or well done—but to medium.

SERVES 4

The Marinade:
¾ cup olive oil
¼ cup fresh lemon juice

The Steaks:
4 rib steaks cut 1 inch thick and weighing about 1 pound each
Salt
Freshly ground black pepper
2 tablespoons olive oil (optional)

The Garnish:
Lemon quarters

Marinating the steak. Pour ¾ cup of olive oil and the lemon juice into a small bowl and beat them together with a whisk until thoroughly combined. Then pour the marinade into a shallow glass or stainless steel dish just large enough to hold the 4 steaks in one layer.

Dip the steaks into the marinade, turning them over two or three times to moisten them thoroughly. Then lay them flat, spoon some of the marinade over them, and cover the dish with plastic wrap. Marinate at room temperature for 4 to 6 hours or in the refrigerator for 6 to 8 hours, turning the steaks over every hour, or whenever you think of it.

Preheating the broiler. When you are ready to broil the steaks, remove the grid from the broiling pan and replace the pan in the broiler about 2 inches from the source of heat. Then turn on the broiler at its highest setting and let it heat for 15 minutes.

Broiling the steaks. Remove the steaks from the marinade and pat them thoroughly dry with paper towels. Set the steaks on the cold grid and return the grid to the broiling pan. The surface of the steaks should be about 1 inch from the source of heat.

Broil the steaks on each side for 3 to 4 minutes for medium, the ideal stage for beef cooked in this fashion, turning them over with tongs. A minute or so before the broiling time is up, test the steaks for doneness, using the touch or cutting method described on page 149.

Serving the steaks. Transfer the steaks to a large heated serving platter and sprinkle them liberally with salt and more discreetly with pepper. Brush each steak with a little of the additional olive oil in the Florentine manner if you like, and garnish the platter with the lemon quarters.

Serve the steaks at once on heated serving plates.

Lamb: Tender and Broilable

Unlike the steer, which yields a comparatively small amount of meat tender enough to be broiled, the lamb is a veritable cornucopia of tender and broilable meats—chops, steaks, legs, and variety meats, particularly the kidneys. In fact, almost every part of the lamb can be broiled in one way or another, simply because most lamb sold in the United States comes from young and tender animals.

Although a few markets sometimes sell, at premium prices, "hothouse" or "baby" lamb that is less than 3 months old, most of the lamb you buy is from animals 3 to 10 months old. Whatever its age, perfectly broiled lamb has incomparable flavor, especially if it is broiled to the state the French call *à point*, that is, to the pink or medium-rare stage. It is also worth noting that only over-cooked lamb has that special flavor disparagingly called "lamby," and that lamb that has been properly broiled has a texture indistinguishable from that of a superior beefsteak, yet with a character all its own.

How to Choose Lamb

When compared with beefsteaks, the broilable cuts of superior lamb have very little variation in texture and flavor. Exceptions, perhaps, are the shoulder cuts, which tend to be less tender than other chops and thus benefit from marination.

Marbling and aging. You should consider marbling and aging when buying lamb for broiling, but to a lesser extent than for beef. Lamb may or may not be aged, depending in part on the maturity of the animal. Marbling of fat throughout the meat is present in varying degrees, too; in general, the younger the lamb, the less interior fat there will be.

Very young lamb that has been milk-fed is pale pink. The color of the flesh—which should always be fine-textured and what is termed "velvety"—darkens in older animals until, in yearlings, the meat may be almost red.

Grades of lamb. The federal grades for lamb are precisely the same as for beef. As when buying beef, you should be primarily concerned with the Prime and Choice grades, or their equivalent in packers' brands.

Externally, a significant difference between lamb and beef is the fell, the thin parchmentlike membrane that lies just under the skin of the lamb. Despite old wives' tales prevalent for so long, the fell has no flavor whatsoever; it is left on as a protection before the lamb is marketed, and the only reason for removing it—for broiling purposes, at least—is to trim away any excess fat that lies beneath it.

Lamb Cuts for Broiling

From the loin. Loin chops are shaped exactly like a porterhouse.

From the ribs (rack). Rib chops are identical in shape to rib beefsteaks, though they have a smaller kernel of meat attached to the bone than a loin chop, so single rib chops are less desirable for broiling than double ones. Frenched rib chops have had the fat trimmed from their long bones.

From the shoulder. Shoulder chops, cut from the meatiest portion of the animal except for the leg, include two categories, both larger in diameter than the chops cut from the loin or the rib: arm chops, with a round bone, and blade chops, with a long bone. They are meaty but chewy, and best when marinated.

From the leg. Boned leg. To serve 6 to 8, a leg should weigh 6 to 7 pounds before boning and fat removal. To serve 4, remove the shank end and any irregular pieces.

From various cuts. Ground lamb may be made from good-quality, lean shoulder or shank meat or from trimmings from chops, roasts, or a boned leg.

Preparing Lamb for Broiling

Trimming the meat. The surplus fat should be trimmed from lamb before it is broiled. On chops, leave an outside rim of fat ⅛ inch wide. On a boned, flattened leg of lamb, remove most of the external fat and any clumps of fat elsewhere.

Seasoning. Like beefsteaks, lamb that has not been marinated should not be salted before it is broiled, except, of course, for ground lamb steaks. To salt the uncooked meat would draw moisture to the surface and prevent it from browning as quickly and as well as it should.

Marinating lamb. Rib and loin chops are so tender that they never require marination if the meat is of good quality. Shoulder chops and cubed lamb for shish kebabs are somewhat different; I recommend marination before broiling in order to tenderize these meats.

A Word About Lamb Broiling Time

Broiling times given in the Lamb Broiling Chart (see page 163) are for fresh and defrosted meat and for broilers preheated to 550° F.

If you like rare lamb (135° F.), subtract 2 minutes from the broiling time for "medium" for each side, then test the meat with a "spot-check" thermometer a minute or so before the end of the estimated broiling time for the second side.

Rib or loin lamb chops and ground lamb patties may be broiled while still in their frozen state. Count on broiling frozen chops about twice as long as the recipe directs for unfrozen meat, and place the chops about twice as far from the heat as you ordinarily would. Shoulder chops must be thoroughly defrosted in order to be marinated, and a leg of lamb for broiling must be completely thawed before it can be boned, trimmed, and butterflied in preparation for broiling.

LAMB BROILING CHART

NAME OF RETAIL CUT	THICKNESS	TYPICAL WEIGHT, TRIMMED	NUMBER OF SERVINGS	DISTANCE FROM MEAT SURFACE TO SOURCE OF HEAT	BROILING TIME—MINUTES PER SIDE	
					Medium 140°–145° F.	Well Done 160° F.
RIB CHOPS Single	1 inch	5–6 oz.	2 per person	2 inches	5–6	7–8
Double	2 inches	¾ lb.	1 per person	4 inches	7–8	9–10
LOIN CHOPS Single	1 inch	5–6 oz.	2 per person	2 inches	5–6	7–8
Double	2 inches	¾ lb.	1 per person	4 inches	7–8	9–10
SHOULDER CHOPS	1 inch	½ lb.	2 per person	2 inches	6–7	8–9
BONED LEG, BUTTERFLIED	1½ to 2 inches maximum	4–4½ lbs.	6 to 8	5 inches	15	20
GROUND LAMB STEAKS	2 inches	½ lb.	1 per person	2 inches	6–7	8–9

Servings of lamb are based on ½ pound per serving of boned and trimmed leg of lamb or ground lamb and ¾ pound to 1 pound for chops.

Techniques for Broiling Lamb

From the recipes or from the Lamb Broiling Chart (page 163), note the approximate times for broiling the meat to various states of doneness.

Place the lamb on a cold grid, place it over the preheated broiling pan, and slide the pan into the preheated broiler. Recheck the distance between the surface of the meat and the heat, and begin timing.

Adjusting the broiling time and/or heat. As the lamb broils, it's wise to check it at the points suggested in the recipe so that you can make necessary adjustments in either the broiling time or the distance from the heat.

If, for example, the estimated cooking time for the first side of a double loin lamb chop is 7 to 8 minutes and the chop has barely begun to take on color after 5 minutes, move the broiler pan closer to the heat for the remaining time. If that doesn't result in the glorious shade of brown you want, subtract a minute or so from the time reserved for the other side and broil the first side that much longer. Then turn the lamb over, replace the pan at its original distance from the heat, and broil the second side, subtracting the time you stole for broiling the first side.

If, on the other hand, the lamb appears to be browning too quickly at the midpoint of broiling the first side, either reduce the heat or move the broiling pan farther from the heat for the time remaining for the first side. Then, when you turn the meat over, return the heat or the pan to its original position. At the midpoint of broiling the second side, check again and follow the same procedure as for the first side, if the meat is browning too fast.

Testing for doneness. About 2 minutes before you expect the lamb to be done, test it for doneness by the thermometer, touch, or cutting methods described on page 149.

—◦§§◦—

DILL-STUFFED DOUBLE LOIN LAMB CHOPS

In one sense at least, loin lamb chops—whether single or double —might be compared to porterhouse steaks, if only because both cuts of meat have fatty tails. A competent butcher will, of course, trim most of the excess fat from the tail of the loin chop and coil the remaining strip of meat before securing it to the chop with a small skewer; insist upon having it done, or as a last resort do it yourself. Don't, however, be tempted to remove the tail; a tailless loin chop would be singularly unattractive.

If you lack the time or desire to stuff the lamb chops, omit the stuffing and broil the chops in their natural state, seasoning them only with salt and freshly ground pepper after they are done. The timing remains precisely the same. And should you want to accompany the unstuffed chops with a sauce, Lemon Sauce (page 434), would be most suitable. Stuffed lamb chops, on the other hand, require no sauce at all.

SERVES 4 TO 8

The Stuffing:
8 tablespoons butter (a quarter-pound stick), softened at room
    temperature
1 teaspoon finely chopped garlic
1 teaspoon fresh lemon juice
3 tablespoons finely cut fresh dill, chives, or parsley
¼ teaspoon salt
A few grindings of black pepper
¾ cup fresh bread crumbs

The Chops:
8 double loin lamb chops cut 2 inches thick

Making the stuffing. Cream the butter by mashing it with a wooden spoon against the sides of a large, heavy mixing bowl, or by processing it in the container of a food processor. Beat until the butter is smooth and creamy. Stir in the chopped garlic, lemon juice, dill, chives, or parsley, salt, pepper, and bread crumbs. Taste for seasoning; the mixture may need more salt or pepper, or even a drop or two more of lemon juice.

Stuffing the chops. With a small knife, make a 2-inch gash along the outer fatty rim of each chop, cutting deeply enough for the point of the knife to touch the bone. Spread the opening apart with your fingers and pack into it about a heaping tablespoonful of the stuffing. Pat the fatty edges of the slits together to enclose the stuffing.

Either refrigerate the chops, covered with plastic wrap, for as long as 8 hours, or set the chops aside while you preheat the broiler.

Preheating the broiler. Remove the grid from your broiling pan and set the pan in the broiler about 6 inches from the source of heat. Then turn on the broiler at its highest setting to heat for about 15 minutes.

Broiling the chops. Plan on broiling the chops for 7 to 8 minutes per side for medium (140° to 145° F.), the ideal stage for lamb chops, or for 9 to 10 minutes per side for well done (160° F.).

Set the chops on the cold grid. When you replace the grid in the broiling pan, the surface of the meat should be about 4 inches from the source of heat.

Broil the chops on each side for the time indicated, turning them over with tongs or with a long-handled fork inserted into the fat. Two or 3 minutes before the broiling time is up, test chops for doneness as described on page 149. Transfer the chops to a heated platter and serve them at once on heated plates.

———————————— ❧ ————————————

VARIATION: DOUBLE RIB LAMB CHOPS WITH HERB-CRUMB TOPPING

If you prefer rib to loin chops, you can follow the preceding recipe, substituting 8 double rib chops cut 2 inches thick and making half the stuffing recipe to use as a topping. Three or 4 minutes before the second side is done, test the chops with a thermometer as described on page 149. Then spread each chop with about a tablespoonful of the topping, patting it evenly over the surface of the meat with a knife or a spatula. Quickly slide the chops into the broiler again and broil them for 2 or 3 minutes, or until the topping is golden brown.

Omit the herb-crumb topping, if you like, and broil the chops unadorned, except for salt and pepper added at the end of broiling. The broiling time is the same as for chops with topping.

Although it is a perfectly respectable practice to broil single or double rib chops just as they come from the market, the chops will be far more attractive if you have them Frenched, which means having the ends of the bones trimmed free of fat. And, for a special touch, you can attach paper frills to the chops just before serving (see "Culinary Glossary," page 454).

MARINATED SHOULDER LAMB CHOPS

Shoulder chops tend toward slight toughness, which is the reason why they should never be cut more than 1 inch thick. And whether you buy arm or blade shoulder chops, don't broil them without marinating them first. The marinade will break down any resistant tissues in the lamb and give the chops a delicious and piquant flavor.

Because of the distinctive flavor of these marinated chops, serving a sauce with them is not only unnecessary but definitely unwise.

SERVES 4

The Marinade:
½ cup vegetable oil
¼ cup fresh lemon juice
½ teaspoon salt
Freshly ground black pepper
1 teaspoon crumbled dried oregano
1 tablespoon finely chopped fresh parsley
½ cup thinly sliced onions
2 cloves garlic, peeled and thinly sliced

The Chops:
8 shoulder lamb chops cut 1 inch thick
Salt
Freshly ground black pepper
2 tablespoons butter, cut into bits

Marinating the chops. Pour the oil, lemon juice, ½ teaspoon of salt, and a few grindings of black pepper into a small bowl, and beat them vigorously with a whisk until the vinegar and oil are thoroughly combined. Stir in the oregano, parsley, onions, and garlic. Pour the entire mixture into a shallow glass or stainless steel dish just large enough to hold the chops, preferably in one layer.

Dip the chops into the marinade one at a time, turning them over two or three times to moisten them thoroughly. Lay them side by side, or slightly overlapping if necessary, in the dish and cover it with plastic wrap. Refrigerate the chops for 6 to 8 hours, turning them over in the marinade every few hours, or whenever you think of it.

Preheating the broiler. When you are ready to broil the chops, remove the grid from the broiling pan and set the pan in the broiler about 3 inches from the source of heat. Then turn on the broiler at its highest setting to heat for 15 minutes.

Broiling the chops. Plan on broiling the chops for about 6 to 7 minutes per side for medium (140° to 145° F.), the ideal stage for lamb chops, or for 8 to 9 minutes per side for well done (160° F.).

Remove the chops from the marinade and pat them dry with paper towels. Place the chops on the cold grid and set the grid in the preheated broiling pan. The surface of the meat should be about 2 inches from the source of heat.

Broil the chops on each side for the time indicated, turning them over with tongs. A minute or two before the broiling time is up, test the chops for doneness, using any of the methods described on page 149.

Transfer the chops to a large heated platter or to heated serving plates. Sprinkle them lightly with salt and a few grindings of black pepper, and dot them with the butter bits. Serve the chops at once.

BROILED BONED LEG OF LAMB
WITH LEMON SAUCE

That one can successfully broil a boned and flattened leg of lamb comes as a delightful surprise to many cooks. Lamb cooked in this manner takes on a character entirely different from that of lamb cooked in other ways. For some curious reason, a broiled leg of lamb has a texture akin to that of a beefsteak, but, to my palate at least, its extraordinary flavor has nothing whatever to do with beef.

After the lamb has been boned and flattened, you will notice that some areas are considerably thicker than others. As a result, when you broil the leg, the thickest portion can be cooked to the medium stage (as it should be) and the thinner portions, because they will cook more quickly, will be more or less well done. This offers you the opportunity to serve slices from the thicker part of the leg to guests who prefer lamb to be pink and slices from the thinner portions to others who like their lamb well done.

If you are the least bit dubious about the tenderness of the leg of lamb, you would do well to marinate it for 6 to 8 hours, using the marinade and marinating procedure described in the preceding recipe for Marinated Shoulder Lamb Chops.

And, of course, you may omit the Lemon Sauce and serve lemon quarters in its place.

SERVES 6 TO 8

The Lamb:
1 leg of lamb, boned, weighing 6 to 7 pounds before boning and
    trimming, about 5 pounds afterward
Salt
Freshly ground black pepper

The Accompaniment:
Lemon Sauce (page 434)

Preparing the lamb. Ask your butcher to bone the leg of lamb and trim off the fell and most of the fat, but not to cut the meat completely open by slitting the leg. Cut the boned leg open at its narrowest point, spread it open butterfly fashion, and carefully cut into the larger clumps of meat with the point of your knife, slitting along their natural seams so that the meat lies as flat as possible. Its thickest portions should be about 1½ to 2 inches thick, no more, and its shape somewhat like a butterfly.

Preheating the broiler. Remove the grid from your broiling pan and set the pan in the broiler 6 to 7 inches from the source of heat. Then turn on the broiler at its highest setting to heat for 15 minutes.

Warming the sauce. Warm the Lemon Sauce in the top of a double boiler over barely simmering water while you broil the lamb. If the sauce seems too thick at serving time, you can stir a little chicken broth or water into it.

Broiling the lamb. Broil the lamb about 15 minutes per side for medium (140° to 145° F.), which is the ideal stage for lamb, or about 20 minutes per side for well done (160° F.).

Place the lamb, fat side down, on the cold grid and set the grid into the broiling pan. The surface of the meat should be about 5 inches from the source of heat.

Broil the lamb on each side for the time indicated, turning it over with a pair of large tongs or a long-handled fork when the first side is done.

If the lamb should show signs of burning at any point before the allotted time is up for the first side, reduce the heat if possible, or lower the rack a notch. Compensate for the lessened broiling time for the first side by 3 or 4 minutes. When you turn the lamb, return the rack or the heat to its original level.

About 4 or 5 minutes before the broiling time is up, test the thickest area of lamb for doneness by any of the methods described on page 149.

Serving the lamb. Place the lamb on a heated platter and sprinkle it with salt and a liberal grinding of pepper.

Pour the hot Lemon Sauce into a warmed sauceboat.

At the table, transfer the lamb to a carving board and carve it crosswise in slices from ¼ to ½ inch thick. Arrange the slices of lamb on heated serving plates and pass the sauce separately.

GROUND LAMB STEAKS WITH DILL BUTTER

Any cut of lamb, provided it is almost completely free of fat and contains no gristle, may be ground and used successfully for ground lamb steaks. Lamb, however lean it may appear, tends to have more natural fat than beef, and consequently does not require the addition of fat to keep the ground lamb steaks moist as they broil. Ground lamb should be formed into somewhat firmer patties than ground beef.

You may omit the dill-flavored butter if you like, but the delicious green-flecked aromatic butter does add an attractive note to the steaks that they would otherwise lack.

The Lamb:
2 pounds ground lean lamb
1 teaspoon salt
Freshly ground black pepper

The Accompaniment:
Dill Butter (page 440)

Preheating the broiler. Remove the grid from your broiling pan and set the pan in the broiler about 4 inches from the source of heat. Then turn on the broiler at its highest setting to heat for 15 minutes.

Preparing the ground lamb steaks. Drop the ground lamb into a bowl and toss it lightly with the salt and a few grindings of pepper. Moisten your hands with cold water and shape the lamb into 4 fairly compact ovals about 2 inches thick.

Broiling the ground lamb steaks. Plan on broiling the lamb steaks for 6 to 7 minutes per side for medium (140° to 145° F.), or for 8 to 9 minutes per side for well done (160° F.).

Place the steaks on the cold grid and put the grid in place in the preheated broiling pan. The surface of the steaks should be about 2 inches from the source of heat.

Broil the ground lamb steaks for the time indicated, turning them over carefully with a spatula. Two or 3 minutes before the broiling time is up, test the steaks for doneness by any of the methods described on page 149.

Serving the lamb steaks. Serve the lamb steaks at once on a heated platter or heated plates, placing a spoonful of Dill Butter on each one. Serve any remaining butter separately in a small bowl.

Chicken and Duckling

Chicken farmers have given various descriptive—and often misleading—names to the categories of the chickens they so endlessly produce. The chickens that concern me here are called broilers, fryers, and, in various localities, broiler-fryers. They range in weight between 1½ and 3 pounds and are 2 to 5 months old. For broiling, I prefer chickens weighing 2½ pounds or a little more; they are more succulent than the smaller birds.

In the United States, virtually every "duck" to be found in the markets is actually, and fortunately, a duckling—a young bird at the best and most succulent stage for either broiling or roasting. Ducklings range in weight from about 3 to 5 pounds or so. For broiling, I prefer a duckling weighing from 5 to 5½ pounds.

Broiling a chicken or a duckling successfully confronts you with less of a challenge than broiling beef or lamb. Because poultry must be broiled for a comparatively longer period than meat and must be fully cooked to be edible, browning it well doesn't present a problem; in fact, it tends to brown too deeply.

Frozen poultry. A frozen chicken has little to recommend it. Freezing the bird tends to rob it of character and alter its delicate texture. On the other hand, unless you are fortunate enough to have a nearby source of fresh-killed duckling, you will have to settle for frozen ones; they are available almost everywhere and are quite satisfactory.

Amounts to Buy

Although chickens under 2 pounds or over 3 pounds can be broiled successfully, you will find it more satisfactory to use chickens weighing about 2½ to 3 pounds. One such chicken will serve 4 adequately, if not copiously, and will easily fit the average household broiler.

A duck must be larger than a chicken to serve a given number of persons because of the large amount of bone in the frame. For 4, a 5- or 5½-pound duckling is about right.

Preparing Poultry for Broiling

Cleaning poultry. A high-quality bird, whether federally graded or not, will have been beautifully cleaned and plucked, with seldom a pinfeather showing. Most often your poultry will require no more than a wiping with damp paper towels outside and dry ones inside.

If you feel that you must wash a chicken or duckling before broiling it (the Europeans never do), wash it quickly under cold running water and pat it thoroughly dry inside and out with paper towels.

Three ways to prepare chicken. For really successful broiling results there are only three ways to prepare a 2½- to 3-pound chicken: whole, halved, or quartered. You may, of course, cut it up in other ways—into smaller pieces than the ones I suggest, for example—but your broiled chicken will inevitably be drier and less succulent. Unlike a chicken, a duckling does not tend to dry out when quartered because of its generous amount of fat. Therefore, a duckling for broiling should be quartered, and in the same way as a chicken.

THE WHOLE, FLATTENED BIRD. Preparing the chicken by the whole-bird method ensures its lying flat as it broils, prevents undue and unattractive shrinking of the meat from the bones, and enables you to carve the chicken at the table with ease, however inexperienced a carver you may be.

Lay the chicken, breast down, on your chopping board. With a very sharp knife, cut along each side of the backbone. Remove and set aside the backbone. Grip the chicken firmly, flesh side up, and bend the carcass sharply backward with both hands until the breastbone pops up. Pull out and discard the entire breastbone.

Working from the flesh side, push back the skin over the joint between the drumstick and thigh. With a small sharp knife, cut all the connections inside the joint, leaving the skin intact in order to hold the drumstick loosely in place. Repeat for the other leg.

Search for the main wing joints where the wings join the body. Push back the skin and, without cutting the skin, sever the connections inside the joints just as you did for the legs. Bend the lower part of each wing sharply so that the connection of the second joint snaps inside the skin. Cut off and discard the wing tips.

The chicken will now lie completely flat, seemingly "boneless." Arrange it on the broiler grid as compactly as possible.

THE HALVED BIRD. This is similar to the whole-chicken method, the only difference being that the chicken is cut in half down the center of the breast after it has been prepared as described above.

Do not be tempted to serve half a chicken per diner, as many restaurants do; it is a deplorable practice, at once wasteful and gross. Carve the halves into quarters after they have been broiled.

THE QUARTERED BIRD. To my mind quartering a bird is the least satisfactory sectioning method, but it is useful to know if you plan to broil two chickens at the same time in a small broiler, or plan to broil a duckling.

Prepare the bird as if it were to be broiled whole, as described above. Then cut it in two down the center of the breast and cut each half into two portions, separating the thigh sections from the breast sections. As the chickens broil, the breast sections will be somewhat dry because they take considerably less time to cook than the legs and thighs. I suggest that you baste the breasts more frequently than the dark meat sections. A duckling, on the other hand, is virtually self-basting because of the generous layer of fat beneath the skin.

Frozen poultry. If frozen poultry is the only kind available to you, do not broil it in its frozen state. You must defrost the bird thoroughly—either at room temperature, if it is to be broiled immediately after thawing, or in the refrigerator, which is a rather slow process. However the bird is defrosted, pat all of its surfaces thoroughly dry with paper towels before broiling it.

Techniques for Broiling Poultry

Basting chickens. Unlike a duck, well-marbled steak, or lamb chops, the flesh of young chickens has little interior fat. Consequently, when subjected to the intense heat of the broiler, a chicken must be periodically basted with fat of some kind. Margarine is perhaps the least successful fat for basting purposes because it burns easily and its flavor, to put it kindly, is dull and often unpleasant. Conversely, olive oil has too assertive a flavor and tends to mask the chicken's natural taste. If for any reason you must avoid using butter, use a mild vegetable oil—soybean, cottonseed, peanut, corn, or safflower—as a basting fat, but it is butter, the incomparable fat, which gives a simple broiled chicken its ultimate gloss and perfection.

Adjusting the broiling time and/or heat. Broiling a 2½- to 3-pound chicken should take about 35 minutes in all, and broiling a 5-pound duckling should require about 50 minutes, but the timing can vary a bit depending upon the efficiency of your broiler. There is no advantage in allowing a bird to warm up to room temperature before broiling it.

If your chicken or duckling should show signs of burning at any point, reduce the heat or lower the rack a notch. Compensate for the lessening of the heat by broiling the chicken 3 or 4 minutes longer and the duckling 4 or 5 minutes longer. (And, with chicken, give it another lavish basting for good measure.) If the bird seems a bit pallid, move the rack a little closer to the heat or increase the heat, and broil a few extra minutes.

Testing for doneness. Two or 3 minutes before you think the chicken or duckling is done, test it for doneness in the following way: Pierce the fleshiest part of the thigh with a small sharp knife. The juice that trickles out should be pale yellow. If it is slightly pink, broil the bird a minute or two longer.

BUTTER-BASTED CHICKEN WITH A PAN SAUCE

In this first and simplest method for broiling chicken, salt and pepper are sprinkled on the bird, which is then basted with melted butter to keep the chicken moist as it broils. The pan drippings are subsequently flavored with scallions, parsley, and seasonings and amplified with a little chicken broth, resulting in a delicious and quickly prepared sauce.

SERVES 4

The Basting Butter:
8 tablespoons butter (a quarter-pound stick) cut into bits

The Chicken:
1 broiler-fryer weighing about 2½ pounds, prepared in any of
    the ways described on pages 173–74
2 teaspoons salt
Freshly ground black pepper

The Sauce:
¼ cup finely chopped scallions, including 2 inches of green
    stems
½ cup fresh or canned chicken broth
A few drops of fresh lemon juice
1 tablespoon finely chopped fresh parsley, preferably the
    flat-leaved or Italian variety
Salt
Freshly ground black pepper

Preheating the broiler. Remove the grid from your broiling pan and set the pan in the broiler about 5 to 6 inches from the source of heat. Then turn on the broiler at its highest setting to heat for 15 minutes.

Preparing the basting butter and chicken. In a small saucepan set over low heat, melt the butter bits, but don't let them brown. Remove the pan from the heat and place it, together with a pastry brush, near the broiler.

Pat the chicken dry with paper towels, brush the skin side evenly with about a tablespoonful of the melted butter, and lay the chicken, skin side down, on the cold grid. Brush the other side with another tablespoonful of melted butter, then sprinkle with 1 teaspoon of salt and a few grindings of pepper.

Broiling the chicken. Place the grid laden with the chicken in the preheated broiling pan and slide it under the broiler. The surface of the chicken should be about 4 inches from the source of heat.

With a pastry brush dipped in the butter, baste the chicken lavishly every 5 minutes; do this as quickly as possible to prevent the heat from lowering perceptibly every time you open the broiler door. If your chicken seems to be broiling too quickly or too slowly, adjust the rack or the heat up or down, and add 3 or 4 minutes to the broiling time.

At the end of 20 minutes, the flesh side of the chicken should be golden brown and well on its way to being done.

Return the rack or the heat to its original position, if either has been changed. Then quickly and carefully turn the chicken over with large tongs. Brush the top with about a tablespoonful of melted butter, sprinkle it evenly with 1 teaspoon of salt and a few grindings of pepper, and return the chicken to the broiler.

Baste lavishly with the butter or with pan juices after 5 minutes of broiling. If it seems that the chicken is cooking too fast or too slow on this side, adjust the rack or the heat up or down. At the end of 10 minutes, the skin should be deep golden brown with a hint of char showing in spots. But if the chicken seems a bit pallid, baste the bird once more, using the drippings in the pan if you have run out of butter, and broil a few minutes longer.

If you feel it is necessary, test the chicken for doneness as described on page 175. Then transfer the bird, skin side up, to a heated serving platter. Cover the platter loosely with foil while you make the sauce.

Making the sauce. Remove the grid from the broiling pan, and pour off and discard all but a thin film of fat from the pan, being sure to keep in the pan all the crusty brown glaze that will be visible here and there.

Set the pan over high heat on top of the stove, using two burners if necessary. Add the scallions and, stirring constantly with a wooden spoon, fry them for about 3 minutes, or until they soften and color lightly.

Deglaze the pan by pouring in the chicken broth and bringing it to a boil, meanwhile scraping up and stirring in all the intensely flavored brown bits in the pan. Let the sauce boil for a minute or so, then stir in the lemon juice and parsley. Taste the sauce for seasoning. Add a little salt and pepper or more lemon juice if you think the sauce needs it.

Serving the chicken. Uncover the chicken on its platter, pour the sauce over it, and serve it at once on heated plates.

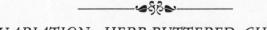

VARIATION: HERB-BUTTERED CHICKEN

This recipe for broiled chicken substitutes highly seasoned, herb-flavored butter for the seasonings and melted butter of the preceding recipe. The delicious juices which will have collected in the pan after the bird has been broiled are poured over the chicken in place of a sauce.

SERVES 4

1 broiler-fryer weighing about 2½ pounds, prepared in any of
    the ways described on pages 173–74
Combination Herb Butter (page 440)
1 tablespoon finely chopped fresh parsley (optional)

Preheating the broiler; preparing the chicken; and broiling the chicken. Follow the directions in the preceding recipe for Butter-Basted Chicken, but baste with the herb butter.

Serving the chicken. When the chicken has been broiled to your satisfaction, transfer it with tongs, skin side up, to a heated serving platter and spoon as much as you like of the pan juices over the bird.

Garnish the chicken, if you like, with the tablespoonful of parsley, sprinkling it over the top. The extra parsley will not only intensify the herbal flavor of the chicken, but will give its crusty golden skin an especially attractive look.

--------- ~❦~ ---------

VARIATION: CHICKEN WITH A DEVILED TOPPING

In this third method of broiling chicken, salt, pepper, and melted butter are used as in the first method, and a savory topping is added to the chicken during the last few minutes of broiling.

SERVES 4

The Basting Butter:
6 tablespoons butter, cut into bits

The Chicken:
1 broiler-fryer weighing about 2½ pounds, prepared in any of
    the ways described on pages 174–75
2 teaspoons salt
Freshly ground black pepper

The Deviled Topping:
4 tablespoons butter, softened at room temperature
1 teaspoon fresh lemon juice
2 teaspoons Worcestershire sauce
½ teaspoon finely chopped garlic
½ teaspoon dry mustard
¼ teaspoon salt
Freshly ground black pepper
¾ cup fresh bread crumbs

Preheating the broiler; preparing the basting butter; and broiling the chicken. Follow the directions in the recipe for Butter-Basted Chicken, page 175, but omit the pan sauce.

Preparing the deviled topping. While you are broiling the chicken, prepare the topping. Cream 4 tablespoons of softened butter by mashing and beating it with a large wooden spoon against the sides of a large heavy mixing bowl until it is creamy and smooth. Then beat in the lemon juice, Worcestershire sauce, garlic, dry mustard, ¼ teaspoon of salt, and a few grindings of black pepper. When the ingredients are well combined, stir—don't beat—in the bread crumbs. Taste for seasoning: the mixture should be quite sharp and piquant—its flavor will be considerably muted after it has been broiled with the chicken.

    Set the topping aside.

About 5 minutes before the chicken is done, spread the deviled topping quickly and evenly over the chicken pieces, using a spatula. Broil for the remaining 5 minutes, or until the topping is a deep golden brown. If you wish, test the chicken for doneness (see page 175), taking care not to dislodge the topping. Crumb side up, transfer the chicken carefully to a heated serving platter and serve it at once.

MARINATED DUCKLING WITH ORANGE SAUCE

Ducklings of the Long Island breed, marketed both fresh and frozen, are particularly suited to broiling because of the thick layer of fat beneath their skins. Not only does the fat dissolve as the bird broils, but the flesh, self-basting as it were, remains moist and succulent. Basting, however, helps brown the bird evenly.

If you purchase a fresh duckling, have the butcher cut it up as directed in this recipe. A frozen bird should be thawed before cooking and before sectioning. Marinate the duckling for at least 6 hours before broiling it, not especially to flavor it but to eliminate any possibility of its being tough.

SERVES 4

The Duckling:
5- to 5½-pound duckling

The Marinade:
¾ cup vegetable oil
¼ cup fresh lemon juice
1 teaspoon salt
½ teaspoon coarsely crushed black peppercorns
2 bay leaves, coarsely crumbled
½ cup thinly sliced onions

For Seasoning and Basting:
4 tablespoons butter, softened at room temperature
2 teaspoons salt
Freshly ground black pepper

The Garnish:
2 large navel oranges, peeled and thinly sliced
Watercress

Preparing the duck for marinating. Ask your butcher to remove the duck's backbone and wing tips, then carefully cut—not chop— the duck into quarters. If you do this yourself, follow the directions on page 447. Trim the quarters with a pair of poultry or kitchen shears, cutting away every bit of fat you see and going a little beneath the skin around the edges, if necessary, to get as much fat as possible.

Making the marinade. Pour the oil, lemon juice, 1 teaspoon of salt, and the crushed peppercorns into a small bowl and beat them vigorously with a whisk until the oil and lemon juice are thoroughly combined. Stir in the bay leaves and onions, and pour the marinade into a shallow glass, stainless steel, or enameled cast-iron baking dish just large enough to hold the duck quarters in one layer.

Dip the quarters, one at a time, into the marinade and turn them over two or three times to moisten them thoroughly. Then lay them side by side in the marinade and cover the dish with plastic wrap. Refrigerate for 6 to 8 hours, turning the pieces of duck over in the marinade every few hours.

Preheating the broiler. Remove the grid from the broiler pan and slide the pan into the broiler about 6 inches from the source of heat. Turn on the broiler at its highest setting to heat for 15 minutes.

Broiling the duck. Remove the duck quarters from the marinade and pat them dry with paper towels. Discard the marinade.

With a pastry brush, coat the pieces evenly with about 2 tablespoons of the softened butter and place the pieces, skin side down, on the cold grid. Sprinkle them evenly with 1 teaspoon of the salt and a few grindings of pepper.

Place the grid with the duck quarters in the broiling pan and slide it under the broiler. The surface of the duck should be about 5 inches from the source of heat.

As the duck broils, brush it lavishly with some of the pan drippings every 10 minutes or so. If it browns too rapidly, reduce the heat, if possible, or lower the rack a notch. Compensate for the lessening of the heat by broiling the first side an extra 4 to 5 minutes and by giving it an extra basting.

At the end of 30 minutes, the flesh side should be golden brown.

Return the heat or the rack to its original setting if either has been changed. Quickly turn the duck quarters over with tongs and brush the skin side with about 1 tablespoon of the butter. Sprinkle evenly with the remaining teaspoon of salt and a few grindings of pepper and return the duck to the broiler.

Baste with the remaining butter or with pan drippings after the skin side has broiled about 10 minutes. If it seems that the duck is cooking too fast or too slow, adjust the heat or the rack up or down.

At the end of 20 minutes' broiling the skin should be deep golden brown with a hint of char showing in spots. But if the duck seems a bit pallid at that point, baste the quarters once more with the pan drippings and broil the duckling a few minutes longer.

Test the duck for doneness by piercing the fleshiest part of the thigh with a small sharp knife. The juice that trickles out should be a pale yellow; if it is slightly pink, broil the duck for 2 or 3 minutes longer.

Serving the duck. With tongs, transfer the duck sections, skin side up, to a large heated platter. Surround the quarters with the sliced oranges and sprays of crisp watercress.

Serve at once on warmed plates.

Fish and Shellfish

Broiling fish is perhaps the quickest and, for some, the most satisfying of all broiling techniques. Yet I have discovered that the almost disarming simplicity of the process often leads many cooks astray.

The terms "rare," "medium," and "well done" have no place here. Like poultry, fish must be thoroughly cooked to reach its optimum flavor and texture. Overcooking fish—a cardinal culinary sin—makes it dry and tasteless; undercooked fish can be decidedly unpleasant.

The flesh of most, if not all, fish is essentially tender to begin with—so tender, in fact, that the Japanese think nothing of serving it raw, as we do our oysters and clams. Therefore, broiling fish to the state of perfect doneness isn't a matter of achieving tenderness.

Because sizes, shapes, and thicknesses of the innumerable fish available to us vary so, the basic principles that I have already discussed for broiling meats and poultry must be applied to fish in crucially different ways.

Fish for Broiling

Fish can be more or less categorized as fat or lean. Fat fish—salmon, mackerel, butterfish, trout, and whitefish, among others—lend themselves most easily to broiling because they are, in effect, almost self-basting. Lean fish of almost any type—members of the sole family, for example—can be broiled quite successfully if they are basted with enough fat to compensate for their essentially dry flesh.

Shellfish are always lean, and broiling them is at best a chancy business; most kinds, I feel, are better cooked in other ways. Broiling a lobster, for example, is to my mind a poor way to treat these superb creatures; the flesh often turns rubbery or stringy when subjected to the intense heat of the broiler. On the other hand, large shrimp and sea scallops can be suitable candidates for the broiler if they are properly handled.

Preparing Fish for Broiling

Unless you are an amateur fisherman given to scaling, eviscerating, and cleaning your own catch, let the fishmonger do the job for you.

There are four so-called dressing methods for fish, and any of them may be used for fish to be broiled. You will find it useful to learn precisely what they are, if only to tell your fishmonger what you want.

A whole fish. A whole fish meant to be broiled should weigh no more than 3 to 3½ pounds after cleaning. Larger fish, although they can be broiled successfully, won't fit into most household broilers. If your broiler is large enough, the fish head may be left on; in this case, the gills must be removed. Although most Americans take a dim view of leaving the head on, it actually helps keep the flesh moist by reducing the area of cut surface.

A split fish. In this method of dressing, the whole fish is split and spread out butterfly fashion. The backbone may be removed or left attached to one side. Try broiling fish with and without the backbone; you may find that the fish has more flavor when the backbone is left in—and it can be easily removed after the fish has been broiled.

Fish fillets. Fillets are split fish with their entire bone structure removed. For broiling, the skin should always be left intact to prevent the flesh from disintegrating as it broils. (Fillets cooked in other ways are almost always skinless.)

Fish steaks. Steaks should be cut no thinner than ½ inch and no thicker than 1½ inches. Steaks cut from swordfish are boneless, but steaks from such fish as salmon, halibut, and cod contain bones, which may be removed before the fish is broiled.

Techniques for Broiling Fish

Preheating the grid and broiler pan. Set the broiling pan, with its grid in place, the designated distance from the heat and preheat the broiler.

Cleaning fish. Just before cooking, wash the fish thoroughly and quickly under running cold water. If it is a whole fish, scrape and rinse away any blood or dark membrane remaining along the backbone. Dry the fish thoroughly before you broil it.

Seasoning. You may season fish with salt and pepper before, during, or after broiling; or add the seasonings to the basting fat. But it is inadvisable to sprinkle fish with lemon juice, as is frequently suggested, before or during the broiling, especially if the fish is a fragile one; the acid in the lemon juice tends to break down the tissues.

For the same reason, I do not recommend marinating fish before broiling it. Flavors similar to those contributed by marinades may be added by serving the fish with a flavored butter or a sauce.

Basting fish. Whether the fish you broil is fat or lean, it must be basted, albeit in varying amounts, with a fat of some kind, preferably butter or vegetable oil. Obviously, a lean fish will require more copious and frequent basting than a fat fish which is, to a degree, self-basting.

Broiling frozen fish. Theoretically, frozen fish may be broiled without defrosting, but timing is tricky. Even though you double the amount of time you would ordinarily estimate for an unfrozen fish of the same size, you may find to your dismay that the center of the piece, if it is a fairly thick one, may still be raw.

You are better off defrosting the fish at room temperature just before cooking. Pat it perfectly dry with paper towels before broiling it. No harm will be done if a few ice crystals remain in the flesh at the start of broiling; complete thawing sometimes results in the loss of too much moisture.

Testing for doneness. There are four ways to test fish for doneness:

BY TOUCH. Fish, like meat, becomes progressively firmer to the touch as it cooks. Because fish is always broiled to the well-done stage, it should be quite firm to the touch when done. The textures of different fish vary considerably, but with practice you should be able to use this touch-testing method accurately.

BY APPEARANCE. The flesh of most raw fish is comparatively glossy. Exposed to heat, the flesh slowly loses its sheen and becomes somewhat dull and opaque. The more opaque the fish, the more likely it is to be done.

BY FLAKING OR CUTTING, IF NECESSARY. These are two other testing methods you can use when all else fails, although I am not enthusiastic about either of them. The first consists of gently jabbing the exposed flesh of the fish with a fork; if the fish flakes easily, it is done. The second should be applied only to fish steaks and scallops. Cut into a scallop or into the side of the steak with a small sharp knife and spread the cut apart. If the flesh is opaque throughout the open area, the fish is done.

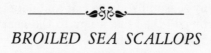

BROILED SEA SCALLOPS

For broiling in the fashion described in this recipe, I prefer the larger, and admittedly somewhat coarser, sea scallops to their small and sweeter relatives, the bay scallops. Larger sea scallops have several advantages, not the least of which is their comparatively low cost and the fact that they can be found almost the year round throughout the country. Both are delicacies far too little known to most Americans and well worth seeking out at your fishmonger's.

Scallops are almost invariably sold shucked. Fresh scallops— I never use frozen ones—should, like fish, be so fresh that their only perceptible odor is a sweet one. Like shrimp, scallops may be creamy white or tinged with pink, orange, or even tan.

For uniform broiling, select scallops that are all about the same size. I prefer those about 1 inch in diameter; if those you buy are much larger or smaller, you may have to adjust the broiling time after checking them for doneness.

All scallops can be cooked in a variety of ways: they can be broiled, poached, sautéed, or fried. Instead of being broiled, for example, the scallops prepared as in this recipe may, after being chilled for at least 20 minutes, be pan fried in 4 tablespoons of vegetable oil and 2 tablespoons of butter, or deep fried in fat heated to a temperature of 375° F.; in either case they will take only 2 or 3 minutes to cook to a golden brown.

SERVES 4

The Scallops:
1½ pounds sea scallops, each about 1 inch in diameter
½ teaspoon salt
Freshly ground black pepper

The Coating:
½ cup flour
2 eggs
2 tablespoons vegetable oil
1½ cups fine dry bread crumbs

The Basting Butter:
8 tablespoons butter (a quarter-pound stick), cut into bits

The Garnish:
Lemon quarters
Parsley or watercress sprigs (optional)

Preheating the broiler. Set your broiling pan, with its grid in place, 4 inches from the source of heat. Place a 10-by-14-inch wire cake rack, feet down, on the grid. Turn on the broiler at its highest setting to heat for 15 minutes.

Preparing the scallops and basting butter. Quickly wash the scallops under cold running water, then spread them out on a double thickness of paper towels and pat them thoroughly dry with more towels.

Place the scallops in a medium-size mixing bowl and sprinkle them with the salt and pepper to taste. With a wooden spoon, toss the scallops about to season them evenly.

Dump the flour into a sturdy brown paper or plastic bag and drop in the scallops. Twist the top of the bag tightly closed and shake the bag vigorously to coat each scallop completely with flour. Pour the contents of the bag into a large sieve and shake the sieve gently from side to side over a sheet of wax paper, leaving the scallops coated with only the thinnest layer of flour.

In a medium-size mixing bowl, beat the eggs and 1 tablespoon of the vegetable oil together with a whisk or a fork only long enough to combine them.

Spread the bread crumbs on a long sheet of wax paper.

Drop all the scallops into the bowl containing the egg mixture. Then lift one scallop at a time with tongs, drain it a second or two, and drop it onto the bread crumbs. Roll the scallop around in the crumbs; it should be thoroughly, but not thickly, blanketed. Set it on a long strip of wax paper. Repeat the process for the remaining scallops.

In a small saucepan set over low heat, melt the butter bits, but don't let them brown. Remove the pan from the heat and place it, together with a pastry brush and the remaining oil, at hand near the broiler.

Broiling the scallops. Using the pastry brush, quickly and thoroughly coat the hot cake rack with the remaining tablespoon of vegetable oil and lay the scallops on the rack. Baste each scallop with about ½ teaspoon of the melted butter, using a bulb baster, then slide the pan under the heat. The surface of the scallops should be about 3 inches from the source of heat.

Broil the scallops for about 5 minutes, basting each one with about ½ teaspoon more of the melted butter after they have broiled about 3 minutes.

Turn the scallops over by placing another 10-by-14-inch cake rack, feet upward, over them; you need not oil this second rack. Firmly grasping the sides of both racks together with sturdy, pliable potholders, quickly invert the two racks enclosing the scallops and replace the racks on the grid. Remove the rack that is now uppermost and again pour about ½ teaspoon of butter over each scallop with the bulb baster.

Broil the scallops for 5 minutes, basting them after 3 minutes with the remaining butter. A minute or so before the broiling time is up, test the scallops for doneness either by touch or by cutting, as described on page 184.

Serving the scallops. Carefully remove the rack of scallops from the broiler. With a large spatula or tongs, transfer the scallops to a heated platter. Serve them at once, garnished with lemon quarters and, if you like, parsley or watercress sprigs.

BROILED WHOLE STRIPED BASS

Broiling a comparatively large whole fish such as a 3-pound bass is not especially demanding, except for the fact that it is so difficult to turn the fish over without damaging it. After much experimentation, I have finally discovered a way to turn a fish by using two wire cake racks that works to perfection. Once you see how miraculously the cake racks work, you will no doubt consider using the method for broiling several small fish at a time and also for fish steaks, both of which, unlike split fish or fillets, must be broiled on both sides.

SERVES 4

The Fish:
2½- to 3-pound whole striped bass (cleaned weight), scaled and
    eviscerated, head and tail left on if your broiler is large
    enough
Salt
Freshly ground black pepper

For Basting and Oiling the Rack:
8 tablespoons butter (a quarter-pound stick), cut into bits
1 tablespoon vegetable oil

The Garnish:
Lemon quarters
Parsley sprigs

Preheating the broiler. Set your broiling pan, with its grid in place, 6 inches from the source of heat. Take a wire cake rack large enough to hold your fish, and place it, feet down, on the broiler grid. Turn on the broiler at its highest setting to heat for 15 minutes.

Preparing the fish and basting butter. Wash the fish thoroughly under cold running water and pat it dry inside and out with paper towels. Then sprinkle it liberally inside and out with salt and more discreetly with pepper.

In a small saucepan set over low heat, melt the butter bits, but don't let them brown. Remove the pan from the heat and place it, together with a pastry brush and the vegetable oil, at hand near the broiler.

Broiling the fish. Pull out the broiling pan. Using the pastry brush, quickly and thoroughly coat the hot cake rack with the vegetable oil and lay the fish diagonally across it. Brush the fish copiously with melted butter and slide the pan back under the heat. The surface of the fish should be about 4 inches from the source of heat.

Broil the fish for 10 minutes, basting it with butter every 3 or 4 minutes. If the fish appears to be browning too rapidly or too slowly, adjust the heat or the broiling pan up or down.

Turn the fish over by placing a second wire cake rack, feet upward, over it. It is not necessary to oil this second rack. Firmly grasping the sides of both racks together with sturdy, pliable potholders, quickly invert the two racks enclosing the fish and set them back on the grid. Remove the rack that is now uppermost and brush the fish thoroughly with butter.

Broil the second side of the fish for 10 minutes, basting it every 3 to 4 minutes with more butter. A few minutes before the fish is done, test it for doneness, using the touch or flaking methods described on page 184.

Serving the fish. Carefully remove the rack and fish from the broiler. With the aid of a large spatula, slide the fish gently from the rack onto a large heated platter. Serve the fish at once, surrounded with lemon quarters and parsley.

To carve the fish, proceed in this fashion: With a broad-bladed knife or other broad-bladed serving implement (a pie server will do very well), cut the uppermost side of the fish into crosswise portions, cutting down only as far as the backbone. Lift off and serve these portions, then lift out the backbone and set it aside. Cut the lower half of the fish into crosswise portions and serve.

BROILED MACKEREL WITH TOMATO BUTTER

Tomatoes and mackerel seem to have a curious affinity: the combination in one dish or another has been used in almost every cuisine throughout the world. Perhaps it is the slightly sweet acidity of the tomatoes that offsets the distinctive, in fact uniquely rich, flavor of the mackerel and makes the two so delicious in tandem.

The tomato butter that is to anoint the broiled mackerel can be made well in advance; simply refrigerate it and then let it return to room temperature before you broil the fish.

Should you decide to omit the tomato butter, as on occasion you may wish to, broil the fish as directed in the recipe and serve it simply with lemon quarters or, more elaborately, with Lemon Sauce (page 434).

SERVES 4

The Tomato Butter:
8 tablespoons butter (a quarter-pound stick), softened at room
    temperature
½ teaspoon salt
Pinch of sugar
2 tablespoons canned concentrated tomato paste

The Fish:
2 mackerel weighing about 1½ pounds each, split
Salt
Freshly ground black pepper

For Basting and Oiling the Grid:
6 tablespoons butter, cut into bits
1 tablespoon vegetable oil

Preheating the broiler. Set the broiling pan, with its grid in place, 3 to 4 inches from the source of heat. Turn on the broiler at its highest setting to heat for 15 minutes.

Making the tomato butter. Cream 8 tablespoons of softened butter in a food processor or by mashing and beating it with a large wooden spoon against the sides of a large, heavy mixing bowl. Continue to beat until the butter is creamy and smooth. Beat in ½ teaspoon of salt and the sugar; then, beating it in a teaspoonful at a time, add the tomato paste. Taste for seasoning.

Preparing the fish and the basting butter. Quickly wash the fish under cold running water and pat them dry with paper towels. Then sprinkle both sides liberally with salt and more discreetly with pepper.

In a small saucepan set over low heat, melt 6 tablespoons of butter bits, but don't let them brown. Remove the pan from the heat and place the vegetable oil, the butter, a pastry brush, and a bulb baster at hand near the broiler.

Broiling the fish. Using the pastry brush, quickly coat the hot broiling grid with the vegetable oil and lay the fish on it, skin side down. Brush the mackerel copiously with butter and slide the pan into the broiler. The surface of the fish should be about 3 inches from the source of heat.

Broil the fish for about 10 minutes, basting with the butter every 3 or 4 minutes, using the bulb baster (or the pastry brush). Two or 3 minutes before the broiling time is up, test the fish for doneness, preferably by the touch method but, if necessary, by the flaking method described on page 184.

Serving the mackerel. Using two wide metal spatulas to support each fish, transfer the mackerel to a large heated platter. Spread the tomato butter over the fish and serve at once.

BROILED FILLETS OF HADDOCK AU GRATIN

The topping of bread crumbs and cheese used in this dish is known as a *gratin*, although many Americans mistakenly think of a "gratin" as a topping that consists of cheese alone.

You may use this gratin, omitting the cheese if you like, on any broiled fish fillets of your choice, but it does especially well as a substitute for the tomato butter in the preceding broiled mackerel recipe.

SERVES 4 TO 6

The Fish:
3 pounds filleted haddock, skin left on
Salt
Freshly ground black pepper

For Basting and Oiling the Grid:
8 tablespoons butter (a quarter-pound stick), cut into bits
1 tablespoon vegetable oil

The Topping:
4 tablespoons fresh bread crumbs
2 tablespoons freshly grated imported Parmesan cheese

The Garnish:
Lemon quarters

Preheating the broiler. Set the broiling pan, with its grid in place, 4 inches from the source of heat. Turn the broiler on at its highest setting to heat for 15 minutes.

Preparing the fish, the basting butter, and the topping. Rinse the fillets quickly under cold running water and pat them thoroughly dry with paper towels. Sprinkle both sides liberally with salt and more discreetly with pepper.

In a small saucepan set over low heat, melt the butter bits, but don't let them brown. Remove the pan from the heat and place the butter, the vegetable oil, a pastry brush, and a bulb baster at hand near the broiler.

In a small bowl combine the bread crumbs with the Parmesan cheese.

Broiling the fish. Using the pastry brush, quickly coat the hot broiler grid with the vegetable oil and lay the haddock fillets on the grid, skin side down. Brush the fish copiously with melted butter and slide the pan into the broiler. The surface of the fillets should be about 3 inches from the source of heat.

Broil the fish for 10 minutes, basting it every 3 or 4 minutes with butter, using the bulb baster or pastry brush. At the end of 10 minutes, test the fish for doneness, using the touch method or, if you must, the flaking method described on page 184.

Quickly scatter the crumb and cheese topping evenly over the surface of the fish. With the bulb baster, moisten the crumb and cheese topping with the remaining butter, and broil for about 2 minutes longer, or until the topping is a light golden brown.

Serving the fish. Using a wide spatula, transfer the fillets to a large heated platter. Serve them at once on warmed plates, accompanied by the lemon quarters.

Vegetables on the Grill

The number of vegetables that can be broiled successfully is comparatively small. But those that can be cooked in this way are sometimes all the better for it. The sheer rapidity of the broiling process ensures a freshness of flavor, a moist texture, and an appealing color often difficult to achieve with other cooking methods.

Broiled tomatoes take only minutes, and the stuffings, toppings, and seasonings with which they can be elaborated make them ideal companions or colorful foils for any of the broiled or roasted meats, poultry, and fish in this book. Mushrooms, too, are one of the simplest vegetables to broil and, moreover, can be filled with a flavored butter or sauce.

Vegetables for Broiling

Most vegetables with a relatively high moisture content respond well to broiling. Among them are zucchini, eggplant, potatoes, and even sweet potatoes. Be forewarned, however, that the more fragile among them will demand your undivided attention, because they easily overcook or burn.

Techniques for Broiling Vegetables

Basting. In choosing a fat for basting any vegetable you broil, the affinity of flavors is the only point to be considered. Butter—to which I am wildly partial—is an excellent choice for all; for some vegetables, such as Broiled Cheese-Topped Eggplant (page 196), olive oil—or, if you prefer, a vegetable oil—is also a good choice. Margarine, to my mind (and taste), is out of the question.
Skewered vegetables. Broiling vegetables threaded on skewers, while undoubtedly attractive, seems to me more of a nuisance than

a necessity. Anchoring them securely is always a problem, and attempting to cook them on the same skewer with other, longer-cooking foods can lead to culinary disasters.

Following are detailed recipes for broiled vegetables which may be served either as a separate course or as an accompaniment for other dishes.

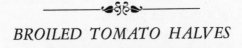

BROILED TOMATO HALVES

Unlike many broiled vegetables that must be served the moment they are done, these halved tomatoes can be broiled an hour or so ahead of time, set aside at room temperature, uncovered, while you prepare the rest of the meal, then reheated for a few minutes in an oven preheated to 400° to 450° F.

SERVES 4

The Tomatoes:
4 fresh ripe but firm tomatoes 2½ to 3 inches in diameter
1 teaspoon salt
Freshly ground black pepper

The Topping:
3 tablespoons freshly grated imported Parmesan cheese
3 tablespoons fresh bread crumbs
2 tablespoons butter, cut into 8 pats ⅛ inch thick

Preheating the broiler. Remove the grid from your broiling pan and set the pan in the broiler about 5 inches from the source of heat. Then turn on the broiler at its highest setting to heat for 15 minutes.

Preparing the tomatoes and the topping. Cut the tomatoes in half crosswise. Then arrange them on the cold grid, cut sides up, and sprinkle them liberally with salt and a few grindings of black pepper.

Combine the Parmesan cheese and bread crumbs in a small bowl and pat the mixture evenly over the tomatoes. Place a pat of butter on each tomato half.

Broiling the tomatoes. Set the grid in the preheated broiling pan and return the pan to the broiler. The tomatoes should be about 3 inches from the source of heat.

Broil the tomatoes for 6 to 8 minutes, watching carefully for any sign of burning; lower the heat or move the broiling pan farther from the heat if necessary.

When the topping is golden brown, test the tomatoes for doneness by pressing their sides gently. They should yield only slightly. Broiled beyond that point, they may fall apart.

Quickly lift the tomatoes from the grid with a large spatula and serve them on a warmed platter.

BROILED ZUCCHINI

SERVES 4

1½ pounds zucchini, each about 2 inches in diameter
4 tablespoons butter, cut into bits
Salt
Freshly ground black pepper

Preheating the broiler. Set your broiling pan, with its grid in place, 4 inches from the source of heat. Turn on the broiler to its highest setting to heat for 15 minutes.

Preparing the zucchini and butter. To remove any possible wax from the zucchini, scrub them with a stiff brush under lukewarm running water. Then trim off their ends with a small sharp knife and cut each zucchini crosswise into 1- or 1½-inch pieces.

In a small saucepan set over low heat, melt the butter, but don't let it brown.

Broiling the zucchini. With tongs, dip each piece of zucchini into the melted butter. Arrange the pieces on the hot grid and sprinkle them lightly with salt and a few grindings of pepper.

Broil the zucchini for 3 to 4 minutes on each side. Using a bulb baster or a pastry brush, baste the pieces with the remaining melted butter at least once on each side as they broil. The zucchini slices are done when they are a light golden brown and still show a slight resistance when squeezed gently between your thumb and forefinger.

Serve the zucchini at once on a warmed platter.

❦

BROILED MUSHROOMS

Broiled Mushrooms can be one of the most delectable accompaniments imaginable for broiled or roasted meats of any kind, and this recipe will show you how easily and quickly they can be prepared with a simple seasoning of butter, salt, and pepper.

Broiled Mushrooms can also be served alone, either as a grand opening for a dinner or as a main course for lunch. If you intend to use them for this purpose, one of the best ways to prepare them is to broil the cap side of the mushrooms; then turn the caps over, drop some Garlic Butter into each cavity, and complete the broiling. Served on rounds of toast, preferably cut from French or Italian bread, these impressive mushrooms, brimming with melted savory butter, come to the table, in the words of a noted food authority, "riding inverted on little rafts of toast."

SERVES 4

16 mushrooms 2 to 2½ inches in diameter
1 or 2 tablespoons butter, softened at room temperature
Salt
Freshly ground black pepper
Garlic Butter (optional; page 441)

Preheating the broiler. Remove the grid from your broiling pan and set the pan in the broiler 5 inches from the source of heat. Turn on the broiler at its highest setting to heat for 15 minutes.

Preparing the mushrooms. Carefully remove the stem from each mushroom by holding the cap securely in one hand and gently bending back and twisting the stem with the other hand until it snaps free. If any part of the stem still adheres to the inside of the cap, cut it away with the point of a very small sharp knife.

Under no circumstances should you wash mushrooms, but you may, if you wish, gently wipe the caps with a lightly dampened towel.

Broiling the mushrooms. If the mushrooms are to be broiled plain, brush the caps inside and out with a little of the 2 tablespoons of softened butter. If you plan to use the Garlic Butter, brush the cap side only with 1 tablespoon of the softened butter.

Place the mushrooms, cap sides up, on the cold grid, set the grid in the broiling pan, and broil the mushrooms, with their tops about 4 inches from the source of heat, for 2 minutes. Then, with tongs, turn the caps hollow sides up and brush them again with the remaining plain butter; or, if you wish, fill each one with about 1 teaspoon of the Garlic Butter.

Broil the mushrooms for 2 or 3 minutes longer, or until they are lightly browned but still retain their shape. When done, they should still be slightly resistant to a gentle squeezing pressure of your thumb and forefinger.

Serving the mushrooms. Season the mushrooms broiled with butter alone with salt and a little freshly ground pepper and serve them at once.

The mushrooms filled with Garlic Butter will require no additional seasoning, but should also be served immediately.

BROILED CHEESE-TOPPED EGGPLANT

To those who love eggplant, that Mediterranean and Middle Eastern vegetable is delectable in any form, but especially so when prepared with cheese or, as here, with two cheeses: Parmesan and mozzarella. Eggplant broiled in this manner is of sufficient stature to be served as a separate course.

SERVES 4

The Eggplant:
2 eggplants weighing about 1 pound each
Salt
Freshly ground black pepper

The Basting Oil:
4 tablespoons olive oil

The Topping:
½ cup freshly grated imported Parmesan cheese
8 to 10 slices mozzarella cheese, cut ¼ inch thick and slightly
     smaller than the eggplant slices

Preparing the eggplant. Cut the unpeeled eggplants crosswise into slices 1 inch thick. Sprinkle the slices generously with salt on both sides and lay them side by side on a large flat platter. Place another flat platter on top of them—or use a flat pan and weight it with a heavy object. Let the slices stand for about 1 hour to drain. Then pour off the bitter liquid accumulated around the eggplant and pat the slices thoroughly dry with paper towels.

Preheating the broiler. Remove the grid from the broiling pan and place the pan about 6 inches from the source of heat. Turn on the broiler at its highest setting to heat for 15 minutes.

Broiling the eggplant. Using a pastry brush, coat the cold broiling grid generously with about a tablespoonful of the olive oil. Lay the eggplant slices on the grid and brush their tops generously with more oil. Then sprinkle them with a little salt (be careful, as the slices may be still somewhat salty from the previous salting) and with a few grindings of pepper.

Place the grid in the preheated pan and slide it under the heat. The surface of the eggplant slices should be about 5 inches from the source of heat. Broil the eggplant for about 5 minutes, or until the slices are lightly browned.

Turn the slices over with a large spatula, salt and pepper the eggplant again, and brush the slices with the remaining oil. Broil the eggplant for about 2 or 3 minutes. Then, working quickly, sprinkle the Parmesan cheese evenly over the slices. Cover the Parmesan on each eggplant slice with a slice of mozzarella and return the pan to the broiler, this time placing it so that the cheese is 3 inches from the source of heat. Broil the eggplant for 2 minutes longer, or just until the cheese is bubbling and lightly browned.

Serving the eggplant. Serve the eggplant at once on a warmed platter or plates, lest the mozzarella topping cool and become stringy.

CHERRY TOMATOES WITH GARLIC AND HERBS

Like the Broiled Diced Potatoes in the following recipe, these cherry tomatoes are not broiled in the accurate sense of the word; instead, they are cooked under direct heat in a baking dish, which prevents air from circulating freely around them. But the results are so delicious that, at the risk of seeming inconsistent, I feel the end justifies the means.

SERVES 4

The Tomatoes:
2 dozen red but not overripe cherry tomatoes about 1 inch in
    diameter
¼ cup olive oil
½ teaspoon salt
¼ teaspoon freshly ground black pepper
1 teaspoon finely chopped garlic

The Garnish:
1 tablespoon finely cut fresh basil
1 tablespoon finely chopped fresh parsley, preferably the
    flat-leaved or Italian variety

Preheating the broiler. Place the broiling pan—it isn't necessary to remove the grid—in the broiler about 4 inches from the source of heat. Then turn on the broiler at its highest setting to heat for 15 minutes.

Preparing the tomatoes. To peel the tomatoes, blanch them by dropping them into a 3-quart pot of rapidly boiling water and leaving them for 15 seconds. Drain the tomatoes immediately in a sieve and run cold water over them to cool them quickly. Then, with the aid of a small sharp knife, carefully slip off their skins.

In a small mixing bowl, stir together the olive oil, salt, pepper, and garlic. Add the tomatoes and toss them gently in this marinade. They need not rest in the mixture, but they may be left in it for 15 to 20 minutes if you wish.

Broiling the tomatoes. Remove the tomatoes from the marinade and arrange them in a shallow flameproof baking dish just large enough to hold them in one layer. Slide the dish into the broiler; the tomatoes should be about 3 inches from the source of heat. Broil the tomatoes until they are lightly flecked with brown, then turn them and broil them until the second side is brown-flecked. Do not overcook them; they should still feel somewhat firm to the touch when done.

Serving the tomatoes. Remove the dish from the broiler and sprinkle the tomatoes with the basil and parsley. Turn the tomatoes about gently with a spoon to coat them with the herbs, then serve them at once in their baking dish or as a garnish.

---◆§◈◈---

BROILED DICED POTATOES

Potatoes broiled in butter until they are golden-crusted and flecked with brown are a superb accompaniment for steak—or, for that matter, for almost any plainly broiled meat or fish that might come to your table.

You can successfully broil sweet potatoes and yams as well as the baking potatoes in this recipe. Use the same amount of butter and follow the same procedure, but omit the final sprinkling of herbs. The yams or sweet potatoes are especially good with chicken.

SERVES 4

The Potatoes:
About 2 pounds baking potatoes, or enough to make 4 cups of
 1-inch cubes
8 tablespoons butter (a quarter-pound stick), cut into bits
1 teaspoon salt
¼ teaspoon freshly ground black pepper

The Garnish:
2 tablespoons finely chopped fresh parsley or finely cut chives
 or dill

Preheating the broiler. Slide the broiling pan, with its grid in place, into the broiler about 6 inches from the source of heat. Then turn on the broiler at its highest setting to heat for 15 minutes.

Preparing the potatoes. Peel the potatoes, dropping them into a bowl of cold water as you proceed to prevent them from discoloring. Then cut them into cubes about 1 inch square. Return the cubes to the cold water until you are ready to broil the potatoes.

Preparing the butter and the baking dish. Over low heat melt the butter bits in a flameproof baking dish just large enough to hold the potatoes in one layer; do not let the butter brown. Remove the dish from the heat.

Drain the potatoes and pat them thoroughly dry with paper towels. Add the potatoes to the melted butter and toss them about with a spoon until they are well coated. Then stir in the salt and pepper.

Broiling the potatoes. Place the baking dish on the grid of the preheated broiler pan, checking to make sure that the top of the layer of potatoes is about 5 inches from the source of heat.

Broil the potatoes for about 20 minutes, turning them with a spoon every 5 minutes or so, until each piece is a crusty golden brown outside and moist within. Watch the potatoes carefully for any signs of burning, and lower the heat, or increase the distance of the dish from the heat, if necessary.

Serving the potatoes. Serve the potatoes at once, sprinkled with parsley, chives, or dill.

Skewered Foods

We generally think of broiling foods on skewers as an outdoor ritual proudly performed over charcoal by the American male in his backyard. You will be delighted to find that skewer broiling can be done quite as successfully, and less messily, in your range broiler or in a portable broiler equipped for the purpose with a special rack.

The advantages of skewer broiling are many. It is not only a simple, picturesque process but a rapid one as well. Because the pieces of food broiled on skewers are comparatively small—never more than about 1½ to 2 inches thick—they cook through quickly, and when you are pressed for time they do equally well as a main course for lunch or dinner, or served as an accompaniment for drinks.

The recipes that follow have been written explicitly enough to serve you as guides in skewer-broiling foods other than the ones specified. Once you have mastered these techniques, you will be able to follow the general methods in developing your own specialties.

Techniques for Broiling Skewered Foods

Preheating pans. Like the steaks and chops discussed in preceding sections, skewered meats, whether marinated or not, are placed on a *cold* grid. The cold grid is then set into a hot broiling pan that has been preheated with the broiler itself. On the other hand, skewered seafood, following the rule for broiling fish and seafood, is placed on a *preheated* grid in a preheated pan and broiler. This allows the seafood to begin to cook on both sides at once.

Marinated foods. Foods that have been marinated in the refrigerator can be broiled in their chilled state. There is no need whatever to bring them to room temperature.

Skewered vegetables. I think it is inadvisable to broil vegetables and meat together on the same skewer; the broiling times are often too disparate, with poorly cooked vegetables the unfortunate result.

However, you may wish to try broiling skewered pieces of zucchini or cucumber, whole cherry tomatoes or mushrooms, or other vegetables of your choice alongside your separately skewered meat. Consult the vegetable recipes that begin on page 193. Then add the skewers of vegetables to the grid at a point during the broiling of the meat that will allow both to be done at the same time.

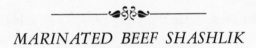

MARINATED BEEF SHASHLIK

This recipe for Marinated Beef Shashlik employs essentially the same culinary procedures as the following one for Marinated Lamb Shish Kebabs. "Shashlik" derives from the Russian and "shish kebab" from the Turkish (*shish*, literally translated, is skewer, and *kebab* is roast meat). But both are skewered cubes of meat which are sometimes marinated before broiling, but just as often not.

In both recipes the meat is marinated because I feel the marinade, besides tenderizing the meat, gives it a piquant and unusual flavor. You can interchange the marinades if you like and decide which of the two you prefer.

In many Eastern countries, shish kebab and shashlik are traditionally accompanied by rice. The platter is often garnished with lemon quarters, red radishes, and scallions. This ensemble is not only colorful, but it offers a harmony of flavors that is extremely effective. Of course, you needn't be limited by tradition; you can serve the skewered meat with whatever accompaniments you like, although I consider the lemon indispensable. Tomatoes, eggplant, and zucchini are particularly good with both dishes.

SERVES 4

The Marinade:
3 tablespoons red wine vinegar
½ cup vegetable oil
½ teaspoon salt
½ teaspoon coarsely ground black pepper
2 tablespoons grated onion
1 teaspoon crumbled dried oregano

The Beef:
2 pounds top sirloin of beef or boneless sirloin steak,
    trimmed of all fat and cut into 1½-inch cubes

The Garnish:
Lemon wedges
Red radishes and trimmed or coarsely chopped scallions
    (optional)

Marinating the beef. Pour the vinegar, oil, and salt into a 3-quart glass or stainless steel bowl and beat them together vigorously with a whisk until the oil and vinegar are thoroughly combined. Then stir in the pepper, onion, and oregano.

Add the meat cubes to the marinade in the bowl. With a large wooden spoon, toss the cubes about in the marinade until they are well moistened on all sides. Cover the bowl and refrigerate it for 6 to 8 hours, turning the meat over in the marinade every few hours.

Preheating the broiler. When you are ready to broil the shashlik, remove the grid from your broiling pan and slide the pan into the broiler about 4 inches from the source of heat. Turn on the broiler at its highest setting to heat for 15 minutes.

Broiling the meat. Remove the meat from its marinade and, dividing the cubes into 4 equal portions, string them through their center on four 14-inch steel skewers. It is not necessary to pat the cubes dry. Press the cubes tightly together and place the skewers side by side on the cold broiling grid. Place the remaining marinade and a pastry brush at hand near the broiler.

Slide the grid into the preheated broiler pan; the skewered meat should be about 3 inches from the source of heat. Broil the meat for about 5 minutes in all for rare, 7 minutes for medium, and 10 minutes for well done. Every 2 or 3 minutes baste the shashlik liberally with the marinade left in the bowl, turning the skewers over after the meat has broiled for half of its allotted time. A few minutes before the broiling time is up, test the meat for doneness by cutting into one of the cubes with a small sharp knife. Spread the cut apart and, depending on what you see, either broil the shashlik a moment or two longer or remove the skewers from the broiler immediately.

Serving the shashlik. Arrange the skewered shashlik on a large heated platter and add the lemon wedges and, if you like, the radishes and scallions. At the table, slide the meat off the skewers, pushing it with a fork or the flat of a knife directly onto heated serving plates.

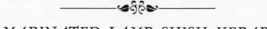

MARINATED LAMB SHISH KEBABS

As much as this lamb dish resembles the Marinated Beef Shashlik in the preceding recipe, there are subtle differences that extend beyond the characteristics of the meats themselves. For the Marinated Lamb Shish Kebabs, lemon replaces wine vinegar as the tenderizing acid, and garlic and rosemary replace the oregano and onion used to season the beef.

Like shashlik, Marinated Lamb Shish Kebabs are most appropriately served with rice.

A delicious variation of this lamb dish can be made by alternating large bay leaves (softened for a few moments in hot water if they are very brittle) with the meat on the skewers. The meat may be marinated or not, as you prefer. In either case the broiling time will remain exactly the same as in this recipe.

SERVES 4

The Marinade:
¼ cup fresh lemon juice
½ cup vegetable oil
½ teaspoon salt
½ teaspoon coarsely ground black pepper
1 large bay leaf, crumbled
4 large cloves of garlic, peeled and thinly sliced
1 teaspoon crumbled dried rosemary

The Lamb:
2 pounds boneless lamb, preferably from the leg, trimmed of
    all fat and cut into 1½-inch cubes

The Garnish:
Lemon wedges
Radishes and trimmed or chopped scallions (optional)

Marinating the meat. Pour the lemon juice, oil, and salt into a 3-quart glass or stainless steel bowl and beat them together vigorously with a whisk until the lemon juice and oil are thoroughly combined. Then stir in the pepper, bay leaf, garlic, and rosemary.

Add the meat to the marinade in the bowl. With a large wooden spoon, toss the lamb cubes about in the marinade until they are well moistened on all sides. Cover the bowl with plastic wrap and refrigerate it for 6 to 8 hours, turning the meat over in the marinade every few hours.

Preheating the broiler. When you are ready to broil the shish kebabs, remove the grid from your broiling pan and slide the pan into the broiler about 4 inches from the source of heat. Turn on the broiler at its highest setting to heat for 15 minutes.

Broiling the meat. Meanwhile, remove the meat from its marinade and divide the cubes into 4 equal portions. String the cubes of lamb through their centers on four 14-inch skewers. It is not necessary to pat the cubes dry. Press the cubes tightly together and place the skewers side by side on the cold grid. Place the remaining marinade and a pastry brush at hand near the broiler.

Slide the laden grid into the preheated broiler pan. The skewered meat should be about 3 inches from the source of heat.

Broil the shish kebabs for about 5 minutes in all for rare, 7 minutes in all for medium, and 10 minutes in all for well done. Every 2 or 3 minutes baste the meat liberally with the marinade remaining in the bowl, using a pastry brush. Turn the skewers over after the meat has broiled for half of its allotted time.

A few minutes before the broiling time is up, test the meat for doneness by cutting into one of the cubes with a small sharp knife and spreading the cut open. Depending on what you see, either broil the shish kebabs for a moment or two longer, or remove them immediately from the broiler.

Serving the shish kebabs. Arrange the shish kebabs, still skewered, on a large heated platter. Garnish the platter with the lemon wedges and, if you wish, with the radishes and scallions.

At the table, slide the meat off the skewers, pushing with a fork or the flat of a knife, directly onto heated serving plates.

SKEWERED SHRIMP WITH GARLIC BUTTER

To be able successfully to skewer shrimp you must choose those that are large, uniform in size, and of the best quality. Fresh shrimp (admittedly difficult to find these days) are infinitely preferable to those that have been frozen, but whether the shrimp are fresh or frozen, their shells and tails must be intact. Small, limp, misshapen shrimp won't do at all because they will be virtually impossible to thread on a skewer.

These unusual skewered shrimp are best served as a first course for dinner or as a main course for lunch or a late supper. And indispensable with them, I feel, is a crusty loaf of French or Italian bread with which to sop up the delicious garlicky juices.

The Garlic Butter:
8 tablespoons butter (a quarter-pound stick), cut into bits
1 tablespoon finely chopped garlic
1 teaspoon crumbled dried oregano

The Shrimp:
16 large shrimp in their shells, each about 3½ to 4 inches long
    (about 2 pounds shrimp)
Salt
Freshly ground black pepper

For Oiling the Grid and the Skewers:
1 to 2 tablespoons vegetable oil

The Garnish:
2 tablespoons finely chopped fresh parsley
Lemon quarters

Preheating the broiler. Slide your broiling pan, with its grid in place, into the broiler 3 inches from the source of heat. Turn the broiler to its highest setting to heat for 15 minutes.

Preparing the garlic butter. In a small saucepan set over low heat, melt the butter bits, but don't let them brown. Remove the butter from the heat and stir in the garlic and oregano. Set the pan, together with a pastry brush, at hand near the broiler.

Preparing the shrimp. With a pair of small scissors, cut the shell of each shrimp from top to tail along the curve of the back, leaving the shell and tail attached to the shrimp. Remove the black (it is sometimes white or yellow) intestinal vein by cutting down into the flesh ⅛ inch or so along the same back curve and lifting out the vein with the point of a knife.

Wash the shrimp thoroughly in cold water and pat them dry with paper towels.

Thread 4 shrimp onto each of four 14-inch skewers in this manner: With a pastry brush, lightly coat the skewers with vegetable oil. Then pick up a shrimp firmly between the thumb and fingers of one hand and, starting at the head end, pierce it with the skewer through the center of the body to a point just below the tail.

Broiling the shrimp. Quickly brush the hot grid with the vegetable oil and lay the skewers of shrimp on the grid. Sprinkle them liberally with salt and then, more sparingly, with pepper. Brush the shrimp copiously with the garlic butter.

Broil the shrimp 2 inches from the source of heat for 3 or 4 minutes, basting them again with the garlic butter after the first 2 minutes.

Turn the skewers over, sprinkle the other side of the shrimp with salt and pepper, and baste them again. Broil the shrimp for 2 minutes, then brush the remaining butter over them and broil them for 2 minutes more, or until they are golden brown and firm to the touch.

Serving the shrimp. Slide the shrimp off their skewers onto a large heated platter and pour all the drippings in the broiling pan over them. Sprinkle the shrimp with parsley and serve at once with lemon quarters.

Braising:
A Bit of Kitchen Magic

S ince the processes of braising and stew-
ing are so closely related, it is inevitable that confusion sometimes
arises. Both mean cooking by moist heat, but in stewing, the meat is
completely immersed in liquid, whereas in braising, a minimal
amount of liquid is used. Although braising is normally done in the
oven, it can be done on top of the stove and, conversely, stewing,
which is usually done on top of the stove, can be done in the oven.

   To make matters even more confusing, braising is all too frequently designated as "pot roasting," a nonexistent technique. "Pot
roast" is the name applied to a chunky beef cut, cooked or uncooked,
and is not a cooking method at all. To cook a pot roast, you braise it.

Foods for Braising

Braising, one of the most effective and delicious cooking techniques, is used for meats, fish, game, poultry, and some vegetables.

Meats. Braising is the way to deal with tough cuts of meat, because the magic combination of heat and moisture renders them succulent and tender. The tough cuts come from the well-exercised sections of animals—oxtails, short ribs of beef, lamb breast and shoulder, veal shanks and shoulder, pork shoulder.

Because braising is a moist-heat method of cookery, it is also the ideal way to prepare lean (poorly marbled), tender cuts such as pork chops that would otherwise dry out before they were done. For this same reason, veal, the most delicate of all meats, is particularly suited to braising. Virtually every cut of veal—the tender as well as the not so tender—profits from braising.

Poultry. Many excellent recipes call for braising chickens, sometimes in broth, sometimes in beer. Duckling, too, is especially succulent when braised.

Fish. Whole fish or thick cuts can be braised with great success. The fish best suited to braising are fairly large and firmly fleshed: salmon, carp, halibut, turbot, trout. Use the whole fish, if it is of manageable size; otherwise, use chunks or steaks.

Vegetables. Not all vegetables can, or should, be braised. Of those that can, I have chosen four which I consider exceptionally good, and I give braising recipes for each.

Techniques for Braising

Two methods of braising. Ordinary braising and white braising are the two classic methods.

Ordinary braising applies particularly to beef and mutton. In this method, the meat is sometimes larded, depending on the cut and quality, and often marinated. If the meat is marinated, it must be thoroughly dried, then well seared in hot fat to seal in the juices. The marinade or other liquid and vegetables are added, the pan is covered, and the long, slow cooking begins.

White braising is usually used for poultry, fish, lamb, or veal. As a general rule, the meats are not browned before the braising liquids are added. Cooking authorities, however, are inclined to be quite arbitrary about the question of browning prior to braising and, with the exception of fish, which would not be browned or seared, and red meat, which always is, you will find that the two methods overlap somewhat.

Braising liquids. The braising liquids, which are used sparingly, vary greatly. If water is used—and it frequently is—it needs the support of excellent seasonings. Broth alone or with wine is commonly used, and you will find recipes that call for beer, hard cider, and, in some instances, tomato purée. Each braising liquid makes its own special contribution. To augment the liquids, herbs, vegetables, and sometimes bones are added to give the dish a distinctive flavor.

A covered pot. In general, the braising pot is securely covered to prevent any steam from escaping. The pot can then be placed in a slow oven and almost take care of itself.

There are, however, instances in braising where the dish is finished in the oven without a cover, usually with very tender meat, such as sweetbreads, or with vegetables.

BRAISED SHORT RIBS WITH KIDNEY BEANS

This robust dish combining chili, short ribs, and kidney beans comes out of the Southwest. Traditionally, it is served with boiled rice, which, considering the beans, may seem like too much of a good thing. In fact, the combination is somehow just right.

Although butchers in supermarkets are inclined to crack short ribs, I find ribs much more impressive, and the meat easier to slice, when served whole.

My recipe calls for 3 tablespoons of chili powder, but if you are a true aficionado, you may want to increase the quantity a bit.

SERVES 6

5 to 5½ pounds short ribs of beef
1 tablespoon salt
1 teaspoon crumbled dried thyme
3 tablespoons chili powder
3 tablespoons vegetable oil
2 large yellow onions, peeled and thinly sliced
2 cloves garlic, peeled and minced
2 cups dry red wine
3 cups cooked red kidney beans or 2 cans (1 pound each)
    red kidney beans, drained, thoroughly rinsed in water,
    and drained again
6 to 8 sprigs parsley, finely chopped

Preheating the oven. Slide a shelf into a middle slot of the oven and preheat the oven at 450° F. for 15 minutes.

Preparing the short ribs. Trim any extra fat from the short ribs and dry each rib with paper towels. Spread a long sheet of wax paper on your work surface and on it line up the ribs.

In a small bowl combine the salt, thyme, and chili powder. With your fingers, rub the mixture into the meat, dividing the seasoning as evenly as possible and covering all surfaces of the ribs.

Braising the short ribs. Pour the vegetable oil into a heavy enameled cast-iron casserole—a 5-quart one is satisfactory, although a larger, shallower one would also be suitable. Set the casserole over moderate heat, and when the oil is hot but not smoking, add the onions and garlic, tossing them about with a wooden spoon until they have barely begun to color—a matter of only a minute or two.

Turn off the heat and arrange the ribs in the casserole in one layer, if possible, over the bed of onions and garlic.

Place the casserole, uncovered, in the preheated oven and bake the ribs for about 20 minutes, or until they have begun to turn a light brown. Then, with tongs, turn each rib over and brown the other side for an additional 20 minutes.

When the ribs are a uniform reddish brown, reduce the heat to 350° F. Remove the casserole from the oven so that you can spoon off the inevitable excess fat. If you can't suck up the fat with a bulb baster, you will have to lift out some, or even all, of the ribs. Then add the wine, stirring with a spoon to mix it with the onions. Return the ribs to the casserole if you have removed them.

Cover the casserole, return it to the oven, and braise the meat for about 30 minutes, then turn or redistribute the ribs so that all the meat will be uniformly moist when the braising is complete.

Return the casserole to the oven and braise 30 more minutes. The meat should be very tender; you may even find that some of the meat has fallen off the bones. Braised short ribs are at their best when braised to the point that a fork pierces them with absolutely no resistance. If in doubt, overbraise rather than underbraise, leaving the ribs in the oven for an extra 30 minutes.

When the meat has passed the fork test, distribute the cooked kidney beans over the ribs, re-cover the pot, and continue cooking for another 15 minutes, or until the beans are piping hot.

Warm a large serving platter and the dinner dishes.

Serving the short ribs. Remove the casserole from the oven and arrange the ribs in a row on the heated platter, lifting them out, one at a time, with tongs and shaking them slightly to dislodge any beans clinging to them.

Place the casserole on top of the stove over moderate heat. With a spoon, stir the contents of the pot so that the beans and pan juices are combined. If any fat is visible, tip the pan and quickly spoon off as much as possible. Then add the beans to the platter with the ribs and sprinkle with the chopped parsley. Serve immediately.

OXTAILS BRAISED WITH WHITE GRAPES

From June through November, California white grapes (Perlettes first, then Thompson Seedless) are available, and this, of course, is the time to make this lovely French dish. The French rarely cook with grapes, and the recipe apparently originated with the *vignerons* (winegrowers). It is earthy and robust, but still with a certain elegance.

Fresh oxtails are usually available only in independent markets, but you can always buy them frozen; in my opinion, there is little, if any, difference. When buying fresh oxtails, ask your butcher to cut them at the "pearl" or joint, which will result in pieces about 1½ inches long; frozen oxtails are already cut up. The tail tapers from a diameter of almost 2 inches down to less than an inch, but this disparity in size in no way affects the cooking.

This is one of those splendid dishes that can be made in advance —in fact, it is desirable to make it a day or two ahead of time, because it seems to develop a richer flavor on standing.

SERVES 6 TO 8

4½ to 5 pounds oxtails (2 large oxtails), cut into
   1½-inch sections
¼ pound salt pork
1 tablespoon vegetable oil
2 large yellow onions, peeled and diced (enough to
   make 2 cups)
4 or 5 carrots, peeled and sliced ¼ inch thick (enough to
   make 3 cups)
2 garlic cloves, skin on and smashed with the flat side
   of a heavy knife or cleaver
2 sprigs parsley
2 large bay leaves
½ teaspoon crumbled dried thyme
1 tablespoon salt
Freshly ground black pepper
2¼ pounds white seedless grapes, rinsed in a colander
   and drained

Preparing the oxtails. If you buy frozen oxtails, they will release a considerable amount of blood on thawing. Whether you buy them fresh or frozen, soak them in cold water to cover for about 2 hours to rid them of surplus blood. Drain them in a colander, then, with a sharp knife, cut away as much fat as possible.

Preparing the casserole. With a sharp knife, remove the rind from the salt pork, then cut the pork into ½-inch cubes.

Pour the vegetable oil into a 7-quart enameled cast-iron casserole. Place over moderate heat and, when the oil is hot but not smoking—its surface will look watery and show ripples—toss in the cubes of salt pork. With a wooden spoon, stir for about a minute to separate the cubes. Add the onions and carrots and continue stirring for a minute or so, just until the vegetables are lightly coated with oil.

Lower the heat, cover the casserole, and allow the salt pork and vegetables to simmer for about 10 minutes, or until the fat running from the pork covers the bottom of the pan and the vegetables have softened slightly. Add the garlic, parsley, bay leaves, and thyme. Cook slowly while you season the oxtails.

Sprinkle the salt over all sides of the oxtails and then season with a liberal grinding of pepper. Arrange the pieces, in one layer, if possible, over the bed of vegetables in the casserole.

Cover the casserole, place over moderate heat, and cook for 15 minutes, or until the oxtails have heated through. On uncovering the casserole, you will notice at this point a faint indication of steam building up; this will help tenderize the oxtails.

Preheating the oven. While the oxtails are heating, slide an oven shelf into a center slot and preheat the oven at 300° F. for 15 minutes.

Preparing the grapes. Strip the stems off the grapes. Reserve 25 to 30 of the prettiest grapes to add to the casserole at the end, and place the remainder in a large bowl. With a potato masher (or the bottom of a bottle), crush the grapes very slightly so that they will readily give off their tart-sweet juices.

Braising the oxtails. When the oxtails have heated for about 15 minutes on top of the stove, scatter the crushed grapes over them and cover with two layers of wax paper cut to fit the casserole. Replace the cover, set the casserole in the oven, and allow the oxtails to braise for about 2 hours.

After about 2 hours of cooking, test the oxtails for tenderness at intervals by piercing one or two of the larger pieces with a fork. The fork may go in easily at the first test, but when perfectly braised, the meat will almost fall from the bones; this usually occurs sometime after 2½ to 3 hours of cooking. If you are the least bit uncertain, overbraise the oxtails rather than risk undercooking them.

When the oxtails are very tender, remove the casserole from the oven and turn off the heat. With tongs, lift out the pieces of meat, shaking each so that any clinging grapes fall back into the casserole. Set the meat aside in a bowl.

Completing the sauce. With a large spoon or bulb baster, remove as much fat as possible from the liquid in the casserole.

Place a food mill, with its finest strainer in place, over a large bowl and empty the contents of the casserole into it. Force the vegetables and juices through the mill. Or, lacking a food mill, use a large fine-meshed sieve and force the vegetables through with the back of a wooden spoon or with a rubber spatula.

If the sauce seems too thick, as it may, thin it with a few tablespoons of water.

Return the oxtails to the casserole, pour the sauce over, and bring to a boil on top of the stove. Taste the sauce for seasoning.

Once the sauce has been added to the oxtails, the mixture may be tightly covered with foil and refrigerated for a day or two. Cover and refrigerate the reserved grapes separately. Just before serving, reheat the oxtails and sauce over low heat.

Serving the oxtails. While the sauce and meat are heating, halve the reserved grapes lengthwise, then toss them over the meat and sauce. Continue heating for only a few seconds, just long enough for the grapes to warm through but not long enough for them to lose their fresh, crisp quality.

Serve at once in the casserole or on a large, deep, heated platter.

BRAISED VEAL WITH PRUNES AND MADEIRA

This dish is almost worth making for the sauce alone, an interesting combination of the sweetness contributed by carrots, Madeira wine, and fruity prunes. The sauce demands a vegetable with which to enjoy it, and I suggest tiny new potatoes, glistening with butter and garnished with minced parsley.

Like many other braised dishes, this one can be prepared well in advance and reheated over very low heat.

SERVES 6

12 ounces pitted prunes (a 12-ounce box or bag)
1 cup Madeira wine
3 pounds boned shoulder of veal, trimmed of all fat and
    gristle, cut into 1½-inch pieces about ¼ inch thick
4 to 6 tablespoons vegetable oil
4 to 6 tablespoons butter, cut into bits
2 to 3 carrots, peeled and thinly sliced (enough to
    make 1 cup)
2 to 3 ribs celery, diced (enough to make 1 cup)
About 2 teaspoons salt
Freshly ground white pepper
½ cup heavy cream

Soaking the prunes. Place the prunes in a bowl, add the Madeira, cover the bowl, and set aside to soak for 24 hours. They need not be refrigerated.

Preheating the oven. Slide a shelf into a middle slot of your oven and preheat the oven at 350° F. for 15 minutes.

Preparing the veal and vegetables. Pat the pieces of veal dry with paper towels and set aside.

Combine 4 tablespoons of the vegetable oil and 4 tablespoons of the butter bits in a heavy 12-inch frying pan, preferably one with a nonstick surface. Set the pan over moderate heat. When the butter has melted and the combined fats begin to foam, add the carrots and celery. Cook for about 2 minutes, stirring occasionally with a slotted spoon. Then transfer the vegetables to a 5-quart enameled cast-iron casserole with a tight-fitting lid and spread them so that they cover the bottom.

In the same frying pan, lightly sauté the veal over moderate heat for about 2 minutes on each side. Do not crowd the pan; sauté only as many pieces as will fit into it comfortably. When the veal has turned a pale golden color, transfer the pieces to the casserole with the slotted spoon, and sprinkle them lightly with salt and white pepper. Sauté, salt, and pepper the rest of the veal in the same manner, adding additional vegetable oil and butter to the pan, if necessary.

Drain the prunes and set them aside, pouring the excess Madeira into the frying pan. Quickly bring the contents of the pan to a boil, scraping the bottom with a spoon to loosen any brown particles. Pour the liquid over the meat in the casserole. Then set the casserole over high heat and bring the juices to a boil. Turn off the heat and cover the casserole.

Braising the veal. Place the covered casserole in the oven and braise the meat and vegetables for about 45 to 50 minutes. After 50 minutes, the vegetables should have begun to soften, and the meat should show only slight resistance when pierced with a fork. Now add the prunes, using tongs or your fingers to distribute them over the top of the meat.

Cover the casserole and braise the meat and vegetables for another 20 to 30 minutes, or until the meat is very tender when pierced with a fork and the prunes are plump. Turn off the oven and remove the casserole.

Serving the veal. Using tongs, lift the prunes off the top of the meat and arrange them around the rim of a heated serving platter; arrange the veal slices in the center. Cover the platter with foil and place in the turned-off oven to keep warm while you make the sauce. At the same time, warm the dinner plates and a sauceboat in the oven.

Set a food mill with its finest strainer in place over a large saucepan. Pour the contents of the casserole into the food mill and force the vegetables through it. Lacking a food mill, use a fine-meshed sieve and force the vegetables through, using the back of a spoon or a rubber spatula. The sieved sauce will be rather thick; thin it out with the cream, stirring the mixture with a spoon or whisk as you heat it over moderate heat. Spoon some of the hot sauce over the meat and serve the remainder in a heated sauceboat.

SHOULDER OF LAMB WITH SPINACH STUFFING

The Lamb:
6- to 6½-pound shoulder of lamb
½ pound fresh pork fat, cut into ¼- to ½-inch cubes

SERVES 6

The Spinach Stuffing:
2 packages (10 ounces each) chopped frozen spinach, defrosted
4 tablespoons butter, cut into bits
¼ cup water
1 to 2 yellow onions, peeled and minced (enough to make 1 cup)
¼ cup pine nuts (*pignoli*)
½ cup fine dry bread crumbs
2 teaspoons fresh lemon juice
¼ teaspoon nutmeg
2 teaspoons salt
1 egg, lightly beaten

The Lamb Bones:
4 tablespoons fat rendered from the fresh pork fat
The bones from the shoulder of lamb

The Braising Ingredients:
3 tablespoons fat rendered from the fresh pork fat
2 medium yellow onions, peeled and sliced about ¼ inch thick
1 carrot, peeled and sliced about ¼ inch thick
1 celery rib, sliced about ¼ inch thick
1½ teaspoons salt
Freshly ground black pepper
2 cups water
1 tablespoon butter, softened at room temperature
12 boiling potatoes, peeled

The Garnish:
A few parsley sprigs

Preparing the lamb shoulder. Have the butcher bone the shoulder, leaving a natural pocket, and, at the same time, cut away as much fat as possible. If the butcher is unable to remove all the bones without cutting the meat open, you will have to sew three sides of the roast after you have stuffed it. The shoulder will weigh about 4 pounds after boning. Save the bones to use in braising the lamb.

Rendering the fresh pork fat. Place the cubes of fresh pork fat in a heavy 12-inch frying pan and let them melt slowly over fairly low heat, stirring now and then; do not let the fat brown. Rendering the fat will take about 10 minutes. Pour the melted fat through a fine sieve into a small bowl and set it aside for browning the lamb bones, meat, and vegetables.

Preparing the spinach stuffing. Squeeze the thawed spinach, a handful at a time, to extract as much moisture as possible. Place the spinach in a large mixing bowl and set it aside.

In a 12-inch frying pan melt 4 tablespoons of butter bits over moderate heat and add the water. When the mixture reaches a boil, add the minced onions and cook at a moderate boil, uncovered, for 6 to 8 minutes, or until the onions are soft and all the water has boiled away. Add the onions and butter to the spinach. Then add the pine nuts, bread crumbs, lemon juice, nutmeg, and 1 teaspoon of the salt. Stir all the ingredients together with a fork. Allow the stuffing to cool, then add the lightly beaten egg, mixing it in with a fork. Set the stuffing aside.

Stuffing the shoulder. If there is a natural pocket, rub the remaining teaspoon of salt into it with your fingers. If the meat has been cut open, sprinkle the remaining teaspoon of salt over the surface.

Stuff the pocket with the spinach mixture or spoon it over the cut surface of the meat. In either case, do not pack the stuffing down. Using a large darning needle and extra-heavy white thread, sew up the opening of the pocket with an overcasting stitch. If there is no pocket, fold the meat over on itself to enclose the stuffing, then sew the edges.

When stuffed, the shoulder will be about 11 inches long, 7 inches across, and 3 inches thick at the thickest part. It should be neat and compact, so if there are any stray ends of meat, skewer them to the shoulder.

Browning the lamb bones and meat. Pour 4 tablespoons of the rendered pork fat into the frying pan and place it over moderate heat. When the fat is hot but not smoking, add the bones and brown them on both sides. Remove the lamb bones and set them aside.

Dry the stuffed lamb shoulder with paper towels, then place it in the frying pan to brown it all over. Since the shoulder is somewhat awkward to handle, take care when turning it to avoid any hot spattering fat, and use two wooden spatulas—not a fork or you will puncture the meat—to turn the meat. Browning will take 16 to 20 minutes. Then set the lamb shoulder aside.

Preheating the oven. Slide a shelf into a center slot of the oven and preheat the oven at 325° F. for 15 minutes.

Preparing the braising ingredients. While the lamb is browning, spoon 3 tablespoons of the rendered pork fat into a 9-quart enameled cast-iron casserole. Heat the fat over moderate heat until it is hot but not smoking, then add the sliced onions, carrot, and celery. Stir with a wooden spoon to coat the vegetables with the fat. Continue cooking for 6 to 8 minutes, or until the vegetables are lightly browned. Turn off the heat, but leave the casserole in place on the stove.

With two wooden spatulas place the lamb on the bed of vegetables in the casserole. Arrange the browned lamb bones around the lamb, then sprinkle both with the 1½ teaspoons of salt and liberal grindings of pepper.

Pour off any fat remaining in the frying pan, add the 2 cups of water, and scrape down any brown encrustations in the pan. Bring to a boil over high heat, then pour into the casserole. Bring the contents of the casserole to a boil. Butter a piece of parchment or wax paper cut to fit the casserole, place it, buttered side down, over the lamb, then put the cover on the casserole.

Braising the lamb. Place the casserole in the oven and cook for 1 hour and 10 minutes. By that time the liquid will about half-cover the lamb.

Remove the cover and the buttered paper. Using tongs, lift out and discard the bones, then add the potatoes to the liquid. Return the buttered paper to the casserole, fit the lid, and continue cooking for 20 to 25 minutes, or until the potatoes are tender when pierced with the point of a small sharp knife. Remove the casserole from the oven and raise the heat to 400° F.

Glazing the lamb and potatoes. Using two wooden spatulas, place the lamb in a shallow roasting pan large enough to hold both it and the potatoes. Then, using a slotted spoon, transfer the potatoes to the same pan. Spoon a little of the reserved pork fat over the meat and potatoes. Place the pan in the 400° F. oven for 10 minutes, or until both the meat and potatoes take on a light brown glaze.

Straining the sauce. Place a large fine sieve over a 2-quart saucepan, and through it strain the liquid and vegetables in the casserole. With a big spoon or wooden spatula, press the vegetables against the sides of the sieve to release as much liquid as possible, but do not force any of the vegetables through. Tilt the pan and, using a large metal spoon or bulb baster, remove as much of the fat as possible. Bring the strained sauce to a boil over high heat and taste for seasoning.

Serving the lamb shoulder. Place the lamb on a large heated platter, surround with the potatoes, and garnish with parsley sprigs. Pour the strained sauce into a heated sauceboat. Serve at once.

ROLLED PORK SHOULDER WITH SAUERKRAUT

SERVES 6 TO 8

The Meat:
1 pork shoulder roast, weighing 3½ to 4 pounds when
    boned as described below
½ pound fresh pork fat, cut into ¼- to ½-inch cubes
1 teaspoon salt
Freshly ground black pepper
2 tablespoons minced fresh parsley

The Sauerkraut:
2 pounds sauerkraut
6 tablespoons fat rendered from the fresh pork fat
1 medium carrot, peeled and sliced thin
1 large or 2 medium yellow onions, peeled and sliced thin
2 teaspoons caraway seeds
Bouquet garni: 4 sprigs parsley, 6 peppercorns, 1 large bay
    leaf, all tied in a cheesecloth bag
⅔ cup dry vermouth or dry white wine
½ cup gin
2 cups beef or chicken broth
½ to 1 teaspoon salt
Freshly ground black pepper
1 teaspoon softened butter

Preparing the pork shoulder. When the butcher bones the roast, also have him trim off as much fat as possible, then roll and tie the shoulder. Ask for that fat—and for additional pork fat, if needed, to make a total of ½ pound—which you will use for both the meat and the sauerkraut.

Rendering the fresh pork fat. Place the pork fat cubes in a large heavy frying pan and let them melt slowly over fairly low heat, stirring now and then; do not let the fat brown. This will take about 10 minutes. Pour the melted fat through a fine sieve into a small bowl and set aside.

Preparing the sauerkraut. Drain the sauerkraut in a colander. Place in a large bowl, cover with cold water, and soak for 5 minutes. Drain, again cover with cold water, and soak 5 more minutes. Pour into a colander and continue to drain.

Meanwhile, add 6 tablespoons of the rendered pork fat to a 5-quart enameled cast-iron casserole and place over moderate heat just long enough for a slight haze to begin to form on the surface of the fat. Add the sliced carrot and onion. Stir with a wooden spatula until the vegetables are coated with the fat. Cover, lower the heat, and cook the vegetables slowly for 10 minutes; do not allow them to brown.

Taking one handful of the sauerkraut at a time, squeeze to extract any excess liquid. Add the sauerkraut to the casserole, stirring with a wooden spatula to combine it with the other vegetables and the fat. Cover and cook over low heat for another 10 minutes.

Preheating the oven. Slide one of the oven racks into a center slot and preheat the oven at 325° F. for 15 minutes.

Braising the sauerkraut. Stir the caraway seeds into the sauerkraut and bury the bouquet garni in it. Add the vermouth, gin, beef or chicken broth, ½ teaspoon of the salt, and several grindings of pepper. Bring to a boil on top of the stove.

Using the softened butter, butter a piece of wax paper or foil cut to fit the casserole and place it, buttered side down, on top of the vegetables. Cover the casserole and place in the oven.

Braise for about 15 minutes, then check to determine if the juices are barely bubbling; they should not boil. Continue braising for another 45 minutes, or a total of 1 hour.

Preparing and braising the pork shoulder. Meanwhile, dry the pork with paper towels. Place 2 tablespoons of the rendered pork fat in the large, heavy frying pan over moderate heat. When it is hot but not smoking, add the pork, fat side down. When golden brown, which will take 4 to 5 minutes, turn with wooden spatulas and brown all the other sides. This should take a total of 15 minutes or so. Remove the frying pan from the heat. Sprinkle the meat with 1 teaspoon of salt and several grindings of pepper.

Remove the cover and wax paper from the casserole containing the sauerkraut. Using two spatulas, make a well in the center of the sauerkraut and place the pork shoulder in it. Scrape any fat or juices left in the frying pan over the meat. Replace the wax paper and the cover of the casserole.

Braise the pork and sauerkraut for 2 hours. By that time, the meat should be very tender when pierced with a skewer or kitchen fork and a "spot-check" thermometer should read 165° to 170° F.

Serving the pork shoulder and sauerkraut. Lift the shoulder from the casserole to a preheated platter deep enough to hold the juices that will inevitably drain from the sauerkraut. Cut off and discard the string and sprinkle the pork with the minced parsley. Cover with foil to keep warm.

Remove and discard the bouquet garni. Correct the seasoning; the sauerkraut may need the extra salt. Drain the sauerkraut in a colander, using a pair of forks or tongs to lift it so that it will drain quickly; the sauerkraut should be moist but not wet.

Spoon the sauerkraut around the pork shoulder and serve immediately.

PORK CHOPS BRAISED WITH BACON AND POTATOES

This is one of those wonderful, hearty, meat-and-potato dinners that make a cold winter's night seem warm, and since it's all cooked in one fell swoop, it's easy on the cook. Moreover, it can be completely cooked one day, refrigerated, and reheated the next.

In choosing the potatoes, buy the "boiling" variety because they are mature enough to hold their shape during the long braising period. Hard cider (less than 7 percent alcohol by volume) is often imported from England and is generally available in liquor stores.

½ pound sliced bacon, at room temperature
6 rib pork chops, cut 1 inch thick (preferably not too lean)
2 cloves garlic, peeled and split into thirds
2½ to 3 pounds potatoes, peeled and cut into ¼-inch slices
2 large or 3 medium yellow onions, peeled and thinly sliced
1½ teaspoons salt
Freshly ground black pepper
½ teaspoon crumbled dried thyme
1½ cups hard cider
1 to 2 teaspoons soft butter (optional)
6 to 8 sprigs parsley, chopped

Preheating the oven. Slide one of the oven shelves into a center slot and preheat the oven at 300° F. for 15 minutes.

Cooking the bacon and browning the chops. In a 12-inch frying pan cook the bacon over low heat—separating the slices with a fork as the bacon begins to fry—for about 5 to 8 minutes, or just long enough for the bacon to start to release its fat. Then, with tongs, lift the slices (they will still be limp and by no means fully cooked) from the pan to a large plate or platter.

Pour the bacon fat into a small bowl, leaving about a teaspoon or so in the frying pan. Set the bowl aside; you will use more bacon fat later.

Dry the chops thoroughly with paper towels and, with a small sharp knife, nick the fatty edges to prevent the chops from curling as they cook. With the tip of the same knife, make a small incision close to the bone at the base of each chop and push in a sliver of garlic, pinching the bone and meat together to hold the garlic securely in place.

Reheat the fat in the frying pan until it is hot but not smoking. Add as many chops as the pan will hold without crowding. Over moderate heat fry the chops just long enough to brown them lightly —roughly 4 minutes on each side—turning each chop with tongs when the first side is brown. As the chops brown on both sides, transfer them to the bacon platter.

Discard the fat in the frying pan and place the platter of chops and bacon on your work surface.

Braising the chops and vegetables. Pour a tablespoon or two of the reserved bacon fat into an enameled cast-iron 9-quart oval casserole, tilting it so that the fat coats the bottom with a light film.

Cover the bottom with half the sliced potatoes, scatter half the onion slices over the potatoes, and sprinkle with ½ teaspoon of the salt, then with several generous grindings of pepper.

Arrange the pork chops on top in a single layer, and sprinkle with ½ teaspoon of the salt, the thyme, and a generous amount of freshly ground black pepper. Cover the chops with the remaining potatoes and onions in layers as before. Sprinkle with the remaining ½ teaspoon of salt and more freshly ground black pepper. Arrange the bacon slices in a single layer over the entire surface. Pour in the hard cider; the cider will not cover the contents of the casserole, nor is it intended to.

Cut one sheet of parchment or wax paper to fit the casserole and coat one side of it with fat or, if you prefer, with 1 to 2 teaspoons of butter. Place the paper, buttered side down, over the contents of the casserole. Cover the casserole with a tight-fitting lid and slide it into the oven.

This sturdy, country dish calls for long braising in a very slow oven for about 2½ hours. By that time the bacon on top will be very soft, the potatoes very moist, and the chops, when pierced with a fork, so tender the meat will come away from the bones with no resistance at all. It is worth noting that if for some reason dinner must be postponed briefly, the chops can continue braising for as long as another 30 minutes.

When the chops are cooked, lift the casserole from the oven. As you will see, the liquid and the fat will have increased greatly. Although some fat is desirable, you should spoon off as much as you can. Let the casserole stand for 5 minutes to allow the fat to rise to the top, then tilt the casserole and skim off the excess with a large spoon.

At this point the casserole may be tightly covered with foil and refrigerated for a day or so before serving. To reheat, place the covered casserole in a preheated 350° F. oven for about 30 minutes, or until the juices bubble and the meat and vegetables are piping hot.

Serving the braised pork chops. It seems logical and attractive to me to serve as homely a dish as this straight from the casserole, so with a damp cloth, wipe the exposed inside surface, which has probably become stained with juices. Then sprinkle with the chopped parsley. Serve each person a chop, some bacon, potatoes, and onions, topped with some of those good savory brown juices remaining in the bottom of the casserole.

CHICKEN BRAISED IN BEER WITH MUSHROOMS

SERVES 6 TO 8

2 ready-to-cook chickens, weighing 3 to 3½ pounds each
2½ teaspoons salt
5 to 6 tablespoons vegetable oil
6 tablespoons butter, cut into bits
⅓ cup finely chopped shallots
1 pound mushrooms, including stems, coarsely chopped
   or sliced
12 ounces dark beer
1 cup heavy cream
Freshly ground black pepper
6 to 7 sprigs parsley

Preparing and trussing the chickens. Remove and reserve for another use the necks and giblets (gizzards, hearts, and livers) usually found inside the cavities of dressed birds. Season the cavities, rubbing about ¾ teaspoon of the salt in each with your fingers.

Truss each chicken as described in the "Culinary Glossary," pages 445–46.

Browning the chickens. Pour 3 to 4 tablespoons of the vegetable oil into a heavy 10-inch frying pan or sauté pan and place over moderate heat. When the oil is hot—barely beginning to sputter—place one of the chickens on its side in the pan and brown it lightly until golden. Then, using tongs, turn the bird by lifting it with the trussing string and brown the other side, adjusting the heat, if necessary. Finally, turn the bird on its back. Each chicken will take anywhere from 10 to 15 minutes, and you can't hurry this operation or the fat will burn and the chicken will not brown evenly.

When the chicken is golden brown all over, transfer it from the pan to a large platter. Add about 2 more tablespoons of oil to the pan and brown the second chicken the same way. When both chickens have been browned, discard the oil in the pan and set the chickens aside.

Cooking the shallots and mushrooms. Cut a piece of parchment or wax paper to fit a 9-quart round or oval enameled cast-iron casserole. Butter one side of the paper with about a teaspoon or so of the butter bits, and set it aside.

Add the remaining butter bits to the casserole and place it over moderate heat. When the butter begins to foam—do not allow it to brown—add the shallots and stir them with a wooden spoon for about 2 minutes, or until they have begun to soften slightly. Then add the mushrooms and continue to stir for a minute or two. The mushrooms will quickly absorb all the butter and may seem to be very dry, but don't be concerned. Immediately place the parchment or wax paper, buttered side down, over the mushrooms, cover the casserole and let the mushrooms "sweat" for about 5 minutes over moderate heat. During this period the mushrooms will release their juices and soften considerably.

Braising the chickens. Turn off the heat, set aside the lid and buttered paper, and pour the beer into the casserole. It will foam dramatically. When the foam subsides, add the cream. Stir the contents of the casserole with a wooden spoon for a second or two to combine the two liquids.

Add the chickens to the pot, placing them on their backs. Sprinkle 1 teaspoon of salt over the birds, followed by a liberal grinding of pepper.

Over moderate heat, bring the liquid in the casserole to a boil, then lower the heat so that the liquid simmers. Place the buttered paper, buttered side down, on top of the chickens and cover the casserole.

Braise the chickens, mushrooms, and shallots at an even simmer—the liquid should barely shiver—for 30 to 40 minutes. Adjust the heat, if necessary, to maintain the simmering temperature. After 30 or 40 minutes, remove the lid and the paper. Using tongs, turn the chickens over by their trussing strings so that the breasts are deep in the juices; by this time, the amount of liquid will have increased noticeably. Cover the casserole and continue braising for another 20 to 30 minutes.

To test the chickens for doneness, pierce a thigh deeply with a fork. When juices run clear with no trace of a rosy color, the chicken is perfectly cooked. It is important not to overbraise the chickens if you want the meat to be moist, tender, and delicious. Once the chickens are cooked, lift with tongs to a heated platter and cover with foil to keep warm.

Making the sauce. Place the casserole over high heat and boil rapidly, uncovered, for 5 to 10 minutes, or until the liquid has reduced to about a third and thickened slightly. The sauce will still be rather thin. Taste for seasoning. Then cover and keep the sauce hot over very low heat until ready to serve.

Serving the chickens. If the chickens are to be carved at the table, remove the trussing strings, spoon a little sauce over each bird, and garnish with parsley sprigs. Or the chickens may be cut into serving pieces to begin with: Cut off the leg sections, using a sharp carving knife; separate the drumsticks and thighs, then slice the breast meat about ¼ inch thick. Arrange the meat attractively on a large heated platter, the dark meat in the center, the breast meat at each end. Spoon some of the sauce, together with the mushrooms, over the meat. Mince the parsley, and sprinkle it over the chicken. Pour the remaining sauce into a heated sauceboat.

DUCKLINGS BRAISED IN HARD CIDER

A number of liquids can be used to braise ducklings; this recipe calls for hard cider bolstered with applejack or Calvados (fine Norman apple brandy). Hard cider, which has less than 7 percent alcohol by volume, is often imported from England and is usually available at liquor stores.

SERVES 6

The Ducklings:
2 ready-to-cook ducklings, weighing 4½ to 5 pounds each
2 tablespoons rendered duckling fat or butter
The 2 duckling livers
¼ cup applejack or Calvados
2 teaspoons salt
Freshly ground black pepper
1 bottle (⅘ quart) hard cider
1 cup heavy cream

The Apple Garnish:
3 large apples (Golden Delicious), washed, cored, and
    cut into thirds
Juice of 1 lemon
2 to 3 tablespoons butter, melted
Salt
Sugar

Preparing the ducklings. If you buy fresh ducklings, ask your butcher to quarter them and to save the duckling fat for you. On the other hand, if you buy frozen ducklings, you will have to quarter them yourself after they have thawed. Thaw and quarter the ducklings as described in the "Culinary Glossary," page 447. Remove the giblets and necks from the cavities of the birds as soon as they can be extricated, and discard all except the livers, which you should set aside in a bowl. Dry each duckling part thoroughly with paper towels.

Rendering the duckling fat. Pull out all the loose fat from the cavities of the ducklings and from around the necks. Place this in a heavy 12-inch frying pan over low heat and let the fat melt slowly. When only crisp bits of fat remain, pour the liquid into a bowl and discard the bits.

Browning the ducklings. Add 2 tablespoons of the rendered duckling fat or 2 tablespoons of butter to the 12-inch frying pan and place over moderate heat. When the fat begins to sizzle, add the duck pieces—a few at a time—skin side down, and sauté them for 10 to 12 minutes, or until the skin is a rich brown. Then turn with tongs and brown the other side. The flesh of the breasts will take only a minute but that of the leg sections about 5 minutes. As you finish browning the pieces, place them on a platter and set aside.

Sautéing the duckling livers. Pour off and discard all but 3 or 4 tablespoons of the fat in the frying pan. Dry the livers with paper towels and sauté them for about 2 minutes. The livers should be pink inside. Lift from the pan to a bowl. Chop fairly fine. Refrigerate, covered, until needed for making the sauce.

Preheating the oven. Slide one of the racks into a center slot of the oven and preheat the oven at 350° F. for 15 minutes.

Flaming the ducklings. Place the pieces of duckling in a 9-quart enameled cast-iron casserole, the dark meat or leg sections on the bottom, the breasts on top. Heat the applejack or Calvados in a small saucepan over low heat just until tepid, ignite with a match, then slowly pour the flaming applejack evenly over the ducklings. When the flames die out, sprinkle the duckling parts with 2 teaspoons of salt and generous grindings of pepper. Add the hard cider; it will cover the legs but only part of the breasts. Place the casserole over high heat and bring the contents to a boil.

Braising the ducklings. Cover the casserole and place it in the oven. Braise for 50 to 60 minutes, then test for doneness by plunging a fork into the thickest part of the thigh. If the fork does not go in easily and the juices do not run clear, replace the cover, braise for another 10 minutes, and test again. When the ducklings are cooked, transfer them to a large, heated ovenproof platter and arrange the pieces in one layer. Cover with foil to keep warm. Set aside the braising broth for making the sauce.

Broiling the apple garnish. Preheat the broiler while you prepare the apples. Pour the lemon juice into a small bowl, then dip in each apple piece and arrange on a cold broiling pan. With a pastry brush, coat each piece with melted butter. Sprinkle lightly with salt, then with sugar. Place the pan in the broiler so that the apples are about 4 inches from the source of heat, and broil 3 to 4 minutes, or until the apples have softened and taken on a golden glaze. Remove the apples and set aside.

Turn off the broiler and heat the oven to 400° F. for the final warming of the ducklings.

Making the sauce. Pour the braising broth from the casserole into a medium-size saucepan and add two trays of ice cubes. The fat will congeal around them. Quickly lift out and discard the ice cubes. Because the melting ice will inevitably dilute the broth, place the saucepan over high heat and boil hard for about 5 minutes. Stir in the cream and the chopped sautéed duckling livers. Bring the sauce up to a boil again but do not cook further, lest it curdle.

Serving the ducklings. Spoon the sauce over the pieces of duckling, coating each one, and arrange the apple pieces around the edge of the platter. Place in the 400° F. oven for about 10 minutes, then serve at once.

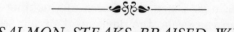

SALMON STEAKS BRAISED WITH WINE AND SHRIMP

Salmon is one of the nicest fish to braise because its meat is firm yet tender, and its flavor is assertive enough not to fade out in the company of braising stock or wine, vegetables, and herbs. Salmon can be braised alone with the simplest of seasonings, or it can be teamed with shellfish. My recipe calls for braising salmon steaks with shrimp in a wine-laced stock—a very happy combination.

The Fish Stock:
1 pound fish bones and trimmings (any kind)
1 carrot, peeled and thinly sliced
1 large yellow onion, peeled and thinly sliced
2 sprigs parsley
½ bay leaf
⅛ teaspoon crumbled dried thyme
1 cup dry white wine
3 cups water
½ teaspoon salt
1 teaspoon peppercorns

The Fish Dish:
4 to 6 tablespoons butter, softened at room temperature
3 medium yellow onions, peeled and very finely diced
2 ribs celery, including the green tops, very finely diced
2 carrots, peeled and very finely diced
6 salmon steaks, ½ to ¾ inch thick, cut from the center
     of the salmon, each weighing about 8 ounces
½ teaspoon salt
Freshly ground pepper, preferably white
1 cup dry white wine
2 cups of the fish stock
1 pound medium shrimp, shelled, deveined, rinsed under
     cold running water, and drained

The Sauce:
2 teaspoons butter, softened at room temperature
2 teaspoons flour
1½ cups of the braising liquid
½ cup heavy cream
2 teaspoons strained lemon juice
Salt
Freshly ground white pepper

The Garnish:
Parsley sprigs

Making the fish stock. In a 2- or 3-quart enameled cast-iron sauce-pan, place the fish bones and trimmings, 1 sliced carrot, sliced onion, 2 parsley sprigs, bay leaf, and thyme. Pour in 1 cup of dry white wine and bring the contents of the saucepan to a boil over high heat. Then add the water. When the liquid returns to a boil, reduce the heat to low. Add ½ teaspoon of salt and the peppercorns, and simmer, covered, for 25 minutes.

Place a large fine sieve over a bowl, strain the contents of the pan into the bowl, and gently press the vegetables and fish bones with the back of a large spoon against the sides of the sieve to release all the juices. Discard the vegetables and bones.

Rinse out the pan, return the strained stock to it, and boil it rapidly, uncovered, until it is reduced to 2 cups. Taste for seasoning, and set it aside.

Preheating the oven. Slide an oven shelf into a middle slot, and preheat the oven to 400° F. for 15 minutes.

Preparing the fish dish. With your fingers, spread 2 tablespoons of the softened butter over the bottom of a shallow roasting pan that is large enough to hold the salmon steaks comfortably in one layer.

Cut a sheet of wax paper to fit the pan, and butter one side with a tablespoon of butter. If the paper is not wide enough for the pan, it may be necessary to use two sheets overlapping, in which case, use additional butter to coat the second sheet. Set the paper aside.

Spread the diced onions, celery, and 2 diced carrots evenly over the bottom of the pan. Arrange the salmon steaks on top of the vegetables and sprinkle with ½ teaspoon of salt and several grindings of pepper. Pour 1 cup of wine and the 2 cups of fish stock evenly over the salmon steaks.

On top of the stove, bring the liquid to a boil over moderate to high heat; if the pan is large, you may have to set it over two heating units. Turn off the heat and place the wax paper over the steaks, buttered side down.

Braising the salmon steaks. Place the pan in the oven, reduce the oven temperature to 350° F., and braise the steaks for 5 to 6 minutes. Then pull the oven shelf forward and set the wax paper aside. Add the shrimp, making sure they are all at least partially immersed in liquid. Cover again with the wax paper and continue cooking for another 3 to 4 minutes, by which time the shrimp will have curled and turned pink. Lift one shrimp out and taste it. It should be slightly firm to the bite. Then test one of the steaks by probing the thickest part with a fork. It should flake easily—that is, the flesh should separate and fall back into its natural divisions. If the steaks are not sufficiently cooked, replace the wax paper and braise for another 2 or 3 minutes. Do not, under any circumstances, overcook, or the fish will be dry and tasteless.

Turn the oven thermostat to its lowest setting, remove the pan from the oven, and set the wax paper aside. Using a wide, flexible spatula, lift the steaks, one at a time, to a large, heated serving platter. If any vegetables cling to the steaks, scrape them off carefully and return them to the pan. Although it is not necessary, you can pull off and discard the skin surrounding each steak. Using a slotted spoon, lift the shrimp from the pan and arrange them on top of and around the salmon. Cover the salmon and shrimp with the wax paper and keep warm in a low oven.

Reducing the braising liquid. Place the pan over high heat—using two units, if necessary—and bring the liquid to a boil. Boil hard, uncovered, for 4 to 5 minutes or until the vegetables are soft. Strain the liquid through a large fine sieve into a large bowl, pressing the vegetables to extract all their juices. If the liquid measures more than 1½ cups—and it probably will—rinse out the pan and return the liquid. Place the pan over high heat and boil, uncovered, until the liquid has reduced to 1½ cups.

Making the sauce. In a small bowl, work 2 teaspoons of softened butter into the flour with your fingers or a spoon to make a beurre manié.

Pour the 1½ cups strained braising liquid into a 1- or 2-quart enameled cast-iron saucepan. Stir in the cream and cook over moderate heat for a couple of minutes. Then add the beurre manié, bit by bit, whisking briskly and constantly with a wire whisk until the sauce has thickened lightly. This will not be a thick sauce in the accepted sense, but it should be thick enough to cling to the whisk when it is lifted. Remove from the heat and whisk in the lemon juice. Taste the sauce for seasoning. You may find it needs more salt and pepper.

Serving the salmon steaks. Lift the platter of fish from the oven and coat both steaks and shrimp with a light film of the sauce. Pour any remaining sauce into a heated sauceboat. Serve at once, garnished with a bouquet of parsley sprigs.

BROWN-BRAISED ONIONS

For this particular recipe, try to find uniform white onions; I suggest 1½ inches as the ideal size. As for the wine, you can use almost any dry wine you have on hand: red, white, rosé, or dry vermouth.

One of the many advantages of this dish is that the onions can be braised in the same oven with meat or poultry, provided the temperature is 325° F. Another is the marvelous flavor, perfect with roasted meat or poultry.

SERVES 6 TO 8

2 quarts water
24 small white onions, unpeeled and about 1½ inches
   in diameter
1 tablespoon butter, softened at room temperature
3 tablespoons vegetable oil
1 cup dry red or white wine
About ½ cup water
1 teaspoon salt
Freshly ground black pepper

Preparing the onions. Bring 2 quarts of water to a boil in a large saucepan. Add the onions and boil briskly 5 to 10 seconds to loosen their skins. Drain through a large sieve, then cool in cold water for easy handling.

With a small sharp knife, trim off the top and bottom of each onion, taking care not to disturb the layers. With your fingers or a paring knife, slip off the outside skin, the first layer of the onion, and the thin film underneath. With the point of the paring knife, make an X at the root end of each onion so it won't burst or split during the braising.

Preheating the oven. Slide a rack into a middle slot of the oven and preheat at 325° F. for 15 minutes.

Braising the onions. Take a shallow flameproof baking dish just large enough to hold the onions in one layer. Coat the bottom of the dish with the butter, then add the onions in one layer and pour the vegetable oil over them. Place over moderate heat, and shake the dish back and forth to roll the onions over and coat them well in the hot butter and oil. When the fat mixture is sizzling, add the wine and boil hard for a few minutes. Then add as much water as is needed to cover the onions by about half. Continue cooking a few minutes until the liquid has thickened slightly. Sprinkle the onions with the salt and several grindings of the pepper mill.

Place the dish in the oven and braise, uncovered, for 1 to 1¼ hours, or until the onions are very tender when pierced with a kitchen fork. Shake the pan two or three times during braising to turn the onions over. Perfectly braised, the onions should hold their shape when served and have turned a deep golden brown.

Serving the braised onions. Pour the onions into a heated serving dish along with all the juices from the pan. Or, if you prefer, serve on a meat or poultry platter, arranging the onions in clusters or garlanding them around the roast so they form a golden, glistening border.

------------&§§&------------

BRAISED BELGIAN ENDIVES WITH BUTTERED WALNUTS

SERVES 6

12 medium Belgian endives with tightly closed leaves,
   2½ to 3 pounds in all
6 tablespoons butter, cut into bits
6 tablespoons coarsely chopped walnuts
½ teaspoon salt
2 tablespoons strained fresh lemon juice

Preheating the oven. Slide an oven rack into a center slot and preheat the oven at 325° F. for 15 minutes.

Braising the endives. Using a sharp knife, trim the endives of all discolored leaves and slice away as much of the roots as you can without cutting the leaves loose.

Using as much of the butter bits as you need, butter well a shallow ovenproof dish that will hold all the endives in one layer. Arrange the endives in the dish and dot them with 2 tablespoons of the butter bits. Cut a piece of wax paper to fit the top of the baking dish and butter one side. Lay the paper, buttered side down, on top of the endives, and cover tightly with foil.

Place the dish in the oven and braise for 45 minutes. At this point, using tongs, turn the endives over so they will brown evenly. Re-cover the endives and continue braising for another 45 minutes, or until they feel extremely tender when pierced with a fork.

Preparing the walnuts. Shortly before the endives have finished cooking, melt the remaining butter bits in a small saucepan. When the butter foams—do not allow it to brown—stir in the chopped walnuts with a fork. Continue stirring until the nuts are well coated with butter and heated through. Set them aside.

Serving the endives. When the endives have finished cooking, remove them from the oven. If your baking dish is not attractive enough to go to the table, arrange the endives in a heated serving dish. Sprinkle them with the salt and lemon juice. Scatter the buttered walnuts over all and add any butter in the saucepan.

BRAISED BRUSSELS SPROUTS AND CHESTNUTS

Perhaps because we raise chestnuts in this country in limited quantities, they are sold fresh only during the late fall and winter. Dried chestnuts are imported all year round from Europe, largely from Italy, and are stocked in Chinese and Italian markets. Once reconstituted, they can be used as you would the fresh—without the arduous chore of peeling.

SERVES 6 TO 8

¼ pound (about 30) dried chestnuts
1¼ pounds (two 10-ounce cartons) Brussels sprouts
6 quarts water
3 tablespoons salt
About ½ cup butter (a quarter-pound stick), softened at
    room temperature
½ cup heavy cream
Freshly ground black pepper
6 to 8 sprigs parsley, minced

Preparing the chestnuts. Rinse the chestnuts in cold water, then place them in a 3-quart saucepan and add enough cold water to cover. Bring to a boil, reduce the heat to a simmer, and cook, uncovered, for 15 minutes, then drain. Repeat the cooking and draining process two more times, cooking, all told, about 45 minutes. At this point, the chestnuts will be firm to the bite and still quite white.

Rinse the nuts in the pan under cold running water. Bits of the brown skin that are tucked into the crevices will float away. However, some will remain, and you should pick those out with the tip of a paring knife. Don't be upset if some of the chestnuts fall apart. Drain the chestnuts and set them aside.

Preparing the Brussels sprouts. Pick over the Brussels sprouts, discarding any that are puffy or soft with wilted or yellow leaves. With a paring knife, trim the base of each sprout, taking care not to cut it so short that the leaves fall off; discard any discolored leaves. Wash the trimmed sprouts in a big basin of cold water, and drain thoroughly.

Pour the 6 quarts of water into a large kettle, add the salt, and bring to a boil. If the sprouts are not of a uniform size—and the chances are they won't be—add the larger ones to the boiling water and boil, uncovered, for 1 minute. Then add all the rest. Boil, uncovered, for 5 minutes, or until the sprouts are almost tender. Pierce with a skewer or taste one to determine its tenderness. Drain the sprouts through a large sieve or colander. If they are not going to be braised immediately, spread them out on paper towels. They will stay bright and green for at least 1 hour.

Braising the sprouts and chestnuts. Using a little of the butter, butter one side of a piece of wax paper, parchment, or foil cut to fit a 2- or 3-quart enameled cast-iron casserole. Set the paper or foil aside for the moment.

Butter the bottom and sides of the casserole well with 3 tablespoons of the butter. Add the Brussels sprouts and drained chestnuts and dot with 3 tablespoons of butter. Place the casserole over moderate heat. When the butter begins to foam, cover with the buttered paper, buttered side down. Add the lid and reduce the heat to very low. Braise for 10 minutes, shaking the casserole every once in a while to turn the vegetables over.

After 10 minutes, take off the lid and test the sprouts with a skewer or the point of a paring knife. If they are not very tender, continue braising until a skewer or knife pierces them easily; it may be as much as 6 to 8 minutes longer. If the vegetables seem at all dry, add the remaining butter.

Once the sprouts are tender, add the cream and cook only long enough to heat it thoroughly and thicken it lightly. Taste for seasoning. You may want to add more salt. Then add several twists of the pepper mill.

Serving the Brussels sprouts and chestnuts. Serve the braised sprouts and chestnuts from the casserole or in a heated vegetable dish, sprinkled with the minced parsley.

BRAISED RED CABBAGE

SERVES **6**

The Cabbage:
2½- to 3-pound head firm red cabbage

The Marinade:
½ cup red wine vinegar
2½ tablespoons sugar
2 teaspoons salt
6 juniper berries, slightly crushed

The Braising Ingredients:
2 to 4 tablespoons vegetable oil
4 to 6 tablespoons butter, cut into bits
2 medium yellow onions, peeled and sliced thin
2 medium apples, peeled, cored, and sliced thin
2½ cups boiling water
⅓ cup dry red wine
⅓ cup red currant jelly
Salt
Freshly ground black pepper

Preparing the cabbage. Trim any coarse leaves from the cabbage, then cut it into quarters from top to bottom and cut out the hard center core. Lay each quarter, flat side down, on a chopping board and slice it crosswise as thin as possible. As you shred the cabbage, place it in a large mixing bowl. You will have about 10 cups of shredded cabbage.

Marinating the cabbage. In a small bowl combine the vinegar, sugar, 2 teaspoons of salt, and juniper berries. Stir with a spoon until the sugar has dissolved. Sprinkle the marinade over the shredded cabbage and toss with your hands to coat all the shreds well. Marinate for about 30 minutes.

Braising the cabbage. Place a heavy 10- or 12-inch frying pan on one heating unit and a 5-quart enameled cast-iron casserole with a lid on the one next to it; do not turn the heat on.

Add 2 tablespoons of the vegetable oil and 2 tablespoons of the butter bits to the frying pan. Turn the heat to moderate. When the fat begins to foam, add the onions, separating the slices with a fork to coat them with the oil and butter. Cook over moderate heat for 5 to 8 minutes, or until the onions are translucent. With a slotted spoon or spatula, transfer them to the casserole. Add 2 more tablespoons of the butter to the pan, then add the apples. Turn them over in the hot fat until they are coated with a film of butter and oil, then transfer them to the casserole.

If there does not seem to be sufficient oil and butter remaining in the pan to coat the cabbage, add another tablespoon or two of each. Heat until foaming, then add the cabbage and toss with a kitchen fork for a minute or two to coat all the shreds well. Transfer to the casserole and mix with the onions and apples.

Pour the boiling water into the casserole; it should reach somewhat beyond half the casserole's depth. Turn on the heat and bring the water to a rolling boil.

Butter a piece of wax paper cut to fit the casserole, and place it, buttered side down, on top of the vegetables. Add the lid and braise over very low heat for 50 to 60 minutes, or until the cabbage is tender to the bite. When the cabbage is cooked, remove the lid and wax paper and stir in the wine. Turn the heat to high and cook, uncovered, another 15 minutes. Then add the currant jelly, mixing it in with a spoon. Cook, uncovered, over moderate heat for another 3 to 4 minutes.

Finishing and serving the cabbage. Place a large sieve over a large bowl and drain the contents of the casserole. Allow the cabbage to drain without pressing, then transfer it to a heated platter. Pour the drained-off liquid back into the casserole; it may be only a couple of tablespoons or as much as ½ cup. Place over high heat and cook down to a fairly thick glaze, taking care to see that it doesn't burn. Return the cabbage to the casserole and toss with the glaze until piping hot. Taste for salt, then add several grinds of the pepper mill. Pepper contributes enormously to the savor of this particular dish.

Serve the cabbage from the casserole, or, if you prefer, from a heated platter.

Roasting:
Most Ancient of
Culinary Arts

*R*oasting, which is cooking by exposure to direct, dry heat (originally that of an open fire) is probably the oldest and certainly one of the best forms of cooking; it was the only method available before the invention of pots, pans, and ovens. Curiously, it is also subject to confused nomenclature. We roast beef and chicken but we bake ham and fish. We also bake potatoes. Culinarily speaking, ham and potatoes are never "baked." They are, in fact, roasted, and I find in a French cookbook in my library recipes for roasted fish which we, in this country, would call baked, a term that we generally apply to breads and pastries. Such indiscriminate use of the terms roasting and baking has led to enormous confusion, and despite extensive research, I can find no adequate explanation, since both methods are done by dry heat.

Although spit roasting goes on in both European and American kitchens, most roasting today is done in the oven. Roasting seems like a relatively simple process, certainly with our modern equipment, yet a surprising number of people seem unable to bring a roast to the table à *point*—that is, at the perfect point of doneness (which obviously means different things to different people).

Suitable Meats and Poultry for Roasting

Beef. Standing rib is, for the majority of Americans, the most desirable beef roast. In addition, there are:

Tenderloin or fillet, considered by many the most glamorous of all beef roasts;

Shell strip cut from the short loin, the same section from which porterhouse steaks are cut;

Rib eye, sometimes called Delmonico, the choice, meaty center part of a rib roast with the outer muscle and all bones removed; weighs from 3 to 6 pounds;

Sirloin tip, called silver tip in some parts of the country; a boneless cut with very little waste from the end of the loin section of the steer, from which we get sirloin roasts and steaks; weighs from 3 to 6 pounds; although not quite as tender as a true sirloin, a prime piece makes an exceptionally fine roast;

Eye round (if prime grade), solid meat with a thin layer of fat, the smallest boneless muscle cut from the round; weighs 2½ to 5 pounds;

Top round (if prime grade), the large, tender boneless top muscle of the round; weighs from 3 to 6 pounds;

Rolled rump of beef (if prime grade), a fairly lean, chunky roast cut from the rump section; weighs from 4 to 6 pounds.

Veal. The choicest roasts are the rib roast, sometimes called rack and similar to a beef standing rib; the crown roast, which is rib sections shaped into a circle, or crown; loin; and sirloin roasts.

Lamb. Most luxurious of all are the whole leg or whole hindquarter. Rib, crown roasts, and loin roasts are also excellent.

Pork and ham. A whole family of delicious large roasts: rib, crown, loin, fresh ham (leg).

Ham, the cured and smoked hind leg of pork, is available in many guises: whole ham, halves (both butt and shank ends), as well as a variety of boneless and semiboneless hams.

Cured and smoked cuts from the shoulder, which are technically not hams although they have similar characteristics: smoked picnic, canned picnic, smoked boneless butt.

Canadian-style bacon, the boned center portion of the loin, sugar-cured and smoked, very lean, which can be baked as you would any ham.

Chicken. The most suitable types for roasting are plump, young, tender, and of top quality. They may be called broilers, fryers, or broiler-fryers and weigh from 1½ to 4 pounds; or they may be called roasters, somewhat older and larger, weighing from 3 to 5 pounds.

Turkey. Turkeys are available in almost every conceivable size—from 5 to 30 or more pounds—and every conceivable form: whole and ready-to-cook, both fresh-frozen and fresh-chilled (but not frozen); frozen prestuffed and prebasted, frozen prebasted and ready-to-stuff; frozen boneless roasts; and frozen turkey parts. The majority of turkeys available today are frozen, to my mind not as good as the fresh.

Duck. Ducklings, no more than 7 to 8 weeks old and weighing from 3½ to 5½ pounds, are excellent for roasting; usually available frozen and ready-to-cook.

Fish and shellfish. Virtually all fish and shellfish can be baked with excellent results.

Amounts to Buy

In buying roasts it is a good idea to think beyond the immediate meal, because certain foods—pork, ham, veal, chicken, turkey—when properly roasted are delicious cold. In buying beef roasts, it is good to remember that the beef will be more succulent if the roast is large.

Since appetites vary, it is difficult to determine exact amounts, but as a rule of thumb, for 1 serving buy 1 pound of bone-in, uncooked meat of any kind, 1 pound of bony meat, and ½ pound of boneless uncooked meat.

When roasting a chicken, allow about ¾ pound of ready-to-cook bird per serving. A 3-pound broiler-fryer will serve 3, perhaps 4, and yield 2½ cups of diced cooked chicken.

One large duckling—5 to 5½ pounds—will serve 3 but could possibly be stretched to serve 4 if the dinner menu is ample.

For turkey, the bigger the bird, the meatier it will be and the more people it will serve per pound. Here is an approximate buying guide:

READY-TO-COOK WHOLE TURKEY (POUND WEIGHT)	APPROXIMATE SERVINGS
5 to 8	6 to 10
8 to 12	10 to 20
12 to 16	20 to 32
16 to 20	32 to 40
20 to 24	40 to 50

Techniques for Roasting

Roasting temperature. In the old days, the cook put her hand in the oven to test the temperature, and if it was good and hot, in went the roast to cook at that same high temperature until "done." But today, we no longer roast meats at a constant high temperature. Currently, there are two schools of thought about how meat should be roasted.

THE SEARING METHOD. Many cooks—and this seems to be particularly true of the French and of chefs—believe in searing a roast at high heat (450° to 500° F.) in a preheated oven, then reducing the temperature to moderate (325° to 350° F.) for the remainder of the roasting period. The theory behind the searing method—and it is one I subscribe to—is that the intense heat seals in the juices and creates a delectable rich surface on the meat.

THE MODERATE HEAT METHOD. In this method, meat is roasted at the same moderate temperature (300° to 350° F.) from start to finish. Economy-minded cooks favor this because there is less shrinkage.

Seasoning roasts. No one seems to be in complete agreement on when a roast should be seasoned. Some cooks salt and pepper after cooking, others rub pepper only into the roast prior to cooking, then salt during the last 15 minutes. Chefs generally salt and pepper the meat before it goes into the oven, and that is my custom, too. The reasoning is that if the meat is seasoned after it is cooked, the seasonings are all around but not in the meat.

Roasting times. The printed charts available that time a roast by weight are not only fallible but practically useless. They should be used as guides only. The cook should learn by proper testing when a roast is done to perfection, and a "spot-check" thermometer is usually the most efficient way to test any roast.

It is nevertheless essential to know the weight of a roast so you will have some idea of its cooking time if your dinner is to be ready all at the same time. This is the principal value of roasting timetables: to indicate when a roast should go in the oven. In the following recipes, I have given approximate cooking times, but these, too, should be used only as guides. Rely on the "spot-check" thermometer to determine when a roast has reached the perfect stage of doneness.

Letting the roast "rest." Because meats and poultry go on cooking internally briefly after they are taken from the oven, they should be allowed to rest on a heated platter in a warm place for 25 to 30 minutes. This helps the juices settle and gives the collagen (a protein contained in the connective tissue of meat), which has softened to a gelatinous state during cooking, a chance to firm up, thereby making the carving easier. It also gives the cook a few extra minutes in which to make sauces and dish up the vegetables.

ROAST SIRLOIN TIP

Rather than the standing ribs of beef, the British prefer to roast the sirloin, which we usually cut into steaks. In this recipe, I have specified sirloin tip as the cut I prefer; however, the recipe is a generic one—that is, it can serve as a model should you prefer to use one of the following four cuts of beef: rib eye, called Delmonico in some markets; eye round, if prime grade; top round, if prime grade; or rolled rump of beef, if prime grade. Any of them would be delicious prepared this way.

SERVES **6**

3- to 3½-pound sirloin tip, or another cut of your choice,
    covered with a thin layer of barding fat tied on
Marchand de Vins Butter (page 441)
A bouquet of parsley

Preheating the oven. Slide one of the oven racks into a center slot and preheat the oven for 15 minutes at 500° F.

Roasting the meat. Place the meat in a roasting pan with a rack, and roast for 15 minutes at 500° F. Then reduce the heat to 350° F. and continue roasting for another 40 minutes, or a total of 55 minutes. At this point, test the roast with a "spot-check" thermometer;

it should read 120° to 125° F. for medium rare. For medium, cook until the thermometer registers 125° to 130° F., and for well done —and I do not recommend this—roast the meat until the thermometer reads 145° to 150° F. When the meat is done to your taste, take it out of the oven.

Serving the sirloin tip. Place 4 tablespoons of the Marchand de Vins Butter on a heated serving platter. Cut the string from the meat, lift it off, and discard the fat. Using two spatulas, place the meat on the serving platter on top of the melting butter, and allow it to rest there for 10 to 15 minutes or so before carving.

Before taking the roast to the table, spoon some of the juices in the bottom of the platter over the meat and tuck a bouquet of parsley under one end of the roast.

At the table, pass the remaining Marchand de Vins Butter separately so each person can serve himself, placing pats on top of the hot slices of roast beef. They melt on contact, creating a savory sauce.

STANDING RIB ROAST OF BEEF WITH YORKSHIRE PUDDING

Because rib roasts vary by name across the country, what many of us call a standing rib roast is variously known as beef rib roast, easy-to-carve rib roast, king roast, rolled rib roast (when boned and rolled), rib eye roast, and Delmonico roast. It all depends on where you live.

Since Yorkshire puddings, like soufflés, "fall" at the glance of an eye, it makes sense to prepare the batter in advance—standing does it no harm—so you can put the pudding in the oven as soon as the roast comes out. By the time the roast has rested and then been carved, the pudding is ready to be taken from the oven and presented at its best.

SERVES ABOUT 6

The Beef:
6-pound standing rib roast
1 teaspoon salt
Freshly ground black pepper

The Yorkshire Pudding:
6 tablespoons beef drippings from the roasting pan or butter
3 eggs
1½ cups milk
1⅓ cups all-purpose flour, not sifted but measured accurately
½ teaspoon salt

The Garnish:
Sprigs of watercress

Preparing the beef. Ask your butcher for the first three ribs from a piece of prime meat, but have him remove the short ribs, which you can use in another recipe (see page 211). The roast should not be boned, but the chine or backbone should be removed and tied back on. This not only contributes flavor but gives the meat a natural platform on which to sit and makes carving easier.

Preheating the oven. Slide an oven shelf into the lowest slot and preheat the oven for 15 minutes to 500° F.

Roasting the beef. Mix together 1 teaspoon of salt and several grindings of pepper. Rub the mixture over the outer fat covering as well as into the lean meat.

Place the roast—curved fat side up, so that the ribs act like a natural stand—in a shallow roasting pan with a rack. Slide the pan into the oven and roast the meat undisturbed for 20 minutes. Reduce the temperature to 350° F. and continue roasting for 1 hour longer, or until a "spot-check" thermometer reads 120° to 125° F. for medium rare, 125° to 130° F. for medium, or 145° to 150° F. for well done.

When the beef is roasted to your taste, remove the pan from the oven and, using two large forks, lift the roast to a heated serving platter or wooden serving board. Allow the roast to rest for 20 minutes while you make the Yorkshire pudding.

Preheating the pudding pan. As soon as the roast comes from the oven, turn the heat up to 450° F. and slide the rack into a center shelf.

Take an ovenproof baking dish measuring about 13½ by 8¾ by 1¾ inches—preferably one that can go to the table—and add 6 tablespoons of beef drippings from the roasting pan. If there are not enough drippings, add enough butter to make up the difference. Place the pudding pan on the middle rack of the preheated oven and let it heat for about 5 minutes. If you prefer, the pudding can be baked and served in six 8-ounce ramekins instead of the baking dish. Spoon 1 tablespoon of beef drippings into each ramekin, set them on a jelly-roll pan, and heat for 3 or 4 minutes in the 450° F. oven.

Making the Yorkshire pudding. If you use an electric blender or food processor: Break the eggs into the container. Add the milk, cover, and mix for 5 seconds (at high speed in the blender). Turn off the machine and add the flour and ½ teaspoon of salt. Cover, turn the machine on, and process for 10 seconds (at low speed in the blender). With a rubber spatula scrape down any clinging flour from the sides of the container. Re-cover and process the batter for a few seconds longer (at low speed in the blender), but do not overblend. The batter should have the consistency of heavy cream.

If you use an electric beater: Break the eggs into a medium-size bowl. Add the milk and beat a few seconds until combined. Then add the flour and ½ teaspoon of salt and beat with the electric beater at high speed for a full minute. Using a rubber spatula, scrape down any flour clinging to the sides of the bowl and beat again for about 1 minute. The finished batter should have the consistency of heavy cream.

Baking the pudding. Pull the rack holding the pudding pan forward and pour the pudding batter into the hot fat in the pan or fill each ramekin about half full. Slide the rack back into the oven, shut the door, and bake the pudding for 15 minutes in the pan or about 12 to 15 minutes in the ramekins. By that time the pudding will have puffed somewhat like a soufflé, although it will not have an even surface.

Reduce the heat to 350° F. and bake for another 15 minutes in the pan, or 12 to 15 minutes in the ramekins. The pudding should be served at once, but you can leave it in the oven, with the heat turned off, for another 5 minutes if dinner must wait. No longer, though, or the pudding will collapse.

Serving the roast. Place the roast on a large heated platter, the larger end down, so it will sit firmly when carved. Remove any suet (layers of beef fat), which protected the meat while roasting.

Steady the roast with a fork, cut along the bone with the tip of a very sharp carving knife to separate the meat from the bone, and start slicing across the meat toward the ribs. Beef is usually sliced thin in France and England but somewhat thicker in this country. As you carve the slices, arrange the servings on warmed dinner plates, adding a sprig of watercress and a spoonful of the drippings and natural juices, as well as a portion or an individual ramekin of Yorkshire pudding.

BONED LEG OF LAMB FLAMED WITH GIN

Curiously, lamb, one of the most delectable of meats, has only recently begun to gain popularity in this country. This is possibly because, as a nation, we have never learned to cook it with the same finesse as the French. Here, as in England, we are inclined to roast lamb "well done," thus sacrificing its delicate and unique flavor.

Every food authority as well as every nationality has ideas on how long to roast lamb. I, along with the French, subscribe to pink (120° to 125° F. on a meat thermometer). I must point out, however, that because of its unusually delicate flavor and extreme leanness, this does not apply to "hothouse" or "baby" lamb, which, like very young veal, is best cooked until all pinkness has disappeared (to about 155° F.).

The whole leg and the whole hindquarter, a recipe for which follows this one, make the most luxurious roasts. This boned leg of lamb, in fact, must be started two days before the feast. Although lesser cuts such as the shoulder and breast can also be roasted, I think they are better braised.

SERVES 8

The Lamb:
1 leg of lamb weighing 6½ to 7 pounds before boning and
   trimming, about 4½ pounds after
2½ teaspoons salt
Freshly ground black pepper
4 tablespoons butter, softened at room temperature

The Stuffing:
½ cup (1¼ ounces) juniper berries
½ cup gin

Preparing the lamb. Have the butcher trim all but a ¼-inch layer of fat from the leg of lamb, then bone it so that the meat will lie flat.

Preparing the stuffing. In a small jar with a tight-fitting cover, combine the juniper berries and gin. Cover the jar and allow the berries to soak in the gin for 24 hours. At the end of that time, the berries will have plumped considerably and the gin will be slightly tinged with color.

Stuffing and marinating the lamb. Place a small strainer over a bowl and drain the juniper berries, then pour the drained gin back into the jar and set it aside.

Place the lamb, boned side up, on your work surface. Sprinkle 1 teaspoon of the salt all over the meat, then several liberal grindings of pepper. Distribute the juniper berries over the surface of the lamb as evenly as possible. Fold over the flaps of the meat and roll up, tucking in or cutting away any loose pieces. Turn seam side down. Tie loops of soft string around the circumference in four or five places to hold the roll in shape, and once or twice lengthwise, making butcher's knots as described on pages 443–44.

Season the outside of the meat with another teaspoon of the salt, rubbing it over the entire surface with your hands. Then sprinkle generously with fresh grindings of pepper.

Place the roast in a large bowl or pan and add the gin in which the berries soaked. Refrigerate for 24 hours or overnight, turning the meat occasionally.

Preheating the oven. Fifteen minutes before you plan to roast the lamb, slide an oven shelf into a center slot and preheat the oven at 450° F.

Roasting the lamb. Remove the lamb from the bowl or pan. Pour the marinade into a small saucepan and set it aside.

Pat the meat dry with paper towels, then coat the entire outside surface of the meat with the softened butter, using your hands. Sprinkle the lamb with the remaining ½ teaspoon of salt and more freshly ground black pepper.

Place the lamb on a rack in a roasting pan, set the pan in the oven, and sear the lamb at 450° F. for 15 minutes. At the end of this period the roast will have begun to brown and release some of its fat. Using a long-handled spoon or pastry brush, baste the roast with the pan drippings. Reduce the heat to 350° F. and continue roasting for another 30 minutes. At this point, plunge the "spot-check" thermometer into the center of the roast; if it reads 120° to 125° F., the lamb is medium rare or "pink," the degree of doneness which I recommend. If necessary, roast the meat another 10 minutes, then check with your thermometer again. If you do not have a thermometer, figure on about 12 minutes per pound, or a total of 50 to 55 minutes for this 4- to 4½-pound roast.

When the lamb has finished roasting, take it out of the oven, cut and discard the string, and place it on a heated platter. Cover lightly with foil or place in a keep-warm oven (140° F.) and allow it to rest for 10 to 15 minutes. At the same time, warm the dinner plates. Because lamb cools more quickly than other meats, it is particularly important that it be served on preheated plates.

Remove the rack from the roasting pan and place the pan over high heat. On another burner, heat the reserved marinade in the saucepan, ignite it with a match, and pour it flaming into the roasting pan. When the flames die out, bring the mixture to a boil, stirring in all the pan juices with a wooden spoon or spatula. Taste for seasoning, then pour into a heated sauceboat.

Serving the lamb. To serve, slice the lamb rather thin, cutting straight down through the meat. Spoon a few of the juniper berries onto each plate along with some of the sauce. Juniper berries, like olives, are a cultivated taste but are surprisingly good.

STUFFED HINDQUARTER OF LAMB

The whole hindquarter is, to my mind, the most unusual lamb roast, and one so spectacular that I urge you to try it the next time you are giving an important dinner. It consists of the entire leg with the loin and flank attached. You will not find it already prepared in a supermarket, but any good butcher can prepare it if given a few days' notice.

As you might assume, this is a very long roast requiring a very large roasting pan and an equally large platter. But don't let that deter you. Borrow or beg, if you must, both the pan and the platter.

SERVES ABOUT 8

The Lamb:

1 hindquarter of lamb, weighing about 8½ to 9 pounds when
trimmed and cut as described below

Salt

Freshly ground black pepper

The Stuffing:

4 cups fresh bread crumbs

⅛ teaspoon salt

⅛ teaspoon pepper

⅓ cup finely chopped fresh mint or 1 tablespoon dried mint

6 tablespoons melted butter

For Roasting:

2 tablespoons softened butter

2 large carrots, peeled and thinly sliced

2 large yellow onions, peeled and thinly sliced

2 cloves garlic, peeled and slivered

The Sauce:

Pan drippings and vegetables from the roast

1½ cups beef broth

The Garnish:

A bouquet of watercress

Preparing the hindquarter. When the butcher prepares the hindquarter, it is essential that the flank be left completely attached to
the loin. However, the flank should be carefully trimmed of extra
fat and, if you explain that you plan to stuff the loin and use the
flank to cover the stuffing, your butcher will be careful not to cut
into the flank beyond removing the excess layers of fat. Also, ask
him to cut carefully—not crack—the bones at the base of the loin
so that serving the chops from this section will be easier for the
carver.

In addition, the butcher should remove as much excess fat as
possible from the leg. However, if you prefer, the fell (the thin
parchmentlike skin that covers the leg) can be left on. This is a
purely personal matter, but many people prefer to keep the fell for
the certain crispness it adds to the roasted lamb.

When you are ready to roast the hindquarter, dry it thoroughly
with paper towels and trim away any fat the butcher may have
overlooked.

Place the meat on your work surface so that the hollow part of the loin faces up. Sprinkle the entire side with salt and pepper. Leave the lamb in place while you prepare the stuffing; no need to refrigerate it.

Preparing the stuffing. In a 3- or 4-quart mixing bowl combine the bread crumbs, ⅛ teaspoon of salt, ⅛ teaspoon of pepper, mint, and melted butter. Toss them lightly with a fork only enough to mix the ingredients thoroughly. The stuffing should not be too moist and will be crumbly. Taste for seasoning, but do not oversalt the stuffing; the mint flavor should dominate.

Preheating the oven. Slide a rack into a center slot, and preheat the oven to 450° F. for at least 15 minutes.

Stuffing and skewering the lamb. Lay the stuffing in the hollow that begins at the loin and continues to the beginning of the leg, spreading it as evenly as possible. Lift the flank over the stuffing, stretching and positioning it so that it covers the stuffing as completely as possible. Then secure it by inserting small metal skewers or toothpicks at 1-inch intervals along the edge, pulling the flank over the severed bones as needed to enclose the stuffing.

Roasting the lamb. A pan at least 18 by 12 by 2 inches is necessary for this unusually long roast. Butter it with the softened butter and scatter the carrots, onions, and garlic over the surface. Place the lamb over the vegetables, arranging it, if necessary, at a slight angle so that it will fit into the pan. Then sprinkle the lamb with salt and pepper.

Place the roast in the 450° F. oven and sear it for 20 minutes. After this roasting period, the lamb will have begun to brown and release some of its fat. Reduce the heat to 350° F. Stir the vegetables in the pan with a long-handled spoon to coat them with the fat and, if the roast appears to be dry, spoon a few tablespoons of the pan juices over it at the same time. Further basting is not absolutely necessary, although you can, if you like, baste the roast occasionally during the next 50 minutes of roasting.

At this point, after the lamb has roasted for a total of 70 minutes, a "spot-check" thermometer inserted into the thickest part of the leg section should read 120° to 125° F., which is the correct temperature for lamb roasted to the pink stage. The chops coming from the smaller loin section will be slightly past the pink stage. If you insist on lamb well done, continue roasting until the thermometer reads 145° to 150° F.

When the lamb is roasted to your taste, remove the pan from the oven and, with the aid of two spatulas, lift the roast onto a large heated serving platter or wooden serving board. Carefully remove the skewers or toothpicks and allow the roast to rest for about 20 minutes while you prepare the sauce and warm the dinner plates and sauceboat.

Making the sauce. Tip the pan and, with a large spoon, remove and discard as much fat as possible, or suck up the fat with a bulb baster. Add the beef broth to the pan, then place it over high heat; you will probably need two burners. Rapidly bring the contents of the pan to a boil, stirring to incorporate the vegetables in the pan with the broth. After about 5 minutes of rapid boiling, the stock will have reduced considerably.

To strain the sauce, set a food mill (use the finest strainer) over a saucepan large enough to hold it securely. Process the contents of the roasting pan in the food mill. Lacking a mill, use a fine-meshed sieve and force the vegetables through with the back of a spoon or a rubber spatula.

If any visible amount of fat has risen to the top of the strained sauce, spoon off what you can; there should be at least 1½ cups of sauce remaining. Taste for seasoning, adding more salt and pepper if necessary. Bring the sauce to a boil before pouring it into a preheated sauceboat.

Serving the lamb. Garnish the lamb with a big bouquet of watercress. Because this is such a dramatic dish, carve it at the table, as follows:

First, cut the chops down vertically (across the grain), then carve the leg in thin slices parallel to the bone. So that you have both a good grip on the leg and a comfortable angle for carving it, raise the shank slightly by spearing it with a fork or by holding the bone with your hand.

Serve each person one of the stuffed chops, a slice or two of the leg, and a tablespoon or so of sauce. The combination of the two cuts in this splendid roast demonstrates the textural and flavor subtleties of lamb.

---◆§᠈◈᠈◆---

CROWN ROAST OF PORK WITH
APPLE-SAGE STUFFING

In recent years, farmers have been producing leaner hogs and, thus, less lavishly fat-streaked pork. In a sense, the pig has been put on a reducing diet. As a result, these new "meat-type" animals have less fat and fewer calories than yesterday's "lard-type" pigs. But they are no less luscious.

Because fresh pork has always carried the stigma of trichinosis (the disease caused by microscopic organisms present in some raw pork), people have been inclined to cook the meat almost literally to death, resulting in fibrous, stringy, unappetizing meat. Research conducted at Iowa State University has now established 170° F. as the most desirable internal temperature for roast pork as against 185° F., which was once recommended. Personally, I roast my fresh pork to 165° F., 5° short of the recommended temperature, for delicious, succulent meat.

Escoffier, the great chef who dominated French cooking for three-quarters of a century, once said that fresh pork should be served only at family meals. Escoffier notwithstanding, my recipe for Crown Roast of Pork is certainly elegant enough for your most distinguished parties.

SERVES 6

The Meat:
5½-pound crown roast of pork (12 ribs)
1½ teaspoons salt
Freshly ground black pepper

The Stuffing:
¾ pound ground pork, put through the grinder twice
6 tablespoons butter, cut into bits
1 medium yellow onion, peeled and chopped fine
¼ cup water
1 large rib celery, chopped fine
1 large tart apple, peeled, cored, and diced
½ cup fresh bread crumbs (about 1½ slices firm white bread)
6 tablespoons minced fresh parsley
1 teaspoon salt
2 teaspoons crushed dried sage
1 teaspoon freshly ground black pepper

The Garnish:
A bouquet of watercress or parsley

Preparing the crown roast. Ask the butcher to make the crown with 12 rib chops cut from the center of the rib section, trimming away as much excess fat as possible and sawing off the pointed rib ends around the base of the crown.

Making the stuffing. Place the ground pork in a 10- or 12-inch heavy frying pan, preferably one with a nonstick surface, over moderate heat. With a kitchen fork, break up the meat as it cooks. After 2 or 3 minutes, the pork will begin to lose its pinkness and will have separated into small pieces. Continue stirring and breaking it up for another 2 minutes.

Place a large strainer or colander over a bowl and lift the ground pork with a spoon to the strainer to drain off any surplus fat.

Pour off and discard any fat remaining in the frying pan, then add 4 tablespoons of the butter bits. Add the chopped onion and the water. Place over moderate heat and bring to a boil. Boil for about 3 minutes, then add the chopped celery and continue to cook 4 to 5 minutes longer, or until the onions are soft and translucent, the celery has lost its crispness, and all the water has boiled away, leaving only the butter. With a slotted spoon, lift the vegetables to a large mixing bowl.

Add the remaining butter bits to the frying pan and stir in the diced apple. Cook over moderate heat, stirring occasionally, until it is quite soft but not brown—3 to 4 minutes. With a rubber spatula, scrape the butter and apple into the mixing bowl. Then add the drained pork (discard the fat), the bread crumbs, minced parsley, 1 teaspoon of salt, sage, and 1 teaspoon of pepper. Mix all the ingredients together lightly with your hands.

Preheating the oven. Because of the height of the roast, it may be necessary to place the oven shelf at its lowest position. If not, slide the shelf into a middle slot. Preheat the oven at 350° F. for 15 minutes while you stuff the roast.

Stuffing the crown roast. Rub both the inside and the outside of the crown with 1½ teaspoons of salt and generously with freshly ground black pepper, using your fingers. Place the roast on the rack of a roasting pan. Using your hands, fill the center of the crown with the stuffing, piling it so that it mounds in the center. Do not pack it down. Cut a circle of foil just large enough to cover the stuffing and place on top. Then, to prevent the rib ends from charring, cut 12 pieces of foil, each 3 inches square, and place one over the tip of each rib bone, pinching it so that it fits the rib snugly.

Roasting the crown. Place the pan with the crown in the oven and roast for about 2 hours, then remove the foil covering the stuffing to allow it to brown. At this point, suck up some of the pan juices with a bulb baster and baste the stuffing. Continue roasting another 30 minutes for a total of 2½ hours, or until a "spot-check" thermometer inserted in the meat registers 165° to 170° F. Remove the crown from the oven and allow it to rest for 10 to 15 minutes before carving. Turn the oven off and warm the dinner plates.

Serving the crown roast. Lift the crown to a large heated platter. Remove and discard the foil from the rib tips and replace them with paper frills (see page 454 on how to make your own). Garnish the platter with a bouquet of watercress or parsley and bring it to the table to carve.

To carve the crown roast, steady the roast on the platter by inserting a large fork into one side. Then, with a sharp carving knife, cut down along each rib so that the roast is neatly divided into chops. Serve 1 or 2 chops to each person along with a generous spoonful of the stuffing.

STUFFED SPARERIBS

SERVES 6

The Spareribs:
2 pork spareribs, weighing about 2½ pounds each, and each in
    one piece
1 clove garlic, skin on but split
4 teaspoons salt
1 teaspoon dried rosemary
2 tablespoons vegetable oil
Freshly ground black pepper
½ cup water

The Stuffing:
6 tablespoons butter, cut into bits
2 or 3 medium yellow onions, peeled and coarsely chopped
    (about 2½ cups)
½ cup water
3 cups fresh bread crumbs
1 teaspoon salt
1 teaspoon crumbled dried rosemary
2 tablespoons minced fresh parsley
Freshly ground black pepper

Preparing the spareribs. Ask your butcher for small lean ribs all in one piece. Try to get one left and one right rack of spareribs, if possible. Then have him crack the base of the ribs about an inch or so but no more; otherwise the ribs will not hold the stuffing properly. At the same time, ask the butcher to cut away all excess fat, connective tissue, and skin.

Preparing the stuffing. Melt the butter bits in a 12-inch frying pan over moderate heat, but don't allow it to brown. Add the onions and ½ cup of water. Bring to a boil and continue boiling until all the water has boiled away and the onions are soft and translucent. Scrape the butter and onions into a large mixing bowl with a rubber spatula. Add the bread crumbs, 1 teaspoon of salt, 1 teaspoon of crumbled rosemary, the parsley, and several grindings of pepper. Toss with a fork to mix well.

Preheating the oven. Slide a rack into a middle slot and preheat the oven at 325° F. for 15 minutes.

Stuffing the ribs. Rub both sides of each rib with the split clove of garlic, then discard the garlic. Next, using your fingers, rub each side with ½ teaspoon of salt. Then rub the outside only (the nonfatty side) of each set of ribs with ½ teaspoon of rosemary and the vegetable oil.

Place one set of spareribs, oil side down, on the rack in a roasting pan. Distribute the stuffing over the length of the ribs. Place the second set of spareribs on top, oil side up. If you were able to buy one left and one right rack of spareribs, they will fit exactly. With small butcher-type skewers, secure the ribs in about five places down one side, then down the other, using as many skewers as needed to hold the stuffing in place during the roasting period. Sprinkle the top with 1 teaspoon of salt and several grindings of pepper. Pour ½ cup of water into the pan.

Roasting the ribs. Place the pan in the oven and roast for about 30 minutes. Then, using a bulb baster, begin to baste the ribs with the pan drippings every 30 minutes or so. After the ribs have been in the oven about 1 hour and 15 minutes, they must be turned over. This is rather awkward to accomplish, and I suggest you use either two wooden spatulas or a pair of tongs. In any event, try not to disturb the filling. Now sprinkle the bottom side with the remaining teaspoon of salt and a generous amount of pepper. Continue roasting for another hour and 15 minutes—a total of 2½ hours— or until the meat is beautifully brown and shiny.

Serving the ribs. With a good sharp carving knife, cut through the top spareribs, the filling, and the bottom ribs, allowing several ribs for each serving. In the event you can't cut straight through, cut the ribs singly, top and bottom, and serve the dressing on the side. As a matter of fact, this may be the best way to serve all the ribs, since most aficionados like to pick them up to eat.

BAKED HAM WITH APRICOT GLAZE

Although half hams are readily available, they never seem to me quite as succulent and delicious as whole hams, and, obviously, they do not make such a spectacular presentation, which is of some importance if you are giving a dinner.

And there is this further advantage: cold baked ham. It is one of our more delectable meats, perfectly marvelous with scalloped oysters or potato salad accompanied by *mostarda di frutta*, the commercial mustard fruits from Italy.

SERVES 12

The Ham:
12- to 13-pound ham, bone in
1 cup dry white wine (optional)
1 tablespoon whole cloves

The Apricot Glaze:
1½ cups (one 12-ounce jar) apricot jam

The Garnish:
A bouquet of watercress or parsley

Preparing the ham. Scrape off and discard any labels on the ham. Then, with a small sharp knife, loosen about 2 inches of the skin at the shank end by sliding the knife between the skin and the fat. Using sharp kitchen scissors, cut a sawtooth design into the edge of the loosened skin all the way across. This finish is purely aesthetic.

Preheating the oven. Slide a shelf into a middle slot and preheat the oven at 325° F. for at least 15 minutes.

Baking the ham. Place the ham, fat side up, on a rack in a large roasting pan and slide it into the oven. Bake the ham for 3 hours, basting with drippings or, if you prefer, with the wine, using a bulb baster or large metal spoon. You should baste every 30 minutes or so. During this long, slow baking period, the fat on the surface of the ham will turn a rich golden brown.

Preparing the apricot glaze. While the ham is baking, heat the apricot jam in a small saucepan over very low heat until it has melted. Using a rubber spatula, push the jam through a fine sieve into a bowl to eliminate any fruit pulp.

Glazing the ham. After 3 hours, lift the pan with the ham from the oven and, with a sharp knife, score or cut the fat about ⅛ inch deep into a diamond pattern. Push a whole clove into the center of each diamond. Spoon the apricot glaze over the fat on the ham. Because the ham is very hot, some of the glaze will inevitably run down the sides and into the pan. Continue spooning the glaze over the fat until it has all been used and sticks to the ham.

To set the glaze, return the ham to the oven for another 30 minutes (a total of 3½ hours' baking time). Do not baste after adding the glaze. The apricot glaze gives the ham a brilliant, golden, and professional finish.

Serving the ham. Remove the ham from the oven. If it is to be served hot, place it on a heated serving platter, with the decorated side up, and allow it to rest for 25 to 30 minutes before carving. If the ham will be served at room temperature—rather than refrigerator cold, which I find less delicious—place it on a large unheated platter. Before serving the ham, either hot or cold, garnish with a crisp bouquet of watercress or parsley tucked under the shank end.

For carving, place the shank end at the carver's right (or, if he is left-handed, at the left). Cut 2 or 3 lengthwise slices from the thin edge of the ham, then cut straight down through the ham from the decorated top to the bone, making the slices fairly thin. To free the slices, turn the knife and cut along the bone. Then lift the slices out.

A BRACE OF CHICKENS, STUFFED AND ROASTED

For roasting, the most suitable birds are plump, young, tender, and top quality.

The Chickens:
2 ready-to-cook chickens, weighing 3 to 3½ pounds each
1 lemon, quartered
2 teaspoons salt
2 large bunches parsley (about 20 stalks each), rinsed and
dried
½ cup butter, softened at room temperature
Freshly ground white pepper
Juice of 1 lemon

The Sauce (optional):
½ cup heavy cream

The Garnish:
Parsley bouquets

Preheating the oven. Slide a rack into a center slot and preheat the oven at 450° F. for 15 minutes.

Stuffing the chickens. As soon as the birds are in the house, remove the giblets (gizzard, liver, and heart, usually in a small bag) and the neck from each body cavity. These can be frozen, suitably wrapped, to use at some future time. Rub the cavity for each chicken with a lemon quarter, then with your fingers rub each with ¾ teaspoon of salt. Next, rub the skin of each chicken all over with a lemon quarter. Stuff each chicken with a bunch of parsley, stems and all. Then truss them, following the directions on pages 445–46. Rub 2 tablespoons of the butter into the skin of each chicken, then sprinkle them with ¼ teaspoon of the salt and several grindings of pepper.

Roasting the chickens. Place the chickens, breast up, on the rack of a roasting pan, leaving as much space as possible between them. Slide the pan into the oven and roast for 15 minutes.

Meanwhile, melt the remaining 4 tablespoons of butter in a small saucepan over low heat. Do not allow it to brown. Add the lemon juice and set aside.

At the end of the 15-minute roasting period, poor the lemon butter over the two chickens, dividing it as evenly as possible.

Continue roasting for another 30 minutes, basting with a bulb baster every 10 minutes with the pan juices.

After 45 minutes, test the chickens for doneness by squeezing the legs. They should feel soft when pressed. Or plunge a kitchen fork into the thigh to see if the juices run clear. If not, continue to roast a few minutes longer. A "spot-check" thermometer inserted into the center of the thigh, not touching bone, should register 175° F. If it is necessary to roast the chickens longer and they seem to be browning too much, cover them lightly with a "tent" made of foil. Test again for doneness after 10 minutes or so.

When the chickens have finished roasting, remove them from the oven and cut off and discard the trussing strings. Lift to a heated serving platter and let them rest while you prepare the sauce and warm the dinner plates.

Making the sauce. With all those good juices in the pan, you may want to make a sauce. If so, lift the rack from the roasting pan and add the cream. Place over high heat. With a wooden spatula, stir loose all the rich brown encrustations and continue to cook until the sauce has thickened slightly. Taste for seasoning, then pour into a heated sauceboat.

Serving the chicken. Tuck a parsley bouquet in the tail of each bird as it rests on the platter, then carve the chickens at table as follow: Cut off each leg as close to the body as possible, separate thighs and drumsticks, and slice off the dark meat. Remove the wings and disjoint them. Thrust a carving fork firmly into the side of the rib cage and slice down along the breast, first on one side, then on the other.

An alternate way to carve the breast is to slide the knife down along the ribs so that the breast meat can be lifted out intact and sliced on the platter.

------------&⟨§⟩&------------

ROAST TURKEY WITH CORN BREAD STUFFING

Turkey, once the holiday *pièce de résistance*, has become an all-year all-purpose bird because most turkeys available today are frozen, to my mind not as good as the fresh. If you are using a frozen turkey, take extra care in its thawing and preparation, as explained on the following pages.

SERVES 8 TO 10

The Turkey:
10- to 12-pound turkey
2 teaspoons salt
Freshly ground black pepper
½ cup butter (a quarter-pound stick), softened at room
    temperature

The Corn Bread Stuffing:
6 cups crumbled day-old corn bread
1 cup butter (2 quarter-pound sticks)
The uncooked turkey liver, chopped fine
2 cups chopped onions (about 2 medium yellow onions)
2 cups chopped celery
1 cup chopped green pepper
1 big pinch crumbled dried thyme
⅓ cup minced fresh parsley
1½ teaspoons crumbled dried basil
1 teaspoon salt
¾ teaspoon or more freshly ground black pepper

The Giblet Sauce:
The uncooked turkey gizzard, heart, and neck
1 cup water
½ cup dry white wine
1 teaspoon salt
3 or 4 peppercorns
1 or 2 sprigs parsley
1 carrot, washed and coarsely chopped
1 onion, peeled, cut in half, and each half stuck with a clove

The Garnish:
Small bouquets of parsley

Preparing the turkey. Buy a fresh-chilled turkey, if possible, and remove the giblets and the neck at once. If you must accept a frozen bird, thaw as follows, and remove the bag of giblets and the neck as soon as they can be extricated.

An unstuffed frozen turkey can be safely thawed at room temperature *if left sealed in its plastic bag and placed in a closed paper bag.* Do not thaw a frozen turkey at room temperature without the paper bag. The closed bag allows the turkey to thaw completely while keeping its surface temperature low enough to discourage bacterial growth. With this slow thawing method, there is less weight loss and the cooked turkey is juicier, according to the U.S. Department of Agriculture.

To thaw a frozen turkey in the refrigerator, leave it in the original wrapper and set it on a tray. Allow 1 to 3 days, depending on the size of the bird.

Still another way to thaw frozen turkey is to place the bird, sealed in its original package (or, if torn, in a waterproof plastic bag), under cold running water. Small birds thaw in 3 to 4 hours; larger ones in 6 to 7 hours. Never use warm water.

Once you have thawed your turkey, cook it within 1 to 3 hours, or store it in the coldest part of the refrigerator and cook it within 1 or 2 days. Never refreeze a thawed uncooked bird.

Making the corn bread stuffing. Place the crumbled corn bread in a large mixing bowl. Heat ½ cup of the butter in a heavy 12-inch skillet.

Combine the chopped turkey liver, chopped onions, celery, green pepper, the thyme, minced parsley, basil, 1 teaspoon of salt, and ¾ teaspoon of freshly ground black pepper. Be generous with the pepper—its flavor is vital to this stuffing. Cook over moderate heat for about 20 minutes, stirring with a wooden spatula. Then add the remaining ½ cup of butter. When the butter melts, combine the mixture with the crumbled corn bread in the mixing bowl and mix thoroughly with a fork.

Preheating the oven. Slide a rack into a center slot and preheat the oven at 425° F. for 15 minutes.

Stuffing the turkey. Using your fingers, rub the inside of the turkey with 1 teaspoon of salt and several grindings of pepper. Spoon the stuffing lightly into the body cavity. Do not pack it in. Close the vent with skewers or sew with a large needle and strong white kitchen thread. Then stuff the neck and pull the neck skin underneath the body, fastening it with a skewer. Truss the turkey, following the instructions for trussing a bird on pages 445–46. Rub the turkey all over with ½ cup of softened butter and sprinkle with the remaining teaspoon of salt and some freshly ground black pepper.

Roasting the turkey. Place the turkey, breast side down, on a rack in a roasting pan and roast it for 30 minutes at 450° F. Reduce the heat to 350° F., and continue roasting for another 2½ hours, basting frequently with pan juices. About 1 to 1½ hours before the turkey will be done, turn it breast side up and continue basting.

Preparing the giblet sauce. At least 1 hour before the turkey will be done, place the turkey gizzard, heart, and neck in a medium-size saucepan, cover with cold water, and bring to a boil. Immediately strain through a sieve, discarding the water. Rinse out the pan to remove any clinging bits or scum.

Return the gizzard, heart, and neck to the pan, and add 1 cup of water, the wine, 1 teaspoon of salt, the peppercorns, parsley sprigs, carrot, and onion halves. Bring to a boil, reduce the heat to a simmer, cover the saucepan, and cook very slowly for 1 hour. Then strain the broth through a fine sieve into a bowl. Discard the contents of the sieve. Set the broth aside.

Finishing the turkey. When the turkey has roasted about 2½ hours, test it for doneness by squeezing the leg, using several thicknesses of paper toweling to protect your fingers. The leg should feel soft. Or plunge a "spot-check" thermometer into the thigh, not touching the bone; it should register 175° to 180° F., and the turkey juices should run clear. If not, continue roasting, testing frequently, until the turkey is cooked. I caution you not to overcook it or you will have a dry, tasteless bird.

When the turkey is cooked perfectly, remove it from the oven and lift carefully to a heated platter or a carving board. Remove the skewers and/or thread and trussing string and let the turkey rest for 20 minutes while you finish the sauce. Turn the oven off and warm the dinner plates, sauceboat, and serving platter, if you are using one.

Finishing the giblet sauce. Pour the broth you have set aside into the empty roasting pan. Place the pan over high heat and cook the mixture down, scraping all the brown particles in the pan with a wooden spatula and combining them with the broth, until you have about 2 cups of sauce. If necessary, add a little more wine. Taste for seasoning, add salt and pepper if needed, then pour the finished sauce into a heated sauceboat.

Serving the turkey. Place the turkey on the heated platter or on a carving board, and garnish with small bouquets of parsley. Carve the turkey at table as follows:

Cut off each leg as close to the body as possible, separate thighs and drumsticks, and slice off the dark meat. Remove the wings and disjoint them.

Thrust a carving fork firmly into the side of the rib cage and slice down along the breast, first on one side, then on the other.

An alternate way to carve the breast is to slide the knife down along the ribs so that the breast meat can be lifted out intact and sliced on the platter.

ROAST DUCKLING WITH LIVER STUFFING

About one hundred years ago, so the story goes, one drake and a harem of six ducks survived a long journey from China and became the progenitors of the millions of ducklings now raised on Long Island every year, which supply half of America's ducklings (the remainder come from the Middle West).

Although roasted duckling is usually served hot, in this instance it is served at room temperature accompanied by fresh lemon compote, which is, in reality, a sauce. The sweet sharpness of the sauce contrasts deliciously with the richness of the duck meat—a perfect combination.

SERVES 3

The Duckling:
5-pound duckling
2 teaspoons salt
Freshly ground black pepper
1 tablespoon butter, melted

The Liver Stuffing:
2 chicken livers
The duckling liver
3 slices bacon, cut into fine dice
2 tablespoons butter
5 to 6 button mushrooms, chopped
2 shallots, peeled and minced
½ cup dry bread crumbs
1 egg, slightly beaten

The Fresh Lemon Compote:
2 large lemons
⅓ cup boiling water
⅓ cup sugar
2 sprigs fresh tarragon (optional)

The Garnish (optional):
1 bunch fresh watercress

Preparing the duckling. Thaw the duckling if it is frozen (for thawing directions, see the "Culinary Glossary," page 447). Remove the neck and giblets, reserving the liver. Pull out and discard any loose fat from the body cavity. Cut off the wing tips. Prick the skin around the thighs, back, and lower breast with a fork or skewer to allow surplus fat to escape. With paper toweling, dry the bird thoroughly inside and out. Then, using your fingers, rub the cavity with 1½ teaspoons of the salt and set the duckling aside.

Making the liver stuffing. With a sharp French knife, chop the chicken livers and the duckling liver as fine as possible, then place them in a medium-size bowl.

Fry the bacon until crisp, then drain on paper toweling.

In a heavy skillet heat 2 tablespoons of butter over high heat. When it begins to foam, add the chopped mushrooms and cook, tossing and shaking the pan, for 4 to 5 minutes. When the mushrooms begin to brown, add the shallots. Reduce the heat to moderate and continue to cook for about 2 minutes. With a rubber spatula, scrape the mixture into the bowl with the livers. Then add the bread crumbs and bacon, combining the mixture with a fork. Finally, stir in the slightly beaten egg.

Preheating the oven. Slide an oven shelf into a middle slot and preheat the oven at 425° F. for 15 minutes.

Stuffing the duckling. Spoon the stuffing into the prepared duckling, then sew up the vent, using a sturdy needle and strong white thread. Rub the remaining ½ teaspoon of salt over the duckling, and sprinkle with freshly ground black pepper. Place the bird, breast side up, on the rack of a roasting pan, and pour the tablespoon of melted butter all over the duckling, coating all surfaces.

Roasting the duckling. Place the duckling in the oven and sear for 20 minutes. Then reduce the oven temperature to 350° F. and turn the duckling on its side. To do this, take several thicknesses of paper toweling in your hand, take hold of one leg, and flip the duckling over. About 20 minutes later, turn the duckling on its other side. Continue roasting for another 20 minutes, then turn the duckling breast side up again. During the next 40 minutes—the duckling should roast a total of 1 hour and 40 minutes—baste occasionally with pan drippings. When properly cooked, remove the pan from the oven and allow the duckling to cool on the rack.

Making the fresh lemon compote. This can be prepared while the duckling roasts; it requires about 1 hour to complete.

Using a vegetable peeler or lemon zester, peel off the rind of the lemons in broad pieces, taking care not to pick up any of the white skin. Pile 3 or 4 pieces on top of each other at a time, then cut into thin strips with a sharp knife. Place these julienned lemon peel strips in a small bowl and cover with the boiling water. Set the bowl aside.

Now, with a sharp knife, cut away all the white skin from both lemons, slice enough off both ends of each lemon to expose the flesh, then slice each lemon as thin as possible; you should have at least 12 slices. Remove any seeds with the tip of a small knife. Place the slices in a sieve over a bowl and allow them to drain for about 30 minutes.

Pour the lemon juice that has drained from the slices into a measuring cup, and to it add enough of the water in which the julienne strips have soaked to make ⅓ cup of liquid. Pour the liquid into a small saucepan and stir in the sugar. Place the pan over moderate heat, bring to a boil, and boil for 8 to 9 minutes, or until it has thickened. A candy thermometer inserted into the boiling liquid should read 220° F. Add the julienne and boil 1 minute longer.

Pat the lemon slices dry with paper towels. Place them in a serving dish and pour the syrup over all. If you have fresh tarragon, strip the leaves from 2 sprigs and scatter them over the top.

Serving the duckling. Place the duckling on a carving board breast side down, wings facing you. With a sharp boning knife, cut off the wings, twisting them slightly at the joint as you cut them away. Turn the duckling on its back and cut off the entire leg section—drumstick and thigh—from each side. Next, cut off each breast in one piece by cutting first on one side of the breastbone, then on the other. Then slice each breast into thirds lengthwise.

Because the stuffing is an important part of the meal, you must extricate it from the cavity of the bird. Remove the breastbone by forcing it back on itself and cutting away the rib sections. You can lift out the stuffing, which is quite firm, all in one piece and much like a pâté. It, too, should be sliced.

Finally, turn the duckling over and you will discover the "oysters," two little nuggets of delicious meat on the lower back. They, too, should be cut out for serving.

Arrange the carved pieces on a generous platter along with the sliced stuffing and, if you like, a garnish of fresh watercress. Pass the serving bowl of fresh lemon compote.

~§§~

RED SNAPPER STUFFED WITH CRABMEAT

SERVES 5 TO 6

The Crabmeat Stuffing:
½ pound crabmeat, flake crab or the more expensive
    lump or backfin
1 cup fresh bread crumbs
4 tablespoons butter, cut into bits
¼ cup water
1 rib celery, finely minced
3 or 4 scallions, with 1 inch of green tops, finely minced
15 to 20 sprigs parsley, finely minced
½ teaspoon salt
Freshly ground white pepper
2 to 3 tablespoons heavy cream

The Fish:
5-pound fresh red snapper (or other firm white fish:
    bass, pompano, haddock, or rockfish), eviscerated,
    boned, and scaled but with head and tail left on
4 to 6 tablespoons butter, softened at room temperature
1½ teaspoons salt
Freshly ground white pepper

The Garnish and Accompaniment:
Bouquet of parsley
Lemon wedges
Sauce Rémoulade (page 437)

Making the crabmeat stuffing. Spread the crabmeat out on wax paper and pick over it to remove any shells or cartilage. Place the crabmeat in a medium-size mixing bowl, add the bread crumbs and toss the two together with a fork.

Place the 4 tablespoons of butter bits in a 10- or 12-inch frying pan with the water. Add the celery and bring to a boil over moderate heat, then simmer for a couple of minutes. Stir in the scallions and continue to simmer until the celery is soft and all the water has boiled away. With a rubber spatula, scrape the vegetables into the bowl of crabmeat and crumbs. Add the minced parsley, ½ teaspoon of salt, and several twists of the pepper mill, and toss together with a fork. Dribble the cream over the mixture, using just enough to make the stuffing a good consistency, and mix it in with a fork. Taste for seasoning; you may want to add salt or pepper or both. Set the stuffing aside.

Preheating the oven. Slide an oven rack into a middle slot and preheat the oven at 400° F. for 15 minutes.

Preparing the pan. You will need a shallow pan a couple of inches longer than the fish. A 5-pound red snapper should fit into a 16-by-11-by-2-inch pan perfectly, or you can use a somewhat shorter pan and place the fish diagonally in it to accommodate both the head and tail.

To make removal of the cooked fish relatively easy, cut two pieces of foil several inches longer than the width of the pan. Fit them into the pan, overlapping at the center. Spread 2 tablespoons of the softened butter over the foil. Set the pan aside.

Stuffing the fish. Sprinkle the inside of the fish with 1 teaspoon of the salt. Distribute the stuffing as evenly as possible down its entire length. If there seems to be a surplus, stuff the head. Sew the fish together with a sturdy needle and heavy white thread, using an overcast-type stitch, or secure it every inch or so with skewers and tie with white string.

With your fingers, spread 1 tablespoon of the remaining butter over the skin, then sprinkle with ¼ teaspoon of the remaining salt and a sprinkling of pepper. Turn the fish over carefully and butter and season the other side, using the final tablespoon of butter and ¼ teaspoon of salt and another sprinkling of pepper.

Baking the fish. With two wide metal spatulas, lift the fish to the prepared pan, then place it in the oven. Bake for 30 minutes, brushing several times with the pan drippings. If the skin seems at all dry, melt the 2 extra tablespoons of softened butter, and coat the fish with it.

Warm a serving platter and dinner plates.

Serving the fish. To remove the fish from the pan, take hold of the foil on both sides where it overlaps and lift to a heated serving platter. To remove the foil, slide a spatula under the tail to lift it slightly, then pull away the foil. Remove the other piece of foil the same way, sliding the spatula under the head. Pull out the thread or skewers and cut off any string.

Garnish the platter with a bouquet of parsley and lemon wedges.

To serve the fish, use a sharp knife and cut straight down through the fish so that each person receives 2 pieces of fish with the stuffing enclosed between them. Because this is a very rich dish, servings should be no wider than an inch and a half. Pass the Sauce Rémoulade in a bowl or sauceboat.

Baking:
Breads and Biscuits

*B*efore the days of packaged breads, biscuit mixes, and ready-to-bake biscuits, buns, and rolls, baking "from scratch" was, of necessity, an almost daily ritual in virtually every American home. Women spent hours every week making endless varieties of yeast breads for the family, working under what we would consider primitive kitchen conditions. Every batter and dough required beating or kneading by a strong arm; and ingredients, such as homemade yeast, were often unpredictable. Baking temperatures were usually determined by thrusting a hand into the hot wood- or coal-burning oven. Obviously, those courageous cooks were not deterred by any of these difficulties, judging by the vast legacy of baking lore they left behind.

Present-day baking, while it requires knowledge and practice, makes fewer demands on the cook. Standardized ingredients, thermostatically controlled ovens, electric blenders and food processors, and high-powered electric mixers make baking a joy while not in the least diminishing its drama.

Nevertheless, breadmaking requires special techniques that are related to the part that yeast plays in baking. Therefore, an understanding of the characteristics and behavior of yeast is helpful.

Yeast cells, like all living plants, need moisture, the correct temperature, and nutrients—in this case, sugar and starch—in order to grow. In my yeast bread and cake recipes, the life cycle of dormant yeast resumes when sweetened water or milk is heated to 110° to 115° F. and is then stirred into a mixture of dry yeast, salt, and a small amount of flour. At that temperature—too much heat will kill the yeast—the yeast cells begin to feed on the sugar in the liquid and the starch in the flour and produce the carbon dioxide gas that will leaven the dough, plus a small amount of alcohol.

As more flour is beaten into the dough, gluten starts to develop from two protein substances in the flour called gliadin and glutenin. Sticky and gluey in its isolated form, gluten in a dough has the singular ability to increase in elasticity, or, to use a culinary term, "develop." With further beating or kneading, the gluten becomes elastic enough to expand but strong enough to entrap the carbon dioxide bubbles produced by the yeast cells. These bubbles cause the dough to rise when it is placed in an area with a favorable temperature, which ideally is between 80° and 90° F.

The function of the risings specified in the recipes is twofold: to develop the flavor of the dough and to allow the carbon dioxide bubbles produced by the yeast to transform a dense mass into a porous one. Obviously, the more risings the dough is subjected to— up to a maximum of three—the lighter the finished bread or yeast cake will be. However, if dough is allowed to rise for too long at one time or to rise at too high a temperature, the resulting bread will have an excessively yeasty flavor and may be dense and low in volume as well.

Those of you who are already familiar with baking will find startling departures from conventional methods in some recipes. These innovations are not shortcuts in the usual sense, but are simplifications that will help to ensure the success of your efforts. The results will convince you that baking remains, even today, the noblest of the culinary arts.

Ingredients for Breads and Biscuits

Flour. If any ingredient has the power to make or break your breads and biscuits, it is surely flour. Wheat flour—the flour most commonly used in baking—is available in many varieties, each composed of hard winter wheat or soft spring wheat or a combination of the two. All wheat flours have at least one element in common—gluten. Since hard wheat has a much higher gluten content than soft wheat, the type of flour you use and to what point you allow its gluten to develop will affect to a significant degree the quality and texture of your breads and biscuits.

Each recipe specifies which kind of flour to use for ideal results: all-purpose, cake, whole-wheat (graham), rye, or corn meal. Never substitute one for another, or you will upset the careful balance among ingredients.

You will also note that for some breads I prefer to use flour without sifting it—this includes so-called presifted flour—rather than flour which has already been sifted; this is an important distinction because a cup of sifted flour contains a little more air and thus a little less flour than does the same measure of unsifted flour.

Yeast. I prefer dry yeast to compressed fresh yeast because it presents no spoilage problems and is easier to mix into doughs. One quarter-ounce package of dry yeast is sufficient for any bread recipe calling for about 6 cups of flour. Two packages are required for a sweet yeast dough made with an equivalent amount of flour. Although a little sugar in a bread dough encourages the growth of yeast, a much larger amount inhibits it; hence the need for extra yeast.

Some experienced bakers, however, deliberately double, triple, or even quadruple the amount of yeast so that a dough, sweetened or not, will rise more quickly. This doesn't affect the flavor of the dough if the risings are correctly controlled, but there is the ever-present danger of over-rising, so I suggest that you play it safe and use precisely the quantity of yeast I recommend for each recipe.

Baking powder. I specify double-acting baking powder, which releases only a fraction of its gas into the batter when moistened, reserving the rest of its leavening power until the batter is exposed to heat. If you must use single-acting baking powder for any reason, there should not be a moment's delay between the mixing of the batter and baking it if you would have the batter rise to its full height.

Baking soda. Baking soda is always used when a batter is made with an acid liquid such as buttermilk or sour cream; they interact to produce carbon dioxide gas that leavens the mixture.

Eggs. Eggs are by no means an indispensable ingredient for breads and biscuits in general. They give yeast breads a delicate yellow color, a definite flavor, a soft cakelike crumb, and a tender crust. However, I do not use eggs in American White Bread, Whole-Wheat

Bread, and other breads of this type. Biscuits require eggs only when they are meant to be rich and crumbly, like scones.

Butter. Every recipe in this section requires butter except the one for pizza, which naturally calls for that most Italian of fats, olive oil.

While margarine and vegetable shortening may be substituted measure for measure in any baking recipe, the results, though satisfactory, will be far from spectacular.

Liquids. Doughs and batters would be impossible to make without liquid of some kind. In addition to their primary function of binding the flour particles together, liquids have other effects upon breads and biscuits. Water will give yeast breads a very crisp crust and a fairly dense crumb, whereas milk, or a combination of water and milk, will give a softer crust and a more luxurious crumb.

Sugars and other sweeteners. When *sugar* is listed without further description, ordinary granulated sugar is meant; other sweeteners —confectioners' sugar, for example—are indicated by name.

Confectioners' sugar is used mainly for dusting the tops of yeast breads and cakes.

Molasses should be the dark kind and unsulfured. Blackstrap molasses is unpleasantly bitter and not suitable for baking. Molasses and other liquid sweeteners are not interchangeable with dry sugars for baking purposes; they are used for their particular flavors and the extra moisture that they contribute.

Salt. Small quantities of salt are used in yeast doughs to slightly inhibit the action of the yeast and thus help prevent over-rising. And salt also strengthens the gluten of flour.

Note: Fuller descriptions of most of these ingredients will be found in the "Culinary Glossary."

Techniques for Making Bread

Measuring ingredients. All measurements of ingredients for the bread recipes are made in the standard ways, with the exception of flour. When I specify unsifted flour, measure it by dipping a dry-measuring cup into the flour container, filling the cup to heaping, then leveling it with the edge of a spatula or the back of a knife.

Sifting dry ingredients. When the recipe requires that you sift dry ingredients together, set the sifter in a large bowl, then measure the ingredients into the sifter. This prevents the loss of any part of an ingredient.

Kneading basic bread dough by hand. Once you have combined the ingredients and mixed the dough, find a comfortable work surface on which to knead the dough. A table 30 to 32 inches high will be much more comfortable for most people than the standard counter height of 36 inches. The best kneading surfaces are marble, Formica, or a polyethylene slab, because they require little flour to prevent the dough from sticking. If you must use a pastry board, don't wash it: clean it with a baker's scraper. A wooden board will absorb water, increasing the likelihood that the dough will stick.

Flour the kneading surface lightly, then gather the dough into a ball and flatten it slightly. Using the lightly floured heel of one hand (or both hands, if you prefer), push the dough away from you, starting close to the near edge. Fold the far edge forward to meet the near edge. Give the dough a quarter-turn so the fold will be at one side, then push the dough away from you again. Repeat the sequence of pushing, folding, and turning—the basic kneading technique—for the time specified in the recipe, or until the dough is smooth and very elastic.

As you knead, flour your hands and the work surface only when necessary.

Kneading soft yeast doughs by hand. If you are kneading soft yeast doughs, scrape the dough from the mixing bowl onto the floured work surface with a rubber spatula. Flour the hand that you will use for kneading as well as the baker's scraper that you will wield with the other hand.

With the heel of the floured hand, push the dough firmly away from you. With the baker's scraper, return the spread-out dough, folding it toward you, roughly in half.

Lightly flouring your work surface, hand, and scraper when necessary, repeat the sequence of pushing, returning, and folding the dough for 10 minutes. Then gather the dough into a ball and, using the technique for kneading basic bread dough described above, push, fold, and turn the dough for the time specified in the recipe, or until the dough is smooth and elastic.

For the best texture in your finished yeast breads, use as little extra flour as possible during kneading. Each recipe specifies the maximum amount of flour to use; how much of that amount you will need will vary from time to time, depending on the absorbency of the flour and even on the humidity of your kitchen.

Machine kneading. A heavy-duty, professional-type mixer equipped with a dough hook can simplify and shorten the mixing and kneading of yeast doughs and batters. The manufacturer's instructions will indicate recommended mixing and kneading times for various mixtures, as well as the speed settings on the machine. These settings are always rather low because too high a speed can cause gluten in a dough to break down.

Follow my recipes precisely for preparing ingredients and making the dough or batter, but mix and knead for the time periods recommended by the manufacturer for similar doughs. Because mixers vary in power from model to model, it is impossible to give precise directions for their use in the bread recipes that follow—hence these general notes:

· Don't try to knead a dough containing more than 6 or 7 cups of flour in even the most powerful mixer, lest you find yourself with a mass of dough spinning wildly in the bowl and then immobilizing itself around the beater.

· You may find, as I do, that you prefer to top off machine kneading with a few strokes of hand kneading to consolidate the mass, or even that you prefer to mix by machine and knead by hand.

· You may find that the additional flour listed in each recipe under "For Kneading the Dough" will not be necessary. But if the dough should seem unusually sticky, you may want to add a little flour to the bowl at the start of kneading, adding more later only if it seems necessary.

Freezing dough. Yeast doughs may be frozen at any point after kneading has been completed. Simply punch the dough down, wrap it securely in aluminum foil, and freeze it—ideally at 0° F. or less—for as long as a week. Let the dough thaw completely before you continue with the recipe from the point at which you left off.

Letting the dough rise. The ideal place for yeast doughs to rise has a temperature between 80° and 90° F. and is free from drafts. Some likely spots to test with a room thermometer are: an unlit oven, preferably one with a pilot light, with the oven door either open or closed; a kitchen cabinet with its door open or closed; a closet, particularly one near a source of heat.

Cover the rising dough with a protective foil tent constructed in the following way: Cut a sheet of aluminum foil at least 6 inches longer than the diameter of the bowl. Pleat it crosswise at 1- or 2-inch intervals. Crimp the pleated sheet firmly to the rim of the bowl, then pull up each pleat to form a dome-shaped "tent."

Let the dough rise for the length of time specified, or to the bulk specified, in the recipe. To make sure it has risen sufficiently, gently poke two fingers about ½ inch into the dough. The indentations will remain if the dough is ready. If they disappear, re-cover the bowl and let the dough continue to rise until it passes this test.

If for any reason you must interrupt the rising of yeast doughs, simply punch down the dough (see below), cover it tightly with plastic wrap, and refrigerate it for as long as 6 to 8 hours. It will continue to rise slowly in the refrigerator. If the rising is still only partially completed when you get back to your breadmaking, return the dough to the 80° to 90° F. environment and proceed with the rising. If the rising has been completed during refrigeration, continue with the recipe from that point.

Punching down the dough. When the dough has risen to the bulk specified in each recipe, punch it down between risings to prevent over-rising, often the cause of poor flavor, texture, and volume. To do this, sink your fist vigorously into the dough as many times as necessary to deflate it, then turn the dough mass over in the bowl, replace the foil tent, and allow rising to resume.

The baking pans. Be sure to use the size pan specified in each recipe. Should you use a larger or smaller pan, you run several risks: If the pan is too small, the dough may overflow during baking; if it is too large, the dough may bake too quickly.

Baking the bread. Bake the bread in a preheated oven, following the instructions in the individual recipes. If you find that your breads and biscuits tend to brown unevenly, some areas in your oven are hotter than others. To cope with these hot spots, wait until the bread has risen to its full height—this usually requires about 15 minutes, especially in a deep pan—then shift the pan or pans quickly about from time to time for even browning.

If you like breads crusty on all sides, remove the loaves from their pans 5 minutes before they should be done and set them on the oven rack to finish baking.

For high-altitude baking, consult the "Culinary Glossary" (page 453).

Yeast Breads

In the following pages you will find recipes for yeast breads of three different types: basic yeast breads, sweet yeast breads, and yeast batter breads.

The basic yeast breads are purely American with the exception of Italian pizza, which has virtually become American by adoption. In the recipes for sweet yeast breads and batter breads I have wandered much farther afield to include breads from Portugal,

Poland, Austria, and France, in addition to a few characteristic breads of our own.

Basic yeast breads and sweet yeast breads demand more effort and time than yeast batter breads. Their doughs must be kneaded after they are mixed and they must be set aside to rise a specified number of times before they are baked. However, mixing the dough is simple enough, and the risings require time but no effort.

Kneading, however, is another matter—delightful or arduous, depending on your point of view. I, for one, find it pleasantly relaxing. Nothing quite rivals the feel of dough as you rhythmically knead it on a slab or a board, almost bringing it to life. For those of you who don't share this feeling, there is the alternative of kneading dough by machine.

If you have neither the inclination for kneading by hand nor a dough hook for kneading by machine, try yeast batter breads which require no kneading at all. Although the batters must be beaten vigorously to develop their gluten—sometimes for as long as 10 minutes—this can be done by the beaters of a fairly high-powered electric mixer.

Basic Yeast Breads

The following four recipes for basic yeast breads—American White Bread, Oat Bread, and Whole-Wheat Bread, plus an Italian Pizza—are structured in much the same manner. This similarity is deliberate and intended to make breadmaking an easy and understandable task for those cooks who have never before worked with yeast.

All four breads are made with active dry yeast. In each recipe the yeast is combined with flour and other dry ingredients in a simplified procedure which, after much experimentation with more conventional methods, I find successful and delightfully easy.

Each of the four doughs requires kneading, and each requires rising periods—the number varies from bread to bread—and all of them, therefore, take several hours to make. However, as you will see, relatively little of that period is working time.

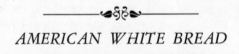

AMERICAN WHITE BREAD

As recently as two hundred years ago—a short span of time in the history of breadmaking—white flour was a rare and expensive commodity, which only the most affluent could afford. Breads made with it were considered a luxury. Today, Americans take white bread for granted, as well they might—many millions of loaves are produced in the nation's commercial bakeries daily. These breads, with very rare exceptions, are inferior to the ones you can make at home.

American White Bread made by this recipe is one of the best I know. It is a fine all-purpose bread with a buttery flavor, suitable for any meal of the day; and with its tender, velvety crumb, it makes excellent toast.

MAKES TWO 9-BY-5-INCH LOAVES

The Dough:
6 cups unsifted all-purpose flour
1 package (¼ ounce) active dry yeast
1 tablespoon salt
2 cups milk
2 tablespoons sugar
4 tablespoons unsalted butter, cut into small bits

For Kneading the Dough:
½ cup unsifted all-purpose flour

For Buttering the Bowl and the Pans:
2 to 3 teaspoons butter, softened at room temperature

The Glaze:
1 egg
1 tablespoon milk

Preparing the ingredients: Measure 5 cups of the flour into a bowl and set it aside. Pour the remaining cup of flour, the yeast, and the salt into a 4-quart mixing bowl and stir them together thoroughly with a fork.

In a 1-quart saucepan, combine 2 cups of milk, sugar, and butter bits. Set the pan over moderate heat and, stirring occasionally, heat the milk mixture until a candy thermometer registers between 110° and 115° F., or until the milk feels very warm, but not quite hot, when you dip your finger into it.

Mixing the dough. Slowly pour the warm milk into the yeast and flour mixture, stirring constantly with a wooden spoon until the batter is smooth. Then stir in the reserved 5 cups of flour, ½ cup at a time, thoroughly incorporating each addition. If at any point you find stirring too difficult, work in the remaining flour with your hands.

Kneading the dough. Using only as much as you need of the ½ cup of unsifted flour reserved for kneading, flour your work surface and your hands. Knead the dough for 8 to 10 minutes, then shape it into a compact ball.

The first rising. With a pastry brush, coat the inside of a 4-quart stainless steel or glass bowl with about a teaspoonful of the softened butter. Drop in the ball of dough and turn it about until it is coated on all sides.

Cover the bowl with a foil tent and place it in an area where a temperature of 80° to 90° F. can be maintained. Within 1 to 1½ hours the dough will have doubled in bulk, an indication that it has risen sufficiently. To make sure, gently poke two fingers about ½ inch into the dough. The indentations will remain if the rising is complete. If the dough is still so elastic that the dents disappear, replace the foil tent and let the dough continue to rise until it passes the test.

The second rising. Punch the dough down with several blows of your fist and turn the mass over in the bowl. Replace the foil tent and let the dough rise again, still in the same warm rising area, for 45 minutes to 1 hour. Test by poking the dough with two fingers after 45 minutes. This rising will not be quite as lofty as the first.

Dividing the dough. Punch the dough down, remove it from the bowl, shape it into a compact ball, and place it on your work surface. With a sharp knife, cut the dough in half and pat each half into an oval. Cover the ovals loosely with foil and let the dough rest for 10 minutes.

Buttering the pans. With a pastry brush, butter the bottoms—but not the sides—of two 9-inch loaf pans, using the remaining softened butter.

Shaping the loaves. Lightly flour your work surface and place one of the ovals of dough on it. With a lightly floured rolling pin, roll the dough into a rectangle measuring about 9 by 7 inches.

Fold the long sides so that they meet in the center, the second fold overlapping the first by about ½ inch. With the heels of both hands, press down firmly all over the dough to expel any entrapped air.

Pinch the dough firmly together along its center fold, then gently pat the ends and sides of the dough inward to form a plump, evenly shaped 9-inch loaf. Place it, seam down, in one of the pans, gently pressing on the dough, if necessary, so that both ends of the loaf touch the ends of the pan.

Shape the second loaf as you did the first and place it in the other pan.

The third rising. Cover each pan with a foil tent and place the pans in the warm rising area. Let the dough rise until it fills the corners of the pans snugly and mounds about ½ inch above their rims; this will take 30 minutes to an hour. This third rising is crucial because it determines the height of the baked loaves.

Preheating the oven. About 15 minutes before you judge that the last rising will be complete, slide an oven shelf into a middle slot and preheat the oven at 400° F.

Glazing the bread. Beat the egg and tablespoon of milk together with a whisk or fork. Using a pastry brush, gently coat the exposed surface of each loaf with the glaze.

Baking the bread. Set the pans about 2 inches apart in the oven. Bake the bread for 30 minutes, then test the loaves for doneness: Turn them out of the pans on a cake rack or your work surface and thump their bottoms sharply with your knuckles. The sound should be a hollow one; if it is the slightest bit muted, return the loaves to the pans and bake them for about 5 minutes longer, or until a repeated test indicates that they are done.

Cooling the bread. Place the finished loaves, right side up, on a wire cake rack and let them cool to room temperature before serving or storing the bread.

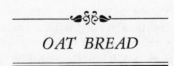

OAT BREAD

I first tasted this old-fashioned American bread on a farm in the Middle West. The original recipe called for oat flour, now almost impossible to find. As an alternative I used rolled oats and produced a bread as good as the one I remembered—deliciously flavorful and of substantial texture. Note that quick-cooking oats will not do for this recipe.

MAKES TWO 9-BY-5-INCH LOAVES

The Dough:
5½ cups unsifted all-purpose flour
2 cups regular rolled oats (not the quick-cooking kind)
1 package (¼ ounce) active dry yeast
2 teaspoons salt
2 cups milk
¼ cup unsulfured dark molasses
1 teaspoon sugar
4 tablespoons unsalted butter, cut into small bits

For Kneading the Dough:
½ cup unsifted all-purpose flour

For Buttering the Bowl and the Pans:
2 to 3 teaspoons butter, softened at room temperature

The Glaze and Topping:
1 egg
1 tablespoon milk
3 tablespoons rolled oats

Preparing the ingredients. Measure 4½ cups of flour into a bowl and set it aside. Pour the remaining cup of flour into a 4-quart mixing bowl and, with a wooden spoon, stir in thoroughly 2 cups of rolled oats, the yeast, and the salt.

In a 1-quart saucepan, combine 2 cups of milk, molasses, and sugar, and stir with a rubber spatula until the molasses dissolves. Then add 4 tablespoons of butter. Set the pan over moderate heat and, stirring occasionally, heat the milk until a candy thermometer registers between 110° and 115° F., or the milk feels very warm, but not actually hot, to the touch.

Mixing the dough. Slowly pour the warm milk mixture into the mixture of dry ingredients, stirring with a wooden spoon until well blended. Then stir in the reserved 4½ cups of flour, ½ cup at a time, incorporating each addition thoroughly. If stirring becomes too difficult after several additions of flour, work in the remaining flour with your hands.

Kneading the dough. Using only as much as you need of the ½ cup of flour reserved for kneading, flour your work surface and your hands. Knead for 8 to 10 minutes, then shape the dough into a compact ball.

The first rising. With a pastry brush, coat the inside of a 4-quart stainless steel or glass bowl with about 1 teaspoon of the softened butter. Drop in the ball of dough and turn it about until it is coated on all sides.

Cover the bowl with a foil tent and place it in an area where a temperature of 80° to 90° F. can be maintained. Within 1 to $1\frac{1}{4}$ hours the dough will have doubled in bulk, an indication that it has risen sufficiently. To make sure, gently poke two fingers about $\frac{1}{2}$ inch into the dough. The indentations will remain if the rising is complete. If the dough is still so elastic that the dents disappear, replace the foil tent and let the dough continue to rise until it passes the test.

The second rising. Punch the dough down with several blows of your fist and turn the mass over in the bowl. Replace the foil tent and let the dough rise again, still in the same warm rising area, for $1\frac{1}{4}$ to $1\frac{1}{2}$ hours. Test by poking the dough with two fingers after 45 minutes. This rising will not be quite as lofty as the first.

Dividing the dough. Punch the dough down, remove it from the bowl, shape it into a compact ball, and place it on your work surface. With a sharp knife, cut the dough in half and pat each half into an oval. Cover the ovals loosely with foil and let the dough rest for 10 minutes.

Buttering the pans. With a pastry brush, butter the bottoms—but not the sides—of two 9-inch loaf pans, using the reserved softened butter.

Shaping the loaves. Lightly flour your work surface and place one of the ovals of dough on it. With a lightly floured rolling pin, roll the dough into a rectangle measuring about 9 by 7 inches.

Fold the long sides so that they meet in the center, the second fold overlapping the first by about $\frac{1}{2}$ inch. With the heels of both hands, press down firmly all over the dough to expel any entrapped air.

Pinch the dough firmly together along its center fold, then gently pat the ends and sides of the dough inward to form a plump, evenly shaped 9-inch loaf. Place it, seam down, in one of the pans, gently pressing on the dough, if necessary, so that both ends of the loaf touch the ends of the pan.

Shape the second loaf as you did the first and place it in the other pan.

The third rising. Cover each pan with a foil tent and place the pans in the warm rising area. Let the dough rise until it fills the corners of the pans snugly and mounds about ½ inch above their rims; this will take about 45 minutes to 1 hour. This third rising is crucial because it determines the height of the baked loaves.

Preheating the oven. About 15 minutes before you judge that the third rising will be complete, slide an oven shelf into a middle slot and preheat the oven at 375° F.

Glazing the loaves. Beat the egg and tablespoon of milk together with a whisk or a fork. With a pastry brush, lightly paint the exposed tops of the loaves. Then sprinkle each loaf with 1½ tablespoons of rolled oats.

Baking the bread. Place the pans about 2 inches apart in the oven. Bake the bread for 40 minutes, then test the loaves for doneness: Turn them out of their pans on a cake rack or your work surface, and thump their bottoms sharply with your knuckles. If they produce a muted rather than a hollow sound, return the loaves to the pans and bake them for about 5 minutes longer, or until they pass the test.

Cooling the bread. Turn out the loaves and place them, right side up, on a wire cake rack. Let the loaves cool to room temperature before serving or storing the bread.

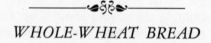

WHOLE-WHEAT BREAD

Here is a bread nourishing enough to fulfill any nutritionist's dream. It is made entirely of whole-wheat flour (some similar breads have a proportion of white flour added), and it requires only two risings instead of the usual three. This produces the slightly rough and grainy texture I like.

If you prefer a whole-wheat bread with a lighter texture, allow the dough to rise three times, as described in the recipe for American White Bread, page 280.

MAKES TWO 9-BY-5-INCH LOAVES

The Dough:
5½ cups unsifted whole-wheat flour
1 package (¼ ounce) active dry yeast
1 tablespoon salt
1 cup milk
1 cup water
¼ cup unsulfured dark molasses
4 tablespoons unsalted butter, cut into small bits

For Kneading the Dough:
½ cup unsifted whole-wheat flour

For Buttering the Bowl and the Pans:
2 to 3 teaspoons butter, softened at room temperature

Preparing the ingredients. Measure 4½ cups of flour into a bowl and set it aside. Pour the remaining cup of flour, the yeast, and the salt into a 4-quart mixing bowl. Thoroughly stir the ingredients together with a fork.

In a 1-quart saucepan, combine the milk, water, and molasses, and stir with a rubber spatula until the molasses dissolves. Add the butter bits. Set the pan over moderate heat and, stirring occasionally, heat the liquid until a candy thermometer registers between 110° and 115° F., or until the liquid feels very warm, but not actually hot, to the touch.

Mixing the dough. Slowly pour the warm liquid over the flour and yeast mixture, stirring with a wooden spoon until the batter is free of lumps. Then stir in the reserved 4½ cups of flour, ½ cup at a time. After several additions of flour you may find stirring too difficult. At that point, incorporate the rest of the flour with your hands.

Kneading the dough. Using only as much as you need of the ½ cup of flour reserved for kneading, flour your work surface and your hands. Knead the dough for 8 to 10 minutes, then shape the dough into a compact ball.

The first rising. With a pastry brush, coat the inside of a 4-quart stainless steel or glass bowl with about a teaspoonful of the softened butter. Drop in the ball of dough and turn it about until it is coated with butter.

Cover the bowl with a foil tent and place it in an area where a temperature of 80° to 90° F. can be maintained.

Within 1 to 1½ hours the dough will have more or less doubled in bulk. To make sure it has risen sufficiently, gently poke two fingers about ½ inch into the dough. The indentations will remain if the dough is ready. If they disappear, replace the foil tent and let the dough continue to rise until it passes the test.

Dividing the dough. Punch the dough down, remove it from the bowl, shape it into a compact ball, and place it on your work surface. With a sharp knife, cut the dough in half and pat each half into an oval. Cover the ovals loosely with foil and let the dough rest for 10 minutes.

Buttering the pans. With a pastry brush, butter the bottoms—but not the sides—of two 9-inch loaf pans with the remaining softened butter.

Shaping the loaves. Lightly flour your work surface and place one of the ovals of dough on it. With a lightly floured rolling pin, roll the dough into a rectangle measuring about 9 by 7 inches. Fold the long sides so that they meet in the center, the second fold overlapping the first by about ½ inch. With the heels of both hands, press down firmly all over the dough to expel any entrapped air.

Pinch the dough firmly together along its center fold, then gently pat the ends and sides of the dough inward to form a plump, evenly shaped 9-inch loaf.

Place the loaf, seam side down, in one of the pans, gently pressing on the dough, if necessary, so that both ends of the loaf touch the ends of the pan.

Shape the second loaf in the same fashion and place it in the other pan.

The second rising. Cover each pan with a foil tent and place the pans in the warm rising area. Let the dough rise until it fills the corners of the pans snugly and mounds just slightly above their rims; this will take about 1 to 1½ hours. This rising is crucial because it determines the height of the baked loaves.

Preheating the oven. About 15 minutes before it appears that the last rising will be complete, slide an oven shelf into a center slot and preheat the oven at 375° F.

Baking the bread. Place the pans about 2 inches apart in the oven. Bake the bread for 40 minutes, then test the loaves for doneness by turning them out of their pans and thumping their bottoms with your knuckles. If they produce a muted, rather than a hollow, sound, return the loaves to the pans and bake them for about 5 minutes longer, or until they pass the test.

Cooling the bread. Place the finished loaves, right side up, on a wire cake rack and let them cool to room temperature before serving or storing them.

PIZZA: A PIE WITH A CRUST OF BREAD DOUGH

Most of us have seen professional pizza bakers twirling large rounds of dough in midair before fitting them into pans. Despite these dramatic and difficult maneuvers, an Italian pizza is much easier to make than it looks, and you will find described in this recipe a much simpler technique that works just as well.

A pizza—in Italian, the word means "pie"—basically consists of a crust of bread dough, topped with tomato sauce and cheese. Omit the mozzarella, if you wish, and before the Parmesan is sprinkled on the pizza, add any embellishments of your choice: sliced peperoni or other Italian sausage, anchovies, olives, mushrooms, red or green peppers—the possibilities are endless.

MAKES TWO ROUND 12-INCH PIZZAS

The Sauce:
4 tablespoons olive oil
1 cup coarsely chopped onions
1 teaspoon finely chopped garlic
1 teaspoon crumbled dried basil
1 teaspoon crumbled dried oregano
1 can (1-pound 12-ounce size) tomatoes, preferably imported
    Italian plum tomatoes
1 tablespoon tomato paste
½ to 1 teaspoon sugar
½ teaspoon salt
Freshly ground black pepper

The Dough:
3 cups unsifted all-purpose flour
1 package (¼ ounce) active dry yeast
¼ teaspoon sugar
1 teaspoon salt
1 cup water
¼ cup olive oil

For Kneading the Dough:
½ cup unsifted all-purpose flour

For Oiling the Bowl:
2 teaspoons olive oil

The Cheese Topping:
½ pound mozzarella cheese, coarsely shredded (about 2 cups)
4 tablespoons freshly grated imported Parmesan cheese
2 to 3 tablespoons olive oil

Making the sauce. Pour 4 tablespoons of olive oil into a heavy 10-inch frying pan and add the onions. Stirring occasionally with a wooden spoon, cook over low heat for 5 to 8 minutes, or until the onions are translucent; do not allow them to brown.

Stir in the garlic, basil, and oregano and, stirring constantly, cook for about 2 minutes. Then add the can of tomatoes, juice and all. Stir in the tomato paste, ½ teaspoon of sugar, ½ teaspoon of salt, and a liberal grinding of pepper.

Raise the heat to high and let the sauce come to a boil, meanwhile breaking up the tomatoes with the spoon. Lower the heat to moderate and cook, uncovered, stirring occasionally, for 20 minutes. Then purée the sauce through a food mill, or rub it through a sieve with the back of a spoon.

Return the puréed sauce to the pan and cook uncovered over moderate heat for 10 to 15 minutes, or until the sauce has thickened enough to flow sluggishly off a spoon. There should be about 1½ cups of sauce.

Taste for seasoning and enliven the sauce with more salt and pepper if you think it needs it. Depending upon the acidity of the tomatoes, you may need the additional ½ teaspoon of sugar as well. Let the sauce cool to room temperature.

Preparing the ingredients for the dough. Measure 2 cups of the flour into a bowl and set it aside. Pour the remaining cup of flour, the yeast, ¼ teaspoon of sugar, and 1 teaspoon of salt into a 4-quart mixing bowl. With a fork, stir the ingredients together thoroughly.

In a small saucepan, combine the water and ¼ cup of olive oil. Over moderate heat, warm the mixture until a candy thermometer registers between 110° and 115° F., or until the liquid feels very warm, but not hot, to the touch.

Mixing the dough. Slowly pour the warm liquid over the yeast and flour mixture, stirring it constantly with a wooden spoon until smooth. Then stir in the reserved 2 cups of flour, ½ cup at a time. After you have added most of the flour, you may find stirring difficult; if so, incorporate the rest of the flour with your hands.

Kneading the dough. Using only as much as you need of the ½ cup of flour reserved for kneading, lightly flour your hands and work surface, and knead the dough for about 10 minutes. Then shape the dough into a compact ball.

The first rising. With a pastry brush, coat the inside of a 4-quart mixing bowl with 2 teaspoons of olive oil. Drop in the dough and turn it about until it is coated with oil.

Cover the bowl with a foil tent and place it in an area where a temperature of 80° to 90° F. can be maintained.

Within 1 to 1¼ hours the dough will have approximately doubled in bulk. To make sure, gently poke two fingers about ½ inch into the dough. The indentations should remain. If they don't, replace the foil tent and let the dough continue to rise until it passes the test.

Dividing the dough. Punch the dough down, remove it from the bowl, shape it into a compact ball, and place it on your work surface. With a sharp knife, cut the dough in half. Pat each half into a round about 5 to 6 inches in diameter.

The second rising. Place the dough rounds on a baking sheet about 4 to 5 inches apart. Cover loosely with foil, leaving at least 2 inches of space above the dough.

Let the dough rise in the warm rising area for about 30 minutes, or until you can judge by eye that it has almost, but not quite, doubled in bulk.

The resting period. Transfer each round of dough to the center of a 12-inch pizza pan. With the flat of your hand, pat out the dough rounds until they are about 8 inches in diameter. Cover each pan with foil and let the dough rest for 10 minutes.

Preheating the oven. While the dough is resting, preheat the oven to the highest temperature possible (500° or 550° F.). In an electric oven, place a shelf in the lowest slot; in a gas oven, remove the shelves so that the pizza pan can be set directly on the oven floor.

Shaping the crusts. Using your fingertips or the palm or heel of your hand, push one round of dough outward from the center toward the edges of its pan. Should the dough tear at any point, pinch it together and pat it flat. When the dough covers the entire bottom of the pan, use your knuckles to force it up against the sides of the pan to make a rim about ½ inch high. Repeat for the other pizza. (Unlike bread dough that is formed into loaves and rises in the pan, dough for pizza crust is baked in an almost unrisen state.)

Filling the pizzas. Pour half of the cooled sauce (about ¾ cup) into the center of each pizza. Then, with the back of a spoon, swirl the sauce outward in concentric circles, stopping when you come to within ¾ inch of the rim.

Scatter the mozzarella evenly over the two pizzas. Then sprinkle each with half the Parmesan. Finally, dribble 1 to 1½ tablespoons of olive oil over each pie.

Baking the pizzas. If you have only one oven, you can bake only one pizza at a time. In that event, bake the second pizza immediately after the first one is done.

Bake the pizza for 10 to 12 minutes. It is done when its edges are a crusty golden brown and the cheese topping has melted completely.

Serving the pizza. Cut the pizza into wedges with a pizza cutter, a pastry wheel, or a very sharp knife, and serve the slices immediately from the pan. If you are using a nonstick pizza pan, slide the pizza onto a board before cutting it to avoid possible damage to the nonstick surface.

Sweet Yeast Breads

These three sweet yeast breads of European origin—Gugelhopf, Portuguese Sweet Bread, and Babka—have an undeniable kinship. Eggs, butter, and sugar give them a golden color, a tender texture, and a delicate sweetness. In fact, they might with equal justice be called cakes rather than breads.

Traditionally, doughs for sweet yeast breads are softer than basic bread doughs, although they, too, usually require kneading.

This holds true for the Babka and the Portuguese Sweet Bread, but not for my version of the famed Gugelhopf, which must be beaten with some vigor rather than kneaded.

If your preference in breads is for those on the sweet side, these three are among the best I know. Certainly they are all ideal accompaniments for morning coffee or afternoon tea.

GUGELHOPF

Gugelhupf, kugelhupf, kugelhopf, even suglhupf—it is almost as difficult to choose the preferred spelling as it is to document the exact origin of this cakelike bread. Certainly Gugelhopf—to use the spelling I prefer—is one of the oldest of the sweet leavened breads. Although generally thought of as Austrian in origin, it is said to have been made as early as 1609 in Poland. In the eighteenth century, it became a favorite in France.

At any rate, this sweet yeast bread or coffeecake has long been such a favorite that a baking pan was named for it. The fluted Gugelhopf pan, sometimes called a "turkshead mold," is also used for other sweet breads, including Babka.

MAKES ONE 9½-INCH CAKE

The Batter:
4 cups sifted all-purpose flour
2 packages (¼ ounce each) active dry yeast
1 teaspoon salt
⅓ cup water
⅔ cup milk
¾ cup granulated sugar
1 tablespoon finely chopped lemon peel
4 eggs, at room temperature
½ pound unsalted butter (2 quarter-pound sticks), cut into
    bits and softened at room temperature
1 cup white raisins

For Preparing the Pan:
2 teaspoons butter, softened at room temperature
2 tablespoons flour
15 to 18 blanched whole almonds

For Dusting the Cake:
Confectioners' sugar

Preparing the ingredients. Measure 2 cups of the flour into a bowl. Pour the remaining 2 cups of flour, the yeast, and 1 teaspoon of salt into a 4-quart mixing bowl, and stir them together thoroughly with a fork.

In a 1-pint saucepan, combine the water, milk, granulated sugar, and lemon peel. With a small wooden spoon, stir them together until the sugar has dissolved. Over low heat warm the liquid until it feels very warm, but not hot, to the touch, or until a candy thermometer registers between 110° and 115° F.

Mixing the batter. Pour the warm liquid into the yeast and flour mixture, stirring constantly with a wooden spoon. One at a time, beat in the eggs, using the electric mixer. Then add the remaining 2 cups of flour, $\frac{1}{2}$ cup at a time, beating well after each addition. A few bits at a time, beat in the butter bits. Continue to beat vigorously for 8 to 10 minutes, or until the batter is very elastic and shines with a perceptible gloss. Add the raisins and stir the batter only long enough to distribute them evenly.

Preparing the pan. With a pastry brush and the softened butter, coat the inside of a 10-cup (9$\frac{1}{2}$-inch) Gugelhopf pan, including the cone. Sprinkle in 2 tablespoons of flour and tip the pan to coat it with a film of flour, then invert it and rap it sharply to dislodge the excess. Place an almond in each groove of the pan.

The rising period. Scrape the batter into the pan with the aid of a rubber spatula and smooth the top.

Cover the pan with a foil tent and place it in an area where a temperature of 80° to 90° F. can be maintained.

Checking frequently after the first hour, let the dough rise until it reaches a point $\frac{1}{2}$ inch from the rim of the pan; the batter must not rise further or the Gugelhopf will mushroom over as it bakes. This rising will take about 1$\frac{1}{2}$ hours.

Preheating the oven. About 15 minutes before you judge that the rising will be complete, slide an oven shelf into a middle slot and preheat the oven at 350° F.

Baking the Gugelhopf. Bake the cake for about 1 hour, or until a cake tester comes out clean. Remove the cake from the oven and let it rest for 5 minutes.

Unmolding and serving the cake. To free the Gugelhopf from the pan, run the flat of a long thin knife all around the cone. Place a wire cake rack over the pan and, grasping pan and rack together with potholders, invert them. Lift off the pan.

Let the Gugelhopf cool for at least 3 to 4 hours. Before serving it, dust the fluted top lightly with confectioners' sugar.

BABKA

Babka is Polish in origin—its name is the diminutive of the word *baba*, meaning old woman—and it bears a family resemblance to the Gugelhopf on page 293.

MAKES ONE 9½-INCH CAKE

The Dough:
3 cups sifted all-purpose flour
1 package (¼ ounce) active dry yeast
½ teaspoon salt
½ cup milk
⅓ cup granulated sugar
2 eggs, at room temperature
2 egg yolks, at room temperature
8 tablespoons unsalted butter (a quarter-pound stick), cut into
    bits and softened at room temperature
1 tablespoon finely chopped lemon peel
1 tablespoon finely chopped orange peel
½ cup white raisins

For Kneading the Dough:
1 cup unsifted all-purpose flour

For Buttering the Bowl and Pan:
4 teaspoons butter, softened at room temperature

The Glaze:
1 cup sifted confectioners' sugar
3 tablespoons milk
1 teaspoon vanilla

Preparing the ingredients. Measure 2 cups of the sifted flour into a bowl. Pour the remaining cup of sifted flour, the yeast, and the salt into a 4-quart mixing bowl and stir them together thoroughly with a fork.

In a 1-pint saucepan combine ½ cup of milk and the granulated sugar and stir with a small wooden spoon until the sugar dissolves. Over low heat warm the liquid until it feels very warm, but not actually hot, to the touch, or until a candy thermometer registers between 110° and 115° F.

Mixing the dough. Pour the warm liquid into the yeast and flour mixture, stirring constantly with a wooden spoon. Continue to stir for 2 to 3 minutes, or until the mixture becomes thick and smooth.

One at a time, beat in the eggs, then the egg yolks, using an electric mixer, if you have one. Half a cup at a time, add the 2 cups of sifted flour, beating well after each addition. Beat in the 8 tablespoons of softened butter a few bits at a time, continuing to beat until all the butter is absorbed. The dough will be very sticky.

Kneading the dough. Using only as much as you need of the 1 cup of unsifted flour reserved for kneading, lightly flour your work surface, hands, and baker's scraper, and knead the dough for 10 minutes in the manner described for soft yeast doughs (page 277). Then knead for 15 minutes in the usual fashion for basic yeast breads, pages 276–77, using the scraper occasionally if needed. When kneaded enough, the dough will be smooth and glossy.

Shape the dough into a ball.

The first rising. With a pastry brush, coat the inside of a 4-quart stainless steel or glass bowl with 2 teaspoons of the softened butter. Drop in the dough and turn it about until it is coated with butter.

Cover the bowl with a foil tent and place it in an area where a temperature of 80° to 90° F. can be maintained.

Within 1½ to 2 hours the dough will have doubled in bulk. To test it, gently poke two fingers about ½ inch into the dough. The indentations should remain. If they disappear, replace the foil tent and let the dough continue to rise until it passes the test.

Adding the fruits. Punch the dough down and turn it out on your floured work surface. Pat the dough out about 1 inch thick and sprinkle it evenly with the chopped lemon peel, the chopped orange peel, and half the raisins. Fold the dough in half and knead it lightly for a minute or two. Again flatten the dough and sprinkle it with the remaining raisins. Repeat the folding and kneading just until the fruits are evenly distributed throughout the dough.

If you are using a heavy-duty mixer with a dough hook, punch the dough down after its first rising, return it to the mixer bowl, and incorporate the lemon peel, orange peel, and all the raisins at a slow speed, being careful not to overmix lest the raisins become bruised and the dough discolored.

After you have incorporated the fruits, shape the dough into a ball, cover it loosely with foil, and let it rest for 10 minutes.

Buttering the pan. Using a pastry brush and the remaining softened butter, coat the inside of a 10-cup (9½-inch) Gugelhopf pan, including its cone.

Shaping the dough and filling the pan. Lightly flour your kneading surface and shape the dough by rolling it back and forth under your palms to make a sausagelike roll about 18 inches long. Make a ring by joining the ends of the roll and pinching and patting the joined spot until smooth.

Lift up the ring with both hands and lower it into the pan. Pat the dough, if necessary, to distribute it evenly around the cone; otherwise the babka will rise unevenly.

The second rising. Cover the pan with the foil tent and place it in the warm rising area. Let the dough rise for 1 to 1½ hours, or almost to the rim of the pan.

Preheating the oven. About 15 minutes before the final rising should be complete, slide an oven shelf into a middle slot and preheat the oven at 375° F.

Baking the babka. Bake the babka for about 40 minutes, or until a cake tester comes out clean and dry. Check after about 25 minutes; if the top appears to be browning too deeply, cover it loosely with a sheet of foil.

Glazing and serving the babka. Allow the babka to rest in the pan for 3 to 5 minutes. Then, to free it from the pan, run the flat of a long thin knife all around the cone. Place a wire cake rack over the pan and, grasping pan and rack together with potholders, invert them. Lift off the pan.

Pour the confectioners' sugar into a bowl. Add the milk and vanilla, and beat with a whisk until smooth.

Pour the glaze slowly over the fluted top of the warm cake while it is still on its rack, letting it drip down the sides. Serve the babka while it is still slightly warm. If it has cooled, preheat your oven to 325° F., wrap the babka in foil, and reheat it for a few minutes. This will not totally restore the pristine quality, but it will help considerably.

————————— ❧❦❧ —————————

PORTUGUESE SWEET BREAD

For years, during summers spent in Provincetown, Massachusetts, on Cape Cod, I was tempted daily by the Portuguese bread of a remarkable local baker. But like many before me, I failed to pry his recipe from him; and it is rumored that when he closed the bakery several years ago he took the secret back with him to his native Portugal.

This recipe, arrived at after many tries, produces loaves that are close kin to the Portuguese bread I first tasted in Provincetown. They require no special pans—the dramatically plump and handsome loaves can be shaped on a baking sheet. And any bread remaining the day after baking—this will require a certain vigilance on your part—can be toasted with extremely good results.

MAKES TWO ROUND 8- TO 9-INCH LOAVES

The Dough:
4 cups sifted all-purpose flour
2 packages (¼ ounce each) active dry yeast
½ teaspoon salt
⅓ cup milk
6 tablespoons sugar
4 eggs, at room temperature
8 tablespoons unsalted butter (a quarter-pound stick), cut into
    bits and softened at room temperature

For Kneading the Dough:
½ cup unsifted all-purpose flour

For Buttering the Bowl and Baking Sheet:
4 teaspoons butter, softened at room temperature

The Glaze:
1 egg
1 tablespoon milk

Preparing the ingredients: Measure 3 cups of the flour into a bowl and set it aside. Pour the remaining cup of flour, yeast, and salt into a 4-quart mixing bowl and stir them together thoroughly with a fork.

In a 1-pint saucepan, combine ⅓ cup of milk and the sugar,

and stir with a small wooden spoon until the sugar dissolves. Over low heat warm the liquid until it feels very warm, but not actually hot, to the touch, or until a candy thermometer registers between 110° and 115° F.

Mixing the dough. Pour the warm liquid into the yeast and flour mixture, stirring constantly with a wooden spoon until smooth. One at a time, beat in 4 eggs. Then stir in the reserved 3 cups of flour, ½ cup at a time. When stirring becomes too difficult, incorporate the remaining flour with your hands.

Now, a few bits at a time, work in the 8 tablespoons of butter, using a wooden spatula or your hands. Don't fuss with this too much, because the butter will be thoroughly distributed when you knead the dough.

Kneading the dough. Using only as much as necessary of the ½ cup of flour reserved for kneading, lightly flour your work surface, your hands, and your baker's scraper. Knead the dough for 10 minutes in the manner described for soft yeast doughs, page 277. Then knead for about 10 minutes more in the usual fashion for basic yeast breads, pages 276–77, using the scraper when necessary and adding a minimum of flour. When kneaded enough, the dough will be smooth and glossy.

Shape the dough into a compact ball.

The first rising. With a pastry brush, coat the inside of a 4-quart stainless steel or glass bowl with 2 teaspoons of the softened butter. Drop in the dough and turn it about until it is coated with butter.

Cover the bowl with a foil tent and place it in an area where a temperature of 80° to 90° F. can be maintained.

Within 1 to 1½ hours, the dough will have approximately doubled in bulk. To make sure that the rising is complete, gently poke two fingers about ½ inch into the dough. The indentations should remain. If they don't, replace the foil tent and let the dough continue to rise until it passes the test.

Buttering the baking sheet. With a pastry brush, coat a 17-by-14-inch baking sheet with the remaining softened butter.

Shaping the loaves. Punch the dough down, shape it into a compact ball, and place it on your floured work surface. With a sharp knife, cut the dough in half and pat each half into a round about 4 to 5 inches in diameter and mounded slightly in the center.

Place the rounds 6 inches apart on the buttered baking sheet.

The second rising. Cover the baking sheet loosely with foil and let the loaves rise in the warm rising area until they are almost doubled in size, in 45 minutes to 1 hour.

Preheating the oven. About 15 minutes before you judge that the rising will be complete, slide an oven shelf into a center slot and preheat the oven at 350° F.

Glazing the bread. Beat the egg and tablespoon of milk together with a fork or whisk. Using a pastry brush, gently coat the loaves with the glaze.

Baking the bread. Bake the loaves in the oven for about 45 minutes, testing them after 35 or 40 minutes. They are done when a cake tester comes out clean and dry.

Cooling the bread. Transfer the loaves to a cake rack and let the bread cool to room temperature before you serve or store it.

Yeast Batter Breads

Batter breads are, to my mind, a cross between conventional yeast breads and quick breads: they require no kneading, but they do require time for their doughs to rise. In choosing to make batter breads you need not feel that you are making a compromise in any way. Batter breads have a very special quality all their own, not the least of which is a wonderful homemade taste. They are best served when freshly baked, and I prefer to slice them just a little thicker than the kneaded breads.

BRIOCHE

A traditional French brioche can be made in many ways, all of them fairly strenuous and time-consuming. Usually a dough must be mixed, set aside to rise a number of times, and then chilled before being formed into any of the numerous classic brioche shapes.

In this recipe I have bypassed many of these procedures. This Brioche is made with a batter instead of a dough, hence its somewhat unconventional inclusion in the batter-bread category. Although the batter must be beaten vigorously for 8 to 10 minutes, you can stop the beating at any point, rest a few minutes, and then resume. It is much less arduous, of course, to use a heavy-duty mixer with a pastry arm or dough hook. Even an ordinary electric mixer can be used if it is a high-powered one.

The batter requires only two risings—the first in a bowl and the second in the coffee cans in which the loaves are baked. The final result will be a tall, round brioche (in French, a *brioche mousseline*) with a light, even, springy texture and a pale golden crust.

MAKES TWO TALL, ROUND LOAVES
4 INCHES IN DIAMETER

The Dough:
4 cups sifted all-purpose flour
1 package (¼ ounce) active dry yeast
2 teaspoons salt
½ cup milk
1 tablespoon sugar
7 eggs, at room temperature
12 tablespoons unsalted butter (1½ quarter-pound sticks), cut into bits and softened at room temperature

For Buttering the Cans and Foil Collars:
2 tablespoons butter, softened at room temperature

Preparing the ingredients. Sift 1 cup of the sifted flour, the yeast, and the salt together into a 4-quart mixing bowl. Measure 3 cups of sifted flour into another bowl.

In a 1-pint saucepan, stir together the milk and sugar. Over low heat warm the milk until it feels very warm, but not hot, to the touch, or until a candy thermometer reads between 110° and 115° F.

Mixing the batter. Slowly pour the warm milk into the yeast and flour mixture, stirring constantly with a wooden spoon. Beat in the eggs, one at a time, making sure that each is absorbed before adding the next. Beat in the remaining flour, ½ cup at a time, beating well after each addition. Now, a few bits at a time, beat in the 12 tablespoons of butter.

After all the butter has been incorporated, beat the dough vigorously for 8 to 10 minutes, until it is very elastic and shines with a perceptible gloss.

If you use an electric mixer, set it at slow speed to make the basic batter, then use medium speed after all the ingredients have been added, beating about 6 to 8 minutes, or until the batter is elastic and glossy.

The first rising. Scrape the dough down from the sides of the mixing bowl with a rubber spatula. Cover the bowl with a foil tent and place it in an area where a temperature of 80° to 90° F. can be maintained.

In about 2 to 2½ hours the dough will have approximately doubled in bulk. Depend on your eye rather than on the finger-poking method described in preceding recipes; the brioche dough is too fragile and porous. If in doubt, settle for the minimum rather than the maximum rising time to avoid the risk of your brioche having a yeasty flavor.

Preparing the cans and collars. While the dough is rising, butter the insides of two tall 1-pound coffee cans, using a pastry brush and about 1½ teaspoons of the softened butter for each can.

To make collars for the cans, cut two 12-by-14-inch pieces of foil. Fold each piece lengthwise in thirds to make 4-by-14-inch strips. Brush one side of each strip with about 1½ teaspoons of softened butter. Wrap a collar, buttered side in, around the top of each can, adjusting the foil so that it rises about 1½ inches above the can rim. Tie each collar to its can securely with string.

Filling the cans. When the dough has completed its first rising, vigorously beat it down to its original volume with a wooden spoon. Now divide the dough—it will be elastic and difficult to manage—between the two cans.

Lift up a heaping spoonful of the dough, then, with the aid of a rubber spatula, flip it into a can. Spoonful by spoonful, add dough alternately to each can. It will fill each can about half full. With a rubber spatula, scrape down any dough clinging to the sides of the can.

The second rising. Cover the cans loosely with foil and place them in the warm rising area. Checking frequently after the first 20 minutes, let the dough rise for 30 to 45 minutes, or until it reaches to within about ½ inch of the rims. It must not rise beyond that point or the brioches will mushroom over as they bake.

Preheating the oven. About 15 minutes before you judge that the last rising will be complete, slide an oven shelf into the lowest slot and preheat the oven at 375° F.

Baking the brioches. Set the can 2 or 3 inches apart on the oven shelf. Bake the brioches for 35 minutes, then test for doneness by turning the loaves out of their cans and thumping their bottoms with your knuckles. If the sound is even slightly muted, rather than hollow, remove the foil collars, return the loaves to the cans and bake them for about 5 minutes longer, or until they produce a hollow sound when thumped.

Cooling the brioches. Turn the loaves out of the cans and set them right side up on a wire cake rack. Let them cool to room temperature before serving or storing them.

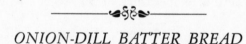

ONION-DILL BATTER BREAD

I prefer this bread with an onion topping—I feel that its rough peasant aspect is intensified by the brown-flecked baked onions—but you may substitute additional dill seeds or anything else you like, or you may omit the topping altogether and brush the baked loaf with softened butter while the bread is still warm.

MAKES ONE ROUND 8-INCH LOAF

The Batter:
2½ cups unsifted all-purpose flour
1 package (¼ ounce) active dry yeast
1 teaspoon salt
1 teaspoon dried dill weed
1 tablespoon dill seeds, slightly bruised or crushed
½ cup milk
¾ cup water
1 teaspoon sugar
2 tablespoons unsalted butter, cut into bits

For Buttering the Pan:
1 teaspoon butter, softened at room temperature

The Topping:
¼ cup coarsely chopped onions

Preparing the ingredients. Pour the flour into a 4-quart mixing bowl. Add the yeast, salt, dill weed, and dill seeds. Stir the ingredients together thoroughly with a fork.

In a 1-pint saucepan, combine the milk, water, sugar, and 2 tablespoons of butter. Over low heat warm the liquid until it feels warm, but not actually hot, to the touch, or until a candy thermometer registers between 110° and 115° F.

Mixing the batter. Slowly pour the warm liquid into the flour and yeast mixture, stirring constantly with a wooden spoon until well combined. Then beat the batter vigorously for 2 minutes. You may find the beating easier if you first allow the batter to rest for 5 minutes. Scrape down the sides of the bowl with a rubber spatula.

The first rising. Cover the bowl loosely with a foil tent and place it in an area where a temperature of 80° to 90° F. can be maintained.

Within 45 minutes to 1 hour, the batter will have nearly tripled in bulk; since you cannot test this soft mixture by poking it with your fingers, depend on your eye to judge when it has risen enough.

Buttering the pan. With a pastry brush, coat the inside of a round 8-inch cake pan with the softened butter.

The second rising. When the batter has completed its first rising, beat it down to its original volume. With a rubber spatula, scrape the batter into the cake pan and let it rest for 5 to 10 minutes. Then, if necessary, tilt the pan from side to side until the batter covers the entire surface of the pan. Sprinkle the chopped onions evenly over the top.

Cover the pan loosely with the foil tent and let the batter rise in the warm rising area for 30 to 45 minutes, or until it has risen about ½ inch above the rim of the pan. Check the rising frequently after the first 30 minutes.

Preheating the oven. About 15 minutes before you judge that the batter will have risen fully, slide an oven shelf into a middle slot and preheat the oven at 350° F.

Baking the bread. Bake the bread for 1 hour, or until the top is golden brown and feels firm to the touch.

Cooling the bread. Turn out the loaf and set it on a cake rack. Cool it to room temperature before serving or storing it.

RYE BATTER BREAD

The reason there is no recipe for a rye loaf among the basic yeast breads is that I am so enthusiastic about this Rye Batter Bread, I prefer to reserve rye for this category.

With its flavoring of caraway seeds, this is a robust bread. I like to serve it with sweet butter cut in the rather thick slices that I prefer for batter breads.

MAKES ONE 9-BY-5-INCH LOAF

The Batter:
2 cups unsifted all-purpose flour
1 package (¼ ounce) active dry yeast
2 teaspoons salt
1 tablespoon caraway seeds, slightly bruised or crushed
1¼ cups water
2 tablespoons unsulfured dark molasses
2 tablespoons unsalted butter, cut into bits
1¼ cups unsifted rye flour

For Buttering the Pan:
1 teaspoon butter, softened at room temperature

For Dusting the Loaf:
1 tablespoon rye flour

Preparing the ingredients. Measure the all-purpose flour into a 4-quart mixing bowl. Add the yeast, salt, and caraway seeds. With a fork stir the ingredients together thoroughly.

In a 1-pint saucepan, combine the water and molasses and stir with a rubber spatula until the molasses dissolves. Then drop in 2 tablespoons of butter bits. Over low heat warm the liquid until it feels very warm, but not actually hot, to the touch, or until it registers between 110° and 115° F. on a candy thermometer.

Mixing the batter. Slowly pour the warm liquid into the flour and yeast mixture, stirring constantly with a wooden spatula until well combined. Then beat the batter vigorously for 2 minutes. Add 1¼ cups of rye flour, ¼ cup at a time, beating well after each addition. With a rubber spatula, scrape down any batter clinging to the sides of the bowl.

The first rising. Cover the bowl with a foil tent and place it in an area where a temperature of 80° to 90° F. can be maintained.

Within 1 to 1¼ hours, the batter will have doubled in bulk. You will have to judge by eye, since you cannot test the soft mixture by poking it with your fingers.

Buttering the pan. With a pastry brush, coat the inside of a 9-inch loaf pan with the softened butter.

The second rising. When the first rising is complete, beat the batter down to its original volume. Then, with a rubber spatula, scrape the batter into the loaf pan, spreading it out evenly.

Sprinkle 1 tablespoon of rye flour over the top and, with your fingers, pat the batter until it fills the corners of the pan. Now press down all around the sides of the batter, forcing it to mound slightly in the center.

Cover the pan loosely with the foil tent and let the batter rise in the rising area for 45 minutes to 1 hour, or until the center mounds about ½ inch above the rim.

Preheating the oven. About 15 minutes before you judge that the rising will be complete, slide an oven shelf into a middle slot and preheat the oven at 375° F.

Baking the bread. Bake the bread for 50 minutes, then test it for doneness by turning the loaf out of its pan and thumping the bottom with your knuckles. If the sound is even slightly muted, rather than hollow, return the loaf to the pan and bake it 5 minutes longer, or until it passes the test.

Cooling the bread. Turn out the loaf and cool it, right side up, on a wire cake rack. Let the bread cool to room temperature before serving or storing it.

Quick Breads

Quick breads, as their name indicates, are the easiest of all breads to make. Because they contain no yeast, and thus require no risings, they are quick to prepare, relatively quick to bake, and, incidentally, usually quick to be consumed.

The fact that I include popovers in the same section with corn bread and Irish soda bread may come as a surprise. To me, however, popovers—whose rising is caused by steam—fit the basic description of quick breads: breads that are leavened by agents quicker-acting than yeast.

POPOVERS

Food scientists explain that it is steam that makes popovers pop and puff; the batter doesn't simply rise, it explodes. Some believe that the steam is generated more quickly if the batter is very cold and the oven and pans very hot when baking begins.

Other popover aficionados just as firmly believe that all ingredients and the pan should be at room temperature.

There is also a school that favors allowing the batter to rest for 30 minutes so that the gluten may relax, as it were, to produce popovers with a slightly more tender texture.

I have experimented with many different methods, including the startling one of pouring the batter into a cold pan in a cold oven, and only then turning on the heat. However, the rather old-fashioned method described here is the one I find the most satisfactory.

Many recipes direct the cook to pierce the popovers before the last 5 minutes or so of baking. I have omitted this step for the simple reason that I do not think it necessary. If you like your popovers to be very crisp and dry, a few minutes' additional baking is an easier way to achieve that result.

MAKES 11 POPOVERS

The Batter:
2 eggs
1 cup milk
1 cup sifted all-purpose flour
¼ teaspoon salt
2 tablespoons unsalted butter, melted and cooled

For Preparing the Pan:
2 tablespoons butter, softened at room temperature

Preheating the oven. Slide an oven shelf into the lowest slot and preheat the oven at 450° F. for at least 15 minutes.

Mixing the batter. If you are using a blender or food processor: In the container of the machine combine the eggs, milk, flour, salt, and 2 tablespoons of melted butter. Cover the container and process for about a minute (at high speed in the blender). Then turn the machine off and scrape down the sides of the container with a rubber spatula. Re-cover the container and process for another minute (at high speed in the blender). If the container is unwieldy to pour from, transfer the batter to a pitcher or a quart-size measuring cup.

If you are using an electric mixer, rotary beater, or whisk: In a medium-size mixing bowl, beat the eggs for about a minute, or until they are frothy. Pour in the milk, flour, salt, and 2 tablespoons of melted butter, and beat for 2 or 3 minutes longer, or until the batter is smooth and has the consistency of heavy cream; don't overbeat. Transfer the batter to a pitcher or a quart-size measuring cup.

Heating, buttering, and filling the pan. Place an 11-cup popover pan in the preheated oven for 5 minutes. Then remove the heated pan from the oven and, with a pastry brush and the softened butter, quickly and generously butter each cup. Immediately pour in the batter, dividing it as equally as possible; each cup should be a little more than half full.

Baking the popovers. Without wasting a moment—the pan mustn't cool—return the pan to the lowest shelf of the preheated 450° F.

oven. Bake the popovers for 15 minutes, then reduce the heat to 375° F. and continue to bake them for 20 to 25 minutes longer, or 30 to 45 minutes in all.

You might do well to check the popovers for doneness after 30 minutes, but don't be tempted to open the oven door sooner or the popovers may fall. They are done when they are a deep golden brown and have puffed about 2 inches above the rims of the cups. If you are the least bit doubtful, or if you like popovers to be very crisp, bake them slightly longer.

Serving the popovers. Remove the pan from the oven and the popovers from their cups. Should any of them tend to stick, quickly run the flat of a knife around the sides of the cups to loosen them. Serve the popovers at once. I do not recommend that you try to reheat popovers—they will never regain their initial glory.

CORN BREAD WITH CRACKLINGS

The combination of corn meal and cracklings is a deep-rooted part of our American culinary heritage. Corn, which was introduced to the early settlers by the Indians, was a staple of the colonists. The crisp bits—cracklings—left from the rendering of lard from pork fat at hog-killing time were soon found to be a delicious addition to corn bread. Today, diced salt pork, cooked until crisp, is an excellent substitute for the cracklings of frontier days.

Eaten while still warm, this crackling-enriched corn bread is, I am convinced, as good as that made by our forebears.

MAKES ONE SQUARE 8-INCH LOAF

The Salt Pork:
½ pound salt pork
2 cups water
¼ cup vegetable oil, or amount needed to make ½ cup when
    combined with fat rendered from pork (see below)

For Preparing the Pan:
2 teaspoons butter, softened at room temperature
2 tablespoons flour

The Batter:
1 cup unsifted all-purpose flour
1 tablespoon double-acting baking powder
1 tablespoon sugar
1 teaspoon salt
1½ cups yellow corn meal, preferably stone-ground
2 eggs
1 cup milk
4 tablespoons unsalted butter, melted then cooled to room
    temperature

Blanching the salt pork. Remove and discard the rind from the
salt pork, then cut the pork into ¼-inch dice. To remove excess
salt, blanch the pork in the following manner: In a 1-quart saucepan, bring the water to a full boil over high heat. Drop in the salt
pork and boil steadily, uncovered, for 2 minutes. Drain the pork in
a sieve, then spread the pieces on a paper towel and pat them dry
with another towel.

Preparing the cracklings. Drop the pork dice into a cold 8-inch
frying pan and set it over moderate heat. Stirring frequently with
a wooden spoon, fry until the pieces are crisp and golden and have
released all their fat. Pour the pork and the fat into a sieve set
over a bowl and drain the pork well. Reserve the fat. Spread the
pork dice, now cracklings, on a paper towel and pat them dry with
another towel.

Measure the rendered fat; if you have less than ½ cup, add
vegetable oil to make up the amount.

Preheating the oven. Slide an oven shelf into a middle slot and
preheat the oven at 375° F. for 15 minutes.

Preparing the pan. With a pastry brush and the softened butter
coat the inside of a square 8-inch baking pan. Sprinkle 2 tablespoons

of flour into the pan and tip it from side to side to coat the butter. Then invert the pan and rap it sharply to dislodge the excess flour.

Mixing the batter. Sift together into a 3-quart bowl 1 cup of flour, the baking powder, sugar, and salt. Add the corn meal and stir the ingredients together thoroughly with a fork.

In a small bowl, beat the eggs lightly with a fork. Then add the milk, the melted butter, and the ½ cup of reserved fat or combined fat and oil. Beat together only long enough to combine them.

Slowly pour the liquid over the corn meal and flour mixture, stirring constantly with a wooden spatula. Beat the batter briskly for a minute or two, just until the ingredients are well combined. Then, with a rubber spatula, scrape it into the pan and smooth the top. Scatter the cracklings evenly over the batter, then press them down gently with the rubber spatula to partially submerge them.

Baking the corn bread. Bake the bread for 25 minutes, or until a cake tester comes out clean.

Serving the bread. Remove the bread from the oven and let it cool in the pan for about 5 minutes. Then cut it into 2-inch squares, lift the squares from the pan with a small metal spatula, and serve them at once.

Leftover corn bread may be wrapped in foil and reheated in a warm oven.

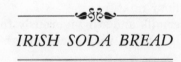

IRISH SODA BREAD

Originally, Irish soda bread was baked in an iron pot over a peat fire burning on the hearth. Today, it is still being baked in farmhouses and homes all over Ireland, and whether baked on the hearth or in an oven, it continues to be one of the Emerald Isle's most popular breads.

No two Irish housewives are likely to be in total agreement about the ingredients of soda bread, but certainly all will agree that it must include buttermilk and soda (and sometimes baking powder), but never yeast. Some versions are flavored with caraway seeds, some include raisins (or currants, which I prefer), and some have both.

The Irish serve freshly baked soda bread with great amounts of their marvelous sweet butter, together with frequently filled cups of strong, hot tea to which milk is added. In all, this makes for a truly glorious afternoon tea.

MAKES TWO ROUND 7-INCH LOAVES

The Dough:
4 cups unsifted all-purpose flour
1 tablespoon double-acting baking powder
½ teaspoon baking soda
1 teaspoon salt
1 tablespoon caraway seeds, slightly bruised or crushed
  (optional)
1 cup currants or raisins
2 cups buttermilk

For Kneading the Dough:
¼ cup unsifted all-purpose flour

For Buttering the Baking Sheet:
1 teaspoon butter, softened at room temperature

Preheating the oven. Slide an oven shelf into a middle slot and preheat the oven at 375° F. for 15 minutes.

Mixing the dough. Sift together into a 4-quart bowl 4 cups of flour, the baking powder, baking soda, and salt. Add the caraway seeds, if you like, and currants or raisins, and stir until they are distributed throughout the flour mixture.

Pour in the buttermilk and stir vigorously for a minute or two with a wooden spatula, until a very sticky dough is formed.

Kneading the dough. Flour your work surface with part of the ¼ cup of unsifted flour reserved for kneading.

Using a rubber spatula, scrape the dough out of the bowl and onto the floured surface. With lightly floured hands, shape the dough into a rough ball, then cut the ball in half with a large sharp knife.

Using only as much as you need of the remaining flour to dust your hands, the work surface, and your baker's scraper, knead each half of the dough briefly—about 8 or 10 times—in the manner described for soft yeast doughs (page 277). Shape each half into a round about 6 inches in diameter, slightly mounded in the center.

Buttering the baking sheet. With a pastry brush, coat the surface of a 17-by-14-inch baking sheet with the softened butter.

Baking the bread. Place the two loaves at least 4 inches apart on the baking sheet. With a large sharp knife, cut a cross about ¾ inch deep in the top of each loaf, extending the incisions almost to the edges of the dough.

Bake the loaves for about 35 to 40 minutes, or until they are a pale golden color and the crust feels firm to the touch.

Cooling the bread. Cool the loaves on a wire cake rack for at least 30 minutes before serving them. Any leftover bread will make excellent toast the next day, or even the day after that.

Biscuits

The word "biscuit" has so many meanings to those who use it that it is almost impossible to define it precisely. The British—and the French and Italians, too—tend to think of biscuits as cookies, as crackers, or as small, shaped cakes, some sweetened and flavored, some not. We Americans, with typical disregard for the culinary classifications of other lands, tend to limit the term "biscuits" to small cakes of leavened dough, crusty outside and moist within and nearly always served hot.

Since pioneer days, when they were part of almost every meal, American hot biscuits have increased rather than decreased in popularity. And it is easy to understand why. They are simple to make, take only minutes to bake, and the results are always predictably delicious.

Do not confuse the three hot biscuits that follow with the ready-to-bake biscuits that you find in supermarket cold cases; those commercial products can't compare in quality with the biscuits you can easily make yourself. The same holds true for the Scones, Shortbread, Sesame Seed Crackers, and Cheddar Cheese Rounds, inferior versions of which can also be bought ready prepared.

———————— ⋅⊰§⊱⋅ ————————

BAKING POWDER DROP BISCUITS

These are, by far, the quickest of all hot biscuits to make. The rapidity with which you can drop the dough, spoonful by spoonful, onto a baking sheet may tempt you to make them often.

These rich biscuits will be irregular in shape, but such lack of uniformity is, for me, part of their charm. If any biscuits are left over, rather than reheating them in the oven, split, butter, and toast them.

MAKES ABOUT 20 SMALL BISCUITS

1½ cups sifted all-purpose flour
2 teaspoons double-acting baking powder
¾ teaspoon salt
4 tablespoons chilled unsalted butter, cut into bits
4 tablespoons chilled shortening
⅔ cup milk

Preheating the oven. Slide an oven shelf into a middle slot and preheat the oven at 425° F. for at least 15 minutes.

Mixing the dough. Sift the sifted flour, baking powder, and salt together into a 3-quart mixing bowl. Add the butter and shortening. With a pastry blender, cut in the fat with small chopping motions until the mixture looks like coarse dry meal. Pour in the milk and, with a wooden spatula, stir just until a fairly smooth dough is formed. Don't overmix.

Shaping the biscuits. Scoop up a heaping teaspoonful of the batter and push it with the back of another teaspoon onto an unbuttered 17-by-14-inch baking sheet. Continue to drop mounds of dough onto the sheet, leaving about 1 inch between them. There should be about 20 when all the dough has been shaped.

Baking the biscuits. Bake the biscuits for about 15 minutes, or until they have puffed to twice their size and the tops are golden brown. Serve them at once.

HAM AND BUTTERMILK BISCUITS

Although these biscuits were first conceived as a way to use up leftover ham, I have grown so fond of them that if there is too long an interval between hams, I have been known to buy a quarter-pound of it just so that I can enjoy this delectable hot bread.

Ham-flavored biscuits are a very good accompaniment for scrambled eggs in the morning or for an omelet at lunch. With a hearty soup, they make a meal that requires only a light dessert—perhaps fresh fruit.

MAKES ABOUT SIXTEEN 2-INCH BISCUITS

The Dough:
2 cups sifted all-purpose flour
2 teaspoons double-acting baking powder
½ teaspoon baking soda
½ teaspoon salt
1 teaspoon dry mustard
⅛ teaspoon cayenne pepper
4 tablespoons chilled unsalted butter, cut into bits
About ¼ pound finely chopped lean boiled or baked ham
    (½ cup, packed down)
¾ cup buttermilk

For Preparing the Baking Sheet:
1 teaspoon butter, softened at room temperature

For Rolling the Dough:
2 tablespoons flour, or amount needed

Preheating the oven. Slide an oven shelf into a middle slot and preheat the oven at 425° F. for at least 15 minutes.

Mixing the dough. Sift 2 cups of sifted flour, the baking powder, baking soda, salt, dry mustard, and cayenne pepper together into a 4-quart bowl.

Add 4 tablespoons of chilled butter and, with a pastry blender, cut the butter bits into the flour with small chopping motions until the mixture looks like coarse meal. With a spoon, stir in the chopped ham and buttermilk. Stir only until the mixture is evenly moistened and can be gathered into a ball.

Buttering the baking sheet. With a pastry brush, coat the surface of a 17-by-14-inch baking sheet with the softened butter.

Rolling out the dough and cutting the biscuits. Lightly flour a pastry cloth and the sleeve on your rolling pin. Roll the dough out about ½ inch thick. With a 2-inch cookie cutter, cut out as many rounds as you can and place them about 1 inch apart on the baking sheet. Gently gather the remaining dough into a ball, roll it out, and cut more rounds, repeating until all the dough has been used. You should have about 20 biscuits when you are finished.

Baking the biscuits. Bake the biscuits for 18 to 20 minutes, or until they are golden brown and crusty and have almost doubled in size. Serve them at once.

WHIPPED CREAM BISCUITS

Do not be deceived into thinking that these are sweet biscuits because of the whipped cream that they contain. On the contrary, they may accompany any meal with which a hot bread would be suitable. The cream merely takes the place of butter or shortening and gives these plump biscuits a velvety softness.

MAKES 15 TO 18 BISCUITS

For Preparing the Baking Sheet:
1 teaspoon butter, softened at room temperature

The Dough:
1½ cups sifted all-purpose flour
1½ teaspoons double-acting baking powder
½ teaspoon salt
1 cup heavy cream, chilled in a medium-size mixing bowl

For Rolling the Dough:
2 tablespoons flour, or amount needed

Preheating the oven. Slide an oven shelf into a middle slot and preheat the oven at 425° F. for at least 15 minutes.

Buttering the baking sheet. With a pastry brush, coat a 17-by-14-inch baking sheet with the softened butter.

Mixing the dough. Sift 1½ cups of sifted flour, the baking powder, and salt together into a medium-size mixing bowl.

Using a wire whisk or a rotary or electric beater, beat the cream until it is stiff enough to hold its shape on the lifted beater.

With a rubber spatula, gently stir the flour mixture into the cream, ½ cup at a time. After the last addition of flour mixture, you may find stirring too difficult. In that event, incorporate the remaining flour mixture into the dough with your hands, handling it as lightly as possible in order to preserve its airiness.

Shape the dough gently into a rough ball.

Rolling out the dough and cutting the biscuits. Without losing a moment, lightly flour a pastry cloth and the sleeve on your rolling pin. Roll the dough out ¾ inch thick. With a 2-inch cookie cutter, cut out as many rounds as you can and place them about 1 inch apart on the baking sheet. Then gently gather the remaining dough together, roll it out again, and cut more rounds, repeating the process until all the dough has been used. You should have 15 to 18 biscuits.

Baking the biscuits. Bake the biscuits for about 15 minutes, or until they are golden brown and have puffed to almost double their original size. Serve them at once.

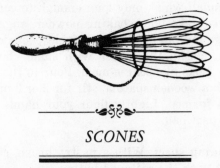

SCONES

Scones are Scottish in origin, although the derivation of their name, which goes far back in the history of the British Isles, is uncertain. What *is* certain is that scones of several kinds are still enjoyed as an accompaniment to afternoon tea.

Scones are sometimes described along seasonal lines—winter scones are baked in the oven, while summer scones are baked on a griddle. Crisp and brown on the outside, and soft and white when split open, scones are traditionally spread with a thick berry jam. If any scones remain after the initial serving (rather unlikely), they are almost as good split and toasted the following day.

The Dough:
2 eggs
⅓ cup heavy cream
2 cups sifted cake flour
2 teaspoons double-acting baking powder
2 teaspoons sugar
½ teaspoon salt
4 tablespoons chilled unsalted butter, cut into bits

For Buttering the Baking Sheet:
2 teaspoons butter, softened at room temperature

For Rolling the Dough:
2 tablespoons flour, or amount needed

The Glaze:
1 egg, lightly beaten

Preheating the oven. Slide an oven shelf into a middle slot and preheat the oven at 375° F. for 15 minutes.

Mixing the dough. Break 2 eggs into a small bowl, add the cream, and beat with a small whisk only long enough to combine them.

Sift the sifted cake flour, baking powder, sugar, and salt together into a large mixing bowl. Add 4 tablespoons of butter. With a pastry blender, cut in the butter with small chopping motions until the mixture looks like coarse meal. Pour in the egg and cream mixture and, with a wooden spatula, stir for 2 or 3 minutes, or until a moist dough is formed. Lightly flour your hands and shape the dough into a compact ball.

Buttering the baking sheet. With a pastry brush, coat a 17-by-14-inch baking sheet with the softened butter.

Rolling out the dough and cutting the scones. Lightly flour a pastry cloth and the sleeve on your rolling pin. Roll the dough out about ½ inch thick. With a 2-inch cookie cutter, cut out as many rounds as you can and place them about an inch apart on the baking sheet. Then gently gather the remaining dough together, roll it out, and cut more rounds, repeating the process until all the dough has been used. You should have about 12 rounds in all.

Glazing and baking the scones. Dip a pastry brush into the lightly beaten egg and brush the tops of the scones lightly.

Bake the scones for 18 to 20 minutes, or until they are golden brown and almost doubled in size.

Serving the scones. Serve the scones at once; or, if you prefer, transfer them to a wire cake rack and let them cool to lukewarm before serving.

SHORTBREAD

Shortbread is another Scottish specialty. It is often baked in molds with fluted edges especially designed for this rich, crumbly cake made entirely from sweet butter (no other kind will do), sugar, and flour.

MAKES A ROUND 9- OR 10-INCH CAKE

½ pound unsalted butter (2 quarter-pound sticks), cut into bits
    and softened at room temperature
½ cup sugar
2½ cups sifted all-purpose flour

Preheating the oven. Slide an oven shelf into a center slot and preheat the oven at 350° F. for 15 minutes.

Mixing the dough. Place the butter in a 4-quart bowl and beat it with a wooden spatula for a minute or two, just until it is creamy. Then stir in the sugar, and cream the mixture vigorously for about 5 minutes, until it is light and fluffy.

Half a cup at a time, add 2 cups of the flour, beating well after each addition. Then, with your hands, knead in the remaining ½ cup of flour. Continue to knead for a minute or two, until the dough is smooth.

Filling the pan. Place the dough in an unbuttered round 9- or 10-inch cake pan, preferably one with a nonstick surface. With your fingers, pat the dough over the bottom of the pan. Still using your fingers, or a small metal spatula if you like, make the surface as smooth as possible.

With a small sharp knife, score the dough into 16 wedge-shaped sections, cutting almost but not quite through the dough.

Baking the shortbread. Bake the shortbread for 30 minutes, or until the top is pale gold and the center still feels slightly soft to the touch. Be careful not to overbake; it will become very firm as it cools.

Cooling the shortbread. Remove the shortbread from the oven and let it remain in its pan until completely cool. Then run the flat of a knife around the sides of the pan to free the bread.

To unmold, invert a cake rack over the pan and, grasping the pan and rack together, carefully turn them over. Lift off the pan. Invert a plate over the bread, and holding the plate and rack together, turn the bread right side up. Remove the rack and cut the shortbread into the scored wedges.

Serve the shortbread at once, or store it in a cool place in a tightly covered canister. It will keep for at least a week, but after 2 or 3 weeks may lose its fresh flavor.

SESAME SEED CRACKERS

The use of sesame seeds in American cooking began in colonial times in the South, where they are still often called "benne seeds." Sesame seeds can be purchased in jars put out by many of the leading spice companies.

Toasted until lightly browned, the seeds give a tantalizing nut-like flavor to sesame crackers. The crackers go well with cocktails and, as with peanuts, it is very difficult to eat just one.

MAKES ABOUT SIXTY 2-INCH CRACKERS

The Dough:
½ cup sesame seeds
2 cups sifted all-purpose flour
1 teaspoon double-acting baking powder
½ teaspoon salt
8 tablespoons chilled unsalted butter (a quarter-pound stick),
    cut into bits
⅓ cup milk (more if needed)

For Rolling the Dough:
2 tablespoons flour, or amount needed

Topping (optional):
Coarse salt

Preheating the oven. Slide one oven shelf into a middle slot and another into an upper slot, then preheat the oven at 375° F. for 15 minutes.

Toasting the sesame seeds. Pour the sesame seeds into an 8-inch frying pan and set the pan over moderate heat. Stirring them constantly with a wooden spoon, toast the seeds for about 3 to 5 minutes, or until they are lightly browned. Pour the seeds into a bowl and let them cool.

Mixing the dough. Sift 2 cups of sifted flour, the baking powder, and ½ teaspoon of salt together into a large mixing bowl. With a pastry blender, cut in the butter bits with small chopping motions until the mixture looks like coarse meal. Stir in the cooled sesame seeds.

Pour in ⅓ cup of milk and, with a wooden spatula, stir for 2 to 3 minutes, or until a moist dough is formed. If the dough tends to crumble, add more milk, 1 teaspoon at a time, up to a total of 3 teaspoons. Lightly flour your hands, and gather the dough into a compact ball. With a large sharp knife, cut the ball of dough in half.

Rolling out the dough and cutting the crackers. Lightly flour a pastry cloth and the sleeve of your rolling pin. Place half the dough on the cloth and roll it out until it is as thin as possible. With a 2-inch cookie cutter, cut out as many rounds as you can and place them ½ inch apart on an ungreased 17-by-14-inch baking sheet. Gather the scraps of dough together and set them aside.

Roll out and cut rounds from the second half of the dough in the same manner and place the rounds on a second baking sheet.

With the prongs of a table fork, prick each cracker two or three times to prevent them from puffing unevenly as they bake. Sprinkle each cracker with a few crystals of coarse salt, if you like.

Baking the crackers. Bake the crackers for about 8 minutes on the two oven shelves. Do not overbake them; when done, the crackers should have colored only faintly and their centers should feel somewhat soft to the touch.

Cooling the crackers. Let the crackers cool on the baking sheets. They will firm considerably as they cool.

Using the remaining dough. While the first two batches are baking and cooling, gather all the dough scraps into a compact ball. Either wrap the dough in wax paper and refrigerate it for later use—it will keep for 2 or 3 days—or roll it out, cut it into rounds, place the crackers on the now thoroughly cooled pans, and bake them at once.

Serving or storing the crackers. Serve the crackers at once, or store them in a closely covered canister in a cool place; they will keep for at least a week. The crackers often benefit by rewarming, especially after they have been stored. Spread them on a baking sheet, heat just until warmed through in a 350° F. oven, then cool them.

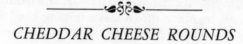

CHEDDAR CHEESE ROUNDS

Cheddar Cheese Rounds should only be made with a good sharp Cheddar-type natural cheese, never a processed variety. Although I find these cheese rounds absolutely perfect when salt and dry mustard are the only seasonings, you can, if you like, substitute for the mustard, or use in addition to it, a pinch of cayenne pepper, a dash of Tabasco or Worcestershire sauce, or any other spicy ingredient you like.

If you don't want to bake the entire batch of cheese rounds at one time, simply roll the dough into cylinders and chill it, then cut and bake only as many rounds as you want. The remaining dough, well wrapped in foil or plastic, will keep for several days in the refrigerator or for several weeks in a freezer. Thaw frozen dough before you try to slice it.

MAKES ABOUT 6 DOZEN

The Dough:
8 tablespoons unsalted butter (a quarter-pound stick), cut into
    bits and softened at room temperature
½ pound sharp Cheddar-type natural cheese, finely grated
    (about 2 cups, packed down), at room temperature
½ teaspoon salt
½ teaspoon dry mustard
1 cup sifted all-purpose flour

For Flouring the Work Surface:
1 to 2 tablespoons flour, or amount needed

Mixing the dough. In a 3-quart bowl, beat the butter with a wooden spatula for a minute or two, until creamy. Add the grated cheese, salt, and dry mustard, and beat the mixture vigorously until well combined, a matter of 2 or 3 minutes.

Beat in 1 cup of flour, ¼ cup at a time. Then beat for another minute or two, until the dough is malleable enough to be shaped into a compact ball.

Shaping and chilling the dough. With a sharp knife, cut the ball of dough in half. Squeeze each half into a rough cylinder.

Flour your work surface lightly and place one of the cylinders on it. Then, with the palms of your hands, roll the dough back and forth into a compact, evenly shaped roll about 7½ inches long and 1 inch in diameter. As you roll, pat both ends inward frequently to make them as flat as possible. Shape the second half of the dough the same way.

Wrap each roll in wax paper, plastic, or foil, and refrigerate for at least an hour, or until firm.

Preheating the oven. Slide one oven shelf into a middle slot and another into an upper slot, and preheat the oven at 350° F. for 15 minutes.

Slicing the rounds. Using a serrated knife, cut one of the rolls into ¼-inch slices; one roll makes about 36 rounds. Arrange the rounds about 1 inch apart on two ungreased 17-by-14-inch baking sheets.

Baking the cheese rounds. Bake the rounds for 8 to 10 minutes. They are done when their edges have colored to a light golden brown and their centers still feel slightly soft to the touch. Watch them carefully after 7 minutes or so lest they scorch.

Remove the rounds from the baking sheets with a small metal spatula and cool them on wire cake racks.

If you intend to bake rounds from the second roll immediately, be sure to let the pans cool thoroughly before placing the second batch on them.

Serving or storing the cheese rounds. Serve the cheese rounds at once, or store them in a tightly covered canister in a cool place. They will keep for at least a week, when properly stored. To serve them after they have been stored, spread them on a baking sheet and heat them in a 350° F. oven just until warmed through, then cool them.

Baking: Cakes

*W*hen I first contemplated the task of choosing cake recipes for this book, I thought of the countless cakes I have eaten here and abroad, to say nothing of the ones I have baked in my own kitchen. As I considered each delicious cake in turn, it became clear that the collection must include not only the best of our own American cakes, but those of other countries, all of which should be in the repertory of every baker.

To be sure, the cakes I finally chose reflect my personal taste, but I have a larger aim in presenting them in this book. Each recipe illustrates a particular cakemaking technique or a combination of techniques—creaming, beating, whipping, folding—and the ways of using those techniques to produce cakes that vary greatly in texture.

The recipes also show you how widely individual cakes differ, not only in texture but in form. The shape of a cake, besides often being a clue to its identity, seems to affect its character as well. A

German Sandtorte (sand cake), for example, wouldn't taste quite the same to me were it baked in a loaf pan instead of a traditional mold. By the same token, a pound cake should be baked in a loaf pan, and a multilayered coconut cake would be far less majestic were it square rather than round.

The fillings in this section range from the simplest—sweetened whipped cream—to a tart filling based on English lemon curd. In the sponge roll, the pineapple cream filling is perhaps more important than the cake; the sponge is merely a light cloak for the filling.

The frosting on the cake is, for many people, the raison d'être for the cake itself. There are frostings in this section that are sweet enough to satisfy the most intense craving—especially the chocolate frosting on the Black-on-Black Chocolate Layer Cake and the white frosting, which is basically an Italian meringue, on the Coconut Layer Cake.

Ingredients for Cakes

Flour. The recipes in this section specify either all-purpose flour or cake flour. Never substitute one for the other. To assure you of as much predictability as possible in my recipes that call for all-purpose flour, I have used the same brand (Gold Medal) of flour in all my tests, primarily because it is widely available. If you can't find it, try other brands until you find one that gives good results.

Cake flour is a finely milled white flour with a low gluten content that makes it eminently suitable for cakes. Make sure that the cake flour you buy is not "self-rising," which, like self-rising all-purpose flour, contains baking powder and salt and is actually a mix.

Baking powder. Baking powder should be double-acting so as to release a fraction of its gas into the batter when moistened, and the rest of its leavening power when the batter is exposed to heat. If you must use single-acting baking powder, there should be no delay between the mixing of the batter and baking it if you would have the batter rise to its full height.

Baking soda. When a batter is made with an acid liquid such as buttermilk, sour milk, or sour cream, baking soda is always used, often together with baking powder. When baking soda encounters the acid in the liquid, it produces carbon dioxide gas that leavens the mixture.

Eggs. In cakes, the indispensable egg plays a starring role. Besides enriching, coloring, and moistening a cake, eggs also act as a leavener. Whole eggs added to a batter have the singular ability to expand slightly when exposed to heat. And the air held in stiffly beaten egg whites expands—and thus leavens—to a much greater degree.

Ideally, eggs for a cake should be 3 or 4 days old. New-laid eggs, for complex chemical reasons, cannot be beaten to the maximum volume for their size. The eggs in all my recipes should be the "large" size.

Butter. The best butter for baking—and for that matter, everything else—is unsalted ("sweet") butter made from sweet cream and graded AA or A by the U.S. Department of Agriculture. Although even the best grade of salted butter made from sweet cream is undesirable for baking, it will not necessarily be catastrophic if you use it, even though the amount of salt varies a great deal from brand to brand. If you must use salted butter, make sure it is as mildly salted as possible and reduce by one-half the salt called for in any of the recipes.

Margarine may be substituted measure for measure for butter in any cake recipe, but the results, though satisfactory, will not be spectacular.

Liquids. The soft, moist, and often very rich texture of cakes usually results from their having been moistened in large part, or even wholly, with eggs. The eggs are, in effect, the liquid in the batter. When a true liquid is used in a cake, it is usually milk, buttermilk, or sour cream. Water is rarely used in cake batters.

Milk gives cakes a soft crust and a luxurious crumb. Buttermilk or sour cream, when combined with baking soda (and often baking powder as well), tends to form more carbon dioxide gas in a cake batter than sweet milk in combination with baking powder does. Consequently, buttermilk or sour cream is frequently used in a comparatively dense batter to give the extra leavening power needed for lightness.

Sugars and other sweeteners. Sugar, or a sweetener of some other kind, is used in most of the recipes in this section. When sugar is listed without further description, ordinary granulated sugar is meant; other sweeteners—superfine sugar, for example—are indicated by name.

When a recipe calls for brown sugar, I mean dark-brown sugar, not light-brown sugar and not granulated brown (or Brownulated) sugar, which I find unp edictable when used in baking.

Confectioners' sugar, frequently called "powdered sugar," is used mainly in frostings or for dusting the tops of cakes.

Liquid sweeteners, such as molasses and corn syrup, are not interchangeable with dry sugars for baking purposes. They are used for the particular flavor and extra moisture they contribute. Molasses should be the dark kind and unsulfured; blackstrap molasses is unpleasantly bitter and not suitable for baking. Corn syrup should be the light kind; dark corn syrup is too sweet for these recipes.

Do not, under any circumstances, substitute one sweetener for another in whatever it is you are baking. Different types of dry sugars and liquid sweeteners have different sweetening powers.

Salt. At first glance, salt and sugar might appear to be antithetical when they appear together in a list of recipe ingredients. Yet the reverse is true. Salt, in minimal amounts, has the curious ability to intensify flavors without making itself known as salt. Moreover, salt added to the creamed butter, sugar, and eggs for a cake stabilizes certain elements in the butter and eggs, thus making it less likely that the mixture will curdle.

In view of these facts, it is imperative that you use exactly the amount of salt called for in each recipe, reducing the quantity by half *only* when you must use salt butter in place of the sweet butter specified in the recipes.

Note: Fuller descriptions of most of these ingredients are given in the "Culinary Glossary."

Techniques for Making Cakes

Sifting dry ingredients. When a recipe requires that you sift dry ingredients together, set the sifter in a large bowl, then measure the ingredients into the sifter. This prevents the loss of any part of an ingredient.

Beating egg whites. The best way is to beat egg whites in an unlined copper bowl, if possible, with a balloon whisk or rotary beater; any other bowl will do, if it must, except an aluminum one. Or, if you prefer, you can use an electric mixer.

Mixing the batter. All the cake recipes in this section have been written for an electric mixer, but you can easily make the cakes by hand. Except for the extra effort and time, there is really little difference in procedures. Creaming butter and sugar by hand, for example, will take at least 10 to 12 minutes rather than the 7 minutes or so that I indicate in the recipes. Similarly, count on more time to whip cream or to beat eggs with a whisk or a rotary beater.

Incorporating eggs, liquid, and flour, if you hand beat vigorously, will take only 2 or 3 minutes longer than if you were to use a machine.

As for beating the finished batter, I would suggest that you underbeat rather than risk overbeating, if there is any question in your mind. For, unlike bread doughs, in which the gluten in the flour must be developed by beating and kneading, cake batters are at their best when the gluten is least developed. Pay particular attention to the machine-beating time indicated in the recipes, and do not overdo hand beating if you don't use an electric mixer.

The cake pans. Be sure to use the size pan specified in each recipe. Should you use a larger or smaller pan, you run several risks. If the pan is too small, the dough may overflow during baking; if it is too large, the dough may bake too quickly.

Filling the cake pans. Spoon heavy batters in the pan, then spread them with a rubber spatula. If the batter doesn't contain beaten egg whites, lift the pan 4 inches above the counter and drop it two or three times to drive out air bubbles.

Pour fluid cake batters into the pan to prevent air bubbles from forming.

Baking the cake. If you find that your cakes tend to brown unevenly, your oven has some areas that are hotter than others. To cope with these "hot spots," wait until the cake has risen to its full height—this usually requires about 25 minutes or so, especially if it is in a deep pan—then shift the pan or pans quickly about from time to time for even browning.

To determine when a cake has finished baking, insert a cake tester into the center of the thickest part of the cake. On removal, it will be clean and dry if the cake is done, damp or crumby if not.

For high-altitude baking, consult the "Culinary Glossary" (page 453).

Cooling the cake. Unless a recipe specifically directs otherwise, always cool cakes on wire racks where the air can circulate freely. If a cake is allowed to remain in its pan for more than a short "resting" period, it continues to cook.

Storing the cake. In general, the moister the cake the longer it will keep. Among the cakes in this section that can be stored for several days in a cool place, loosely wrapped in foil or plastic, are the Sandtorte, pound cake, applesauce ring, and chocolate cake.

SANDTORTE

Sandtorte, or "sand cake," in its English translation, seems a strange name for what is really a rather rich cake, a bit reminiscent of pound cake. It is a favorite not only with the Germans, but with the Danes and Russians, too. The term "sand" no doubt stems from the slightly grainy texture of the original cake, which was (and sometimes still is) made with potato flour.

This recipe is based on a German version which traditionally calls for half cornstarch and half flour as the basic dry ingredients. In Germany, Sandtorte often appears at the late-afternoon kaffee klatsch, where it is served with the strong coffee the Germans so cherish.

MAKES ONE 8-INCH CAKE

For Preparing the Pan:
2 teaspoons butter, softened at room temperature
2 tablespoons flour

The Cake Batter:
1¼ cups sifted cake flour
¾ cup sifted cornstarch
2 teaspoons double-acting baking powder
½ pound unsalted butter (2 quarter-pound sticks), softened at room temperature
1 cup granulated sugar
¼ teaspoon salt
4 eggs
2 teaspoons vanilla
1 tablespoon finely chopped lemon peel

For Dusting the Cake:
Confectioners' sugar

Preparing the pan. With a pastry brush, spread 2 teaspoons of softened butter on the bottom and sides of an 8-cup (9½-inch) Gugelhopf pan, including its cone. Add 2 tablespoons of flour and, holding the pan sideways over a sheet of wax paper, rotate it so the flour spreads evenly over the buttered surfaces. Invert the pan and rap it to dislodge excess flour.

Preheating the oven. Slide an oven shelf in a middle slot and preheat the oven at 325° F. for 15 minutes.

Mixing the batter. Sift the sifted cake flour, sifted cornstarch, and baking powder together, and set aside.

In the large bowl of your electric mixer, cream ½ pound of

softened butter at medium speed for about 1 minute, then slowly pour in the granulated sugar and the salt, continuing to beat.

Stop the machine after 2 minutes and scrape down the sides of the bowl with a rubber spatula. Increase the speed to high and beat for another 5 minutes, or until the mixture has lost most of its granular texture and is fluffy and light.

Lower the speed to medium and beat in ¼ cup of the reserved flour mixture. Then, one at a time, beat in the eggs, incorporating each one completely before adding the next. Beat in the vanilla and chopped lemon peel. Beat in the remaining flour mixture ½ cup at a time, lowering the speed before each addition, then raising it to incorporate the flour.

After all the ingredients have been added, stop the machine and scrape down the sides of the bowl with a spatula. Then beat the batter at high speed for about a minute.

Baking the cake. With a rubber spatula, scrape the batter into the prepared pan, then smooth the top. To eliminate any air pockets in the batter, lift the pan about 4 inches above your work surface and drop it two or three times.

Bake the cake for 1 hour, or until a cake tester comes out clean and dry.

Remove the cake from the oven and let it rest in the pan for 5 minutes.

Unmolding and serving the cake. To free the cake from the pan, run a long thin knife all around the cone. Invert a wire cake rack over the pan and, grasping pan and rack together with potholders, turn them over. Lift the pan off. Cool the cake to room temperature.

Just before serving, dust the fluted top of the cake with confectioners' sugar.

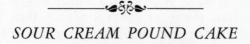

SOUR CREAM POUND CAKE

In Finland, this spicy loaf cake is called *kermakakku* and is a national favorite. Americans of Finnish ancestry dust the cake with confectioners' sugar and cut it into very thin serving slices. You may wish, as many Finns do, to add about a teaspoonful of ground cardamom or ginger to the batter.

For Preparing the Pan:
2 teaspoons butter, softened at room temperature
2 tablespoons flour

The Cake Batter:
1¾ cups sifted all-purpose flour
2 teaspoons double-acting baking powder
1 teaspoon baking soda
½ teaspoon ground cinnamon
8 tablespoons unsalted butter (a quarter-pound stick), softened
    at room temperature
1 cup granulated sugar
⅛ teaspoon salt
3 eggs
1 cup sour cream
1 teaspoon vanilla

For Dusting the Cake (optional):
Confectioners' sugar

Preparing the pan. With a pastry brush, spread 2 teaspoons of softened butter on the bottom and sides of a 9-by-5-inch loaf pan. Add the 2 tablespoons of flour and, holding the pan sideways over a sheet of wax paper, move it from side to side to spread the flour evenly over all buttered surfaces. Invert the pan and rap it to dislodge the excess flour.

Preheating the oven. Slide an oven shelf into a middle slot and preheat the oven at 350° F. for 15 minutes.

Mixing the batter. Sift the sifted flour, baking powder, baking soda, and cinnamon together, and set aside.

In the large bowl of your electric mixer, cream 8 tablespoons of butter at medium speed for about a minute, then, continuing to beat, slowly pour in the granulated sugar and the salt.

Stop the machine after 2 minutes and scrape down the sides of the bowl with a rubber spatula. Then increase the speed to high and beat for another 5 minutes, or until the mixture is fluffy and light.

Lower the speed to medium and, one at a time, beat in the eggs, incorporating each one completely before adding the next. Beat in the sour cream and vanilla.

Beat in the reserved flour mixture ½ cup at a time, lowering the speed before each addition, then raising it to incorporate the flour. Stop the machine and scrape down the sides of the bowl with a rubber spatula. Then beat the batter at high speed for about a minute.

Baking the cake. With the aid of a rubber spatula, scrape the batter into the prepared pan, then smooth the top. To eliminate any air pockets in the batter, lift the pan about 4 inches above your work surface and drop it two or three times.

Bake the cake for 1 hour or until a cake tester comes out clean and dry. Remove the cake from the oven and let it rest in the pan for 5 minutes.

Turning out and serving the cake. To remove the cake from the pan, first run the flat of a knife around the sides of the pan. Then invert a wire cake rack over the cake and, grasping rack and pan together with potholders, turn them over. Lift off the pan and turn the loaf right side up. Let the cake cool to room temperature.

If you wish, dust the cake generously with confectioners' sugar just before serving it.

APPLESAUCE, DATE, AND PECAN RING

This might very well be considered a year-round fruit cake. Lighter than traditional fruit cakes, it has many of the same qualities. I suspect that once you try it, you may very well add it to your list of cakes treasured for holiday giving.

The ring keeps very well for 2 or 3 days at room temperature, covered loosely with foil or plastic wrap. (The flavor actually improves after a day or two.) For a longer period, storage in the refrigerator is preferable; there the cake will keep almost indefinitely if well wrapped. And it can, of course, be frozen.

Although the recipe calls for the use of a ring mold—I prefer the smaller slices this makes possible—a 9-inch loaf pan may be substituted. In that event, increase the baking time by 10 to 15 minutes, testing the cake frequently for doneness.

MAKES A 9½-INCH RING OR A 9-BY-5-INCH LOAF

For Preparing the Pan:

1 tablespoon butter, softened at room temperature

2 tablespoons flour

The Batter:

1½ cups applesauce

1 cup dried currants

2 cups boiling water

24 pitted dates (about 1 cup)

1 cup pecan halves

2 cups sifted all-purpose flour

½ teaspoon double-acting baking powder

½ teaspoon baking soda

½ teaspoon ground cloves

1 teaspoon ground cinnamon

8 tablespoons unsalted butter (a quarter-pound stick), softened
   at room temperature

1 cup sugar

⅛ teaspoon salt

1 egg

1 teaspoon vanilla

Preparing the ring mold. With a pastry brush, spread 1 tablespoon
of softened butter on the bottom and sides of a 6-cup ring mold. Add
2 tablespoons of flour and, holding the pan sideways over a sheet
of wax paper, rotate it so the flour evenly covers the buttered surfaces. Invert the pan and rap it to dislodge the excess flour.

Preparing the ingredients. Place the applesauce in a fine-meshed
sieve set over a bowl. Let it drain for at least 15 minutes. Then
discard the liquid in the bowl and measure out 1 cup of the drained
applesauce, setting aside any excess.

Soak the currants in the boiling water for 10 minutes. Drain
them in a sieve, spread them on a double layer of paper towels, and
pat them dry with more towels.

Using kitchen scissors, cut the dates into ¼-inch pieces. Then,
with a large sharp knife and a chopping board, chop the pecans as
fine as possible.

Sift 2 cups of sifted flour, the baking powder, baking soda,
cloves, and cinnamon together, and set aside.

Preheating the oven. Slide an oven shelf into a middle slot and
preheat the oven at 350° F. for 15 minutes.

Mixing the batter. In the large bowl of your electric mixer cream 8 tablespoons of butter at medium speed for about a minute; then, still beating, slowly pour in the sugar and salt.

Stop the machine after 2 minutes and scrape down the sides of the bowl with a rubber spatula. Increase the speed to high and beat for about 6 minutes, or until the mixture has lost most of its granular texture and is fluffy and light.

Lower the speed to medium and in succession beat in the egg, vanilla, and drained applesauce.

Lowering the speed before each addition, then raising it afterward to incorporate the flour, beat in the flour mixture ½ cup at a time. When all the flour has been added, stop the machine, scrape down the sides of the bowl with the spatula, then beat at high speed for 2 minutes. Stir in the currants, dates, and pecans.

Baking the cake. With the aid of the rubber spatula, scrape the batter into the prepared mold and smooth the top. To eliminate any air pockets in the batter, lift the pan about 4 inches above your work surface and drop it two or three times.

Bake the cake for 50 minutes, or until a cake tester comes out clean and dry. If the tester is damp, bake the cake for 5 to 10 minutes longer, or until it passes the test.

Remove the cake from the oven and let it rest in the pan for 10 minutes.

Unmolding and serving the cake. To free the cake from the mold, run the flat of a long thin knife around the sides of the pan and around the cone. Invert a wire cake rack over the mold and, grasping mold and rack together with potholders, turn them over. Lift off the mold and turn the ring right side up on the rack, protecting your hands with a cloth.

Let the cake cool to room temperature on the rack before serving it. It will, however, have a superior flavor if it is allowed to rest for at least 4 to 5 hours.

FRENCH CHERRY CUSTARD CAKE

This should probably not be called a cake at all, but I am far too enamored of it to deprive you, for purely semantic reasons, of the recipe for one of the easiest and most charming desserts I know.

Like its progenitor, the French *clafouti*, this custard cake is made with what is essentially a pancake batter poured over fruit and baked. However, because my recipe calls for less flour and more eggs, the result is more custardlike than the traditional *clafouti*.

If the dish in which it is baked is an attractive one, you can serve the warm "cake," sprinkled with confectioners' sugar, directly from the dish. However, I prefer to unmold it. And I must caution you to expect the dessert to fall as it cools; this is basic to the nature of the batter.

Although the recipe lists 2 cups of cherries, you can limit the cherries to 1 cup if you prefer, or you can substitute any fruit you like. You must, however, be absolutely certain that the fruit is not only thoroughly drained, but as free of surface moisture as possible.

MAKES A SQUARE 8-INCH CAKE

For Buttering the Baking Dish:
2 teaspoons butter, softened at room temperature

The Batter:
2 cups cherries (canned Bing cherries, pitted and drained; or frozen sweet cherries, thawed and drained; or fresh sweet cherries, pitted)
4 eggs
1½ cups milk
½ cup sifted all-purpose flour
¼ cup granulated sugar
⅛ teaspoon salt
1 tablespoon vanilla

For Dusting the Cake:
Confectioners' sugar

Preheating the oven. Slide an oven shelf into a middle slot and preheat the oven at 350° F. for 15 minutes.

Preparing the baking dish. With a pastry brush and the butter, coat the inside of a cake pan 8 inches square and 2 inches deep.

Preparing the cherries. Spread the drained cherries out in a single layer on a double thickness of paper towels and pat them thoroughly dry with more towels. Spread the cherries evenly in the baking dish.

Mixing the batter. If you are using a blender or food processor: In the container combine the eggs, milk, flour, granulated sugar, salt, and vanilla. Cover the container and process in the blender at high speed for about a minute, or in the food processor for 15 to 20 seconds. Turn off the machine and scrape down the sides of the container with a rubber spatula. Replace the cover of the container and process the batter for another minute at high speed in the blender and another 15 to 20 seconds in the food processor.

If you are using an electric mixer, rotary beater, or whisk: Place the eggs in a medium-size mixing bowl and beat for about a minute, or until they are frothy. Pour in the milk, flour, granulated sugar, salt, and vanilla, and beat the batter for 2 or 3 minutes longer, or until it is smooth.

Slowly pour the batter over the cherries in the baking dish.

Baking the cake. Bake the cake for about 1½ hours. Begin testing after 1¼ hours; the cake is done when the batter has set into a custardlike mass and a cake tester comes out clean.

Let the cake cool in its pan until lukewarm.

Unmolding and serving the cake. Run the flat of a knife around the sides of the pan to free the cake. Invert a large serving platter over the pan and, grasping pan and plate together, turn them over. Lift off the pan.

Dust the cake with confectioners' sugar and serve it at once.

PINEAPPLE CREAM SPONGE ROLL

Ideally, this sponge roll, one of the most delicate of desserts, should be served as soon as it is assembled, although it can be refrigerated for up to 30 minutes.

The chief component—the sponge cake—may be prepared hours in advance. You may also prepare the pineapple, cover it with plastic wrap, and refrigerate it. Then, before serving time, all you have to do is whip the cream, combine the filling, and assemble the roll; with practice, this can be accomplished in a matter of minutes.

For Preparing the Pan:
2 tablespoons butter, softened at room temperature
2 tablespoons flour

The Sponge Cake:
6 egg yolks
½ cup granulated sugar
1 teaspoon vanilla
6 egg whites
¼ teaspoon salt
¾ cup sifted all-purpose flour
1 teaspoon double-acting baking powder

For Sugaring the Cake:
2 tablespoons granulated sugar

The Filling:
1½ cups drained, finely chopped canned pineapple, preferably
    packed in its own juice (a 20-ounce can)
1 tablespoon light corn syrup
1 cup heavy cream, chilled in a medium-size bowl

For Dusting the Roll:
Confectioners' sugar

Preheating the oven. Slide an oven shelf into a middle slot and preheat the oven at 375° F. for 15 minutes.

Preparing the pan. With a pastry brush, butter the bottom and sides of a 12-by-18-inch jelly-roll pan with 1 tablespoon of the softened butter. Then cut a sheet of wax paper 24 inches long. Pat it down securely in the pan, allowing a few inches of paper to extend over each end. Brush the wax paper in the pan evenly with the remaining butter; don't butter the overhanging ends. Sprinkle 2 tablespoons of flour into the lined pan and tip the pan in all directions to spread the flour evenly. Then invert the pan and rap it sharply to dislodge the excess flour.

Mixing the batter. Combine the egg yolks, ¼ cup of granulated sugar, and vanilla in the large bowl of your electric mixer. Beat at high speed for 3 to 5 minutes, or until the mixture is thick and pale yellow.
    Pour the egg whites and salt into a large mixing bowl, preferably one of unlined copper; any other bowl will do except one made of aluminum. With a balloon whisk or a rotary beater, beat the whites for a moment or two, until they thicken lightly and begin

to foam. Then pour in the remaining ¼ cup of granulated sugar and continue to beat until the whites form firm peaks on the beater when it is lifted. With a rubber spatula, scrape the whites over the egg yolk mixture.

Working quickly, combine the sifted flour and baking powder and sift them over the egg whites. Then fold the ingredients together with a rubber spatula, stopping as soon as no streaks of flour are visible.

Pour the batter into the prepared pan, using the rubber spatula to spread the batter lightly and evenly over the entire surface and into the corners. Do not fuss with this too much or you will deflate the airy mixture.

Baking the cake. Bake the cake for 13 to 15 minutes. The cake is done when it is well puffed and the center feels springy to the touch.

Cooling the cake. Remove the cake from the oven and let it rest in the pan for 2 or 3 minutes. During this period the cake will lose its puffiness. Sprinkle 2 tablespoons of granulated sugar evenly over the cake.

Unmold the cake in the following fashion: Place two 24-inch-long sheets of wax paper in a double layer over the sugared cake. Then, protecting your hands with potholders, grasp the two ends of the pan, hold the covering paper taut, and turn the paper-covered cake over onto your work surface, one of the long sides facing you. Gently lift off the pan and carefully peel the wax lining paper away from the cake. With a sharp knife, cut away all four crusty edges from the sheet of cake.

Loosely roll up the cake, together with the doubled wax paper on which it rests, beginning with the long edge nearest you. Cover it with a kitchen towel to prevent it from drying out. The roll may rest in this fashion for up to 6 hours before filling; or you may fill it as soon as it has cooled thoroughly.

Making the filling. In a small bowl, stir together the drained pineapple and the corn syrup.

Using a whisk or a rotary or electric beater, beat the cream in its chilled bowl until it is stiff enough to stand in firm peaks. Gently fold in the pineapple mixture with a rubber spatula.

Assembling and serving the sponge roll. Remove the towel and carefully unroll the cake and smooth out the wax paper on which it rests. With a rubber spatula, spread the pineapple filling evenly over its entire surface. Then roll up the cake and its filling in this way: Grasp the edge of the wax paper nearest to you and parallel to the length of the cake, and lift the paper, causing the cake to roll gently away from you; end with the seam side down. With two large spatulas, lift the cake onto a long jelly-roll board or a serving platter.

Ideally, the roll should be served at once. If necessary, you may refrigerate it for up to 30 minutes; kept any longer, the roll may become soggy.

Just before serving, dust the roll with confectioners' sugar.

ORANGE GINGERBREAD UPSIDE-DOWN CAKE

Rarely have I been so charmed by any bit of Americana as I was by a small cookbook published by The Great Smoky Mountains Natural History Association; and I must confess that a recipe in it inspired this gingerbread. However, with my passion for butter, I have of course substituted it for the original shortening, and I have also changed the original fruit—apples—to the thin orange slices, which give this upside-down cake its very unusual character.

MAKES ONE ROUND 8-INCH CAKE

For Preparing the Pan:
2 tablespoons butter, cut into bits
½ cup granulated sugar
¾ teaspoon ground cinnamon
2 medium unpeeled navel oranges, cut crosswise into ¼-inch
    slices and end slices discarded

The Batter:
1¼ cups sifted all-purpose flour
¾ teaspoon baking soda
¾ teaspoon ground ginger
½ teaspoon ground cinnamon
4 tablespoons unsalted butter, softened at room temperature
¼ cup dark-brown sugar
¼ teaspoon salt
1 egg
½ cup unsulfured dark molasses
½ cup buttermilk

The Whipped Cream:
1 cup heavy cream, chilled in a medium-size bowl
2 teaspoons confectioners' sugar
1 teaspoon vanilla

Preheating the oven. Slide an oven shelf into a middle slot and preheat the oven at 350° F. for 15 minutes.

Preparing the pan. Melt 2 tablespoons of butter in a round 8-inch cake pan set over low heat; don't let the butter brown. Remove the pan from the heat. As evenly as possible, sprinkle the granulated sugar over the butter, then sprinkle the sugar with ¾ teaspoon of cinnamon.

Place an orange slice in the center of the pan, then overlap the other slices around it in a circle that covers most of the bottom. If the oranges are quite large, you may wish to cut the rounds in half before overlapping the slices.

Mixing the batter. Sift together the sifted flour, baking soda, ginger, and ½ teaspoon of cinnamon, and set aside.

In the large bowl of your electric mixer, cream 4 tablespoons of softened butter at medium speed for about 1 minute, then, continuing to beat the butter, slowly pour in the dark-brown sugar and salt.

Stop the machine after 1 minute and scrape down the sides of the bowl with a rubber spatula. Increase the speed to high and beat for another 3 minutes, or until the mixture is fluffy and light. Lower the speed to medium and drop in the egg. When it has been thoroughly absorbed, slowly pour in the molasses and continue to beat until the dark mixture becomes a light and uniform mocha color.

Lower the speed and beat in about half the reserved flour mixture, then raise the speed to incorporate the flour. Add the buttermilk, first lowering the speed, then raising it again. Varying the speed in the same fashion, add the remaining flour, then beat the batter at high speed for about a minute longer, or until it is completely smooth.

With the aid of a rubber spatula, scrape the batter over the oranges in the prepared pan, spreading it out evenly.

Baking the cake. Bake the cake for 20 minutes in the middle of the preheated 350° F. oven. Then turn down the heat to 325° F. and bake the cake for 25 minutes longer. Now check the cake with a cake tester. If it comes out dry, the cake is done; if it comes out the slightest bit damp, bake the cake for 5 minutes longer, or until it passes the test.

Let the cake rest for 5 minutes before turning it out of the pan.

Unmolding and cooling the cake. Run the flat of a thin knife all around the sides of the pan to free the cake. Invert a round cake plate over the pan and, grasping pan and plate together with potholders, turn them over. Still holding them firmly, rap plate and pan on the table; the cake should drop out easily.

If any bits of glaze should cling to the pan, you can easily transfer them to the cake with a small spatula. Let the cake cool to lukewarm.

Serving the cake. Just before serving the cake, whip the cream in its chilled bowl with a whisk or a rotary or electric beater, beating it just until it forms soft peaks. Then add the confectioners' sugar and vanilla and continue to beat until the cream holds its shape on the lifted beater.

Transfer the cream to an attractive bowl and serve it separately with the cake.

WALNUT TORTE

In Vienna it is said, "A torte is a round cake, but not every round cake is a torte."

The "round cake" that follows is very much in the Viennese tradition. It is less ephemeral, perhaps, than certain of the Viennese tortes calling for great baking skill, but even when undertaken by a baker of only modest experience, my Walnut Torte is almost certain to succeed.

A further merit of this torte is that it will keep for several days, loosely covered with foil or plastic wrap. Then it is an easy matter to whip the cream and fill and frost the torte just before serving time.

For Preparing the Pan:
2 teaspoons butter, softened at room temperature
1 tablespoon flour

The Torte:
3 egg yolks
½ cup granulated sugar
1 teaspoon vanilla
½ cup ground walnuts (ground in a rotary nut grater or food
   processor, not in a blender)
¼ cup graham cracker crumbs, finely crushed
3 egg whites
¼ cup sifted all-purpose flour
½ teaspoon double-acting baking powder

The Filling and Frosting:
1 cup heavy cream, chilled in a medium-size mixing bowl
2 teaspoons confectioners' sugar
1 teaspoon vanilla

The Garnish:
1 tablespoon ground walnuts or 8 small candied violets
   (optional)

Preheating the oven. Slide an oven shelf into a center slot and preheat the oven at 375° F. for 15 minutes.

Preparing the pan. With a pastry brush, spread the softened butter on the bottom and sides of a round 8-inch cake pan. Add 1 tablespoon of flour and, holding the pan sideways over a sheet of wax paper, move it from side to side to distribute the flour evenly over the buttered surfaces. Invert the pan and rap it sharply to dislodge excess flour.

Mixing the batter. Combine the egg yolks, ¼ cup of the granulated sugar, and 1 teaspoon of vanilla in the large bowl of your electric mixer. Beat at high speed for 2 or 3 minutes, or until the mixture is thick and pale yellow. Then stop the machine, add ½ cup of ground walnuts and the graham cracker crumbs, and beat at medium speed for about 1 minute.

Pour the egg whites into a medium-size mixing bowl, preferably one of unlined copper (any other bowl will do, except one of aluminum). With a balloon whisk or a rotary beater, beat the whites for a moment or two, until they thicken lightly and begin to foam. Then pour in the remaining ¼ cup of granulated sugar and continue to beat until the whites form firm peaks on the lifted beater. With a rubber spatula, scrape the whites over the reserved egg yolk mixture.

Working quickly, combine the sifted flour and baking powder and sift them over the egg whites. Then fold the ingredients together with the rubber spatula, stopping as soon as streaks of flour no longer show.

Pour the batter into the pan and spread it evenly with a spatula.

Baking the torte. Bake the torte for 25 minutes, or until it has puffed above the rim of the pan and a cake tester comes out clean.

Cooling the torte. Remove the torte from the oven and let it rest in the pan for 1 minute.

Run the flat of a knife around the sides of the pan to free the torte. Invert a wire cake rack over the pan and, grasping rack and pan together with potholders, turn them over. Lift off the pan. Cool the torte to room temperature.

Whipping the cream. No more than 30 minutes before serving time, whip the cream in its chilled bowl, using a whisk or a rotary or electric beater, until it forms soft peaks. Then add the confectioners' sugar and 1 teaspoon of vanilla and continue to beat until the cream is stiff enough to hold its shape on the lifted beater.

Filling, frosting, and serving the torte. Using small sawing motions of a serrated knife, carefully cut the torte crosswise into two equal layers.

Invert the top layer onto a serving plate in this way: Slip one hand, fingers spread, under the upper layer. With the other hand, hold the inverted serving plate over the layer. Hold the layer in place against the plate while quickly turning the plate right side up.

With a rubber spatula, spread the layer evenly with about a third of the whipped cream. Spread one hand over the bottom layer and with your other hand lift and invert the cake rack, leaving the layer resting on your hand. Set this layer, cut side down, on top of the whipped cream. Spread the remaining cream on the top and sides of the torte.

If you like, sprinkle the tablespoonful of ground walnuts over the torte, or dot the cream fancifully with candied violets.

Ideally, the torte should be served at once, but you may, if you must, refrigerate it for up to 30 minutes. Don't refrigerate it longer or it will become soggy.

---◆⧏⧐◆---

BLACK-ON-BLACK CHOCOLATE LAYER CAKE

Everybody has at least one favorite chocolate cake recipe, and this one is the one I like best. The batter combines chocolate with coffee, giving the cake a subtle flavor; the apricot jam filling further contributes to the cake's subtlety, and both these elements are greatly complemented by the rich, glossy frosting made with old-fashioned sweet baking chocolate.

I would like to emphasize that the chocolate used in the batter must be semisweet, while that for the frosting must be German's sweet chocolate. For best results, do not attempt to substitute another type for either of them.

MAKES A ROUND 9-INCH TWO-LAYER CAKE

For Preparing the Pans:

1 tablespoon butter, softened at room temperature
2 tablespoons flour

The Batter:

3 ounces semisweet chocolate, coarsely chopped
¾ cup strong coffee, cooled (2 teaspoons instant espresso
  powder dissolved in ¾ cup boiling water)
2¼ cups sifted cake flour
1½ teaspoons baking soda
¾ teaspoon double-acting baking powder
12 tablespoons unsalted butter (1½ quarter-pound sticks),
  softened at room temperature
2 cups dark-brown sugar
¾ teaspoon salt
3 eggs
¾ cup sour cream
2 teaspoons vanilla

The Frosting:

8 ounces (two 4-ounce bars) German's sweet chocolate,
  coarsely chopped
8 tablespoons unsalted butter (a quarter-pound stick), cut into
  bits and softened at room temperature
½ cup sifted confectioners' sugar

The Filling:

¾ cup apricot jam, beaten with a whisk until smooth

Preheating the oven. Slide an oven shelf into a middle slot and preheat the oven at 350° F. for 15 minutes.

Preparing the pans. With a pastry brush, spread 1 tablespoon of softened butter on the bottom and sides of two round 9-inch cake pans. Add 1 tablespoon of flour to each pan. In turn, hold each pan sideways over a sheet of wax paper and move it from side to side to distribute the flour evenly over the buttered surfaces. Invert pan and tap it to dislodge excess flour.

Mixing the batter. In a small heavy saucepan, combine the semi-sweet chocolate with the cooled coffee. Stir constantly over low heat until the chocolate has melted. Transfer the mixture to a bowl and cool it to room temperature.

Sift together the sifted cake flour, baking soda, and baking powder, and set aside.

In the large bowl of your electric mixer, beat 12 tablespoons of softened butter at medium speed for about a minute, then, still beating, slowly pour in the dark-brown sugar and salt. Still at medium speed, cream the mixture, stopping the machine after 2 minutes to scrape down the sides of the bowl with a rubber spatula. After about 2 more minutes of beating, the mixture should look like mocha-colored whipped cream.

One at a time, beat in the eggs, beating until each is absorbed before adding the next. Then slowly pour in the chocolate and coffee mixture and beat for about 30 seconds.

Lower the speed, add about ½ cup of the reserved flour mixture, then raise the speed to medium until the flour has been incorporated. Repeat the process until all the flour mixture has been added, then beat in the sour cream and vanilla. When all the ingredients have been added, beat at high speed for about 1 minute, or until the batter is perfectly smooth.

Using a rubber spatula, divide the batter equally between the two cake pans and smooth it evenly.

Baking the cake. Bake the layers for 30 minutes, or until the layers have begun to shrink slightly away from the sides of the pan and a cake tester comes out dry and clean.

Let the layers rest in their pans for 2 or 3 minutes. Then run the flat of a knife around the sides of the pans. Invert a wire cake rack over each pan and, grasping rack and pan together with potholders, turn them over. Lift off the pans and let the layers cool to room temperature.

Making the frosting. Place the sweet chocolate in a heavy 2-quart saucepan and set the pan over low heat. Stir the chocolate constantly with a rubber spatula until it has melted completely and is smooth. Be careful not to overheat it, or the chocolate may scorch.

Off the heat, use a small whisk to beat in 8 tablespoons of softened butter a few bits at a time. Then beat in the confectioners' sugar ¼ cup at a time, continuing to beat until the frosting is smooth.

Assembling the cake. Place one of the layers, top side down, on a cake plate. Place about five 6-by-12-inch sheets of wax paper under the edges of the layer, slipping each sheet about 1 inch under the cake and overlapping the sheets slightly.

With an icing spatula, spread the beaten apricot jam over the layer, smoothing it to the very edges. Then carefully place the second layer, top side up, over the first.

Again using an icing spatula, spread the top and sides of the cake with the still-warm frosting. It will be quite soft, and you should have no difficulty in spreading it evenly.

Place the cake in a cool place—but not in the refrigerator—for 2 or 3 hours, or until the frosting is firm.

COCONUT LAYER CAKE

This majestic cake is purely American, based on an old family-style recipe that was often referred to as "one of butter, two of sugar, three of flour, and four of eggs." I have added an extra egg, but generally have stuck very closely to the easily remembered "1-2-3-4" formula.

With its tart lemon filling, its moist white frosting, and its magnificent masking of coconut, this is a nostalgic cake, the kind that one remembers as the hit of church suppers or old-fashioned birthday parties. Ideally, the cake should be served at once, but it may safely rest, uncovered, on its plate for up to 4 hours or so; the frosting will remain deliciously moist.

MAKES A ROUND 8-INCH THREE-LAYER CAKE

For Preparing the Pans:
2 tablespoons butter, softened at room temperature
3 tablespoons flour

The Batter:
3 cups sifted all-purpose flour
1 tablespoon baking powder
½ pound unsalted butter (2 quarter-pound sticks), softened at
   room temperature
2 cups sugar
¼ teaspoon salt
4 egg yolks
1 whole egg
1 teaspoon vanilla
1 cup milk
4 egg whites

The Filling:
3 egg yolks
½ teaspoon arrowroot
⅓ cup sugar
⅓ cup fresh lemon juice
1 teaspoon finely chopped lemon peel
3 tablespoons unsalted butter, cut into bits and softened at room
   temperature

The Frosting:
3 egg whites
⅛ teaspoon cream of tartar
⅛ teaspoon salt
1 cup light corn syrup
1½ teaspoons vanilla

The Topping:
1½ cups shredded coconut, preferably fresh

Preheating the oven. Slide an oven shelf into a middle slot and
preheat the oven at 350° F. for 15 minutes.

Preparing the pans. With a pastry brush, spread 2 tablespoons of
softened butter on the bottoms and sides of three round 9-inch cake
pans. Add 1 tablespoon of flour to each pan. In turn, hold each pan
sideways over a sheet of wax paper and move it from side to side

to distribute the flour evenly over all buttered surfaces. Invert each pan and rap to dislodge excess flour.

Mixing the batter. Sift together the sifted flour and baking powder, and set the mixture aside.

In the large bowl of your electric mixer, cream ½ pound of softened butter at medium speed for about a minute, then slowly pour in 2 cups of sugar and ¼ teaspoon of salt, continuing to beat.

Stop the machine after 2 minutes and scrape down the sides of the bowl with a rubber spatula. Increase the speed to high and beat for another 5 minutes, or until the mixture has lost most of its granular texture and is fluffy and light.

Lower the speed to medium and, one at a time, beat in 4 egg yolks and 1 whole egg, incorporating each thoroughly before adding the next. Add 1 teaspoon of vanilla. Lower the speed and add ¾ cup of the reserved flour mixture, then raise the speed to medium until the flour is absorbed. Alternating speeds in the same manner, beat in ¼ cup of the milk, then repeat alternate additions of flour and milk in similar amounts. When all of the ingredients have been added, beat the batter at high speed for 1 minute.

Pour 4 egg whites into a medium-size mixing bowl, preferably one of unlined copper (but not aluminum). With a balloon whisk or a rotary beater, beat the whites until they are stiff enough to form unwavering peaks on the lifted beater.

With a rubber spatula, scoop the beaten whites over the batter. Then fold the two together with the spatula, stopping as soon as streaks of egg white no longer show. Do not overfold.

Baking the cake. Bake the cake for 25 to 30 minutes, or until each layer has risen fully and begun to shrink slightly from the sides of the pan, and a cake tester comes out dry and clean.

Cooling the layers. Let the layers cool in their pans for 2 to 3 minutes. Then run a knife around the sides of each pan. Invert a wire cake rack over each pan and, protecting your hands with potholders, grasp rack and pan together and invert them. Lift off the pans and let the cakes cool to room temperature.

Making the filling. In a heavy 1-quart saucepan, beat 3 egg yolks and the arrowroot together with a small whisk. When the arrowroot has been absorbed, beat in ⅓ cup of sugar, lemon juice, chopped lemon peel, and finally, a few bits at a time, 3 tablespoons of softened butter.

Set the pan over moderate heat and, whisking it constantly,

cook the mixture slowly until it begins to thicken slightly. At this point begin to raise the pan from the heat every few seconds to cool it slightly, then whisk the filling over the heat again; the mixture must at no time even approach a boil or it will inevitably curdle.

When the filling has thickened heavily, immediately remove the pan from the heat and, with a rubber spatula, scrape it into a bowl. Cool to room temperature, then cover the bowl with plastic wrap and refrigerate it for about 30 minutes, or until the filling is thoroughly chilled and quite firm.

Making the frosting. Just before you assemble the cake, make the frosting. Place 3 egg whites, cream of tartar, and ⅛ teaspoon of salt in the large bowl of your electric mixer and beat them at medium speed until the whites thicken to a light foamy mass. Then increase the speed to high and beat uninterruptedly for 2 to 3 minutes, or until the whites stand in firm unwavering peaks on the lifted beater.

Pour the corn syrup into a small heavy saucepan and bring it to a boil over high heat. Boil the syrup for 5 minutes, or until a candy thermometer registers 238° F.

Immediately start beating the stiff egg whites again, this time at medium speed, and pour the hot syrup into the bowl in a slow steady stream. When all the syrup has been added, raise the speed to high and beat the mixture for about 5 minutes.

The frosting is done when it has cooled and become a thick mass resembling marshmallow cream; if in doubt, beat it a longer rather than a shorter time—this Italian meringue almost literally cannot be overbeaten. Beat in 1½ teaspoons vanilla.

Assembling and serving the cake. Place one of the layers, top side down, on a cake plate. Slip about five 6-by-12-inch sheets of wax paper under the edge of the layer around its entire circumference, overlapping them slightly.

With an icing spatula, spread half of the chilled lemon filling over the top of the layer, smoothing it to the very edges. Then place the second layer, top side down, over the first and spread the remaining filling over it. Add the final layer, top side up.

Again using an icing spatula, spread the frosting over the top and sides of the cake. Then sprinkle the top with about ½ cup of the coconut and gently pat the remaining coconut around the sides. Carefully pull out the sheets of wax paper one at a time and brush stray bits of coconut from the plate.

⊷§§⊷

ALMOND MERINGUE CAKE

This cake is an adaptation of a European confection known by a variety of names, among them *Dacquoise, broyage suisse, gâteau japonais.* But by whatever name it is called, the classic cake usually consists of thin disks of crisp nut-flecked meringue enclosing a very rich butter cream filling flavored in any of a number of ways.

Because I think butter cream is too overpowering for these delicate layers, I have chosen instead to fill them with a velvety chocolate cream of my own devising.

Most baked meringues cannot be refrigerated without turning soggy, but this meringue is an exception. The cake is usually at its best when served shortly after being assembled, but you may refrigerate it for as long as 6 hours, if you must. Make sure, however, to let it rest at room temperature for about 30 minutes after it comes from the refrigerator or the filling will be too firm.

MAKES A 10-INCH CAKE

For Preparing the Baking Sheets:
1 tablespoon butter, softened at room temperature
4 tablespoons flour

The Almond Meringue Layers:
1 tablespoon cornstarch
¾ cup superfine sugar
¾ cup finely ground toasted almonds (ground with a rotary nut
   grater or food processor, not in a blender)
1 cup egg whites (whites of about 8 eggs), at room temperature
⅛ teaspoon salt
¼ teaspoon cream of tartar

The Chocolate Cream Filling:
1 cup heavy cream
8 ounces semisweet chocolate, coarsely chopped
2 tablespoons Grand Marnier or other orange-flavored liqueur

For Dusting the Cake:
Confectioners' sugar

Preparing the baking sheets. With a pastry brush, spread 1 table-spoon of softened butter on the bottoms of two 17-by-14-inch baking sheets. Sprinkle 2 tablespoons of flour on each sheet. In turn, shake each sheet from side to side to distribute the flour evenly over the buttered surfaces, then invert over a piece of wax paper and rap to dislodge excess flour.

Place a 10-inch cake pan or plate on each sheet in turn and run the tip of a knife around its rim to outline a circle.

Preheating the oven. Slide an oven shelf into a middle slot and another into a lower slot. Then preheat the oven at 250° F. for 15 minutes.

Making the meringue mixture. Sift the cornstarch through a fine-meshed sieve into a small bowl. Add 2 tablespoons of the superfine sugar and the ground almonds. Stir together thoroughly with a fork and set aside.

Place the egg whites, salt, and cream of tartar in the large bowl of your electric mixer and beat at medium speed until the whites thicken to a light foamy mass. Still beating at medium speed, very slowly pour in the remainder of the superfine sugar.

Then increase the speed to high and beat uninterruptedly until the meringue stands in firm unwavering peaks and has lost most of its gloss. This will take about 5 minutes (or 10 minutes if you make the meringue by hand, using a rotary beater or a whisk). If in doubt, overbeat rather than underbeat. Remove the bowl from the machine.

Scatter the reserved almond mixture over the meringue. With a rubber spatula, gently fold the two together, just until the al-monds are evenly distributed. Do not overfold.

Shaping the meringues. With the rubber spatula, scoop half of the meringue mixture into each of the circles marked on the baking sheets. Then lightly shape the meringue into flat 10-inch rounds about ½ inch thick. Don't worry about making perfect shapes; any uneven edges will be trimmed away later.

Baking and drying the meringues. Bake the meringues on the middle and lower shelves of the preheated 250° F. oven for 45 to 50 minutes, or until the meringues are the palest imaginable golden brown and their centers are still slightly sticky to the touch.

Turn off the heat and let the meringues cool in the closed oven for about 30 minutes to 1 hour, or until their centers feel dry to the touch.

Remove the baking sheets from the oven. Gently slide a metal spatula under each meringue to free it from the pan. Carefully place the meringues on wire cake racks. Set them aside and prepare the filling.

Making the chocolate cream filling. Pour the cream into a 2-quart saucepan and add the semisweet chocolate. Set the pan over moderate heat and stir with a wooden spoon until the chocolate has melted. Don't let the mixture boil or it may separate; if by some mischance this should happen, beat the mixture with a whisk to recombine it. Stir in the liqueur.

Pour the chocolate cream into the small bowl of your electric mixer and, stirring it occasionally, let it cool to lukewarm. Then cover the bowl with plastic wrap and refrigerate it for about 30 minutes, or until the filling is cold and thick.

Assembling and serving the cake. With your electric mixer set at medium speed, beat the chilled chocolate cream for a minute or two, until it is velvety smooth.

Place one of the cooled meringues on a sheet of foil and, with a spatula, spread the chocolate cream evenly over it. Then carefully set the other meringue on top.

To trim the cake, place the original 10-inch pan or plate on top of the meringue. Using a large sharp knife and gentle sawing motions, cut all around the cake, pressing the flat of the knife against the rim of the pan or plate to guide you.

With two large metal spatulas, transfer the cake to a serving plate and refrigerate it for about 30 minutes to allow the filling to set. If the cake is refrigerated for several hours, be sure to bring it back to room temperature before you serve it.

Just before serving the cake, dust it with confectioners' sugar.

At the table, carefully cut the cake into small wedges, using the sharpest and thinnest knife you own.

Baking: Pies, Tarts, and Chou Puffs

*T*he common denominator linking such enticing culinary terms as pies, tarts, and chou puffs is the word "paste." And paste—whether it is called pastry in English, *pâte* in French, *pasticcería* in Italian, or *pastelería* in Spanish—is a comparatively flavorless composition of flour, fat, and liquid, and, on occasion, eggs. This simple mixture has been prepared and baked in one form or another for centuries: the German *strudel*, the paper-thin Greek *phylo*, or the many-leaved French puff pastry, *feuilletage*, are only a few examples.

Although the international guises that pastry can take are virtually limitless, I am concerned here with my versions of three classic pastries that are as satisfying and delicious as any you can imagine: flaky-crusted American pies, French tarts and tartlets with velvety fillings, and puffs as fragile and as ephemeral as the air they contain. I have also included appropriate fillings for these pastry constructions served as hors d'oeuvre, main dishes, and desserts.

The homely expression "easy as pie" may be oversimplifying matters a bit, but the techniques of making simple doughs, wielding a rolling pin, and baking pastries are by no means as complicated as some cooks—novice and skilled—fear them to be. Your successes will depend more on precision and practice than on any God-given gift for pastrymaking.

Ingredients for Pies, Tarts, and Chou Puffs

Flour. The recipes in this section require all-purpose flour—not cake flour, self-rising flour, bread flour, instant (granulated) flour, or pastry flour. Like other wheat flours, all-purpose flour contains gluten, which will develop a certain amount of elasticity in every pastry you make; too much elasticity, however, is the common cause of tough crusts. To prevent pastry from developing too much elasticity, use speed and dexterity in mixing, handling, and rolling it—in other words, use "a light hand with pastry."

Fats. Use butter or solid vegetable shortening, either separately or in combination, because they produce the best pastries—flaky, rich, and easy to handle before baking.

BUTTER. Except in American pie crusts, I am unconditionally committed to butter—sweet butter—for most cooking purposes, and particularly for tarts and puffs. However, salted butter is also acceptable, and if you use it, reduce the salt called for by one-half.

Never use the product called whipped butter for pastrymaking. Although it serves well enough as a spread, the air whipped into it replaces part of the fat, reducing its shortening power and changing its texture so that it will make only a leaden and rather oily pastry.

You may substitute margarine for butter; it will produce inferior but still palatable pastry.

SOLID VEGETABLE SHORTENING. The standard brands—Crisco, for example—have no animal fat, little or no flavor, needn't be refrigerated, and keep almost indefinitely without deteriorating. Do not substitute vegetable oils for solid vegetable shortening. Pastries made with oil—for my palate, at least—leave a great deal to be desired, and the results do not justify learning the techniques involved.

LARD. Lard can lend a distinctive flavor to pastry, but most

packaged lard today has been so emulsified, hydrogenated, and refined to ensure its stability that few brands, if any, have the special
flavor and richness of old-fashioned leaf lard, which is now almost
impossible to find. However, if you insist on using packaged lard,
you may substitute it for vegetable shortening measure for measure,
or you can combine shortening and lard in any proportion you like.
I would suggest, however, that you master the pastrymaking techniques, using the ingredients specified in each recipe, before experimenting with substitutions.

Eggs. The freshness of eggs is important to the success of many
dishes, but in making pastries and fillings, it is not essential that
the eggs be new-laid. In fact, eggs a few days old are preferable
to really fresh eggs for making meringues. And as for the whole
eggs in custard fillings, their age will make very little difference.
Whenever I specify eggs, I mean the "large" size.

Sugar. When sugar is indicated in any recipe, it means standard
granulated sugar unless another sugar is specified, as for example,
confectioners' sugar or light-brown sugar. Do not substitute one
type of sugar for another.

Thickenings. Most pie fillings, especially those made with fruit,
need a thickening agent to help prevent the bottom crust from
becoming soggy and to make it possible to cut the finished pie into
fairly compact but still juicy servings.

The best thickeners for fruit-filled pies are cornstarch, arrowroot, tapioca, and flour. Each recipe suggests a specific thickener
for a specific fruit. Cornstarch, arrowroot, and tapioca can be used
interchangeably in the same amounts to achieve the same general
density of the finished filling, but if you substitute flour for any of
them, double the amount of thickener specified.

Liquids. All pastry requires moisture of some sort to make the
particles of flour adhere to each other, and water—iced to prevent
the fat in the pastry from softening too much—is the most reliable
binder. Some cooks mistakenly believe that fruit juices can be substituted for water to improve the flavor. Not only will the fruit
flavor be virtually lost in the pastry, but the acidity of the juice
may break down the structure of the flour and make the pastry,
whatever its type, almost impossible to handle.

Pastry mixes. Instant pie-crust and cream-puff mixes are dubious
preparations that bear only a slight resemblance to the real thing.
Furthermore, my American pie crust is cheaper, better, and not
much more difficult to make, and I seriously doubt if anything even
remotely approaching my tart and tartlet pastries is available in a
mix. Needless to say, I would avoid all of them.

Packaged and canned pie fillings. I have no enthusiasm for packaged or fully cooked canned pie fillings, despite their convenience; they are generally tasteless, overly thickened, and have synthetic overtones. Sour red cherries in water are the only canned fruit I really prefer to fresh for pies.

In the absence of fresh fruit, frozen fruit—thoroughly defrosted and drained—makes an excellent substitute.

Note: Fuller descriptions of many of these ingredients are given in the "Culinary Glossary."

❧❧

American Pies: An International Heritage

Almost every country in the world has for centuries taken pride in its pies—whatever their fillings, no matter how bizarre or multitudinous their shapes. There is the Moroccan *bastila*, tissue-thin layers of pastry, sometimes triangular, filled with pigeon meat and aromatic spices; the French *pâté en croûte*, a rectangular box of pastry filled with a compact mixture of ground meats and herb seasonings; the Italian pizza.

But the English, whose cuisine is perhaps the most maligned of any in the world, surely raised piemaking to its most fanciful and poetic heights with their beef and kidney pies, their Christmas mincemeat pies, their deep apple pies baked in a bowl, their pillow-shaped Cornish pasties, and such conceits as latticed parsnip pies festooned with primroses. Then the Americans came along.

Almost from the beginning, America, with an inexhaustible bounty of fruit and vegetables at hand, produced pies that were increasingly different from those of other countries. Little by little, American cooks modified, simplified, and transformed the pastry-making principles brought from their ancestral homelands until, by some mysterious alchemy, the typical shallow, circular, flaky-crusted American pie evolved.

Although we think of most standard American pies as two-crusted—that is, having a lower and an upper crust sealed together to enclose a filling and baked in a pan—this does little justice to Yankee or Southern ingenuity. American cooks experimented with fruit pies of every description, to say nothing of chiffon pies, custard pies, pecan pies, lemon pies, all as American as the land that produced them.

Despite the many recipes for pie pastry made with hot water, oil, eggs, cream cheese, and what not, I am convinced that early American cooks knew what they were doing when they kept their pastry simple and used only flour, shortening, salt, and water. I have, therefore, concentrated on what I consider to be a fine, successful, standard American pastry recipe; and you will find various adaptations of it for double-crusted pies, deep-dish pie lids, and fully baked pie shells. This pastry is one of the easiest to handle, and you will find it invaluable once you have mastered it.

Techniques for Making Pies

Whether you are preparing dough for a double-crusted pie, a single pie, a prebaked pie shell, or a pastry lid for a deep-dish pie, the basic techniques remain the same. The essential differences are in the quantities of the ingredients and the size of the rolled-out dough. These, and other specific information, appear with each recipe.

Preparing the ingredients. Always sift flour—even flour labeled "presifted"—before measuring it, unless otherwise directed; dry ingredients, especially flour, tend to settle and thus increase in density when kept very long or when stored in a damp atmosphere. Then spoon the sifted flour lightly into a dry-measuring cup and scrape off the surplus with the back of a knife. Never rap the cup containing the flour to settle it or you will increase the quantity of flour disastrously.

When combining two or more dry ingredients, sift them together to mix completely. You can't achieve the same uniformity merely by stirring them with a spoon or a whisk.

Some pastry ingredients should be chilled, others should be at room temperature, so read the recipe completely before you begin so that all ingredients will be at the correct temperature.

Making the pastry. Add the chilled shortening to the sifted dry ingredients, tossing the shortening about lightly to dust it with the flour.

With small chopping motions, use your pastry blender to cut through the shortening and distribute it throughout the flour. Run the blender around the bowl to incorporate any flour clinging to the sides, and occasionally slide a table knife across the blender to free any shortening lodged in the wires. Continue to cut in the shortening until small rice-size pellets are formed. They needn't be uniform. As an alternative, you can cut the shortening into the flour with two knives, but you will achieve greater uniformity of texture with the pastry blender.

Pour the ice water over the fat-flour granules and, with a fork, toss together lightly to make a moist crumbly dough. Quickly gather the dough together with your hands, then pat and shape it into a compact ball.

At this point you can wrap your pastry securely in plastic wrap and refrigerate it for at least 2 days. Before using it, let it soften at room temperature to a pliable state. Or you can wrap it closely in foil and freeze it for at least 2 months; naturally, you must defrost the pastry before rolling it out.

Rolling the dough. Slip a rolling pin sleeve over the rolling pin and thoroughly hand rub it with flour before each use. Rub enough flour into your pastry cloth to give the canvas a very smooth surface.

Hold the ball of dough in one hand and, with the other, sprinkle it lightly and evenly with unsifted flour. Place the dough on your floured pastry cloth and pat it into a circle about 4 inches in diameter. For a double-crusted pie, cut the ball of dough in half and set one half aside.

Position your rolling pin, encased in its floured sleeve, across the center of the dough and roll it away from you in one firm continuous stroke, lifting the pin as you near the edge. If you apply the pressure of your rolling pin all the way to the outer edge of the pastry circle, the dough will become brittle and thin.

Return the pin to the center of the dough and, shifting your direction slightly to the right, again roll it away from you precisely as before. Never roll back and forth except when patching; this toughens the pastry because it overdevelops the gluten. For the same reason, it is unwise to turn pastry over and roll it on the other side.

Continue this rolling procedure all around the circle, slightly overlapping each preceding stroke by about an inch. Your strokes will circle the pastry like a hand around the face of a clock. If your pastry begins to stick to the sleeve or the pastry cloth, rub a little extra flour into the sleeve or, if necessary, into the pastry cloth. Keep the extra flour to a minimum; too much of it can toughen the pastry. If the pastry tears while you are rolling it, pull off a small piece from the edge, place it over the torn place, and firmly roll back and forth over it until the surface is smooth.

When you have completed the circle and are at the point where you began rolling the dough, measure its diameter with a ruler to see if it is the size specified in the recipe. If the circle is too small, repeat the entire rolling process. Never pull or stretch the dough to enlarge its area; this will increase its elasticity and cause the pastry to retract, like a rubber band, to its original shape as it bakes. The finished circle will probably be ragged around the edge but will be trimmed later.

Lining the pie pan. To avoid the precarious procedure of transferring the pastry to the pie pan with your hands, use the easier (and safer) rolling pin method: Set the pin horizontally across the pastry about 4 inches away from the edge closest to you. Lift the near edge of pastry and double it over the rolling pin, which will roll away as you lift the pastry. The rolling pin, its handles exposed, will be enclosed in a half-moon of pastry, and you can securely proceed to line the pan.

Set the pie pan before you. Lift the rolling pin by its exposed handles and, using your thumbs to prevent the pastry from rolling off, hold the pin over the pan and a few inches beyond its center. Then lower the pastry and unroll it from the pin, letting it fall slackly into the pan. Ideally, the center of the pastry should fall in the center of the pan.

To fit the slack pastry snugly into the crease of the pie pan, run the back of a teaspoon around it, using just enough pressure to mold the pastry without stretching it.

At this point you can trim the overhanging edges of dough, then wrap the pan and pastry securely in foil and freeze it. You can bake the crust in its frozen state, but increase the baking time somewhat.

Filling the pie. If a pie is to contain a moist filling, brush the bottom crust with 1 or 2 teaspoons of softened butter before pouring in the filling. This, and adding the filling at the last possible moment, will help to prevent sogginess.

The top crust. After filling the pie, roll the reserved half of the pastry dough out to the dimensions specified in your recipe. Lift the top crust pastry onto your rolling pin and unroll it over the filling in the same manner as the lower crust was unrolled over the pan.

Holding the pan on the palm of one hand, with the other, rotate it slowly and trim the overhanging edges of the upper and lower crusts together, using short strokes of a small sharp knife pressed firmly against the rim of the pan.

Sealing a double-crusted pie. To seal the two crusts together, set the pie down and press the back of the prongs of a table fork all around the rim to crimp it. Don't press too firmly or you may push the fork through the pastry altogether.

Fluting is a more intricate technique for sealing edges than simply crimping them with a fork. It does, however, produce a charming decorative effect. After the pie has been filled, cover it with a top crust rolled out to a diameter about 3 inches larger than the pan. Then, with a pair of small scissors, trim both layers of overhanging pastry evenly about 1 inch beyond the rim of the pan. Now lift the two layers of pastry, a small section at a time, and fold them under, thus making a four-layered edge resting on the flat rim of the pan.

To make the fluting, spread the thumb and forefinger of one hand about an inch apart and set them lightly on the pastry rim. With the forefinger of your other hand, push against the pastry on the rim as you pinch simultaneously with the first hand, thus forming an upstanding fluted ridge. Move all around the edge in this fashion. If you like, go around a second time to deepen the fluting.

Letting out the steam. All double-crusted pies must have some kind of opening in the top crust to release the steam formed by the filling as it cooks. In whatever shape you choose to cut these openings, always make them either in or as close to the center of the pie as you can. The filling is almost certain to boil over through openings made near the sides.

Decorating the top crust. If you have leftover pastry as well as the time and inclination to decorate your pie, gather the pastry scraps into a ball, roll it into a thin sheet, and use a small knife, scissors, pastry wheel, cookie cutter, or any other instrument to cut the pastry into small designs of your choice—for example, leaves, triangles, flowers, diamonds.

Secure the pastry cutouts to the unbaked crust by brushing their undersides lightly with cold water or milk, then pressing them gently onto the crust.

Glazing the top crust. You can give the top of a double-crusted pie interesting highlights and a better color if you brush it lightly with any one of the following glazes: cold milk; light or heavy cream; lightly beaten whole egg; an egg white beaten slightly with 2 teaspoons of cold water; an egg yolk mixed with 2 teaspoons of milk or cream. Each glaze gives the crust a particular sheen, and it is really a matter of taste which of them you prefer.

I should note here that I disapprove of dusting the top of a pie with granulated sugar. The sugar does indeed make the surface glitter, but the glitter is gained at the expense of toughening the crust.

Baking the pie. Always bake a double-crusted pie in the center of the oven, because the pie bakes and browns more evenly when the heat is distributed equally around it.

Always bake a single-crusted pie in the lower third of the oven, because the uncooked single crust requires the greatest amount of heat under it, not above it.

On the other hand, always bake a meringue-topped pie in the upper third of the oven. Since the filling and the crust have been cooked beforehand, you want to brown the meringue quickly by the greater heat near the top of the oven.

Uneven browning is sometimes a problem, so observe your pie as it bakes. If the crust appears to be browning too fast, you can cover the top of a pie loosely with aluminum foil. If one side seems to be browning more rapidly than the other, quickly turn the pale side around to the hotter area. Move or turn the pie gently so as not to damage the crust, and do it quickly so that the oven door is not open long enough to cause the heat to lower appreciably. Shifting the pie will not hurt it a bit, because pies, unlike cakes, will not "fall" if moved during baking.

All fruit-filled pies have a tendency to bubble over as they bake. To protect your oven, place a sheet of aluminum foil on the oven floor—but not on the rack on which the pie is resting. Make sure that the foil doesn't cover any of the air vents in a gas oven, and that it lies flat without touching the heating element in an electric oven.

---------- ❦ ----------

A MODEL DOUBLE-CRUSTED PIE

This recipe is designed to serve as a model for all double-crusted American pies. It is accompanied here by recipes for American Apple Pie, New England Clam Pie, and Lattice-Topped Cherry Pie, which is basically a two-crust pie. After you make any one of these three pies, you can securely take off on your own with any other double-crusted pie; use a favorite family recipe for a sweet or savory filling—mincemeat, for example—and follow the same procedures for making and rolling the pastry, lining and filling the pan, adding and sealing the top crust, glazing and baking the pie. Incredible as it may seem, whatever the filling, the baking time remains precisely the same.

If you want to refresh your pastrymaking skills, all the techniques are described in detail, starting on page 359.

MAKES A 9-INCH DOUBLE-CRUSTED PIE

The Pastry:
2½ cups sifted all-purpose flour
1 teaspoon salt
1 cup chilled vegetable shortening
⅓ cup ice-cold water
¼ cup unsifted flour

The Coating for the Lower Crust:
2 teaspoons butter, softened at room temperature

The Filling:
Any filling of your choice

The Glaze for the Top Crust:
1 tablespoon milk; or 1 tablespoon light or heavy cream; or 1
   lightly beaten whole egg; or 1 egg white beaten slightly with
   2 teaspoons cold water; or 1 egg yolk mixed with 2 teaspoons
   milk or cream

Making the pastry. Combine the sifted flour and salt, and sift them together into a large mixing bowl. Add the shortening and toss it about lightly to dust it with the flour.

With small chopping motions of your pastry blender, cut the shortening into the flour until rice-size pellets are formed.

Pour the ice-cold water over the fat-flour granules and toss them together lightly with a fork to make a moist crumbly dough. Quickly gather the dough with your hands, then shape it into a compact ball. Hold the ball in one hand and, with the other, sprinkle it evenly with the unsifted flour.

Rolling the dough. Cut the ball of dough in half and set one half aside. Place the other on your floured pastry cloth and pat it into a 4-inch circle.

Roll the pastry, always starting with your rolling pin across the center of the dough, working outward in continuous strokes, and lifting the pin as you near the edge of the pastry. Work all around the circle of dough, overlapping each preceding stroke by about 1 inch, until you reach your starting point. The finished rough circle of pastry should be about ⅛ inch thick and 14 inches in diameter. If it is smaller, repeat the entire rolling process.

Lining the pan. Drape the pastry in a half-moon over your rolling pin, then unroll it from the pin over the pie pan, letting it fall slackly across the pan. Run the back of a teaspoon around the sides and crease of the pan to fit the pastry snugly without stretching it.

Coating the lower crust. Using a pastry brush, coat the bottom and sides of the pastry evenly with the softened butter.

Preheating the oven. Slide an oven shelf into a center slot and preheat the oven for 15 minutes at 450° F.

Filling the pie. Fill the pie with your prepared pie filling.

Adding the top crust and sealing the pie. Roll out the reserved half of the dough precisely as you did for the bottom crust, but roll it only to a diameter of 11 inches for the top crust.

With a pastry brush dipped into the glaze of your choice, lightly paint the lip of the lower crust—that is, the pastry that lies over the flat rim of the pan—ignoring the overhanging edge.

Lift the pastry for the top crust onto your rolling pin and let it fall gently into place over the filling. Trim the overhanging pastry with a sharp knife and crimp the crusts together with a fork to seal them.

Cut two 1-inch slits or a ¾-inch circle out of the center of the pastry to vent the steam.

Glazing and baking the pie. Dip a pastry brush into the glaze and brush the entire top surface lightly and evenly.

Bake the pie for 10 minutes at 450° F. Then lower the heat to 350° F. and bake the pie for 40 minutes longer, or until the crust is light golden brown and firm to the touch. Remove the pie from the oven and let it cool to lukewarm or to room temperature before serving it.

AMERICAN APPLE PIE

Of all the apples that are found in this country in such colorful profusion, I much prefer Greenings to any other variety for my version of this classic American pie. If Greenings are unavailable, use any tart, crisp cooking variety; do not use such "eating apples" as McIntosh and Delicious—they are much too soft in texture and tend to fall apart when they are cooked.

MAKES A 9-INCH PIE

The Filling:
2½ to 3 pounds tart cooking apples, or enough to make 7 cups cubed apples
2 tablespoons butter
½ cup granulated sugar
½ cup light-brown sugar
½ teaspoon ground cinnamon
¼ teaspoon nutmeg, preferably freshly grated
2 to 4 tablespoons heavy cream (optional)

The Pastry:
2½ cups sifted all-purpose flour
1 teaspoon salt
1 cup chilled vegetable shortening
⅓ cup ice-cold water
¼ cup unsifted flour

The Coating for the Lower Crust:
2 teaspoons butter, softened at room temperature

The Glaze for the Top Crust:
1 tablespoon milk

Making the filling. Peel and quarter the apples and cut out the cores. Then cut each quarter into ½-inch cubes. (Cubes will retain their shape after cooking better than slices will.) Don't try to make the cubes uniform in shape; the pieces need only be about the same size.

Over moderate heat, slowly melt 2 tablespoons of butter in a heavy 12-inch frying pan or skillet, preferably with a nonstick lining. When the butter is completely melted but not brown, add the apples and sprinkle them with the granulated sugar. Toss the mixture about with a rubber spatula to coat the apples evenly. Then, still over moderate heat, cook the apples for 2 or 3 minutes, turning them over continuously with the spatula until a slight film of liquid covers the bottom of the pan. Don't overcook the apples; they should barely have begun to soften.

Pour the contents of the frying pan into a large sieve set over a mixing bowl and let all the liquid drain through. Discard the juice, and transfer the drained apples to the mixing bowl.

Cool the apples to room temperature, or refrigerate them until you are ready to fill the pie.

Making the pastry; rolling the dough; lining the pan; coating the lower crust; and preheating the oven. Follow the directions in the preceding recipe for A Model Double-Crusted Pie.

Filling the pie. Drain the apples once more and spread them evenly over the pastry-lined pan. In a small bowl combine the brown sugar, cinnamon, and nutmeg, and stir them together with a fork, breaking up any lumps in the sugar. Sprinkle the mixture over the apples.

Adding the top crust and sealing the pie. Follow the directions in the preceding recipe for A Model Double-Crusted Pie.

To allow steam to escape as the pie bakes, cut a $3/4$-inch circle out of the center of the pastry.

Glazing and baking the pie. Dip a pastry brush into the tablespoon of milk and brush the entire top surface of the pastry lightly and evenly.

Bake the pie for 10 minutes in the preheated 450° F. oven. Then lower the heat to 350° F. and bake the pie for 40 minutes longer, or until the crust is light golden brown and firm to the touch. Remove the pie from the oven and let it cool to lukewarm, or to room temperature if you prefer, before serving it.

Serving the pie. Just before you serve the pie you may, if you like, insert a small funnel or a plain pastry tip into the center opening of the pie and slowly pour into it the 2 tablespoons of cream (or use as much as 4 tablespoons if you like your pie really moist). Then remove the funnel and slowly tilt the pie from side to side to distribute the cream evenly beneath the crust.

Alternatively, serve the pie with a pitcher of heavy cream, but not, I implore you, with ice cream. Where this barbaric practice originated I don't know, but placing a scoop of ice cream on top of your pie will chill its delicate flaky crust to the texture of papier-mâché. If you must have ice cream with your pie, serve it in a separate dish.

NEW ENGLAND CLAM PIE

If you are fortunate enough to find fresh clams, they are, of course, preferable to canned ones for this regional favorite. The number you will need to make 1½ cups of drained minced clams will naturally depend upon the size of the clams.

SERVES 4 TO 6

The Filling:
1½ cups drained minced clams (three 8-ounce cans) or chopped
   freshly shucked clams
½ cup juice drained from the clams
3 eggs
½ cup cream
½ cup milk
¼ pound baked or boiled ham, cut into slivers about ½ inch
   long, ⅛ inch thick (about 1 cup)
½ cup coarsely crumbled crackers (preferably pilot crackers,
   but Uneeda Biscuits or unsalted Krispy Crackers or Saltines
   are also suitable)
1 teaspoon fresh lemon juice
4 to 6 drops Tabasco
2 tablespoons finely chopped fresh parsley
¼ teaspoon salt
Freshly ground black pepper
2 tablespoons butter, cut into small bits

The Pastry:
2½ cups sifted all-purpose flour
1 teaspoon salt
1 cup chilled vegetable shortening
⅓ cup ice-cold water
¼ cup unsifted flour

The Coating for the Lower Crust:
2 teaspoons butter, softened at room temperature

The Glaze for the Top Crust:
1 egg white
2 teaspoons water

Making the filling. Place the clams in a large strainer set over a mixing bowl and drain them thoroughly, shaking the strainer repeatedly to rid the clams of all possible juice. If you are using fresh clams, line the strainer with cheesecloth, or use a fine-meshed sieve, to catch all the sand. Pour ½ cup of the clam juice into a measuring cup and discard the rest.

Break 3 eggs into the same mixing bowl and, using a fork or a small whisk, beat them just long enough to combine the yolks and whites. Then stir in the cream, milk, and the clam juice. Stir gently until the ingredients are well combined. Add the drained clams, ham, crackers, lemon juice, 4 drops of Tabasco, parsley, salt, and a liberal grinding of pepper. Stir together thoroughly, then taste for seasoning. Add the extra drops of Tabasco and more salt and pepper if you think the filling needs it.

Refrigerate the filling while you make and roll out the pastry and line the pan.

Making the pastry; rolling the dough; lining the pan; coating the lower crust; and preheating the oven. Follow the directions in the recipe for A Model Double-Crusted Pie (pages 364–65).

Filling the pie. Remove the filling from the refrigerator and stir it gently with a rubber spatula, then pour it into the pastry-lined pan. Use your spatula to spread out the solid ingredients, then dot the top evenly with the 2 tablespoons of butter bits.

Adding the top crust and sealing the pie. Follow the directions in the recipe for A Model Double-Crusted Pie (page 365), using a pastry brush dipped into water instead of milk to moisten the edges of the pastry before sealing them.

Instead of cutting a circle out of the top crust to vent the steam, you may prefer to make two 1-inch slits close to the center of the pie.

Glazing and baking the pie. In a small bowl, using a whisk or a fork, beat the egg white with 2 teaspoons of water only long enough to combine them. Using a pastry brush, lightly coat the top crust with the mixture.

Bake the pie for 10 minutes in the preheated 450° F. oven. Then lower the heat to 350° F. and bake the pie for 40 minutes longer, or until the crust is light golden brown and firm to the touch.

Serving the pie. Clam pie is equally good served warm or lukewarm, and some New Englanders prefer it at room temperature, or even cold. I never serve it cold, and if I have any leftover pie, I reheat it in a preheated 325° F. oven for about 15 minutes, or until the crust and the filling are hot.

LATTICE-TOPPED CHERRY PIE

Although the lattice top gives this pie a charming and dramatic appearance, it is basically a double-crusted pie. There are numerous ways to make a lattice—some call for the skill of a weaver—but I prefer to keep the lattice simple because the final effect (and certainly the taste) is more or less the same. The lattice technique may be confidently used as a basic pattern for a pie containing any other filling.

MAKES A 9-INCH PIE

The Filling:
2 cans (1 pound each) pitted sour red cherries (3½ cups after
    draining)
1¼ cups juice drained from the cherries
½ teaspoon almond extract
1 cup sugar
3 tablespoons arrowroot
2 tablespoons coarsely chopped toasted almonds
1 tablespoon butter, cut into bits

The Pastry:
2½ cups sifted all-purpose flour
1 teaspoon salt
1 cup chilled vegetable shortening
⅓ cup ice-cold water
¼ cup unsifted flour

The Coating for the Lower Crust:
2 teaspoons butter, softened at room temperature

The Glaze for the Lattice:
1 tablespoon milk

Making the filling. Pour the cherries and their juice into a large sieve set over a mixing bowl and drain them thoroughly, shaking the sieve from time to time.

Then spread the cherries on a double layer of paper towels and gently pat them dry with more paper towels. Measure 1¼ cups of cherry juice and discard the rest.

Combine the cherry juice, almond extract, sugar, and arrowroot in a heavy 2-quart saucepan. Stir them together briskly with a wire whisk and set the pan over moderate heat. Stirring constantly, bring the mixture to a boil, lower the heat, and, still stirring, simmer it for 2 or 3 minutes, until it is smooth and thick. Add the drained cherries and remove the pan from the heat.

Cool the filling to room temperature before you proceed. You may allow it to cool in the pan, or you can hasten the cooling by pouring the filling into a previously chilled bowl.

Making the pastry; rolling the dough; lining the pan; coating the lower crust; and preheating the oven. Follow the directions in the recipe for A Model Double-Crusted Pie (pages 364–65).

Filling the pie. Pour the cherry filling into the pastry-lined pan and spread the fruit out evenly with a rubber spatula. Sprinkle the almonds over the top and dot with the tablespoon of butter bits.

Making and glazing the lattice top. With a small pair of scissors, cut away the excess pastry of the lower crust, leaving a uniform overhang of about ½ inch beyond the edge of the pan.

Roll out the other half of the dough precisely as for the first half, to a diameter of about 14 inches. Using a ruler as a guide, cut the pastry with a small sharp knife or a plain or jagged pastry wheel into 18 strips ½ inch wide.

Dip a pastry brush into the milk and paint the rim of the filled lower crust. Coat the latticing strips lightly but evenly with the milk, then carefully place one of the longest strips horizontally across the center of the pie. Set another long strip over it vertically, thus forming a cross. Lay 4 more pastry strips about ½ inch apart on one side of the horizontal strip and 4 more on the other side, spacing them similarly. Lay the remaining strips in the opposite direction to form a lattice.

At first try, your finished lattice may lack the perfection you will soon achieve; in any case, I prefer the slightly irregular homemade look to the machine-made appearance of a commercial baker's lattice top.

Sealing the pie. With scissors, trim the overhanging strips to match the ½-inch overhang of the bottom crust.

Now lift the bottom pastry and the overhanging strips together, a small section at a time, and fold them under to fit precisely on the lip of the pan. To seal the layers together, lightly press the back of the prongs of a table fork all around the rim.

Baking the pie. Bake the pie for 10 minutes in the preheated 450° F. oven. Then lower the heat to 350° F. and bake it for 40 minutes longer, or until the lattice top is golden brown.

Remove the pie from the oven and let it cool to lukewarm or to room temperature before serving it.

A FULLY BAKED SCALLOPED PIE SHELL

Making a fully baked unfilled pie shell—which professionals often call a "blind shell"—is unquestionably a challenge. The tendency of the pastry to shrink in the pan as it bakes has driven even skillful cooks to the brink of despair. I think you will find my solution to this problem fascinating technically, the results virtually foolproof, and the finished scalloped-edge pie shell handsome and unusual. My double-crusted pie pastry, in reduced amounts, is used for this, as are the same pastrymaking techniques described in detail beginning on page 359.

MAKES A 9-INCH SHELL

1¼ cups sifted all-purpose flour
½ teaspoon salt
½ cup chilled vegetable shortening
3 tablespoons ice-cold water
2 tablespoons unsifted flour
2 teaspoons butter, softened at room temperature

Making the pastry. Combine the sifted flour and salt and sift them together into a large mixing bowl. Add the vegetable shortening and toss it about lightly to dust it with the flour.

With small chopping motions of your pastry blender, cut the shortening into the flour until small rice-size pellets are formed.

Pour the ice-cold water over the fat-flour granules and toss them lightly with a fork to make a moist crumbly dough. Quickly gather the dough together with your hands, then shape it into a compact ball.

Hold the ball in one hand and, with the other, sprinkle it evenly with 2 tablespoons of unsifted flour.

Rolling the pastry. Place the ball of dough on your floured pastry cloth and pat it into a 4-inch circle.

Roll the pastry, always starting with your rolling pin across the center of the dough, working outward in continuous strokes, and lifting the pin as you near the edge. Work all around the circle of dough, slightly overlapping each preceding stroke by about 1 inch, until you complete the circle and reach the point where you began.

The finished rough circle of pastry should be about 15 or 16 inches in diameter. If it is smaller, repeat the entire rolling process.

Making the scalloped edge. Invert a 9-inch pie pan and place it in the center of the pastry circle, rim down. Starting 2 inches out from the edge of the rim, use a small sharp knife to cut out a 14-inch circle; a ruler will help maintain the 2-inch distance from the pan. Remove the pan.

Fold the pastry circle in half by lifting up the near edge of the pastry and folding it away from you to make a double layer in the shape of a half-circle. With a small knife or scissors, cut scallops or notches about ½ inch deep all around the curved edge of the doubled pastry.

To transfer the scalloped pastry to the pan, slide both hands under the half-circle of pastry, lift it, and lay it flat in the upper half of the pie pan. Turn back the upper layer of pastry and let it fall into place. The pastry should lie slackly in the pan, the scalloped edges extending evenly beyond the rim.

To fit the slack pastry snugly into the crease of the pie pan, run the back of a teaspoon—not your fingers—around it, using just enough pressure to mold the pastry without stretching it.

Preheating the oven. Slide an oven shelf into a center slot and preheat the oven for 15 minutes at 450° F. Meanwhile, continue with the construction of the shell.

Lining and baking the shell. Using a pastry brush and the softened butter, coat a sheet of heavy-duty aluminum foil about 14 inches wide and 18 inches long. If you don't have wide foil on hand, use two narrower strips, overlapping them slightly.

Gently but tightly fit the pastry-filled pan with the foil, buttered side down. Place a second 9-inch pan on top of the foil, and allow the excess foil to extend straight out all around between the doubled pans.

Holding the pans together, carefully turn them over and gently pat the pastry scallops out flat on the extended foil. Push the upper pan down onto the lower one to enclose the pastry firmly.

Transfer this intricate-sounding—but in fact quite simple—construction to the preheated 450° F. oven, placing it directly on the shelf; the pie pans will be upside down. Bake the shell undisturbed for 8 to 10 minutes, or until its exposed scalloped edge is golden brown.

Removing the shell from the oven. To take the baked shell out of the oven requires care to prevent its scalloped edge from breaking. Pull the oven shelf out and, with both hands holding the sides of the foil, slide the construction toward you. When the pan partially clears the shelf, slip your hand (protected by a potholder) under the lower pie pan and remove the construction—two pans, foil, and shell—from the oven.

Place the construction on a table and let it cool for a few minutes for easier handling. Then turn the doubled pans right side up and, using the foil edges as handles, lift off the upper pan, exposing the pastry.

If by some mischance a scallop or two should crumble after you have baked a pie shell, simply cut away the remaining scallops with a small knife. Although this will destroy the decorative effect, the shell itself will be intact.

Cool the shell in its pan and fill it as directed in your recipe.

LEMON MERINGUE PIE

Even the most expertly made meringue—that favorite American topping of stiffly beaten egg whites and sugar, browned in the oven—almost inevitably produces an inordinate amount of liquid that collects over the filling and runs down into the bottom crust as the pie cools. This is called "weeping," and the term is apt.

Until now, no foolproof way to control weeping has been generally known. Cream of tartar alone added to the egg whites really doesn't do the trick. After countless experiments I have found that if I add a small amount of dicalcium phosphate and an equal amount of cream of tartar to the egg whites while beating them, the finished meringue will shed at most only a few tears.

Dicalcium phosphate is a tasteless, inexpensive nutritional supplement that keeps indefinitely and does not affect the silky texture of the meringues in any way. If you can't find dicalcium phosphate powder in easily opened capsules at your drugstore, buy the tablets and crush them with a mortar and pestle or the back of a spoon.

MAKES A 9-INCH PIE

The Pastry:
A Fully Baked Scalloped Pie Shell (page 372)

The Filling:
1 cup sugar
5 tablespoons cornstarch
¼ teaspoon salt
2 cups water
5 egg yolks
2 tablespoons very finely chopped lemon rind
2 tablespoons butter, cut into bits and softened at room
   temperature
⅓ cup strained fresh lemon juice
4 tablespoons finely crushed gingersnap crumbs

The Meringue:
½ cup sugar
¾ teaspoon cream of tartar
¾ teaspoon dicalcium phosphate
5 egg whites

Making the filling. In a heavy 2-quart saucepan, combine 1 cup of sugar with the cornstarch, salt, and water. Stir with a whisk until the sugar and cornstarch are dissolved, then cook over high heat, continuing to stir constantly, until the mixture comes to a boil and thickens. Lower the heat and continue to whisk for another 3 minutes, or until the mixture is very thick, shiny, and translucent. Remove the pan from the heat.

Then, one at a time, quickly whisk the egg yolks into the mixture, making sure that each yolk has been thoroughly absorbed before adding the next one. Stir in the chopped lemon rind. Now cook the mixture over very low heat for 10 minutes, stirring constantly. To prevent the mixture from boiling, lift the pan off the heat every 3 minutes or so to cool it slightly, then return it to the heat.

If the mixture should become lumpy at any point, remove the pan from the heat, beat the filling vigorously until it is smooth again, then resume the cooking.

When the filling has cooked for 10 minutes, beat in the butter, a few bits at a time. Then stir in the lemon juice. Immediately pour the filling into another bowl, and cool it until it is only slightly warm to the touch, whisking it now and then to keep it smooth.

Scatter the gingersnap crumbs evenly over the bottom of the baked pie shell and slowly pour in the still slightly warm filling, smoothing the top with a rubber spatula.

Refrigerate the pie for about 30 minutes, or until the filling is firm.

Preheating the oven. Slide an oven shelf into an upper slot of the oven and preheat the oven for 15 minutes at 325° F.

Making the meringue. In a small, fine-meshed strainer set over a bowl, combine ½ cup of sugar with the cream of tartar and dicalcium phosphate; shake the strainer, stirring to remove any lumps, until the mixture has been sieved into the bowl.

Using an electric mixer, a rotary beater, or a balloon whisk and copper bowl, beat the egg whites briskly until they are thick and foamy. Then, still beating, add the sugar mixture a tablespoonful at a time. Continue to beat until the egg whites—now a meringue —are firm enough to hold stiff peaks on the beater when it is lifted. If you have any doubt about the consistency of the meringue, overbeat rather than underbeat it.

Remove the pie from the refrigerator. With a rubber spatula, cover the entire surface of the filling with the meringue, making sure it extends ¼ inch over the rim of the pastry as well. Then swirl small decorative peaks all over the surface of the meringue with the spatula.

Baking the meringue. Bake the pie in the preheated oven for 20 to 25 minutes, or until the top of the meringue is a light golden brown with some marbling of white still showing.

Cool the pie to room temperature before serving it.

Ideally, a lemon meringue pie should never be refrigerated. However, if the weather is very warm, you can refrigerate any leftover pie, but let it return to room temperature before serving it again.

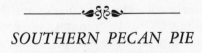

SOUTHERN PECAN PIE

The pecan is indigenous to America and is, in fact, closely related to the hickory nut. It grows in great profusion in the southern Mississippi valley, and anyone with a sweet tooth owes an enormous debt of gratitude to the creative Southern cook who made the first pecan pie.

MAKES A 9-INCH PIE

The Pastry:
A Fully Baked Scalloped Pie Shell (page 372)

The Filling:
2 cups dark corn syrup (a 16-ounce bottle of dark Karo syrup)
5 eggs
1 tablespoon butter, cut into bits
1 teaspoon vanilla
2 cups shelled pecan halves (a 6-ounce can)

The Topping (optional):
1 cup chilled heavy cream, whipped

Preheating the oven. Slide an oven shelf into an upper slot and preheat the oven for 15 minutes at 325° F.

Making the filling. Pour the corn syrup into a heavy 2-quart saucepan. Over high heat, bring the syrup to a turbulent boil. Then remove the pan from the heat.

Break the eggs into a medium-size bowl and beat them with a whisk just until they are well combined but not foaming. Then, a tablespoonful at a time, pour 4 tablespoons of the hot syrup into the eggs, whisking well after each addition. Slowly pour the egg mixture, now slightly heated, in a thin stream into the pan of hot syrup, stirring constantly. Add the butter bits. Continue to stir for 5 minutes, still off the heat; then add the vanilla.

Filling the pie. Pull your oven shelf partway out and on it set the fully baked pie shell, still in its pan. Then, slowly and carefully, pour the hot filling into the shell. Sprinke the pecan halves over the top, spreading them out evenly with a spoon or spatula.

Baking the pie. Gently slide the shelf back into the preheated oven and bake the pie for 30 to 40 minutes, or until the filling has browned slightly on top. Remove the pie from the oven carefully to protect the extended scalloped edge of the pastry.

Cool the pie to room temperature before serving it.

The optional topping. If you like to be traditional, serve the pie with a bowl of unsweetened whipped cream. Or spoon the whipped cream into a pastry bag fitted with a No. 9 star tip and pipe the cream around the edge of the pie in as fanciful a pattern as you wish.

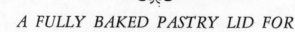

A FULLY BAKED PASTRY LID FOR
DEEP-DISH FRUIT PIES

In traditional deep-dish pies, such as the chicken pie for which I give a recipe later, the filling and the top crust are baked at the same time; and this technique works very well indeed for a savory filling. However, deep-dish fruit pies made this way tend to bubble over, no matter how much care you exercise. Therefore, I have departed entirely from tradition for the deep-dish fruit pies that follow.

It is perhaps unorthodox to bake the pastry first, cook the filling separately, and then combine the two, but the result is almost miraculous. The heat of the fruit seals the prebaked lid to the filling, creating the illusion that the filling and pastry have been baked together—while you, the cook, are spared the unpleasant chore of cleaning the inevitably fruit-blackened oven.

The recipe for the baked pastry lid is followed by two recipes for deep-dish fruit pies: blueberry and rhubarb. In fact, there is no end to the variety of fruits you can combine for deep-dish fruit pies. Incidentally, I have devised these recipes with frozen fruit, so you need no longer wait for spring to make delectable fruit pies. And because defrosting frozen fruit takes at least 2 hours, you may want to defrost the fruit for the filling before you proceed to bake the pastry lid.

If you want to refresh your pastrymaking skills, all the techniques used in the following recipe are described in detail, starting on page 359.

MAKES A PASTRY LID FOR A 9-INCH PIE

The Pastry:
1¼ cups sifted all-purpose flour
½ teaspoon salt
½ cup chilled vegetable shortening
3 tablespoons ice-cold water
2 tablespoons unsifted flour

The Glaze for the Crust:
1 tablespoon milk

Making the pastry. Combine the sifted flour and salt, and sift them together into a large mixing bowl. Add the vegetable shortening and toss it lightly about to dust it with the flour.

With small chopping motions of your pastry blender, cut the shortening into the flour until small rice-size pellets are formed.

Pour the ice-cold water over the fat-flour granules and toss them together lightly with a fork to make a moist crumbly dough. Quickly gather the dough with your hands, then shape it into a compact ball. Hold the ball in one hand and, with the other, sprinkle it evenly with the unsifted flour.

Rolling the dough. Place the ball of dough on your floured pastry cloth and pat it into a 4-inch circle.

Roll the pastry, always starting with your rolling pin across the center of the dough, working outward in continuous strokes, and lifting the pin as you near the edge of the pastry. Work all around the circle of dough, overlapping each preceding stroke by about 1 inch, until you reach your starting point. The finished rough circle of pastry should be about 11 inches in diameter. If it is smaller, repeat the entire rolling process.

Preheating the oven. Slide an oven shelf into a center slot and preheat the oven for 15 minutes at 450° F.

Making, glazing, and baking the pastry lid. Invert a 9-inch glass pie plate and place it directly in the center of the pastry circle. With a small sharp knife, cut through the pastry about ¼ inch beyond the rim of the pie plate. Remove the plate and gently transfer the pastry to an ungreased cookie sheet with your hands or a large spatula. To prevent the pastry lid from puffing as it bakes, prick it all over with a fork, or perforate it in a decorative pattern such as a star or flower head. Then paint the surface lightly with a pastry brush dipped in the milk.

Bake for about 10 minutes in the preheated oven until the lid is light golden brown and feels firm to the touch. Slide it onto a wire cake rack to cool.

Making pastry lids for individual fruit pies. If you prefer, you can make individual deep-dish pies in custard cups or other dishes; this recipe for a 9-inch lid and either of the fillings that follow will make either 4 individual pies in 10-ounce custard cups, or 8 individual pies in 5- or 6-ounce custard cups.

To make the pastry lids for individual pies, roll the pastry circle to a diameter of 15 or 16 inches, and use your custard cup, inverted, as a guide in cutting out the pastry. Just as you did for the large pastry lid, cut each pastry circle ¼ inch outside the rim of the custard cup, then prick, glaze, bake, and cool them in the same manner. The smaller lids may require a moment or so less baking time because the pastry will probably be somewhat thinner than the single large pastry lid.

DEEP-DISH BLUEBERRY PIE

If you want to vary the fruit filling slightly, substitute one small package of sliced frozen peaches, thoroughly defrosted and drained, for a little of the hot blueberry filling in the pie dish before topping the pie with its baked pastry lid.

MAKES A 9-INCH PIE

The Pastry:
A Fully Baked Pastry Lid (page 378)

The Filling:
3 packages (10 ounces each) frozen unsweetened blueberries
1 cup juice drained from the berries
¾ cup sugar
2 tablespoons cornstarch
2 tablespoons fresh lemon juice
½ teaspoon ground cinnamon

Making the filling. Defrost the blueberries completely in a sieve set over a large bowl. Shake the sieve occasionally to drain the berries thoroughly as they defrost. Measure the blueberry juice; if you have less than 1 cup, add water as needed.

In a heavy 12-inch frying pan, combine the blueberry juice with the sugar, cornstarch, lemon juice, and cinnamon. Mix thoroughly.

Over moderate heat, bring the mixture to a boil, stirring constantly with a whisk. Lower the heat and simmer until it is thick and smooth, about 2 minutes. Then stir in the drained blueberries and simmer the mixture for 3 to 5 minutes, or until the berries are tender but still intact. Taste for sweetness; you may want to add a little more sugar.

Assembling and serving the pie. While the filling is still hot, pour it into a 9-inch glass pie plate. Then immediately—and carefully—lift up the baked pastry lid and place it over the filling.

Serve the pie while it is still warm. If it cools too much before serving time, heat it for 10 minutes in a preheated 325° F. oven, making certain that the filling never comes to a boil, or it will spill over disastrously.

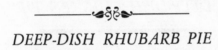

DEEP-DISH RHUBARB PIE

If you like the combination of rhubarb and strawberries, substitute one 9- or 10-ounce package of frozen sliced strawberries, defrosted and drained, for a little of the hot rhubarb filling after placing it in the pie dish and before topping the pie with its baked pastry lid.

MAKES A 9-INCH PIE

The Pastry:
A Fully Baked Pastry Lid (page 378)

The Filling:
2 packages (1 pound each) frozen unsweetened rhubarb
2 cups juice drained from the rhubarb
¾ cup sugar
2 tablespoons quick-cooking tapioca

Making the filling. Defrost the rhubarb completely in a sieve set over a large bowl. Transfer the drained rhubarb to a double thickness of paper towels, and pat it dry with more paper toweling. Measure the rhubarb juice; if there is less than 2 cups, add water to make up the amount.

In a heavy 12-inch frying pan, combine the rhubarb juice with the sugar and tapioca. Mix thoroughly. Add the rhubarb and let the mixture rest, uncovered, for 15 minutes.

Over moderate heat, bring the mixture to a boil. Lower the heat and simmer the rhubarb, stirring gently every now and then, for 5 to 10 minutes, or until the sauce thickens slightly and the rhubarb is tender but not falling apart.

Assembling and serving the pie. As soon as the filling is done, pour it into a 9-inch glass pie plate. Immediately—and carefully—cover it with the baked pastry lid.

Serve the pie while still warm. If it cools too much, heat it for 10 minutes in a preheated 325° F. oven, making certain that the filling never comes to a boil.

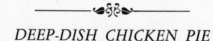

DEEP-DISH CHICKEN PIE

Although this chicken pie is basically a traditional one—that is, the pastry and filling are baked at the same time—it departs from tradition in a significant way. It is unlike most chicken pies in that neither the chicken nor the vegetables require previous cooking. This results in a filling in which the essential flavor of each ingredient is retained to a remarkable degree. And as an added bonus, it is exceedingly simple to make.

SERVES 6

The Filling:

2 pounds chicken breasts, skinned, boned, and cut into ¾-inch cubes

About 2 pounds baking potatoes, peeled and cut into ½-inch dice (2½ cups)

1 cup frozen peas, defrosted and drained

4 tablespoons finely chopped scallions

2 tablespoons canned pimientos, cut into small strips

2 tablespoons dried mushrooms, soaked in hot water for 15 minutes, drained, then finely chopped; or finely chopped drained, canned mushrooms

½ teaspoon crumbled dried thyme leaves

½ teaspoon salt

Freshly ground black pepper

4 hard-cooked eggs, cooled, peeled, and cut in half lengthwise

The Sauce:
4 tablespoons butter, cut into bits
5 tablespoons flour
1½ cups fresh or canned chicken broth
½ teaspoon salt
⅛ teaspoon fresh lemon juice

The Pastry:
1¼ cups sifted all-purpose flour
½ teaspoon salt
½ cup chilled vegetable shortening
3 tablespoons ice-cold water
2 tablespoons unsifted flour

The Glaze for the Crust:
1 egg yolk
2 teaspoons milk

Making the filling. Place the chicken cubes in a 1½-quart soufflé dish. Add the potatoes, peas, scallions, pimiento strips, mushrooms, thyme, salt, and a liberal grinding of black pepper. With either a wooden spoon or your hands, gently lift and toss the ingredients together. Set the dish aside while you prepare the sauce.

Making the sauce. In a heavy 2-quart saucepan, melt the butter bits over low heat, being careful not to let it brown.

Remove the pan from the heat and stir in 5 tablespoons flour; this mixture is called a roux. Blend the butter and flour well, then pour in the chicken broth. With a whisk, beat the roux and broth together until they are well mixed.

Return the pan to high heat and, whisking constantly, bring the sauce to a boil. When the sauce is thick and smooth—a matter of a moment—lower the heat and simmer it for 2 or 3 minutes to rid it of any taste of raw flour.

Stir in the salt and lemon juice. Taste for seasoning.

Pour the sauce over the ingredients in the baking dish. With a rubber spatula, gently lift and toss all the ingredients until they are thoroughly coated with the sauce.

Place the hard-cooked eggs over the filling, laying them cut side down and end to end in a circle around the perimeter of the dish. The eggs should rise slightly higher than the top of the dish so that they will support the crust. Set the dish aside.

Preheating the oven. Slide an oven shelf in a lower slot and preheat the oven for 15 minutes at 450° F.

Making and rolling the pastry. Follow the directions in the recipe for A Fully Baked Pastry Lid (page 379).

To trim the pastry, which has been rolled out to a diameter of 11 inches, invert a 9-inch pie pan over it. With a small sharp knife or a plain pastry wheel, cut all around the pan. This will make a circle 10 inches in diameter. Remove the pan.

Topping, sealing, and glazing the pie. Beat the egg yolk with the milk until they are just combined; then, with a pastry brush, paint the rim of the filled soufflé dish, and paint a band 1½ inches wide around the outside of the dish just below the rim.

Drape the pastry in a half-moon over the rolling pin, then lower it, letting it fall gently over the filling. Adjust the pastry over the dish, with a uniform overhang all around.

Double the overhanging pastry edge under itself and press it against the coated band on the dish to form a thick edge about 1 inch wide. Now, holding a table fork vertically, press the back of its prongs all around the band of pastry to crimp the pastry to the dish.

Using a pastry brush, coat the crust evenly with the remaining glaze. Then, with a small sharp knife, cut a circle ¾ inch in diameter in the center of the pastry, discard the cut-out disk, and insert a small funnel or a plain No. 9 pastry tip into the opening.

Baking and serving the pie. Bake the pie for 10 minutes in the preheated 450° F. oven, then lower the heat to 325° F. and continue baking it for 50 minutes more.

After the pie has baked for about 30 minutes, you will probably find that the sauce is bubbling up into the funnel or pastry tip in the center of the crust. If at any point the sauce threatens to bubble over, use a bulb baster to draw off the excess. Check the pie every 10 minutes or so for the rest of its baking time and remove sauce whenever you think it necessary. Save the sauce, if you like, and reheat it to serve with the pie.

The pie is done when its crust is a golden-flecked brown and firm to the touch. Serve it at once.

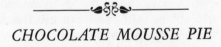

GRAHAM CRACKER PIE CRUST

A graham cracker crust is a purely American concept, as are the crackers themselves, made from a flour invented by Sylvester Graham. In making this crust, you need not be limited to graham cracker crumbs; you may substitute finely crushed zwieback, gingersnaps, or vanilla wafers.

When you want a ready-to-fill pie crust, this is a good alternative to A Fully Baked Scalloped Pie Shell. It is especially delicious with the Chocolate Mousse Pie and Orange-Apricot Chiffon Pie, recipes for which follow.

MAKES A 9-INCH PIE CRUST

1½ cups finely crushed graham cracker crumbs
¼ cup sifted confectioners' sugar
1 teaspoon ground cinnamon
6 tablespoons melted butter

In a large bowl, combine the graham cracker crumbs, confectioners' sugar, and cinnamon. With a wooden spoon stir them together thoroughly. Add the melted butter, and mix the ingredients until the butter is completely absorbed.

Dump the mixture into a 9-inch aluminum pie pan and, using your fingers, press and pat it as evenly as possible over the bottom and up the sides of the pan.

Set a second 9-inch pie pan into the crumb-lined pan and press it down firmly. Remove the upper pan and press any uneven spots smooth with your fingers; this will be likely only around the sides.

To firm the crust, refrigerate the shell for at least 2 hours before filling it. This is absolutely essential.

CHOCOLATE MOUSSE PIE

The chocolate mousse filling is indubitably French and pairs splendidly with a uniquely American graham cracker crust or a fully baked pie shell.

MAKES A 9-INCH PIE

The Crust:

1 chilled Graham Cracker Pie Crust (page 385), or A Fully
Baked Scalloped Pie Shell (page 372)

The Filling:

½ pound semisweet chocolate (preferably Baker's), cut into
small pieces; or ½ pound packaged semisweet chocolate bits

½ cup strong coffee, or 1 tablespoon instant coffee powder
dissolved in ½ cup boiling water

1 teaspoon vanilla

2 egg yolks

2 egg whites

2 tablespoons sugar

½ cup chilled heavy cream

The Border (optional):

1 cup chilled heavy cream

Making the filling. Place the semisweet chocolate in the top of a
double boiler, and add the coffee. Partially fill the lower section
with hot water, and fit the top section over it.

Set the double boiler over moderate heat, and stir the chocolate
and coffee together constantly with a rubber spatula until the chocolate melts and the mixture is smooth. Then take the double boiler
off the heat and remove the upper pan. Stir the vanilla into the
chocolate mixture and set it aside to cool slightly—for not more
than 2 minutes—stirring it once or twice.

Now, with a whisk, beat the egg yolks into the chocolate mixture one at a time, continuing to beat until the yolks are completely
absorbed. Set the filling aside to cool to room temperature.

Beat the egg whites with a rotary or electric beater, or in a
copper bowl with a balloon whisk, until they are thick and foamy;
add the sugar and continue beating rapidly, moving the beater
around the bowl as you beat, until the whites form very firm, unwavering peaks on the beater when it is lifted.

In a chilled bowl, beat ½ cup of heavy cream only until it forms
soft peaks; it should not be stiff. You can use the same beater you
used for the egg whites without washing it.

With a rubber spatula, gently fold the beaten whites into the
whipped cream, keeping the mixture as airy as possible. Then thoroughly stir 2 tablespoons of the combination into the chocolate
mixture to lighten it.

With the spatula, scrape the chocolate mixture over the combined egg whites and cream and gently fold the mixtures together, combining the two by cutting down through both and lifting the heavier mass over the lighter. Mix just until no streaks of white show; do not overmix, or the mousse will be heavy.

Chilling the pie. Pour the mousse into the pie shell, spreading it evenly with your spatula. Refrigerate the pie for at least an hour to allow the mousse to become firm. Like all desserts containing cream, the pie should be kept refrigerated until serving time.

The optional border. If you wish to decorate the pie, whip the cup of chilled heavy cream until it forms firm but still slightly wavering peaks. Spoon the whipped cream around the edge of the pie or pipe it through a pastry bag fitted with a No. 9 star tip in as fanciful a pattern as you wish.

ORANGE-APRICOT CHIFFON PIE

MAKES A 9-INCH PIE

The Crust:
1 chilled Graham Cracker Pie Crust (page 385), or A Fully Baked Scalloped Pie Shell (page 372)

The Filling:
1 envelope (¼ ounce) unflavored gelatin
½ cup water
4 egg yolks
4 tablespoons sugar
½ cup strained fresh orange juice
1 tablespoon finely chopped orange rind
⅛ teaspoon salt
2 cans (1 pound 1 ounce each) pitted apricots, drained and rubbed through a medium-fine sieve or processed in a food processor (about 1½ cups purée)
4 egg whites

The Garnish (Optional):
1 small can (11 ounces) mandarin oranges, thoroughly drained and patted dry with paper towels
½ cup chilled heavy cream, stiffly whipped

Making the filling. Sprinkle the gelatin into a glass measuring cup containing the cold water. Set aside and allow the gelatin to soften for about 5 minutes.

In the top pan of your double boiler, off the heat, beat the egg yolks for 2 minutes with a whisk, then beat in 2 tablespoons of the sugar, continuing to beat for about 2 minutes more, or until the mixture is thick enough to run sluggishly off the beater in a ribbon when it is lifted out of the pan. Now stir in the orange juice, orange rind, and salt.

Partially fill the lower pan of the double boiler with hot water, insert the top pan, and set the double boiler over moderate heat. With a rubber spatula, stir the mixture for about 5 minutes, or until it becomes smooth and fairly thick, like a custard.

Add the softened gelatin to the custard and stir for about 30 seconds to dissolve the gelatin completely. Scrape the mixture into a large bowl and thoroughly combine with the apricot purée.

Refrigerate for about 30 minutes, only until the mixture thickens to a puddinglike consistency. Check it from time to time. If it should become lumpy at any point, beat it briskly with a whisk until smooth, then complete the chilling.

With a rotary or electric beater, or using a copper bowl and a balloon whisk, beat the egg whites for a minute or two, just until foamy. Then add the remaining 2 tablespoons of sugar and continue beating rapidly, moving the beater around the bowl as you beat, until the whites form firm but slightly wavering peaks when the beater is lifted. If in doubt, underbeat rather than overbeat; overbeaten egg whites will make the filling spongy rather than velvety.

Mix 2 heaping tablespoons of the beaten whites into the apricot mixture, then, with a rubber spatula, scrape the mixture over the remaining whites in the bowl. Slowly and gently fold the two together, constantly cutting down and lifting the heavier mass over the lighter mass and running the spatula around the sides of the bowl occasionally. Do not overfold; stop when traces of egg whites no longer show.

Filling and serving the pie. Pour the filling into the chilled pie shell, mounding it slightly in the center and smoothing the surface with a spatula as evenly as you can.

Refrigerate the pie for at least 1 hour, or until the filling is firm. The pie can remain in the refrigerator up to 6 hours before you serve it. It will inevitably sink a bit as it chills, but this will have no effect whatsoever on its light texture.

The optional garnish. You may garnish the chilled pie with overlapping sections of mandarin oranges, laid in a ring around the outer edge. You might mound the whipped cream in the center just before serving the pie.

Tarts and Tartlets

There is an essential difference, theoretically at least, between a French tart and an American pie. A tart is an open-faced, filled pastry shell, which is commonly removed from its pan before it is served. A tart shell—at least in this book—is always baked before it is filled. A pie, on the other hand, is generally thought of as a filled pastry, usually with both a top and a bottom crust, but sometimes with only one or the other. A pie is, of necessity, always left in its pan.

With the passage of years the two culinary categories have overlapped. Although the American pie has rather brazenly taken on some of the characteristics of the French tart, both tarts and tartlets—small individual tarts—have, in some mysterious fashion, retained their original identity. Undoubtedly the French, always rigid classicists when it comes to culinary matters, are responsible for this; they wouldn't dream of concealing their colorful, symmetrically patterned fruit fillings, or the quivering, delicate, savory custards they call quiches.

Techniques for Making Tarts and Tartlets

In general, the same pastrymaking techniques apply to both tarts or tartlets and pie dough. But because French pastry is so short—that is, it contains a large amount of butter in proportion to flour—it is harder to handle than American pie dough and requires some special techniques of its own.

Preparing the ingredients. The success of this rich pastry depends in large measure on having all the ingredients thoroughly chilled, and on combining them speedily. Because the warmth of your fingers will soften the butter as you rub the fats with the flour, it is necessary that the butter, shortening, and water—even the flour and the bowl, if you are a perfectionist—be extremely cold when you begin to work. Plan to chill the ingredients and make the pastry well before you will use it—at least 3 hours, or even a day.

Making the pastry. Add the chilled fats to the sifted dry ingredients, tossing them together with your hands to coat the fats with flour. Then rub the flour and fats together, using the thumbs and first two fingers of each hand in a sliding motion, as if you were counting out money. Do not squeeze or press the dough. Nor should you use a pastry blender to mix tart pastry; the desired texture can be achieved only by rubbing the flour, butter, and shortening together with your fingers to form a fat-flour structure that is quite different from that of American pie crust. For mixing tartlet pastry, however, a pastry blender is more effective than fingers to achieve a fine granular texture, although you may use your fingers if you prefer.

After a moment or two, rub a handful of the mixture between both hands with a sliding motion, letting the flakes fall into the bowl. Then return to the thumb-and-finger operation. Alternating these procedures will aerate the mixture and prevent it from becoming oily. Continue until the fats and flour are fairly well integrated in comparatively dry flakes. Don't try to make the blend too uniform; there should be some small nuggets of flour-coated fat among the blended flakes.

Immediately pour the specified amount of ice-cold water over the mixture, and toss it with your hands until you can gather the dough into a compact ball. Hold the ball of dough in one hand and, with the other, lightly and evenly sprinkle it with unsifted flour.

Chilling the dough. Pack the dough in plastic wrap or a plastic bag and refrigerate it for at least 3 hours, or for a day, or even overnight. This pastry must be thoroughly chilled before it is used. Well wrapped, it may be frozen for up to 2 months at below 0° F.

Rolling the dough. The French traditionally roll their pastry on a hardwood board or a marble slab. You can follow their practice (see page 391) if you wish, but you will find it considerably easier to use a pastry cloth and a rolling pin with a floured stockinette sleeve, as in making American pie crust.

Remove the dough from the refrigerator, unwrap it, and let it rest at room temperature until it softens just enough for you to press a finger into it fairly easily; don't let the dough get too soft.

Place the ball of dough on your floured pastry cloth and pat it into a circle about 4 inches in diameter. If it tends to crack or seems unmanageable, it is still too cold; let it soften before proceeding.

Position your rolling pin, encased in its floured sleeve, across the center of the dough and roll it away from you in one firm continuous stroke, lifting the pin as you near the edge. If you apply the pressure of your rolling pin all the way to the outer edge of the pastry circle, the pastry will become brittle and thin.

Return the pin to the center of the dough and, shifting your direction slightly to the right, again roll it away from you precisely as before. Never roll back and forth except when patching—it would toughen the pastry—and never, for any reason, turn the dough over and roll the underside.

Continue this rolling procedure all around the circle of dough, each time overlapping the last stroke by about an inch. You will, after four or five strokes, reach a point where you must change your direction and roll the dough toward rather than away from you. After a similar number of downward strokes, you will find it again necessary to reverse direction; so roll the dough away from you until you complete the circle and reach the point where you began.

If your pastry begins to stick to the sleeve or the pastry cloth, rub a little extra flour into the sleeve or, if necessary, into the pastry cloth. But keep the extra flour to a minimum; too much of it can toughen the pastry.

If the pastry tears while you are rolling it—and, alas, it often does—merely cut a small piece from the edge, brush it lightly with water, and patch it into place, moistened side down, over the opening. Dust it with a little flour and roll your pin back and forth over it until the surface is smooth again.

When you have finished rolling the dough to the diameter specified in the recipe, check it with a ruler. If the circle of dough is too small, repeat the entire rolling process. Never pull or stretch the dough to enlarge its area; this will increase its elasticity and cause the pastry to retract to its original shape as it bakes.

Rolling the dough the French way. Spread about 2 tablespoons of unsifted flour on your pastry board, Formica-topped counter, or marble slab. Place the dough on the surface and pat it lightly into a 4-inch circle. Dust a little flour over the dough and, starting at the center, roll the pin away from you in one continuous stroke, as described above. However, after each stroke, gently turn the entire circle an inch or two to the right and sprinkle a little more flour under it if it seems to be sticking. Continue to roll from the center, turning the dough and dusting with flour as necessary, until you reach your starting point. If the circle of dough is too small, repeat the entire rolling and rotating process.

Lining the tart pan. Set the rolling pin horizontally across the pastry about 4 inches away from the edge closest to you. Lift the near edge of pastry and double it over the rolling pin, which will roll away as you lift the pastry. The rolling pin, its handles exposed, will be enclosed in a half-moon of pastry.

Lift the rolling pin by its exposed handles and, using your thumbs to prevent the pastry from rolling off, hold the pastry-laden pin over the pan and a few inches beyond its center. Then lower the pastry and unroll it from the pin, letting it fall slackly into the pan.

To fit the pastry fully into the pan, gently lift up a small section of the overhanging edge with your fingers and let it fall easily into the crease of the pan. Continue to ease the pastry without stretching it, section by section, until the pan is lined with pastry lying slackly in place. With a fingertip, gently press the pastry into each fluting of the side of the pan until it fits snugly all around. To form a more definite crease, run the back of a teaspoon all around the pastry where the flutes meet the bottom of the pan.

To remove the overhanging pastry, run your rolling pin across the top of the tart pan. The excess pastry will fall away, leaving a perfectly smooth edge.

You may bake the shell at once, or refrigerate the pastry-lined pan until you are ready to use it. If you want to store pastry for a day or two, cover the pastry-lined pan with plastic wrap before refrigerating it. If you want to freeze the unbaked shell, wrap it securely in heavy-duty foil; it will keep up to 2 months at a temperature below 0° F.

Baking the tart shell. To support the unfilled tart shell as it bakes, you must weight it during its initial baking period. To do this, cut a sheet of foil a few inches wider than, and more than twice as long as, the diameter of the tart pan. Double the foil, butter one side, and place that side over the pastry in the pan, pressing it gently down and into the crease of the pan to support the sides. Pour in about a cupful of small dry beans or rice—even pebbles will do—and spread them evenly on top of the foil. They may be used repeatedly.

After you remove the foil and beans for the final baking period, to prevent the dough from blistering, prick the bottom of the crust lightly all over its surface but not entirely through the crust.

Always bake tart shells in the center of the oven and at a fairly high temperature. After filling, however, set the tart on an upper shelf so that the heat will be greater above the filling than below the previously baked crust. Bake custard fillings at a lower temperature than others in order to prevent them from curdling.

If your oven has "hot spots," you may safely move tarts or

tartlets around to avoid uneven baking, but do it quickly so the oven door is not open long enough to cause the heat to lower appreciably.

Repairing a broken shell. If you are careless or hurried, you may occasionally find that the edge of the baked pastry has crumbled or broken enough to make it impossible to fill the shell, particularly with custard. There is a simple way to line the shell so that it will hold the filling without leakage while it bakes: Build a new edge with a strip of aluminum foil. To make this foil "dam," butter a foil strip wider and longer than the break. Press the buttered side against the inner edges of the flutings; it will contain the filling during baking, and when the filling is fully cooked, you can remove the strip.

Freezing tart and tartlet shells. A baked and unfilled tart or tartlet shell may be frozen if it is securely wrapped in heavy-duty foil, but I don't recommend freezing a fully baked, filled tart of any kind, because the moisture generated during the defrosting process will turn the pastry sodden.

If you have frozen an unbaked tart or tartlet shell, you may bake it without defrosting it. A frozen baked shell must be baked without defrosting; fill it quickly and bake it immediately. In either case, the baking time will be the same as for an unfrozen shell.

Tarts

A FULLY BAKED FLUTED TART SHELL

The pastry I use for tarts is a version of the classic *pâte brisée*, a French short pastry. It is somewhat richer and less flaky than American pastry and contains a considerable amount of butter in addition to shortening. Although it takes some practice to roll out, the result is worth the effort.

You might note, by the way, that this recipe for tart pastry makes more than enough dough to line a 9-inch tart pan. This gives novice cooks an embarrassment of riches, as it were, to play around and experiment with; and any leftover pastry can be frozen. An experienced cook may choose to make half the amount of pastry called for, or to make two tart shells from the original recipe. But, experienced or not, I would suggest that, at least the first time, you make the dough in the quantity I indicate.

MAKES A FULLY BAKED, UNFILLED 9-INCH SHELL

The Pastry:
2 cups sifted all-purpose flour
½ teaspoon salt
8 tablespoons butter (a quarter-pound stick), cut into ¼-inch
     pieces and thoroughly chilled
3 tablespoons shortening, thoroughly chilled
⅓ cup ice-cold water
¼ cup unsifted flour

For Coating the Tart Pan and the Lining Foil:
2 teaspoons butter, softened at room temperature

Making the pastry. Combine the sifted flour and salt, and sift them together into a large mixing bowl. Add 8 tablespoons of butter and the shortening. Toss the ingredients together with your hands to coat the butter and shortening with flour. Then rub the flour and fats together, alternating the two techniques described in detail on page 390. Continue until the fats and flour are fairly well integrated in comparatively dry flakes. Don't attempt to make the blend too uniform; there should be occasional small nuggets of flour-coated fat among the blended flakes.

Immediately pour the ice-cold water over the mixture and toss it with your hands until you can gather the dough into a compact ball. If for any reason it seems crumbly—most unlikely—sprinkle in an additional teaspoon, no more, of cold water.

Hold the ball of dough in one hand and, with the other, sprinkle it lightly and evenly with the unsifted flour.

Chilling the dough. Wrap the ball of dough in plastic wrap or a plastic bag and refrigerate it for at least 3 hours, or for a day, or even overnight.

Rolling the dough. Remove the dough from the refrigerator, unwrap it, and let it rest at room temperature until it softens just enough for you to press a finger into it fairly easily, but don't let the dough get too soft.

Place the dough on your floured pastry cloth and pat it into a 4-inch circle. Position your rolling pin, encased in its floured sleeve, across the center of the dough, and roll it away from you in one firm continuous stroke, lifting the pin as you near the edge. Shift the direction slightly to the right, return the pin to the center of the dough, and again roll it away from you. Continue to roll the dough in this fashion, each time overlapping the last stroke by about 1 inch. Your strokes will circle the pastry like a hand around the face of a clock. When you reach the point where you began, your pastry should be about ⅛ inch thick and about 13 inches in diameter. If the circle is too small, repeat the entire rolling process.

Lining the tart pan. With your pastry brush and 1 teaspoon of the softened butter, coat the entire inside surface of your tart pan.

Drape the pastry in a half-moon over your rolling pin, then unroll it over the tart pan, letting it fall slackly into the pan, as described in detail on pages 391–92. Ease the overhanging pastry into the pan without stretching it, section by section, until the pan is lined with pastry lying slackly in place. With a fingertip, gently press the pastry into each fluting of the pan until it fits snugly, then run the back of a teaspoon all around the crease where the flutes meet the bottom of the pan.

To remove the overhanging pastry, run your rolling pin across the top of the tart pan. The excess pastry will fall away, leaving a perfectly smooth edge.

Preheating the oven. Slide an oven shelf into a middle slot and preheat the oven at 425° F. for 15 minutes.

Baking the tart shell. Cut a sheet of 12- or 14-inch-wide aluminum foil 24 inches long, double it, and paint one side evenly with the remaining teaspoon of softened butter, using a pastry brush. Place the foil, buttered side down, over the pastry, and press it gently down and into the crease to support the sides of the pastry as it bakes. Pour in about a cupful of small dry beans and spread them evenly on top of the foil.

Bake the shell in the preheated 425° F. oven for 10 to 12 minutes, or until you see the rim of the pastry beginning to turn a very pale brown. Then, using both hands, lift out the foil holding the beans.

To prevent the pastry from puffing as baking is completed, prick the bottom of the crust lightly all over its surface, but don't pierce it entirely.

Reduce the oven temperature to 375° F. and bake the shell about 8 minutes longer, or until it is golden brown and firm to the touch. Check the shell after 5 minutes of this final period to make sure that the shell isn't baking too fast.

Let the shell cool in its pan.

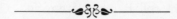

VARIATION: A PARTIALLY BAKED FLUTED TART SHELL

MAKES A 9-INCH SHELL

Make the pastry exactly as described in the preceding recipe and bake the shell for the first period of 10 to 12 minutes. After removing the foil and beans and pricking the surface of the pastry, lower the heat to 325° F. and reduce the second baking time to about 3 minutes. When the partially baked shell has barely begun to brown, remove it from the oven. Let the shell cool in its pan before filling it.

Prebaking a tart shell ensures a crisp crust, but if the filling is to bake longer than 30 minutes, only bake the shell partially so that it won't overcook when baked again with the filling.

HAM AND CHEESE TART

This is essentially a version of the French *quiche Lorraine*, except that it uses ham and cheese instead of cheese alone. You may, if you like, substitute for the ham the same quantity of another meat, such as cooked tongue or fried bacon, with interesting effect.

MAKES A 9-INCH TART

The Pastry:
A Fully Baked Fluted Tart Shell (page 393)

The Filling:
2 eggs
¾ cup milk
¼ cup heavy cream
¾ teaspoon salt
Freshly ground black pepper
½ teaspoon dry mustard
⅓ cup freshly grated imported Parmesan cheese, plus
    2 tablespoons for topping
¼ pound baked or boiled ham, trimmed of all fat and cut into
    ¼- to ½-inch cubes (about 1 cup cubed ham)
1 tablespoon butter, cut into bits

The Garnish:
1 tablespoon finely chopped fresh parsley

Preheating the oven. Slide an oven shelf into the upper slot and preheat the oven for 15 minutes at 325° F.

Making the filling. Break the eggs into a 2-quart mixing bowl and, with a fork or a small whisk, beat them for a few seconds, or only long enough to combine them. Then stir in the milk, cream, salt, a liberal grinding of pepper, the dry mustard, and ⅓ cup of Parmesan cheese. Stir gently until the ingredients are well combined. Taste for seasoning; you may need more salt and pepper.

Filling the tart. Spread the cubed ham in the baked tart shell.

Pull the upper oven shelf forward and place the baked shell on it. Then pour the filling mixture into the shell. If the filling threatens to overflow the rim (the pastry may have contracted a bit too much during baking), stop pouring and discard the surplus custard.

Sprinkle the extra 2 tablespoons of grated Parmesan cheese over the filling and dot it evenly with the butter bits.

Baking the tart. Gently slide the laden shelf back into the preheated 325° F. oven and bake the tart for about 30 minutes, or until the custard is firm and a small table knife inserted into its center emerges almost, but not entirely, dry.

Serving the tart. Remove the tart from the oven and set it on top of a tall cylinder, such as a coffee can, carefully holding on to the sides of the pan. Check to see if the fluted sides of the pan will separate easily from the flat bottom of the pan and the baked shell; if the filling has cooked over at any point, the pastry may adhere to the metal. Free any such areas with the point of a small knife before gently guiding the outer rim down to the tabletop.

Slide the tart, still resting on the metal base of the tart pan, onto a serving platter. Sprinkle the tart with the chopped parsley and serve it at once; or cool it to lukewarm, if you prefer.

CRABMEAT TART

Cooked lobster or cooked shrimp, shredded or chopped, may be substituted for the crabmeat in this tart with equal success. If you use lobster, you might replace the chives with 1 tablespoon of chopped fresh tarragon; with the shrimp, you might use 2 table-spoons of chopped fresh dill.

These three herbs are interchangeable in any version of this tart, depending upon your taste or the fresh herbs you may have on hand. Frozen chopped chives are acceptable in place of fresh chives, but do not use dried herbs. Lacking all else, use fresh parsley, which is always available.

MAKES A 9-INCH TART

The Pastry:
A Fully Baked Fluted Tart Shell (page 393)

The Filling:
1 cup fresh-cooked crabmeat or a 6½-ounce can of crabmeat, thoroughly drained; or 1 cup frozen crabmeat, defrosted and thoroughly drained
2 eggs
¾ cup milk
¼ cup heavy cream
¾ teaspoon salt
⅛ teaspoon white pepper
2 tablespoons finely cut fresh chives or 3 tablespoons frozen chopped chives
2 tablespoons freshly grated imported Parmesan cheese
1 tablespoon butter, cut into bits

Preheating the oven. Slide an oven shelf into the upper slot and preheat the oven for 15 minutes at 325° F.

Making the filling. Remove and discard any bits of shell or carti-lage from the crabmeat. Then, using your fingers, shred the meat coarsely.

For the custard, break the eggs into a 2-quart mixing bowl and, using a fork or a small whisk, beat them for a few seconds, or only long enough to combine them. Then stir in the milk, cream, salt, pepper, and chives. Stir gently until the ingredients are well combined. Taste for seasoning; the mixture may need more salt and pepper.

Filling the tart. Scatter the crabmeat evenly in the baked shell.

Pull the upper oven shelf forward and place the baked shell on it. Then pour in the custard mixture. If the filling threatens to overflow (the pastry may have contracted a bit too much during baking), stop pouring and discard the excess custard. Sprinkle the Parmesan cheese evenly over the filling, then dot it with the butter bits.

Baking the tart. Gently slide the laden shelf into the oven and bake the tart for about 30 minutes, or until the custard is firm and a small table knife inserted into its center emerges almost, but not quite, dry.

Serving the tart. Remove the tart from the oven and set it on top of a tall cylinder, such as a coffee can, carefully holding the sides of the pan. Check to see if the sides of the pan will slip down easily from the flat bottom of the pan and the baked shell; if the filling has cooked over, the pastry may stick to the pan at that point. Free any such areas with the point of a small knife, then gently guide the loose rim of the pan down to the tabletop.

Slide the tart, still on the flat metal base of the tart pan, onto a serving platter. Serve it at once; or let it cool to lukewarm.

SWISS POTATO AND SAUSAGE TART

MAKES A 9-INCH TART

The Pastry:
A Partially Baked Fluted Tart Shell (page 396)

The Filling:
2 pounds baking potatoes
2 eggs
¼ cup heavy cream
1 teaspoon salt
Freshly ground black pepper
4 tablespoons butter, melted
2 teaspoons caraway seed, slightly bruised or crushed
About 1½ pounds peeled sausage, preferably Kielbasa (Polish sausage) ; or any similar garlic-flavored sausage

Preheating the oven. Slide an oven shelf into the upper slot and preheat the oven for 15 minutes at 325° F.

Making the filling. Peel the potatoes, immediately dropping them into a bowl of cold water to prevent discoloration. When all the potatoes have been peeled, remove them from the water one at a time, pat them dry with paper towels, and shred them directly into a mixing bowl, using the tear-shaped teeth of a stand-up four-sided grater, or use a food processor with its grating blade. Work quickly to keep discoloration to a minimum. (Discoloration will not affect the taste of the tart, but it will make it less attractive.)

When all the potatoes have been shredded, squeeze them firmly, a handful at a time, to rid them of as much moisture as possible. Drop each handful into a pint-size glass measuring cup as you finish squeezing it, then pack it down. You should have 2 cups of firmly packed shredded potatoes. If you don't, quickly peel, shred, and squeeze another potato.

Break the eggs into a 2-quart mixing bowl and, using a fork or a small whisk, beat them for a few seconds, or only long enough to combine them. Stir in the cream, salt, and a liberal grinding of black pepper, and continue to stir until the ingredients are well combined. Then add the potatoes and melted butter. Stir the mixture well and taste it for seasoning; it may need more salt.

Filling the tart. Pour the contents of the bowl into the tart shell and spread evenly with a rubber spatula. Sprinkle the caraway seed over the filling. Slice the sausage about 1 inch thick, and place slightly overlapping sausage slices around the edge, spacing them so that they make a complete circle.

Baking the tart. Bake the tart in the preheated oven for 45 minutes. Because some potatoes cook more quickly than others, test the filling for doneness 15 minutes or so before the time is up. The tart is done when the potatoes show no resistance to the point of a small sharp knife.

Serving the tart. Remove the tart from the oven and set it on top of a tall cylinder, such as a coffee can, carefully holding on to the sides of the pan. Check to see if the sides of the pan will move freely down from the flat bottom of the tart pan and the baked shell; if the filling has cooked over at any point, the pastry may cling to the metal. Free any such areas with the point of a small knife before guiding the outer rim down to the tabletop.

Slide the tart, still on the flat metal base of the tart pan, onto a serving platter. Serve it at once.

SPINACH TART

The Pastry:
A Fully Baked Fluted Tart Shell (page 393)

The Filling:
1 package (10 ounces) frozen chopped spinach, defrosted and thoroughly drained; or ½ pound fresh spinach, cooked and thoroughly drained
2 eggs
¾ cup milk
¼ cup heavy cream
2 coarsely chopped hard-cooked eggs
2 tablespoons finely chopped mushrooms; either about 12 dried mushrooms, soaked in warm water for 15 minutes, drained, patted dry with paper towels, and chopped; or canned mushrooms, drained, patted dry, and chopped
2 tablespoons finely chopped scallions
1 teaspoon salt
1 teaspoon fresh lemon juice
⅛ teaspoon ground nutmeg, preferably freshly grated
Freshly ground black pepper
2 tablespoons freshly grated imported Parmesan cheese
1 tablespoon butter, cut into bits

Preheating the oven. Slide an oven shelf into the upper slot and preheat the oven for 15 minutes at 325° F.

Making the filling. A small handful at a time, squeeze the spinach dry; then, using a long sharp knife on a board, chop it as fine as possible.

Break 2 eggs into a 2-quart mixing bowl and, using a fork or a small whisk, beat them for a few seconds, or only long enough to combine them. Then stir in the milk and cream. Add the spinach, hard-cooked eggs, mushrooms, scallions, salt, lemon juice, nutmeg, and a liberal grinding of pepper. With the fork or a rubber spatula, stir together thoroughly. Taste for seasoning.

Filling the tart. Pull the oven shelf forward and place the baked shell on it. Then pour the spinach mixture carefully into the shell.

If the filling threatens to overflow (the pastry may have contracted too much when you baked it), stop pouring and discard the excess filling. Sprinkle the Parmesan cheese over the filling, and dot it evenly with the butter bits.

Baking the tart. Gently slide the rack back into the oven and bake the tart for about 30 minutes, or until the custard is firm and a table knife inserted into its center emerges almost, but not entirely, dry.

Serving the tart. Remove the tart from the oven and set it on top of a tall cylinder, such as a coffee can, carefully holding on to the sides of the pan. Check to see if the sides of the pan will separate easily from the flat bottom of the pan and the baked shell; if the filling has cooked over at any point, the pastry may adhere to the metal. Free any such areas with the point of a small knife before gently guiding the outer rim of the pan down to the tabletop.

Slide the spinach tart, still on the flat metal base of the tart pan, carefully onto a large round serving platter. Serve it at once.

A SAVORY TART WITH TWO CHEESES

For some tastes the blue cheese in this tart may be piquant, and if you prefer a milder flavor, substitute for the blue cheese an equal quantity of Camembert or Liederkranz. Cut away the crust after allowing the cheese to soften at room temperature for about 30 minutes.

MAKES A 9-INCH TART

The Pastry:
A Fully Baked Fluted Tart Shell (page 393)

The Filling:
8 ounces cream cheese, softened at room temperature
4 ounces blue cheese, softened at room temperature
2 tablespoons heavy cream
2 eggs
2 tablespoons finely chopped fresh parsley
1 tablespoon grated onion
½ teaspoon salt
1 teaspoon sweet Hungarian paprika

Preheating the oven. Slide an oven shelf into the upper slot and preheat the oven for 15 minutes at 325° F.

Making the filling. With a large wooden spoon, mash the cream cheese and the blue cheese together against the sides of a large, heavy mixing bowl, then beat them vigorously until the mixture is fluffy and smooth.

Beat in the cream and, one at a time, break in the eggs, beating sturdily after each addition. When not a trace of the eggs remains, stir in the parsley, onion, and salt. Taste for seasoning; it may need more salt.

Filling the tart. Carefully pour the mixture into the tart shell and spread it out evenly with a rubber spatula. Sprinkle the top with the paprika.

Bake the tart for 30 minutes, or until the filling is firm and a table knife inserted into its center emerges almost, but not entirely, dry.

Serving the tart. Remove the tart from the oven and set it on top of a tall cylinder, such as a coffee can, carefully holding on to the sides of the pan. Check to see if the sides of the pan will move freely down from the flat bottom of the pan and the baked shell; if the filling has cooked over at any point, the pastry may cling to the metal. Free any such areas with the point of a small knife before guiding the outer rim down to the tabletop.

Slide the tart, still on the flat metal base of the tart pan, onto a serving platter. Serve it at once.

TOMATO AND CHEESE TART

This is my version of a famous French country tart that I make with Parmesan and Swiss cheese—either Gruyère, which I prefer, or Emmenthal. The French frequently serve it cold, especially at picnics. I personally prefer it hot; and you can choose between the French and me, or compromise by serving it lukewarm.

MAKES A 9-INCH TART

The Pastry:
A Fully Baked Fluted Tart Shell (page 393)

The Filling:
5 firm ripe medium tomatoes (about 1½ pounds), stem ends removed and the tomatoes sliced about ½ inch thick
1 tablespoon salt
¼ pound Swiss Gruyère or Emmenthal cheese, coarsely grated (about 1 cup, packed down)
Freshly ground black pepper
2 tablespoons finely cut fresh basil or 1 tablespoon crumbled dried basil
5 or 6 scallions, coarsely chopped, including 2 inches of green part (about 6 tablespoons)
2 tablespoons freshly grated imported Parmesan cheese
2 tablespoons dry bread crumbs
1 tablespoon butter, cut into bits

Preparing the tomatoes. Sprinkle the tomato slices on both sides with the salt, then place the tomatoes on a wire cake rack set over paper towels or a large shallow pan. Let them drain for 30 minutes. Then spread the tomatoes on a double layer of paper towels and gently pat them dry with more towels.

Preheating the oven. Slide an oven shelf into an upper slot and preheat the oven for 15 minutes at 325° F.

Filling the tart. Spread the Swiss cheese evenly in the tart shell. Arrange the sliced tomatoes in overlapping concentric circles so that they cover the cheese completely. Season the tomatoes evenly with a liberal grinding of pepper, and scatter the basil and scallions over the top.

In a small bowl, combine the Parmesan cheese with the bread crumbs, then sprinkle the mixture evenly over the filling. Dot the top with the butter bits.

Baking the tart. Bake the tart for 30 minutes, or just until the tomatoes are still slightly resistant when pressed with your fingers and the crumb-cheese topping is lightly browned.

Serving the tart. Remove the tart from the oven and place it on top of a tall cylinder, such as a coffee can, carefully holding on to the sides of the pan. Check to see if the sides of the pan will come away easily from the bottom of the pan and the baked shell; if the filling has cooked over at any point, the pastry may stick to the metal rim. Free any such areas with the point of a small knife before guiding the outer rim down to the tabletop.

Slide the tart, still on the flat metal base of the tart pan, onto a round serving platter. Let the tart rest for about 5 minutes, then serve it.

STRAWBERRY TART

Although I have suggested fresh strawberries for this incomparable fruit tart with a custard base, you may, if you prefer, use any other fruit of your choice. You might consider, among others, fresh berries of any kind; or canned, drained fruit halves—peaches, pears, or apricots. Frozen fruits, thoroughly defrosted and drained, make an effective topping, too. Whatever the fruit you use, arrange it as attractively as you can on the custard base.

The glaze, too, may be changed. Simply substitute an equal amount of currant jelly for the apricot jam. It is not necessary to rub the jelly through a strainer; just dissolve it in 2 tablespoons of water and simmer the mixture for a few minutes until it thickens. Cool it to lukewarm before glazing the tart.

The Pastry:
A Fully Baked Fluted Tart Shell (page 393)

The Filling:
2 eggs
3 tablespoons sugar
2 tablespoons flour
Pinch of salt
1 envelope (¼ ounce) unflavored gelatin
1 teaspoon vanilla
1 cup milk
¾ cup chilled heavy cream
1 to 1½ quarts fresh strawberries

The Glaze:
1 cup apricot jam
2 tablespoons water

Preparing the tart for filling. Set the tart shell, still in its pan, on top of a tall cylinder, such as a coffee can, and let the sides of the pan drop down. With a wide metal spatula, lift the pastry shell off its base and slide it onto a round serving platter. Handle the shell gently; if you break off bits of the sides, follow the repair instructions on page 393.

Preparing the filling. With a rotary or electric beater or whisk, beat the eggs in a medium-size mixing bowl for a few seconds, or just long enough to combine them. Then add the sugar and continue beating until the mixture is thick enough to fall in a sluggish ribbon when the beater is lifted out of the bowl. Add the flour, salt, gelatin, and vanilla. Beat once more until the added ingredients are thoroughly absorbed.

In a heavy 2-quart saucepan heat the milk over moderate heat until small bubbles form around the edges.

To make the custard, slowly pour the hot milk into the egg mixture, stirring it continuously with a wooden spoon. Now pour the mixture into the saucepan and set it over low heat.

Cook the custard slowly without ever letting it come to a boil, stirring it constantly with a rubber spatula; occasionally run the spatula around the sides of the pan and especially the crease where the custard tends to coagulate. When the custard has thickened fairly heavily and is smooth, scrape it back into the mixing bowl and refrigerate it, uncovered, for about 15 minutes, or until it has thickened further and cooled completely.

Then, with a rotary or electric beater, whip the cream in a chilled, medium-size bowl until the cream forms firm but still slightly wavering peaks on the beater.

With a rubber spatula, immediately scrape the whipped cream over the custard. Slowly fold the two together, cutting down and bringing the heavier mass up over the lighter one just until no streaks of cream show. If at any point the mixture threatens to become lumpy—as sometimes happens—beat it slowly with the rotary or electric beater until it is smooth. Then pour the custard into the waiting tart shell and smooth it with the spatula.

Refrigerate the tart once more until the custard has become not quite completely firm; it should jiggle when you shake the pan gently.

Meanwhile, hull the strawberries and, one at a time, dip them quickly into cold water. Pat them gently but thoroughly dry with paper towels, then arrange them in concentric rings on the custard, starting around the sides and placing them stem ends down. If you don't have enough berries to cover the custard completely, space them farther apart.

Return the tart to the refrigerator while you make the glaze.

Making the glaze. Place the apricot jam in a sieve set over a small saucepan. Rub the jam through the sieve with the back of a spoon and discard any pulp left in the sieve. Stir 2 tablespoons of water into the apricot purée, then, stirring it constantly with a spoon, simmer the mixture for about 5 minutes, or until it thickens to a syruplike consistency.

Remove the pan from the heat and let the glaze cool only to lukewarm. If you let it cool too much, it will be too thick to pour; if this happens, merely reheat it and let it cool to the proper temperature.

Glazing the tart. Remove the tart from the refrigerator and dribble a light coating of the glaze over each strawberry, letting the excess cover any exposed custard. Refrigerate the tart again for at least 1 hour, or until the glaze sets and the custard is firm.

Serving the tart. The finished tart can safely remain in the refrigerator for 6 to 8 hours. But if it has chilled that long, allow it to rest at room temperature for about 15 minutes before you serve it.

Tartlets

As their name implies, tartlets differ from tarts mainly in the matter of size: they are small tarts. Although French tart pastry may be used to line the tartlet pans, I have included a recipe for an alternative, and richer, pastry dough in which an egg takes the place of water. Do not make the mistake, however, of using tartlet pastry for tarts; it is difficult to handle when lining a large pan.

Chilling the ingredients is not the crucial element that it is in making the French tart pastry. But it is indeed essential that you chill this dough thoroughly *after* you have made it. Because this pastry is so short—or, in other words, because it contains a large amount of butter in proportion to the flour, to say nothing of the egg—you will find it virtually impossible to roll out unless it has been chilled to considerable firmness beforehand.

As for my tartlet fillings, they are similar to those for the tarts, but they are in general more custardy in texture and more piquant in flavor, as befits morsels you will probably serve as accompaniments for drinks.

TARTLET PASTRY

MAKES 24 TARTLETS

1½ cups sifted all-purpose flour
½ teaspoon salt
8 tablespoons butter (a quarter-pound stick), cut into ¼-inch slices and thoroughly chilled
1 egg, slightly beaten
2 tablespoons unsifted flour

Mixing and chilling the dough. Sift the sifted flour and the salt into a large mixing bowl and add the butter. Toss the butter slices to coat them with flour. Then, using a pastry blender, cut into the butter with small, quick chopping motions to distribute it evenly through the flour. A pastry blender is more effective than fingers to achieve a fine granular texture, although you may use your fingers if you prefer.

When the mixture is as uniform as corn meal, pour over it the lightly beaten egg. Now substitute two table knives for the pastry blender and, using a crisscross motion, cut and stir the egg thoroughly into the dough, scraping the knives across each other from time to time to remove the pastry sticking to them.

Gather the dough together in your hands and mold it into a ball. Press the ball against any stray pellets of dough in the bowl and work them in.

Now hold the dough over the bowl and lightly and uniformly sprinkle the 2 tablespoons of unsifted flour over it, rotating the ball until a film of flour covers the dough.

Wrap the dough in foil or plastic wrap, or enclose it in a plastic bag, and refrigerate it for at least 3 hours, or for as long as 2 days.

Rolling the dough. Remove the dough from the refrigerator and let it soften slightly, just until you can press a finger into it fairly easily. Pat it out on a floured pastry cloth to a circle about 4 inches across, then roll it into a circle a little less than ⅛ inch thick, using the technique described on pages 390–91.

With a 3-inch cookie or biscuit cutter, cut out rounds and lay them on a long strip of wax paper.

Quickly gather together the pastry scraps and knead them into a ball, using a little extra flour if the scraps are too soft. Roll them into another circle of the same thickness as the first. Cut out rounds as before. You should have 24 pastry rounds when all the dough has been rolled and cut. (It may reassure you to know that, unlike pie pastry, rolling and rerolling this particular dough will not affect its texture to any appreciable degree.)

Lining the muffin tins. Line each muffin cup with a pastry round in the following fashion: Lay the round over the cup. Then lift up the sides of the round with the fingers of both hands and gently encourage the pastry to fall into place, exerting slight downward pressure. Now run your fingertip around the bottom crease of the cup to mold the pastry gently against the sides. The sides will fold into small pleats, which will give them a somewhat irregular appearance. Don't fuss with this now; your primary concern should be to make sure that the pastry reaches the top of each muffin cup, or even rises above the rim.

Refrigerating the pastry. Refrigerate the pastry-lined muffin tins for at least 30 minutes while you prepare a filling of your choice, such as the cheese and crabmeat fillings that follow. Chilling the pastry will firm it so that you can shape and mold the cups more symmetrically if you wish to improve their appearance.

CHEESE TARTLETS

MAKES 24 TARTLETS

The Pastry:
Two 12-cup muffin tins lined with unbaked Tartlet Pastry (page 408), chilled in the refrigerator for at least 30 minutes

The Filling:
2 eggs
1 cup heavy cream
¼ teaspoon salt
⅛ teaspoon freshly ground black pepper
⅛ teaspoon nutmeg, preferably freshly grated
¼ teaspoon dry mustard
½ cup grated Swiss cheese (Emmenthal or Gruyère), packed down

Preheating the oven. Slide an oven shelf into a slot in the lower third of the oven and preheat the oven for 15 minutes at 450° F.

Making the filling. Break the eggs into a 2-quart mixing bowl and, using a fork or a small whisk, beat them for a moment, or only long enough to combine them. Then add the cream, salt, pepper, nutmeg, and dry mustard, and stir until the ingredients are thoroughly mixed. Taste for seasoning; the mixture may need more salt and pepper.

Filling the tartlets. Remove the lined muffin tins from the refrigerator and put an equal amount—about a teaspoonful—of the grated Swiss cheese into each of the 24 tartlets.

Pour 1 tablespoon of the custard mixture into each tartlet. As the tartlets rest, the cheese will absorb some of the custard and you can go around a second time, adding any remaining custard until the tartlets are filled almost to the brim. Make certain that the filling doesn't overflow.

Baking the tartlets. Carefully transfer the filled tartlet pans to the preheated 450° F. oven and bake them undisturbed for 10 minutes. Then lower the heat to 325° F. and bake them 5 to 8 minutes longer, or until the filling has puffed and the pastry edges have become golden brown.

Serving the tartlets. Run a table knife around the sides of each tartlet, then carefully remove them from their cups. Arrange them on a large platter and serve them at once. The filling will sink a bit as the tartlets cool, but this is as it should be.

CRABMEAT TARTLETS

MAKES 24 TARTLETS

The Pastry:
Two 12-cup muffin tins lined with unbaked Tartlet Pastry (page 408), chilled in the refrigerator for at least 30 minutes

The Filling:
2 eggs
1 cup heavy cream
½ teaspoon salt
⅛ teaspoon white pepper
½ cup fresh crabmeat, packed down; or canned crabmeat (about half of a 6½-ounce can), thoroughly drained and picked over for bits of shell or cartilage; or ½ cup frozen crabmeat, defrosted and drained
2 tablespoons freshly grated imported Parmesan cheese

Preheating the oven. Slide an oven shelf into a slot in the lower third of the oven and preheat the oven for 15 minutes at 450° F.

Making the filling. Break the eggs into a 2-quart mixing bowl and, using a fork or a small whisk, beat them a few seconds, or only long enough to combine them. Then stir in the cream, salt, and pepper. Stir gently until the ingredients are well combined. Taste the mixture for seasoning; it may need more salt and pepper.

Now remove the lined muffin tins from the refrigerator and divide the crabmeat into each of the 24 tartlets, about a teaspoonful in each cup.

Pour 1 tablespoon of the filling mixture into each tartlet. As they rest, the crabmeat will absorb the custard and you can go around a second time, adding any remaining custard until the tartlets are filled almost to the brim. Make certain that the filling doesn't overflow. Now sprinkle a little of the freshly grated Parmesan cheese over the top of each tartlet.

Baking the tartlets. Carefully transfer the filled pans to the pre-heated 450° F. oven and bake them undisturbed for 10 minutes. Then lower the heat to 325° F. and bake them for 5 to 8 minutes longer, or until the filling has puffed and the pastry edges are golden brown.

Serving the tartlets. Run a table knife around the sides of each tartlet, then carefully remove them from their cups. Arrange them on a large platter and serve them at once. The filling will sink a bit as it cools, but this is as it should be.

BREAD TARTLET SHELLS

Despite their simplicity, don't underestimate the extraordinary effect these tiny toasted bread shells create. They take only minutes to make and can be filled with Curried Tuna Pâté (page 418), or Herbed Cream Cheese (page 420), or any of the variations suggested in those recipes.

Fill the Bread Tartlet Shells while they are still warm, mounding the fillings as generously as you like. You need not be limited to the fillings suggested above—you can use any other filling your imagination dictates. For a more robust tartlet, you might even consider as unorthodox a filling as hot baked beans, generously spiked with any seasoning of your choice.

Because the bread cases are so porous, I must caution you, however, about the type of filling that can be baked in the tartlets. You can fill them before baking with any fairly dense cooked filling, but not with a custardy or moist mixture that would seep through the cases during baking.

Whatever filling you choose, these charming constructions make wonderful accompaniments for drinks of any kind.

MAKES 24 BREAD SHELLS

24 slices fresh American White Bread (page 280), or
homemade-type packaged white bread, each about ¼ inch
thick

Preheating the oven. Slide an oven shelf into a center slot and preheat the oven for 15 minutes at 375° F.

Making and baking the shells. Use tiny muffin cups, about 2 inches wide at the top, which usually come 12 cups to a tin.

Stamp out the center of each slice of bread with a 3-inch cookie cutter. Fill each muffin cup with a round of bread in the following fashion: Lay a circle of bread over the muffin cup and, lifting the circle slightly, gently mold it into the cup with your fingers. Then press your forefinger around the bottom crease so that the bread takes on the shape of the cup. Don't fuss with this too much, lest you tear the fragile bread.

Bake the bread tartlet shells in the preheated oven for 10 to 15 minutes, or only until they are light golden brown. They burn easily, so keep your eye on them. When the shells have reached the color you desire and have become fairly firm, remove the muffin tins from the oven and carefully lift each shell out of its cup.

The tartlet shells may be filled at once and served immediately. Or you may refrigerate the filled shells, but let them return to room temperature before serving.

Freezing the shells. The unfilled tartlet shells may be wrapped in aluminum foil or enclosed in a plastic bag and frozen. Don't defrost them before using; simply preheat your oven to 325° F., place the shells on a cookie sheet, and heat them for about 10 minutes, or until they are thoroughly defrosted and crisp.

⊲ঞ⊳

Chou Puffs

Whether the French or the Italians invented these extraordinary cream puffs and savory puffs is a moot point, but the French name, *pâte à choux*, is generally used for the dough. This can be translated loosely as "paste in the form of cabbages," presumably because the small or large puffs made from it look something like cabbages. The name has been shortened in its Anglo-French version to chou puff, and the dough from which it is made to chou paste.

Like pie and tart pastries plain chou pastry is meant to be, almost always, a texture enclosing a taste. Therefore, sweetening it, or adding flavoring when you use the paste in making desserts, is unnecessary. However, when the paste is used in certain recipes, such as that for the Gougère, other ingredients are essential, as you will see.

Chou paste is the easiest of pastries to prepare. It consists of water, butter, flour, and eggs; the butter is melted in the boiling water, the flour is stirred into it to make a paste, and then the eggs are beaten in. This simple preparation, however, has almost magical properties. When baked in the oven it explodes into the most remarkable shapes imaginable.

Chou paste puffs up for entirely different reasons than, for example, a soufflé does. In a soufflé, it is the air beaten into the egg whites that rises when subjected to oven heat. The *pâte à choux* rises in another fashion and for another reason: the eggs become partially cooked as they are beaten into the hot paste. Then, when this rather sturdy paste is again heated rapidly in baking, the steam in the mixture doesn't just cause it to expand—it literally causes an explosion and gives the puffs their fanciful shapes.

I therefore stress the need for speed of preparation, whether you make the paste by hand or in an electric mixer, because the paste must remain hot—but off the heat—while the eggs are beaten into it if they are to undergo this necessary partial cooking. If you add the eggs too slowly and beat the paste too long after each addition, by the time the last egg is added the paste will be too cool. This crucial element of speed makes the difference between glorious success and partial or complete failure.

CHOU PASTE

Once this Chou Paste is made, it may rest for hours before you plan to use it, although it is at its best when used immediately, even while still warm. Do not expect predictable results if you double or halve this recipe. If you need more than the 2 cups of paste my recipe yields, make two separate batches. If you need half the amount, make the full amount and refrigerate the surplus, wrapped in foil, for another use.

MAKES ABOUT 2 CUPS

1 cup water

6 tablespoons butter, cut into pieces

½ teaspoon salt

1¼ cups sifted all-purpose flour

1 cup eggs (4 whole eggs plus, possibly, 1 additional white or part of an additional white, to make precisely 1 cupful), beaten with a whisk only long enough to combine the yolks and whites

Making the paste by hand. By far the most effective method of preparing chou paste is to beat it by hand. This makes it possible to judge the state of the paste at every stage. An electric mixer with a pastry arm may be used if you wish (instructions follow these).

In a heavy 2-quart saucepan, combine the water, butter, and salt. Set over high heat and cook, stirring constantly, until the butter has dissolved and the water has begun to boil all over its surface.

Remove the pan from the heat instantly; if you let the mixture continue to boil, part of the water will evaporate and you will end up with less liquid than you need. Dump in all the flour at once, and stir the ingredients together vigorously with a large wooden spoon. After a few seconds of hard stirring—all around the pan, including the sides—the mixture will have the appearance of somewhat leaden but smooth mashed potatoes.

Return the pan to moderate heat and continue to stir briskly for 4 or 5 seconds—no more—until you can hold the whole mass up in your spoon and the pan is almost clean.

Speed of mixing is now the crucial factor. With your spoon, make a deep hollow in the center of the paste, but not so deep as to expose the bottom of the pan. Using a dry-measuring cup, immediately scoop up about ¼ cup of the lightly beaten eggs and pour it into the hollow. Briskly stir the paste into the eggs and continue to stir for a few seconds, until the slippery strands come together again and become a comparatively firm mass.

Without waiting a second, form another hollow and pour in another ¼ cup of eggs and combine as before. Add the third and fourth ¼ cups of eggs quickly, beating each addition in the same fashion.

After the last addition, beat the mixture vigorously for another moment, and the chou paste is done.

Making the paste in an electric mixer. If you have an electric mixer equipped with a paddle or a pastry arm, you can make the paste with less physical exertion.

Follow the directions for cooking the basic mixture of water, butter, and flour; then, after heating it for the 4 or 5 seconds required, immediately transfer it to a warm mixer bowl. (To ensure predictable results, before cooking the paste, you might fill the mixer bowl with very hot water. Just before adding the hot paste, empty the bowl and dry it.)

Proceed as for the hand-beaten paste, adding the eggs ¼ cup at a time and running the machine at low speed to prevent splattering during each addition until the eggs are partially absorbed, then beating at high speed just until the separated strands of dough have come together. Continue adding the eggs in ¼-cup amounts, lowering, then raising, the speed after each addition. Work as quickly as possible.

After all the eggs have been absorbed, you may beat the mixture 4 or 5 seconds longer for good measure, but don't overdo it. Overbeating will not ruin the paste, but neither will it improve it.

Storing the paste. If you will be using the paste within about 2 or 3 hours, leave it, uncovered, at room temperature. If you will not be using it until a few hours later, cover it with plastic wrap; otherwise, a hard crust will form on the surface, preventing the puffs from rising to maximum volume.

If you want to store the paste, cool it and transfer it to a bowl, cover it closely with plastic wrap, and refrigerate it for as long as a day or two. Be sure to remove it from the refrigerator at least 2 hours before you want to use it, because it must be at room temperature for baking. And don't hasten the warming-up process by heating chilled paste on the stove; even a few seconds' cooking at this point will ruin it.

I do not recommend freezing chou paste in its uncooked state. When defrosted and baked, it will indeed rise again, but to only half the level of unfrozen paste.

CHOU PUFFS

MAKES ABOUT 35 PUFFS ABOUT
1½ INCHES IN DIAMETER

The Chou Puffs:
Chou Paste (page 414)

For Preparing the Pans:
1 tablespoon butter, softened at room temperature
4 tablespoons unsifted flour

The Glaze:
1 egg white
2 teaspoons water

Preheating the oven. Slide an oven shelf into the top slot and another into the lowest slot, then preheat the oven for 15 minutes at 450° F.

Preparing the pans. Using a pastry brush, the butter, and the flour, grease and flour two cookie sheets. Invert each sheet and rap it on a table to knock off the excess flour.

Shaping the puffs. Drop heaping teaspoonfuls of the Chou Paste onto the cookie sheet, using a second spoon as a pusher. Shape the mounds with the back of a teaspoon so that they are higher than they are wide. Don't fuss with this too much; the charm of these puffs is the variety of forms into which they explode. Or you can use a pastry bag and a No. 6 plain tip for shaping the puffs, if you wish. Whichever method you use, leave about 2 inches between mounds; do not crowd the puffs—they need space to double in size as they bake.

Glazing the puffs. In a small mixing bowl, beat the egg white and water with a whisk only long enough to combine them.

With a pastry brush paint each puff lightly, but don't allow any of the wash, as it is called, to drip down onto the baking sheet. This could discourage the puffs from rising as high as they should.

Baking the puffs. Set one cookie sheet on the upper shelf of the 450° F. oven and the other sheet on the lower shelf. Bake the puffs undisturbed for 5 minutes; then lower the heat to 425° F. and bake them for 10 to 15 minutes longer, or until they have puffed to about twice their original size, feel firm to the touch, and have turned golden brown. To make sure they are thoroughly baked, break one puff open. If the inside is doughy, quickly close the oven door and bake the puffs a few minutes longer.

(If the puffs are baking unevenly because of "hot spots" in your oven, they must not be moved around until they have expanded completely, especially during the initial baking period when the high temperature gives them a "blast" to start the exploding process.)

Turn off the oven and, one at a time, remove the pans. Pierce each puff in the side with the point of a small sharp knife. This will allow the steam to escape and prevent the puffs from becoming soggy. Then return the pans to the turned-off oven and let the puffs dry for 5 minutes, with the oven door closed.

Transfer the puffs to wire cake racks and cool them thoroughly.

Unfilled baked puffs that have been cooled may be stored for up to 3 days in an airtight container. Before using them, heat them on a rack in a preheated 350° F. oven for 2 or 3 minutes, and then cool them on the rack until they are crisp.

You may also freeze baked unfilled chou puffs, provided they are wrapped securely in plastic wrap and then in foil. Before using the frozen puffs, bake them briefly, without defrosting, on a cake rack in a preheated 325° F. oven, just until crisp.

SMALL PUFFS FILLED WITH
CURRIED TUNA PÂTÉ

If you prefer another pâté mixture to the tuna, you may substitute one of the following: drained canned salmon; frozen cooked lobster, defrosted and well drained; drained, canned minced clams; or cooked shrimp.

However—and this is important—do not use any of the liquid drained from any of this seafood. Instead, increase the amount of vegetable oil by about 1 tablespoon when you purée the fish.

Seasonings for any of these pâtés may be changed at will. For example, omit the curry powder and use liberal amounts of freshly ground pepper instead. Or stir into the mixture a tablespoon or more of any finely chopped fresh herb you may have on hand.

Any leftover pâté may be spread on toast or crackers to make canapés.

MAKES 35 PUFFS

The Puffs:
35 small Chou Puffs (page 417), baked and cooled

The Filling:
1 can (7 ounces) tuna fish packed in oil, coarsely shredded, with its juices
½ cup coarsely chopped onions (about 1 medium onion)
2 teaspoons fresh lemon juice
3 to 4 tablespoons vegetable oil
8 tablespoons butter (a quarter-pound stick), softened at room temperature
½ teaspoon salt
2 teaspoons curry powder

Making the pâté. Empty the tuna fish and all its juices into the container of an electric blender or food processor. Add the onions, lemon juice, and 3 tablespoons of the vegetable oil. Cover and process at high speed for about a minute in the blender; in the food processor for a few seconds, just until smooth.

Then turn off the machine, scrape down the sides of the container with a rubber spatula, and process a few seconds more. If at any point the blender clogs, stop the machine and add the remaining tablespoon of vegetable oil, then resume the blending. Set the purée aside.

In a medium-size mixing bowl cream the butter. Beat in the salt and curry powder. Then, tablespoon by tablespoon, beat in the tuna fish purée until the mixture is smooth. Taste for seasoning and add more salt and lemon juice if you think it needs it.

The pâté will be quite fluid at this point, but don't be concerned. Simply cover the bowl with plastic wrap and refrigerate the mixture for about 2 hours, or until it is about the consistency of cream cheese.

Filling and serving the puffs. Cut the Chou Puffs in half horizontally, and with a small spoon scrape out any moist paste inside. Fill the bottom of each shell with a teaspoon or more of the pâté and set the upper halves in place, allowing a little filling to show.

These puffs are best if they are served at once. If they must wait, you may cover them with plastic wrap and refrigerate them for up to 6 hours. Before serving them, remove the puffs from the refrigerator and let them rest at room temperature for about 10 minutes. This will allow the pâté to soften a bit to the velvety consistency it should have.

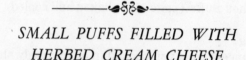

SMALL PUFFS FILLED WITH HERBED CREAM CHEESE

In the filling for these puffs you may, of course, use any other fresh herb of your choice, or finely chopped scallions, in place of the chives. The filling, like the tuna pâté in the preceding recipe, may be spread on toast or crackers or heaped in Bread Tartlet Shells (page 412) to make canapés.

MAKES 35 PUFFS

The Puffs:
35 small Chou Puffs (page 417), baked and cooled

The Filling:
8 ounces cream cheese, softened at room temperature
2 tablespoons butter, softened at room temperature
2 tablespoons heavy cream
½ teaspoon salt
Freshly ground black pepper
1 tablespoon finely cut fresh chives, or 2 tablespoons frozen
   chopped chives

Making the filling. In a medium-size mixing bowl, cream the cream cheese and butter together until the mixture is smooth and fluffy. Beat in the cream, a tablespoon at a time, then stir in the salt, a liberal grinding of pepper, and the chives. Taste for seasoning; the mixture may need more salt or more chives.
    Cover the bowl with plastic wrap and refrigerate the mixture for about 1 hour, or until it is moderately firm.

Filling and serving the puffs. Cut the Chou Puffs in half horizontally and with a small spoon scrape out any moist paste inside. Fill the bottom of each shell with a teaspoonful or more of the filling and set the upper halves in place.
    These are best when served at once. If the puffs must wait, you may cover them and refrigerate them for up to 6 hours. Before

serving them, remove the puffs from the refrigerator and let them rest at room temperature for about 10 minutes. This will allow the cheese filling to soften to a velvety consistency.

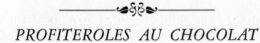

PROFITEROLES AU CHOCOLAT

Cream-filled puffs with a hot chocolate sauce are always listed on French menus as Profiteroles au Chocolat. The origin of the word *profiteroles* is almost impossible to pinpoint precisely, but I do know it was in common use in the sixteenth century and means, literally, "small profit." Why this term was used by the bakers who first made *profiteroles* is a mystery to culinary historians, because the puffs require few ingredients, not one of them rare or exotic. The chocolate, then a great rarity, was a later addition.

MAKES 35 CREAM PUFFS

The Puffs:
35 small Chou Puffs (page 417) baked and cooled

The Hot Cocoa Sauce:
1½ cups granulated sugar
1 cup water
1½ cups unsweetened cocoa

The Filling:
1 cup chilled heavy cream
2 tablespoons granulated sugar
1 teaspoon vanilla

The Topping:
Confectioners' sugar

Making the hot cocoa sauce. In a 2-quart saucepan, stir 1½ cups of granulated sugar with the water only long enough to combine them. Then cook the mixture over moderate heat until it comes to a rolling boil and boil it briskly and undisturbed for 2 minutes.

Remove the syrup from the heat and, beating it rapidly with a whisk, add the cocoa and continue to beat until the sauce is smooth and thick and has a satiny look.

If the sauce is too thick for your taste, thin it with a little water or, if you like, with heavy cream. If the sauce does not seem sweet enough, add sugar to taste, stirring the sauce constantly over moderate heat until the sugar dissolves.

You may make this sauce ahead of time and reheat it just before serving.

Making the filling. In a chilled 2-quart bowl beat the cream with a rotary beater for a minute or two, or just until it has thickened lightly. Then add 2 tablespoons of granulated sugar and the vanilla, and continue beating until the cream forms firm but still slightly wavering peaks on the beater when it is lifted and held upright over the bowl.

Filling and serving the puffs. Carefully cut each Chou Puff in half horizontally and use a small spoon to scrape out any moist paste inside. Drop a heaping teaspoonful or more of the whipped cream into the lower half of each shell, then gently replace the top. Arrange the puffs on a large serving platter.

Ideally, they should be served at once. Refrigerate them if you must, but for no longer than 10 or 15 minutes or so, or the cream will turn the puffs soggy. On the other hand, never allow cream-filled puffs to sit at room temperature for more than a few minutes for two reasons: the cream tastes best when properly chilled; and warmth may produce souring or, even worse, permit bacteria to multiply to an actually dangerous level.

Just before serving, dust each puff lightly with confectioners' sugar, using a perforated shaker if you have one, or a small flour sifter or sieve.

Serve with a bowl of hot cocoa sauce.

GOUGÈRE

This savory puffed cheese ring, called a *gougère* by the French, originated in Burgundy in the thirteenth century. It was then, and still is, torn into pieces and served with a glass of good Burgundy wine. We in America need not be so traditional. The ring makes a perfect accompaniment to drinks of any kind and may even be served, in place of bread, with a salad. Not the least of its charms is that it can be served either hot or warm; and some people even prefer it at room temperature.

MAKES TWO 9-INCH RINGS

The Pastry:
Chou Paste (page 414)
1 teaspoon prepared mustard
1 teaspoon salt
1¼ cups coarsely grated imported Swiss cheese (Gruyère or Emmenthal) ; or freshly grated imported Parmesan cheese; or a combination of the two in any proportions you like

For Preparing the Pans:
1 tablespoon butter, softened at room temperature
4 tablespoons unsifted flour

The Glaze:
1 egg
2 teaspoons water

Preheating the oven. Slide one oven shelf into the topmost slot and another shelf into the lowest slot, then preheat the oven at 450° F. for 15 minutes.

Making the pastry. Place the Chou Paste in a large mixing bowl and add the mustard and salt. Using a wooden spoon, beat the paste very vigorously for a moment, then beat in 1 cup of the grated cheese.

Preparing the pans. Using a pastry brush, the tablespoon of softened butter, and the 4 tablespoons of unsifted flour, grease and flour two cookie sheets. Invert each sheet and rap it on a table to knock off the excess flour.

Using a 7-inch round pan or plate or lid as a guide, press the outline of a circle on the floured surface of each sheet.

Shaping the rings. Place heaping tablespoonfuls of the Chou Paste side by side around each circle to form two rings. With a spatula, pat the dough into fairly smooth rings about 2 inches thick and 1 inch high. Don't fuss over this; for me, one of the charms of these cheese rings is that no two ever look exactly alike. As an alternative, you may pipe the paste into two rings, using a pastry bag and a plain No. 9 tip.

Glazing the rings. In a small mixing bowl, beat the egg and 2 teaspoons of water with a whisk only long enough to combine them. With a pastry brush, lightly paint the entire surface of each ring with the egg wash, as it is called. Don't allow any of the wash to drip down onto the baking sheets; this might prevent the rings from rising as high as they should. Sprinkle the remaining grated cheese evenly over the tops.

Baking and serving the rings. Set one cookie sheet on the upper shelf of the preheated oven, the other sheet on the lower one. Bake the rings for 10 minutes, then lower the heat to 350° F. and bake for about another 30 minutes. After a total of 40 minutes, the rings should be well puffed and light golden brown in color, and they should feel firm to the touch.

Slide them off their sheets onto a large platter and serve them at once. Or, if you prefer, cool the rings to lukewarm on a wire cake rack before serving them. To serve, either cut or tear the rings into pieces.

PARIS-BREST

This spectacular almond-topped whipped cream ring is one of the great baking specialties of Paris. Although it is traditionally filled with sweetened vanilla-flavored whipped cream, or *crème Chantilly* as the French call it, you may wish to flavor the cream in other ways.

You might, for example, fold a teaspoonful or more of instant powdered coffee into the cream after it has been whipped. Or, if you are as addicted to almonds as I am, you might add a small handful of ground almonds to the cream, or even substitute a small amount of almond extract for the vanilla flavoring.

SERVES 6 TO 8

The Ring:
Chou Paste (page 414)

For Preparing the Pan:
1 tablespoon butter
2 tablespoons unsifted flour

The Glaze and Topping:
1 egg
2 teaspoons water
4 tablespoons blanched almonds, cut into slivers

The Filling:
2 cups chilled heavy cream
2 tablespoons granulated sugar
2 teaspoons vanilla

For Dusting:
1 tablespoon confectioners' sugar

Preheating the oven. Slide an oven shelf into a middle slot and preheat the oven at 450° F. for 15 minutes.

Preparing the pan. Using a pastry brush, the softened butter, and the flour, grease and flour a cookie sheet. Then invert the sheet and rap it sharply on a table to knock off all of the excess flour, leaving only the thinnest of layers clinging to the buttered surface of the cookie sheet.

Using an inverted round 9-inch baking pan as a guide, press the outline of a circle firmly onto the floured surface of the cookie sheet.

Making the ring. Place heaping tablespoonfuls of the Chou Paste close together around the rim of the circle. Then, using a spatula, shape the dough into a fairly smooth ribbon about 2½ inches wide and 1½ inches high. Don't fuss with this too much; one charm of this confection is its irregular surface. Alternatively, you may pipe the Chou Paste into a circle with a pastry bag and a plain No. 9 tip.

Glazing the ring. In a small mixing bowl, beat the egg and water with a whisk only long enough to combine them well; do not over-beat.

With a pastry brush, lightly paint the entire surface of the ring, sides as well as top, with the egg wash, as it is called. Don't allow any of the wash to drip down onto the baking sheet; this might prevent the ring from rising as high as it should. Sprinkle the ring with the slivered almonds, distributing them evenly over the entire surface of the ring, sides as well as top.

Baking the ring. Set the cookie sheet in the preheated oven and bake the ring undisturbed for 10 minutes, then lower the heat to 350° F. and bake it for another 10 minutes. At this point, reduce the heat to 325° F. and bake the ring for 20 minutes more. After a total of 40 minutes, it should be well puffed and a light golden brown in color, and it should feel firm to the touch.

Turn off the oven and remove the cookie sheet. Pierce the sides of the ring with the point of a small sharp knife at intervals of about 2 inches to release the enclosed steam.

Return the sheet to the oven; let the ring dry for another 5 minutes with the oven door closed, then slide it off the cookie sheet and onto a cake rack and cool it for about 10 minutes.

With a large serrated knife, slice the ring horizontally, using small sawing motions; make the cut closer to the top of the ring than to the bottom. With a tablespoon, scrape out any moist dough. Let the halves of the ring cool completely on a cake rack before filling them.

Making the filling. In a chilled 2-quart bowl, beat the cream with a rotary beater for a minute or two, or until it begins to thicken slightly. Add the granulated sugar and vanilla, and continue beating until the cream forms firm but still slightly wavering peaks on the beater when it is lifted.

Gently set the base of the ring on a serving platter, and, using a spatula, pile the whipped cream into it. Or use your pastry bag and the No. 9 star tip to pipe the cream into ornamental swirls. The whipped cream should rise about 1 inch above the edge. Carefully set the top half over the filling like a crown. If you haven't used the pastry bag, swirl the cream on the sides into a pattern, using a spoon or a spatula.

Serving the ring. Ideally, the ring should be served at once; refrigerate it if you must, but not for longer than 30 minutes or the cream will turn the pastry soggy. And never let the filled ring sit at room temperature for more than a few minutes, for two reasons: the cream tastes best when properly chilled; and warmth may produce souring or, even worse, permit bacteria to multiply to an actually dangerous level.

Just before serving, dust the ring with confectioners' sugar; shake it out of a perforated canister if you have one, or distribute it evenly with a small sifter or fine sieve.

A Few
Versatile Sauces

*A*mong the literally thousands of sauces that the cuisines of the world have to offer, there are a few that truly deserve to be called classics. Of those classics, surely Hollandaise, Béarnaise, and Lemon Sauce are among the best known, not only because they are so rich and delicious but because they can be used in so many ways.

A few such classic sauces belong in the repertory of every good cook. And when you use them properly and with discretion, they will glorify your meats, poultry, fish, and vegetables.

As for flavored butters, classically called compound butters, they consist basically of butter that is creamed or beaten until fluffy and then combined with the herbs, spices, or flavorings that give each kind its name. These flavored butters present few, if any, problems in the making, and one of their great advantages is that they can be put together hours ahead, covered closely, refrigerated, and served whenever you need them.

HOLLANDAISE SAUCE

In this recipe I have given you two methods for making Hollandaise. One version is made by hand, the other in a blender or food processor; both require the use of a double boiler. I prefer the hand method because I feel that it produces a Hollandaise that is more velvety in texture than a sauce made in a blender or processor.

When you use the double boiler for making Hollandaise Sauce, or for keeping the machine-made Hollandaise warm, it is imperative that the water in the bottom pan only simmer—it must never boil— and that it not touch the upper pan lest the sauce become too hot and possibly separate. Don't use an aluminum double boiler.

Serve this velvety sauce with poached eggs, fish, artichokes, asparagus, and broccoli.

MAKES ABOUT 1½ CUPS

¼ pound butter (1 stick), cut into bits
4 egg yolks
2 tablespoons cold butter, cut into bits
¼ teaspoon salt
⅛ teaspoon white pepper
4 teaspoons strained fresh lemon juice
1 to 2 tablespoons heavy cream

Making the sauce by hand. Melt the ¼ pound of butter bits in a small saucepan over low heat, but don't let the butter brown. Set the pan aside.

Pour about 2 or 2½ cups of water into the bottom of your double boiler; be sure it will not reach the bottom of the upper pan. Bring the water to a simmer, then lower the heat.

Meanwhile, off the heat, drop the egg yolks into the upper pan of the double boiler and beat them vigorously with a whisk for about 2 minutes, until they are somewhat thicker than heavy cream.

Add 2 tablespoons of cold butter bits to the yolks, together with the salt and white pepper.

Immediately insert the top pan into the base containing the simmering water. With your whisk, beat the eggs, butter, and seasonings for about 2 minutes, until the butter has melted and the mixture has become quite hot and considerably thicker than before. It is imperative that, before you proceed with the next step, the mixture be thick enough to cling to the whisk, yet not so thick that it becomes lumpy or loses all fluidity.

Immediately remove the upper pan from the base and place it nearby, allowing the water in the bottom pan to continue to simmer.

As quickly as possible set the reserved saucepan of melted butter over high heat and reheat it for a few seconds, just until it foams. Then, rapidly stirring the egg mixture—still off the heat—with your whisk, pour in about a teaspoonful of hot butter and whisk for a second or two until it is completely absorbed. Repeat this procedure, teaspoonful by teaspoonful, without ceasing to stir for even a second. When you have added about half the melted butter in this fashion, pour in the remaining butter in a slow thin stream, stirring the sauce constantly. Continue to stir for a few more seconds, until the Hollandaise is thick, smooth, and glossy. Now stir in the lemon juice, a teaspoonful at a time.

Set the pan into the base containing the simmering water. Whisk the sauce again for about a minute, then stir in 1 tablespoon of the heavy cream. The sauce may now be too thick for your taste (it usually is not, for mine) ; if so, thin it with as much of the remaining tablespoon of cream as you like. Taste the sauce for seasoning and serve it at once; or keep it warm in the manner described at the end of the recipe.

Making the sauce in a blender or food processor. Use the ingredients listed above, but change the procedure as follows:

Place the egg yolks, salt, pepper, and lemon juice in the container and cover it.

Then, over high heat, melt all the butter—the ¼-pound stick plus 2 tablespoons more, all cut into bits—until it foams, but don't let it brown. Remove from the heat. Immediately blend the egg yolk mixture for 4 seconds (at high speed in the blender). Turn off the machine and scrape down the sides of the container with a narrow rubber spatula. If you are using a blender, replace the cover and blend again for another 4 seconds; this is unnecessary in the food processor.

Without wasting a moment—the butter must be bubbling hot; reheat it if it has cooled too much—turn on the machine (use high speed in the blender) and ever so slowly pour in the butter. Turn off the machine as soon as all the butter has been added. The container will now hold a thick, heavy Hollandaise.

Pour the required amount of water into the base of your double boiler and bring it to a simmer.

With a narrow rubber spatula, scrape the Hollandaise into the top pan of the double boiler and set it over the simmering water in the base.

Stir in 1 tablespoon of the heavy cream, then thin the sauce with as much as you like of the second tablespoonful of cream.

Stir the sauce constantly for about a minute to heat it through, then taste it for seasoning. Serve it at once, or keep it warm as follows.

Keeping the sauce warm. Because Hollandaise should be served warm but never really hot, it is perfectly possible to make it by either of the two methods just described 10 or 15 minutes before you plan to use it.

Simply leave the sauce in the double boiler, but turn off the heat. Be sure to stir the sauce once or twice every 3 or 4 minutes. Should the sauce become too thick as it rests, thin it with a teaspoonful or more of cream, until it reaches the consistency that you like.

Should the Hollandaise Sauce curdle, either while you are cooking it or during this resting period, the most satisfactory way to reconstitute it is to whisk about a tablespoonful of boiling water into the sauce and continue to whisk it until the butter and eggs have recombined.

Incidentally, I do not approve of reheating leftover Hollandaise that has been refrigerated; the results are unpredictable. You would do far better to use it in its chilled state as a topping for a steak or for any of the hot boiled or steamed vegetables in this book.

VARIATION: BÉARNAISE SAUCE

Béarnaise is another classic sauce—a highly acidulated one flavored with tarragon—which is nothing more, in fact, than a variation of Hollandaise. Although French chefs of the classic school might perhaps disapprove of my simplified method of making it, I am convinced that my results are equal to theirs.

It is a splendid accompaniment to fish, lamb, beef, and a variety of vegetables.

MAKES ABOUT 1½ CUPS

⅓ cup tarragon vinegar
1 teaspoon crumbled dried tarragon
2 tablespoons finely chopped shallots
¼ pound butter (1 stick), cut into bits
4 egg yolks
2 tablespoons cold butter, cut into bits
¼ teaspoon salt
⅛ teaspoon white pepper
1 tablespoon finely cut fresh tarragon or parsley

Make a tarragon essence in the following way:

Combine the tarragon vinegar, dried tarragon, and shallots in a small saucepan and bring the mixture to a boil over high heat.

Let it boil vigorously, uncovered, until it has reduced to 2 tablespoons, more or less. Then pour it into a small, fine-meshed sieve set over a bowl and, to release all the flavor possible, press down hard on the seasonings with the back of a spoon before discarding them.

Make Hollandaise Sauce as directed in the preceding recipe, omitting the lemon juice and cream.

Immediately whisk the essence, a teaspoonful at a time, into the Hollandaise, tasting the mixture occasionally and adding as much of the essence as you wish. About 6 teaspoons give Béarnaise the flavor I like.

Taste the sauce again for seasoning and add more salt and white pepper if you think it necessary. Just before serving, stir into the sauce the fresh tarragon or, lacking that, parsley.

MOCK HOLLANDAISE SAUCE

This mustard-flavored sauce, which goes so well with beef, is known in French as *sauce bâtarde*. In English, with justification, it is called Mock Hollandaise because it does indeed bear a faint family resemblance to a true Hollandaise. However, unlike Hollandaise, whose behavior can be treacherous, to say the least, Mock Hollandaise is the most predictable of sauces. It can be made hours ahead and flavored in almost numberless ways.

You might, for example, omit the mustard and in its place use 1 tablespoon of finely chopped fresh parsley, dill, basil, tarragon, or chives. And for a more piquant flavor, stir into the finished sauce, whether you have flavored it with mustard or herbs, a tablespoon or two of washed, drained, and dried small capers, either whole or coarsely chopped.

MAKES ABOUT 2 CUPS

2 tablespoons butter
2 tablespoons flour
1 cup fresh or canned chicken broth
1 egg yolk
2 teaspoons dry mustard
2 tablespoons heavy cream
¼ teaspoon salt
Pinch of white pepper
2 teaspoons strained fresh lemon juice
4 tablespoons butter, cut into bits

In a 1- or 2-quart enameled cast-iron or stainless steel saucepan set over low heat, melt 2 tablespoons of butter without letting it brown. Remove the pan from the heat, add the flour, and stir with a wooden spoon until the mixture—or roux—is smooth. Then pour over it, all at once, the chicken broth. With a whisk, beat the roux and broth together until they have blended completely.

Return the pan to high heat and, whisking constantly, bring the sauce to a boil. When it is thick and smooth—a matter of seconds—lower the heat and cook the sauce slowly for 2 or 3 minutes to rid it of any floury taste.

In a small dish, mix together thoroughly the egg yolk, dry mustard, and cream. Pour it in a thin stream into the simmering sauce, whisking constantly. Stir in the salt, a pinch of white pepper, and lemon juice, then taste for seasoning, adding more salt and pepper if you think it needs it. Then, bit by bit, beat in 4 tablespoons of butter and set the sauce aside until ready to use.

LEMON SAUCE

This is my version of the famous Greek preparation called avgolemono sauce. It contains no butter whatever, but when you taste it, perhaps for the first time, you will have the illusion that it does.

It is a lovely accompaniment to lamb dishes and fish, as well as asparagus and broccoli.

MAKES ABOUT 2 CUPS

4 egg yolks
1½ tablespoons flour
½ teaspoon salt
⅛ teaspoon white pepper
1½ cups fresh or canned chicken broth
2 tablespoons strained fresh lemon juice

Making the sauce. Drop the egg yolks into a 2-quart enameled cast-iron or stainless steel saucepan or into the top of a double boiler.

Add flour, salt, and pepper. Beat vigorously with a whisk until the flour has been absorbed. Then pour in the chicken broth, beating until the mixture is thoroughly smooth.

Set the pan over moderate heat and, whisking constantly— particularly around the crease of the pan where the eggs are most likely to coagulate—cook the sauce without allowing it to boil or even reach a simmer until it thickens, lifting the pan off the heat every few minutes to prevent boiling.

If the sauce should become lumpy at any point, lift it off the heat and beat it even more vigorously until it is smooth again.

Still stirring, continue to cook the sauce for 2 or 3 minutes after it has thickened to remove any taste of raw flour.

Stir in the lemon juice and taste for seasoning. You may want to add more lemon juice and, possibly, more salt. If you prefer the sauce somewhat thinner, you can stir in a little more chicken broth or water.

Serve the Lemon Sauce at once; or keep it warm in the covered top of a double boiler over barely simmering water.

Reheating the sauce. Leftover Lemon Sauce may be refrigerated and then successfully reheated in the top pan of a double boiler set over simmering water. Stir the sauce with a whisk until it is hot and smooth.

MAYONNAISE

MAKES 2 CUPS

3 egg yolks, at room temperature
1 teaspoon salt
½ teaspoon dry or prepared mustard
1 tablespoon white wine vinegar or lemon juice
1½ cups vegetable oil or olive oil, or a combination in any
    proportion you prefer
2 tablespoons boiling water

In a mixing bowl which has been rinsed in hot water then dried, and using a whisk, rotary beater, or an electric mixer, beat the egg yolks steadily for about 2 minutes until they thicken and cling to the beater when it is lifted from the bowl. Add the salt, mustard, and vinegar or lemon juice, and beat for another minute. Still beating, add ½ teaspoonful of the oil and beat until it is thoroughly absorbed. Then add another ½ teaspoonful of oil and beat it in. Continue beating and adding oil, ½ teaspoonful at a time, in this fashion, until you have incorporated ½ cup of the oil. By this time, the mixture will have thickened considerably and you can add the remaining oil in a slow, steady stream, beating all the while. When all the oil has been added and absorbed, beat in the boiling water, a tablespoonful at a time. Taste for seasoning.

If the mayonnaise should separate at any time, in a clean dry bowl beat 1 additional egg yolk with 1 teaspoon of prepared mustard for about a minute, then into that mixture beat the separated mayonnaise, 1 teaspoonful at a time.

VARIATION: HERB-FLAVORED MAYONNAISE

Prepare Mayonnaise, following the directions in the preceding recipe, then stir in finely cut tarragon, dill, chives, basil, or parsley, alone or in any combination you prefer. To 2 cups of Mayonnaise, plan on adding about 1 teaspoon of chopped chives and about 3 tablespoons of the other herbs, in all. Of course, you may use more or less of any of them, depending on your taste.

VARIATION: SAUCE RÉMOULADE

Because Sauce Rémoulade needs a mellowing period, make it at least 2 hours or longer before you need it.

MAKES ABOUT 1¼ CUPS

1 cup Mayonnaise (page 436), preferably homemade
1 teaspoon Dijon mustard
½ teaspoon anchovy paste
1 tablespoon capers, thoroughly drained and chopped
1 tablespoon chopped gherkins
8 to 10 sprigs parsley, finely chopped
1 tablespoon finely chopped chives (optional)
Salt (optional)

Spoon the Mayonnaise into a medium-size mixing bowl. With a fork or wooden spatula, stir in the mustard, anchovy paste, capers, gherkins, parsley, and, if you wish, chives, mixing only enough—a matter of a minute or so—to combine the ingredients. Taste for seasoning. You may want to add just a pinch of salt.

Place plastic wrap flat on the surface of the sauce; this seals out the air and prevents a skin from forming. Refrigerate the sauce until needed.

HORSERADISH SAUCE

This is a zesty sauce for boiled beef, corned beef, and tongue.

MAKES ¾ CUP

2 tablespoons grated white horseradish, bottled or fresh
2 teaspoons white wine vinegar
½ teaspoon dry mustard
¼ teaspoon sugar
¼ teaspoon salt
Pinch of white pepper
2 tablespoons fresh white bread crumbs
4 to 6 tablespoons heavy cream

Drain the horseradish in a small, fine-meshed sieve. Then transfer it to a clean small kitchen towel and twist the ends firmly to squeeze out all the liquid. You should end up with about 1 tablespoon of dry horseradish; if there is less, simply repeat the draining and squeezing procedure with more horseradish until you have the amount required.

Place the horseradish in a small mixing bowl and, with a table fork, stir in the vinegar. Add the dry mustard, sugar, salt, pepper, and bread crumbs.

Stir the mixture until it becomes a fairly firm paste, then mix in 4 tablespoons of the cream, a tablespoonful at a time. If the sauce is too thick for your taste, thin it with as much of the remaining cream as you like.

Cover the sauce with plastic wrap, and refrigerate it until ready to use.

MARCHAND DE VINS SAUCE

This red wine and shallot sauce, called by the French *sauce marchand de vins*—literally, wine merchant's sauce—is a classic in French cooking and a splendid accompaniment to steaks, roast beef, and hamburgers. The 1-cup quantity is sufficient for a 4- to 5-pound bone-in steak for 4 people, but you may double or triple the recipe as needed.

MAKES 1 CUP

¾ cup finely chopped shallots, or ½ cup finely chopped scallions, white parts only
2 cups dry red wine
2 teaspoons arrowroot
2 tablespoons water
8 tablespoons butter (a quarter-pound stick), cut into bits
¼ teaspoon salt
Freshly ground black pepper
2 tablespoons finely cut fresh or frozen chives

Place the shallots or scallions in an 8-inch enameled cast-iron or stainless steel frying pan. Pour in the wine and bring the mixture to a boil over high heat. Then lower the heat and simmer, uncovered, until the wine has cooked down to about a cupful.

Strain the contents of the pan through a fine sieve set over a bowl, pressing down on the vegetables with the back of a spoon to extract all their juices before discarding them. Return the wine to the frying pan.

Mix the arrowroot with the water in a small bowl. Add the mixture to the wine and, stirring constantly with a whisk, bring the wine to a boil. Lower the heat and simmer the sauce for about 2 minutes, or until it is thick and smooth.

Remove the pan from the heat and, bit by bit, stir in the butter. When all the butter has been incorporated, add the salt, a liberal grinding of pepper, and the chives. Taste for seasoning—the sauce may possibly need more salt.

VINAIGRETTE SAUCE

This is a basic recipe for a vinaigrette sauce to use with cold vegetables and salads.

Good-quality olive oil
Red or white wine vinegar
Salt
Freshly ground black pepper

With a whisk, combine the olive oil and wine vinegar in the proportion of 3 tablespoons of oil to 1 of vinegar. Season with salt and freshly ground pepper.

PARSLEY BUTTER

MAKES ABOUT ½ CUP

8 tablespoons butter (a quarter-pound stick), softened at room temperature
1 tablespoon strained fresh lemon juice
3 tablespoons finely chopped fresh parsley, preferably flat-leafed or Italian variety
Salt
Freshly ground black pepper

Cream the butter in a food processor or by mashing it with a wooden spoon against the sides of a large, heavy bowl. Continue to beat until the butter is smooth and creamy. Then beat in the lemon juice a few drops at a time, following it with the parsley and salt and pepper to taste.

Cover the bowl with plastic wrap and refrigerate until needed.

DILL BUTTER

MAKES ABOUT ½ CUP

8 tablespoons butter (a quarter-pound stick), softened at room temperature
1 tablespoon strained fresh lemon juice
3 tablespoons finely cut fresh dill
⅛ teaspoon salt
Freshly ground black pepper

Cream the butter in a food processor or by mashing it with a wooden spoon against the sides of a large, heavy bowl. Continue to beat it until the butter is smooth and creamy. Beat in the lemon juice a few drops at a time, and when it has all been absorbed, stir in the dill, salt, and a few grindings of pepper. Taste for seasoning.

Cover the dill butter with plastic wrap and refrigerate it until you are ready to use it.

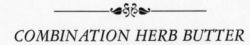

COMBINATION HERB BUTTER

MAKES ABOUT ½ CUP

8 tablespoons butter (a quarter-pound stick), softened at room temperature
1 tablespoon soy sauce
1 teaspoon strained fresh lemon juice
1 teaspoon very finely chopped garlic
2 tablespoons finely chopped fresh parsley, preferably flat-leafed or Italian variety
Salt
Freshly ground black pepper

Cream the butter in the container of a food processor or by mashing and beating it with a large wooden spoon against the sides of a large, heavy mixing bowl. Continue to beat until the butter is creamy and smooth. Then beat in the soy sauce a few drops at a time, following it with the lemon juice, garlic, chopped parsley, and salt and pepper to taste.

Cover the herb butter closely and refrigerate until needed.

GARLIC BUTTER

MAKES ABOUT ½ CUP

8 tablespoons butter (a quarter-pound stick), softened at room temperature
2 tablespoons finely chopped scallions, including 1 inch of green stems
2 teaspoons finely chopped garlic
1 tablespoon finely chopped fresh parsley
⅛ teaspoon salt
Freshly ground black pepper

Cream the butter in the container of a food processor or by mashing it with a wooden spoon against the sides of a large mixing bowl, then beating it vigorously until smooth and creamy. Stir in the scallions, garlic, parsley, salt, and a few grindings of pepper. Taste it for seasoning.

Cover the garlic butter closely with plastic wrap and refrigerate until needed.

MARCHAND DE VINS BUTTER

This is a classic accompaniment for broiled and roasted beef dishes.

MAKES ABOUT 2 CUPS

1½ cups dry red wine
2 tablespoons finely chopped shallots
1 clove garlic, peeled and finely minced
1½ cups (3 quarter-pound sticks) butter, softened at room
    temperature
2 tablespoons minced fresh parsley
2 tablespoons strained fresh lemon juice
Salt
Freshly ground black pepper

In a small enameled or stainless steel saucepan, combine the wine with the shallots and garlic. Place over moderate heat and cook, uncovered, until the wine has reduced to about ½ cup. This will take about 12 minutes. Cool the mixture slightly.

Place the butter in a medium-size mixing bowl. Add the parsley and lemon juice, and work the ingredients together with your hands until they are well combined. Add the wine mixture, beating it in with a wire whisk. Beat in salt—you may need as much as ¾ teaspoon—and freshly ground pepper to taste.

Spoon the butter into crocks and refrigerate until ready to use.

Culinary Glossary

Here you will find terms and definitions, explanations, discussions of foods and ingredients, some basic food preparation techniques, and other miscellaneous information of general interest. If an ingredient or a technique relates only to one recipe, it is discussed where it occurs in the text.

Baking powder. Baking powder is a chemical leavener (unlike yeast, which is a biological one), composed of an alkaline substance—baking soda—combined with one or more acid ingredients and a small amount of starch that serves as a stabilizer. When moistened, these ingredients give off the carbon dioxide gas that leavens doughs or batters.

In each of my recipes that requires baking powder, I specify that it be double-acting. Single-acting (or tartrate) baking powder begins to release its carbon dioxide gas as soon as it is moistened. On the other hand, double-acting baking powder releases only a fraction of its gas into the batter when moistened, reserving the rest of its leavening power until the batter is exposed to heat.

If you must for any reason use single-acting baking powder, there should not be a moment's delay between the mixing of the batter and baking it if you would have the batter rise to its full height.

Baking soda. Baking soda, also called bicarbonate of soda and sodium bicarbonate, is always used, often together with baking powder, when a batter is made with an acid liquid such as buttermilk, sour milk, or sour cream. When baking soda encounters the acid in the liquid, it reacts in the same way that baking powder does when moistened with an ordinary liquid—that is, it produces carbon dioxide gas that leavens the mixture.

Barding fat. These are the thin sheets or strips of fat used to cover a bird or a roast, either to provide automatic basting or to protect delicate parts during cooking.

Beurre manié. Butter and flour worked into a paste, either with your fingers or a spoon, and used as a thickener for some sauces.

Butcher's knots. Butcher's knots are slip knots that make it possible to tighten and loosen string as needed when rolling a boned roast. Make them as follows:

1. Place soft string under the meat with the ball of string (the source end) toward you and the free (cut) end away from you. Bring the free end up over the top of the meat and underneath the source end. Place the index and second fingers of your left hand between the roast and the string, and rotate your hand clockwise, turning the palm down to form a loop.

2. Carry the free end over the top of the string.

3. Pull the free end through the loop and tighten the knot by pulling both source and free ends of the string.

4. Release the free end of the string, hold the roast with your left hand, tighten the string by moving it back and forth with the source end until the knot no longer slips. To secure the knot, tie a second knot the same way.

Butter. The U.S. Department of Agriculture grades or "scores" butter on the basis of such factors as aroma, texture, and flavor. The best butter, made of sweet cream, is scored AA, the next best, A—the packages are so marked. The butter may be either salted or unsalted. Should you find butter scored B—and occasionally you may in some small towns— it will be labeled as being made from sour, or so-called ripened, cream. Despite its slightly acidulated flavor, this somewhat inferior butter may be used in any of my recipes that require butter.

The best butter for baking—and for that matter, everything else— is unsalted ("sweet") butter, graded either AA or A. Although even the best grade of salted butter made from sweet cream is undesirable for baking, it will not necessarily be catastrophic if you use it, even though the amount of added salt varies a great deal from brand to brand.

My objection to the use of salted butter may strike you as illogical, but it is nothing of the sort. I have calculated the precise amount of salt necessary in each recipe when unsalted butter is used. If you must use salted butter, make sure it is as lightly salted as possible, and reduce the salt called for in any of my recipes by one-half.

TO CLARIFY BUTTER, melt the butter over low heat without letting it brown. Let the butter rest for a few minutes off the heat, then tilt the pan and remove as much of the clear liquid butter as you can, discarding the milky solids at the bottom of the pan.

Buttermilk. Buttermilk, as country folk know it, is the liquid that remains after butter has been churned from ripened (soured) cream. Buttermilk that originates in this way is, alas, no longer available in retail markets. What you get when you buy buttermilk today is a cultured product composed of skimmed or partially skimmed milk that has been soured and thickened by a culture of lactic acid bacteria.

Cultured buttermilk can be purchased everywhere, but individual dairies use different cultures. Not surprisingly, the flavor and the thickness will vary from brand to brand. Often buttermilk will be excessively bland or too thin. For the best results with my recipes, try to find a cultured buttermilk that pours out in a thick, smooth stream and has a definitely acidulated but pleasant flavor.

Chicken (also see **Poultry**). Choosing a chicken for quality can be difficult for the nonprofessional cook. It is true that the U.S. Department of Agriculture grades chickens, but having chickens graded is voluntary on the part of the producer, not mandatory. Chickens that have the USDA Grade A seal (usually attached to a wing) are of the best quality. The chicken should be moist and plump and have a fresh wholesome odor. The color of its skin makes no difference at all: yellow-skinned chickens have been fed on corn and white-skinned chickens on milk; both, if they are of the highest quality, have essentially the same flavor.

According to U.S. Government standards, chickens are classified as follows:

BROILERS. Also called *fryers* or *broiler-fryers*, these are young chickens weighing from 1½ to 4 pounds. They can be broiled, sautéed, fried, roasted, and braised.

ROASTERS. These are somewhat older and larger chickens (3 to 5 pounds), delicious when roasted, poached, or braised.

STEWING CHICKENS. Also called *mature, old chickens,* or *hens,* these should be poached or simmered.

CAPONS. Castrated cocks, weighing 6 to 7 pounds or more, these birds are especially desirable for roasting when a large bird is in order.

SQUAB CHICKENS. The *poussins* of France, these are mere babies, weighing about a pound and sufficient for one person. They are usually tender and delicate and are best when roasted whole or split and broiled.

The term "ready-to-cook," often seen on packages of fresh and frozen chicken, means that the bird has been cleaned inside and out, is free of pinfeathers, and eviscerated (the head, feet, and inedible organs were removed before the bird was weighed for pricing). The neck, gizzard, heart, and liver have been washed, trimmed, wrapped, and tucked, most likely, inside the body cavity of the bird.

HOW MUCH CHICKEN TO BUY. For roasting or braising, allow about ¾ pound ready-to-cook chicken per serving. A 3-pound broiler-fryer will serve 3, perhaps 4, and yield 2½ cups of diced cooked chicken.

THAWING CHICKENS. Thaw the chicken in the refrigerator in its original wrapper, allowing a full day for a 3- to 5-pound bird. Or, place the frozen bird, sealed in its original wrapper (if the wrapper is torn, place it in a plastic bag), in a pan under cold running water.

TRUSSING A BIRD. Place the bird on its back so its neck faces you. Holding a drumstick with each hand, force the legs down against the body as far as they will go. Slide a 3-foot length of string underneath the legs so that they are about in the center of it. Then cross the string around the legs, pulling it tight around the drumsticks and then up underneath the breastbone just above. Pull the string toward you along each side of the bird between the leg and body. Turn the bird so its tail faces you and the string ends come up each side between leg and body.

Pull the string ends tight, then slide one end under each wing, bring the strings up along the elbow joints of the wings and across the back where you should tie the string in a knot. Close the neck opening by folding the loose neck skin flat against the back and over the knot, then tie another knot over the neck skin.

Twist the wing tips up over the back, then tuck the tail into the opening just above it. Turn the bird over; it will sit neatly on its haunches. The advantage of this method is that all you have to do to remove the string is to snip it at the drumsticks, then pull it away in one piece.

QUARTERING A CHICKEN. Using a sharp thin knife, cut the legs from the body, then cut along each side of the backbone. Set the backbone aside. Hold the chicken flesh side up, and bend it sharply backward until the keelbone (center breastbone) pops up. Remove the keelbone, then cut the breast in half lengthwise.

Chilling a bowl. To chill a "working" bowl (it should be of stainless steel), dump two trays of ice cubes into a second, larger bowl and set the "working" bowl on top.

Clarified butter. See **Butter**.

Coconut. To prepare a fresh coconut, first puncture the "eyes" in one end of the shell with an icepick or a screwdriver forced through with a hammer. Set the coconut over a cup and let the milk drain out. Then place the coconut in a preheated 400° F. oven and bake it for 15 minutes.

Set the coconut on a chopping board and, with a few sharp blows of a hammer, split the shell. While the coconut is still warm, use a swivel-bladed peeler to strip away all the brown skin. Then grate the coconut on the tear-shaped teeth of a stand-up grater or in a food processor, using the grating blade.

Corn meal. See **Flour**.

Corn Syrup. See **Sugars and sweeteners**.

Court bouillon. An aromatic, quickly made broth composed of water, vegetables, seasonings, and sometimes wine. Although the French always poach fish in a court bouillon, I never use a court bouillon when I poach fish unless I intend to use the broth as the base of a soup or sauce; I find that the exquisite flavor of a truly fresh fish is somewhat muted, rather than enhanced, by a court bouillon.

Cream. When I call for heavy cream (sweet cream), called whipping cream in some parts of the country, I mean cream with a butterfat content of at least 30 percent. When used in making sauces, it can be simmered or actually boiled without any danger of its curdling. Light or medium cream and half-and-half do not contain enough butterfat to produce the density necessity for some classic sauces.

Deglazing. Deglazing is the process of incorporating into a sauce the browned particles of food—the concentrated essences—left in the pan after food has been sautéed or roasted. This is done by removing the food and any fat from the pan, then dissolving the remaining particles in an appropriate liquid—water, stock, cream, wine—to give body and flavor to the accompanying sauce.

Degreasing. To remove fat from a hot liquid quickly, dump a couple of trays of ice cubes into the liquid. The grease will congeal around each cube and can be lifted out. Because there will be some dilution as the ice melts, place the degreased liquid over a fairly high heat and boil down for a few minutes. You can also draw off the fat with a bulb baster or skim it off with a spoon. Or, if you have the time, refrigerate the liquid until the fat congeals on the surface and can be easily removed.

Ducks and ducklings (also see **Poultry**). Ducks no more than 7 or 8 weeks old are correctly called ducklings and weigh from 3½ to 5½ pounds, eviscerated. They are available fresh or frozen, ready-to-cook, the year round, and are excellent for both roasting and braising. Although the modern duckling is being bred for less fat than formerly, fat is the important ingredient that gives a handsome duckling its rich flavor.

HOW MUCH DUCKLING TO BUY. One large duckling (5 to 5½ pounds) will serve 3 but could possibly be stretched to serve 4 if the dinner menu is ample.

THAWING A DUCKLING. If you are preparing a frozen duckling, the thawing will take about 12 hours at room temperature and twice as long in the refrigerator. To speed the process, leave the duckling sealed in its original wrapper, or put it in a waterproof plastic bag and place it in a bowl under cold running water. Remove the giblets and neck from the cavity of the bird and discard, unless you are using them in another recipe.

QUARTERING A DUCKLING. Cut off any loose skin at the neck and place the duckling breast down. Starting at the neck with a sharp boning knife, carefully cut down on both sides of the backbone until you reach the section where the bone begins to fan out or broaden (somewhat past the middle of the duck). From this point on, the cutting is more difficult and you may find it easier to use poultry shears. Keep cutting until you can remove the backbone. Once the backbone is lifted out, pull away as many of the small bones as you can, loosening them from the meat with the boning knife.

Turn the duckling breast side up, grip it firmly, and bend the carcass back until the breastbone pops up. Pull out and discard the bone. Spread the duckling flat and cut it in half, right down the center. Next, cut each half in two, separating the breasts from the leg sections and taking care to cut the skin cleanly.

Eggs. Eggs are sold in the United States in a variety of sizes ranging from small pullet eggs, which are difficult to find these days, to the more available medium, large, extra large, and jumbo eggs, all of which are classified by weight per dozen. When I specify eggs in this book, I always mean "large" eggs, which weigh 24 ounces to the dozen. Should you substitute small (18 ounces per dozen), medium (21 ounces), extra large (27 ounces), or jumbo (30 ounces) eggs, you may find the mathematical adjustments involved insurmountable, and any miscalculation will upset the balance I have created to ensure the success of the recipes.

As for color, it matters not at all if the eggs are brown or white; there is absolutely no difference in quality or flavor between them.

Unless you are fortunate enough to live in a locality where truly fresh eggs from nearby chicken farms are easily available, you will have to depend on the trustworthiness of your dairyman or supermarket manager for the freshness of the eggs you buy. In most recipes the freshness of the eggs is of less importance than their size, but when freshness is of crucial importance or, conversely, when eggs a few days old are desirable, I indicate that in the recipe.

HARD-COOKING EGGS. To hard-cook eggs, let them come to room temperature and then lower them carefully, using a spoon, into a pan containing boiling water to cover them. Reduce the heat to low and simmer the eggs, uncovered, for 15 minutes. Plunge them into a bowl of cold water immediately, then either peel them or let them cool first. Refrigerate the eggs until you are ready to use them.

SEPARATING EGGS. Separating eggs is tricky because even when the greatest care is taken, yolks sometimes break. The safe way is to use three bowls—one for the yolks, one for the whites, and a small bowl over which you separate each egg, thus eliminating the possibility of breaking a yolk into the bowl of whites. Whites will not beat up properly if they contain even so much as a drop of yolks or, for that matter, any fat.

To separate an egg, crack the shell at its midcenter sharply on the edge of the small bowl. Pull the two halves apart, holding them upright, over the bowl. The yolk, because it is heavier, will automatically remain in one half, while the white will run out. Switch the yolk back and forth between the shells until all the white has disengaged itself and dropped into the small bowl. Then pour the white into the bowl in which you intend to beat the whites. Drop the yolk into its proper bowl.

If, by mischance, you should break a yolk and even a small amount of it falls into the white, lift it out with a piece of shell or paper toweling.

EGG WHITES. When properly beaten, egg whites mount to seven or eight times their original volume. They are smooth and glistening (sometimes called "wet"), free from granules, and will hold firm, glossy peaks when the beater is lifted straight up. If they are granular or dry, they have been overbeaten and much of the air will have been lost.

Although many authorities are convinced that you get more volume and stiffness when the egg whites are at room temperature, I have had equally good results with whites that were refrigerator-cold.

For whipping egg whites, traditionalists recommend the big balloon whip (*fouet*, in French) and an unlined copper bowl, with which egg whites mount faster and with greater volume. However, I think it would be ridiculous to ignore the fact that modern beaters—the rotary, the portable electric, and the big electric mixer—are marvelously effective pieces of equipment that, to a large extent, take the work out of cooking. I use them myself, and I particularly recommend to you the big electric mixer for this and many other uses.

HOW TO FOLD EGG WHITES INTO A HEAVIER MIXTURE. Folding means to combine a fragile mixture such as beaten egg whites with a heavier mixture, such as a soufflé base or a cake batter. This is how it's done: Add about a third of the beaten whites to the heavier mixture and whip them in vigorously with a wire whip. This lightens the mixture and makes folding easier. Then, using a rubber spatula, scoop the mixture on top of the remaining egg whites. Still using a rubber spatula, cut down from the top center of the mixture to the very bottom of the bowl, then draw the spatula toward you against the edge of the bowl, rotating the bowl as you work. Working swiftly, repeat this cutting and folding until the whites have been folded in, but do not attempt to be too thorough, especially in making a soufflé; better to have a few unblended patches of egg white than a soufflé that won't rise. You can be more thorough in combining beaten egg whites with a cake batter.

Fats. See **Butter, Margarine, Vegetable shortening.**

Federal inspection and grading of meats and poultry. All meat sold in interstate commerce is federally inspected and will bear the round inspection stamp indicating that it is wholesome and has been processed under sanitary conditions. In addition, a shield-shaped stamp indicates its quality, as graded by the U.S. Department of Agriculture. The two top grades for beef, veal, and lamb (the only two grades that concern us) are *Prime*, the finest quality and most expensive, primarily available in independent markets, and *Choice*, the quality most commonly found in supermarkets. Pork is federally inspected for wholesomeness but is not graded in the same manner.

Federal grading of chickens and ducklings for quality is voluntary, not mandatory. All poultry bearing a shield-shaped grade stamp—Grade A indicates the highest quality and is usually the only grade for sale in retail markets—has also been inspected for wholesomeness.

Fish. Fish may well be the most neglected food in America. Nearly every other country does it homage, and the French, who cook it so magnificently, devote as much attention to fish as they do to meat. There is nothing more delicious than fish perfectly cooked. Sweet and tender, it is a delicate distillation of the sea itself.

Fish cookery calls for precise timing and precise temperatures and, as is true of all cookery, a modicum of common sense. No matter how the fish is to be cooked, you should remember that fish is *not* cooked to tenderize it—it is tender when it comes from the water. In fact, the Japanese often eat their fish raw. The primary reason for cooking fish is to change its texture and develop its flavor, and this can be accomplished in a relatively short cooking time. Overcooking is the crime all too often perpetrated on a delicious piece of fish. Every fish has its own special characteristics, and they determine how the fish should be cooked.

Fresh fish is available in any of the following forms:

WHOLE OR ROUND FISH. These fish are marketed just as they come from the water. Before cooking, they must be scaled and eviscerated. Usually the head, tail, and fins are removed.

DRAWN FISH. Fish in this form have had only the entrails removed. They need to be scaled and have head, tail, and fins removed before cooking.

DRESSED FISH. Also called *pan-dressed*, they are both scaled and eviscerated; usually head, tail, and fins have been removed and the fish are ready for cooking.

STEAKS. The cross-section slices of large dressed fish that are ready for cooking.

FILLETS. These are the sides of dressed fish, cut lengthwise away from the backbone. Practically boneless, they are usually skinned and ready to cook.

CHUNKS. Taken from cross-sections of large dressed fish, they are ready to cook.

Fresh whole or dressed fish should have firm flesh; a fresh mild odor; bright, clear, full eyes; red gills, free from slime; and shiny skin with color unfaded. Fresh steaks, fillets, and chunks should have a fresh-cut look; firm texture without any traces of browning or drying around the edges; and a fresh, mild odor.

HOW MUCH FISH TO BUY. Allow ¾ to 1 pound per person for whole or drawn fish; about ½ pound per person for pan-dressed fish, steaks, or fillets.

STORING FISH. Fresh fish is extremedy perishable. If you cannot use it at once, wash it quickly and pat it dry with paper towels. Wrap it securely in plastic wrap, then in foil, and refrigerate it immediately; it will keep its freshness in this state for not more than 2 days. If for any reason you must keep it longer, seal it in freezer wrap and freeze it at 0° F. or less—ideally at −10° F. A fat fish—salmon, mackerel, trout, among others—will keep in this deeply frozen state for 2 months, a lean variety—sole, for example—for 3 months. But frozen fish, whether you freeze it yourself or buy it already frozen, will never have the pristine quality of fresh fish. The freezing inevitably changes its texture.

COOKING FISH. Whether you are broiling, poaching, or baking stuffed or unstuffed fish, it is the thickness—not the weight—that determines how long fish should be cooked. This method of cooking was discovered by the Bureau of Fisheries in Ottawa, Canada.

Measure the fish at the thickest part—with a stuffed fish, measure after it has been stuffed—and allow 10 minutes of cooking time per inch of thickness. To measure accurately, run a skewer through the fleshiest part so the point touches the table. Grasp the skewer with your thumb and forefinger at the exact point where the skewer emerges from the body of the fish. Pull the skewer out and measure with a ruler the distance between your fingers and the tip of the skewer. Following the cooking rule of thumb, if the distance is 2 inches, cook the fish 20 minutes.

Flour. Simply stated, flour is any fine, often powdery meal obtained by grinding an edible grain. Although flour can be made of any grain besides wheat—rye, rice, or corn, for example, or even from legumes or roots— the flour most commonly used in baking today is made from wheat.

Wheat flour is available in many varieties—bread flour, bleached or unbleached all-purpose flour, cake flour, whole-wheat flour, instant or granulated flour, self-rising flour (actually a mix), and others—each one composed of hard winter wheat or soft spring wheat, or a combination of the two in various proportions.

All wheat flours have at least one element in common: gluten. When flour is moistened and mixed, gluten is developed in the dough from two protein substances in the flour, gliadin and glutenin. Since hard wheat has a much higher gluten content than soft wheat, the type of flour you use and to what point you allow its gluten to develop will affect to a significant degree the quality and texture of your breads, biscuits, cakes, and pies.

ALL-PURPOSE FLOUR. Milled from a mixture of hard and soft wheats, all-purpose flour has a moderate gluten content. It is available throughout the United States and sold under many brand names. They all look alike (except for a difference in the degree of whiteness between bleached and unbleached all-purpose flours), but they have subtly different characteristics that are neither described on their labels nor apparent to the eye: varying proportions of hard and soft wheat, the presence or absence of enrichment, the various processes by which each brand is milled.

To assure you of as much predictability as possible in the recipes that call for all-purpose flour, I have used the same brand (Gold Medal) consistently, not because of any intrinsic superiority of that flour to other all-purpose flours, but simply because it is readily available throughout the country. I would suggest that you either use Gold Medal or experiment with other brands until you find one that gives you the results you like.

CAKE FLOUR. This is finely milled white flour made wholly from soft wheat. Cake flour has a low gluten content, which makes it eminently suitable for delicate biscuits and cakes. No matter what instructions may appear on box labels, it should *not* be used when all-purpose flour is called for—at least, not in my recipes.

Make sure that you don't mistakenly buy cake flour labeled "self-rising"; this, like self-rising all-purpose flour, contains baking powder and salt and should under no circumstances be substituted in my recipes.

WHOLE-WHEAT FLOUR (GRAHAM FLOUR). Whole-wheat flour, as is obvious from its name, is milled from whole grain. It is often called graham flour because its use was widely promoted by the vegetarian Sylvester Graham in the early nineteenth century.

Whole-wheat flour is a powerhouse of vitamins, minerals, and other nutrients, and it has a high gluten content. It has a distinctive nutlike flavor because the germ and the bran of the wheat kernel are not removed as they are in the milling of white flour. Stone-ground whole-wheat flour, which is ground between millstones, has far more flavor than flour that is milled by machine. It is most often available in health food stores.

You might note that whole-wheat flour is quite perishable because of its fat content and should not be purchased if you have reason to believe that it has been in stock longer than a month or so. And you should use it fairly promptly; it has a shelf life of only about 4 months. Kept longer, it may become rancid.

RYE FLOUR. The light-gray flour made from rye has a fairly high gluten content, but the gluten lacks elasticity. For this reason rye flour is usually combined with white flour for home baking. Like the best whole-wheat flour, the best rye flour is stone-ground. It can be found in most health food stores.

CORN MEAL. Not a true flour, this is a coarse meal, yellow or white, ground from corn. It contains no gluten whatsoever, which is why it is always combined with white flour when used for breads. The best corn meal is stone-ground, but it is difficult to find in some places; health food stores are the most likely sources. Like all stone-ground flours, it is quite perishable; it has a shelf life of about a month. Conventionally milled corn meal is quite satisfactory, although it lacks the robust flavor of the stone-ground kind.

Glaze (also see **Deglazing**). The glaze is the drippings left behind when browned foods are removed after sautéing or roasting. A glaze is often used as the base for a sauce or gravy.

Gratin. A topping of bread crumbs and cheese, browned in the oven by baking or broiling, is known in French as a *gratin*. Many Americans mistakenly think of a "gratin" as a topping that consists of cheese alone.

Ham. Pork has not had the cachet of other meats in the culinary world, but ham—fresh pork that has been cured and smoked—has been the delight of epicures ever since 149 B.C., when Cato the Elder wrote specific instructions on the curing and smoking of fresh pork.

Modern processing has speeded up the curing and smoking. No longer soaked in brine as in the old days, most hams today are injected with the curing solution and then smoked. "Injected" is the key word, because if, during the smoking, the ham has not shrunk to its original fresh weight, it must by federal regulations be labeled "Ham, Water Added" or "Imitation Ham." Obviously, this is less desirable meat, and you would be advised when you buy ham to read the label very carefully so that you know exactly what you are getting.

There are only two kinds of cured and smoked hams available in most retail stores: Cook-Before-Eating and Fully Cooked. Although the labels on fully cooked hams say they can be served without further cooking, I do not agree. It has been my experience that long, slow cooking at

325° F. of either type with frequent basting improves both the texture and the flavor of the ham.

High-altitude baking. At altitudes above 5,000 feet, batters and doughs behave differently from the way they do at sea level. You may compensate for the lower atmospheric pressure in several ways.

Increase oven temperature by 25° F.

Shorten rising time for yeast doughs, letting your eye or the finger-poking method be your guide.

In batters containing baking powder, reduce the baking powder by ¼ teaspoon for every teaspoon called for; do not change the amount of baking soda.

In batters containing beaten egg whites, underbeat the egg whites somewhat.

For more information about high-altitude cooking, consult the home economics department of your state university.

Lamb. The quality of lamb in this country is excellent and the meat is generally available year round, making obsolete the old familiar designation "spring lamb." The age of lamb in U.S. markets averages less than 8 months, but it may be as young as 3 months. "Genuine spring lamb" is usually 3 to 5 months old, depending on where it was raised, "lamb" is usually 5 to 10 months old, although it can be a year, or more, older. "Hothouse" will weigh 15 pounds, dressed weight, and "baby," 8 to 10 pounds. Both are sold in quarters only. Lamb that is more than 1½ years old—in short, sheep—is called mutton. Federal grades for lamb are precisely the same as for beef.

Larding. A French technique, larding is a method of threading lardoons—pork fat or bacon of varying lengths and thicknesses—into large cuts of uncooked meat or poultry or game by means of a larding needle in order to flavor or tenderize it. Deriving from the French *larder*, which actually means "to stuff," the term is now used more loosely in that the lardoon need not necessarily be a fat.

Lobster. Lobster is available in many forms—frozen, canned, and as fresh cooked meat—but it is the fresh, live lobster that concerns us here. Note the word "live." A live lobster should not only be alive but lively. When picked up, it will curl its tail underneath.

A 2¼- to 2½-pound live lobster will serve one person amply and, if prepared with a stuffing or crumb topping, two persons, provided they haven't the appetites of trenchermen.

Margarine. Margarine is made by emulsifying oil—usually vegetable oil, although some margarines contain animal fats—with cultured milk, then kneading the resulting fat to a consistency similar to that of butter.

Margarine has no flavor except what it gains from being churned with the milk, plus artificial flavorings.

I shun margarine entirely. From my point of view, there is nothing more delicious than the flavor of pure butter.

Metric equivalents. See pages 459–61.

Molasses. See **Sugars and sweeteners.**

Onions. To peel onions easily and tearlessly, boil them briskly for 5 to 10 seconds, drain in a sieve, then plunge them in cold water to cool them quickly. Trim the tops and bottoms from the onions, taking care not to disturb the layers, then slip off the skins, first layers, and underfilms.

To dice an onion, halve it lengthwise, make even vertical and horizontal cuts through each half, turn the cut side down, and then slice.

Paper frills. Although many meat markets have paper frills and are glad to give them to you, it's very easy to make your own, prettier ones.

First cut a long rectangle of baking parchment or wax paper approximately 25 inches long and 5 inches wide, and fold it lengthwise. Fringe the folded side by making cuts ¼ inch apart into half the depth of the paper. Unfold the paper, lay it flat on a table, then refold the opposite way—that is, with the inside on the outside. Secure each end with a staple or a piece of cellophane tape. Roll the paper up on a pencil or the end of your finger. Fasten with cellophane tape or a dab of glue.

Make as many frills as you need. Slip them over the tips of a crown roast before presenting it, or on pork or lamb chops, or on the legs of a roasted bird.

Parsley. One easy way to chop parsley is to stem it before washing, bunch the tops on a chopping board, then chop it finely with a chopping knife. Wash the parsley snips in a sieve and dry them in a towel. Another way is to stem, then wash the parsley sprigs, and pat them thoroughly dry in a paper towel. Then process them briefly in a blender or food processor, using the cutting blade. Italian parsley, a flat-leafed variety, has a better-developed taste than the more familiar curly parsley that is used as a garnish.

Pastry bag. To use a pastry bag, turn the top back as you would a cuff, then drop the metal tip into place. Fill the bag, using a rubber spatula to spoon in the food. Gather the top of the bag with one hand, then squeeze the bag with the other hand to force the food out.

Pâte à choux. Also called chou paste in its Anglo-French version, it is a paste made of water, butter, flour, and eggs and used to make cream puffs and hors d'oeuvre pastries.

Potatoes. The amount of starch a potato contains is the crucial factor. A potato with a low starch content—loosely categorized as a boiling potato —is most likely to remain firm after cooking. A potato with a high starch content—loosely categorized as a baking potato—will be mealier and fluffier than the boiling type, and it is more likely to fall apart when boiled. It is difficult to identify boiling and baking potatoes by sight, but it is helpful to remember that mature, or old, potatoes, whatever their type, contain more starch than young, new potatoes.

Poultry (also see **Chicken, Ducks and ducklings**). Poultry must be federally inspected for wholesomeness before it can be graded for quality. The official grade shield can be either a label, wing tag, or a stamp on the giblet bag. Of the three grades—A, B, and C—only Grade A, indicating the highest quality, is available in retail markets. You may find the grade shield on any chilled or frozen ready-to-cook poultry.

With any poultry, fresh or frozen and thawed, the giblets and neck should be removed from the body cavity as soon as possible, wrapped in foil or a polyethylene bag, tied securely, and placed in the coldest part of the refrigerator. They should be cooked promptly—particularly thawed frozen giblets which should never be refrozen—because they deteriorate very quickly. You might make it a point of accumulating the fresh livers and freezing them until you have enough for a pâté.

To test roasted poultry for doneness, use any of these three methods: For the finger test, protect your fingers with a couple of thicknesses of paper towels, and press the drumstick and breast; they should feel soft. For the fork test, puncture the skin of the bird at the thigh joint; the juices should run clean. If they are pink, roast the bird a little longer, but take care not to overcook or the bird will be dry. For the thermometer test, plunge a "spot-check" thermometer (see "Equipment and Utensils," pages 4–5) into the thickest part of the thigh, taking care not to touch bone. It should register 170° to 175° F. for a perfectly cooked chicken, 175° to 180° F. for turkey at its juiciest best.

Reduction. This is the process of reducing the quantity of stock or cooking liquid by boiling it rapidly in an uncovered pot, thus intensifying the flavor by evaporation alone. Reduction, a necessary step in making all sauces for sautés, consists of boiling liquids and glaze together, uncovered, so that about half the sauce evaporates, concentrating the flavor.

Roux. A smooth cooked paste of butter and flour, commonly used to thicken many sauces.

Short pastry. Pastry that contains a large amount of butter in proportion to the flour.

Sour cream. Nowadays sour cream is no longer cream that has gone sour by accident or on purpose but, like buttermilk, is a commercially cultured product. Light cream (cream containing from 18 to 20 percent butter-fat) is homogenized and pasteurized, then mixed with a lactic-acid bacteria culture and allowed to ripen until it reaches the desired thickness and degree of acidulation.

Cultured sour cream. like cultured buttermilk, varies in flavor from one dairy to another. Some brands have more body than others when newly made. Sour cream stored in the refrigerator never thins out, but continues to thicken as it stands. Its staying power when properly refrigerated is quite remarkable—it will keep for at least a week. Should you notice an accumulation of watery fluid in the container, simply pour it off before measuring the sour cream.

Stocks and broths. If you lack freshly made chicken or beef stock, a good canned brand—always called broth, incidentally, on the can—will serve almost as well. If the canned broth is a condensed type, follow the directions on the can for diluting with water. There are, however, other brands of chicken and beef broth that do not call for any dilution. I think these, for the most part, are superior to the condensed broths.

Don't use canned consommé, either chicken or beef, as a substitute for broth. Canned consommés are generally too sweet in flavor and may contain added gelatin.

Sugars and sweeteners. When sugar is listed in this book without further description, ordinary granulated white sugar, made from sugar beet or cane, is meant; other sweeteners are indicated by name.

BROWN SUGAR. Brown sugar, both light and dark, has molasses added in varying amounts. When a recipe calls for brown sugar, I mean dark-brown sugar, not light-brown sugar and not granulated brown (or Brownulated) sugar, which pours easily but behaves rather unpredictably in baking and cooking.

SUPERFINE SUGAR is finely granulated white sugar, sometimes called instant sugar, used mainly in drinks and desserts.

CONFECTIONERS' SUGAR. This fine-textured sugar, which contains about 3 percent cornstarch to prevent caking, is used mainly in frostings or for dusting the tops of cakes. It is frequently called "powdered sugar," but the label on the box may read 10X Confectioners' Sugar or XXXX.

LIQUID SWEETENERS. These, such as molasses and corn syrup, are not interchangeable with dry sugars for baking purposes. Liquid sweeteners are used in my recipes for the particular flavor and extra moisture they contribute.

When you buy molasses—I always use the dark kind—make certain it is unsulfured; sulfured molasses has a perceptibly sulfurous flavor. Blackstrap molasses is unpleasantly bitter and is unsuitable for baking.

Corn syrup should usually be the light kind; dark corn syrup is too sweet for most of the recipes in this book.

Turkey. See **Poultry.**

Veal. Veal, which lends itself to innumerable delicious interpretations, has always been more prized in Europe than in this country, undoubtedly because the quality of European milk-fed animals is so exceptional. In this country, where the quality of veal varies greatly, it is frequently impossible to get really good meat.

The best veal is the meat from young, milk-fed animals between 5 and 12 weeks old. After 12 weeks, it is no longer considered veal but "baby" beef and has lost its pure flavor and tenderness.

Because veal comes from very young animals, it has little or no "marbling"—that is, fat within the lean such as you find in beef. Any exterior fat is white and firm. In Normandy, where veal is the great specialty, the natives say, "The white fat of veal smells slightly of milk."

Veal has certain other characteristics that make its cooking somewhat different from that of other meats. Although it is tender, it has considerable connective tissue, which means that a veal roast requires long, slow cooking. Delicate in color, it becomes lighter when it is cooked.

Two of the best methods for cooking veal are roasting and braising. It is excellent sautéed, it can also be cooked in liquid for stews, but it is seldom broiled. Veal is always cooked well done, but *only* until tender yet firm. Do not cook it until all the juices run out and the texture turns coarse.

Vegetable shortening. Made from bland vegetable oils, solid vegetable shortening is generally white or creamy in color. It has little or no flavor; it needn't be refrigerated; and it keeps almost indefinitely without deteriorating.

Warming plates and platters. It might appear inconsistent for me to recommend that you let meats rest before carving, and then tell you to serve the same meat on a heated platter and plates. The fact of the matter is that whereas uncarved meat will retain its internal heat while resting, once the meat is carved, it will cool very rapidly. To compensate for this, it is imperative that hot plates and platters be used.

If you own a dishwasher with a plate-warming setting, you will have no problem at all. But you can just as easily heat your plates and platters by placing them in an oven with its thermostat set at "warm," or at its lowest setting. Or, you can put them on a warming tray.

Wine. When wine is included among the ingredients in a recipe, under no circumstances use so-called cooking wine or a wine that you wouldn't drink. It will taste just as bad in the dish as it would in a glass. Any good domestic wine will do, and only if you feel extravagant need you use an imported wine. However, if you buy wine for use in a recipe, you might—as discriminating diners do—want to drink the remainder of the bottle with the dish.

Yeast. Yeast consists of single-celled plants which are one of the innumerable kinds of fungi. There are about 3,200 billion cells in a pound of yeast. The cells, which can be kept dormant for varying periods by drying, chilling, or freezing, revive and grow under the proper conditions. Like all living plants, yeast cells need moisture, the correct temperature, and nutrients—sugar and starch, in this case—in order to grow.

Yeast today is marketed in two forms, active dry and compressed (or fresh active). Active dry yeast is available everywhere in quarter-ounce foil packages, and it will keep fresh for several months on any cool dry shelf. On each package is stamped the date after which the maker no longer recommends that you use the yeast.

Compressed fresh yeast comes most often in foil-wrapped cakes weighing six-tenths of an ounce (the size meant when a recipe calls for "a cake of yeast"). It is perishable and must be kept refrigerated. In general, it should be kept for no more than about two weeks after purchase lest it deteriorate.

Having used both types of yeast in countless baking tests, I have discovered little if any difference in the results. Because dry yeast presents no spoilage problem and is much easier than fresh yeast to mix into doughs, I call for it in all the recipes for yeast-leavened breads and cakes in this book.

Metric Equivalents
of Weights and Measures

As you convert to the metric system, you will find that in cooking, three kinds of measurements are affected by the change: weight, in which the basic measure will be the gram (g.); temperature, which will be expressed in degrees Celsius (° C.), also called Centigrade; and volume, in which the basic metric unit is the liter (l.). Until you actually start thinking in metric units, the following conversion tables of approximate equivalents will help you find your way between the two systems.

Weight

To convert ounces to grams, multiply by 28.35.
To convert grams to ounces, multiply by 0.035.
To convert pounds to kilograms, multiply by 0.45.
To convert kilograms to pounds, multiply by 2.2.

OUNCES/POUNDS	GRAMS/KILOGRAMS
¼ oz.	7.1 g.
½ oz.	14.17 g.
¾ oz.	21.27 g.
1 oz.	28.35 g.
¼ lb. (4 oz.)	.113 kg. (113 g.)
½ ib.	.227 kg.
¾ lb.	.340 kg.
1 lb.	.454 kg.
2.2 lb.	1 kg.

Temperature

To convert degrees Fahrenheit to degrees Celsius, subtract 32, multiply by 5, and divide by 9.

To convert degrees Celsius to degrees Fahrenheit, multiply by 9, divide by 5, and add 32.

OVEN TEMPERATURES

° F.	° C.	Description
160	71	Warm
170	77	
200	93	
205	96	Simmer
212	100	Boil
225	107	Very slow
250	121	
275	135	
300	149	Slow
325	163	
350	177	Moderate
375	190	
400	204	Hot
425	218	
450	232	
475	246	Very hot
500	260	
525	274	
550	288	

Volume

To convert U.S. quarts to liters, multiply by 0.95.
To convert liters to U.S. quarts, multiply by 1.057.
To convert gallons to liters, multiply by 3.8.
To convert liters to gallons, multiply by 0.26.
To convert pints to liters, multiply by 0.47.
To convert liters to pints, multiply by 2.13.
To convert cups to liters, multiply by 0.24.
To convert liters to cups, multiply by 4.17.
To convert teaspoons to milliliters, multiply by 5.
To convert milliliters to teaspoons, multiply by 0.20.
To convert tablespoons to milliliters, multiply by 15.
To convert milliliters to tablespoons, multiply by 0.07.
To convert fluid ounces to milliliters, multiply by 30.
To convert milliliters to fluid ounces, multiply by 0.03.

LIQUID MEASURE	MILLILITERS
¼ teaspoon	1.25 ml.
½ teaspoon	2.5 ml.
¾ teaspoon	3.75 ml.
1 teaspoon	5 ml.
1 tablespoon	15 ml.
¼ fluid ounce	7.5 ml.
½ fluid ounce	15 ml.
1 fluid ounce	30 ml.
¼ cup	59 ml.
⅓ cup	78 ml.
½ cup	118 ml.
⅔ cup	157 ml.
¾ cup	177 ml.
1 cup	236 ml. or .24 liter
½ pint	236 ml. or .24 liter
1 pint	473 ml. or .47 liter
1 quart	946 ml. or .95 liter
1 gallon	3785 ml. or 3.8 liters

Menus

Consider the following menus only as a guide. They are intended primarily to illustrate some of the foods in this book (indicated by an asterisk) that make felicitous partners at the same meal, some appropriate wines for different menus, and occasionally, a simplicity of menu that is often desirable and frequently overlooked. Needless to say, you are invited to adapt these menus to your own taste and circumstances.

Broccoli*, melted butter and lemon wedges
Filets de Soles à la Meunière*; Boiled New Potatoes*; green salad
Cold Grand Marnier soufflé
Corton-Charlemagne

Small Puffs Filled with Herbed Cream Cheese*
Filets de Soles Amandine*; Boiled New Potatoes*; whole baby
   string beans
Floating Island*
Chablis

Rolled Fillets of Sole* with Lemon Sauce*; Spinach with Pine
   Nuts*; Boiled New Potatoes*; French rolls
Black-on-Black Chocolate Layer Cake*
Pouilly-Fuissé

Liver pâté with baked toast fingers
Salmon Steaks Braised with Wine and Shrimp*; boiled rice;
   cold sliced tomatoes and cucumbers on a bed of watercress
Strawberry Tart*
Chassagne-Montrachet or Pouilly-Fuissé

Red Snapper Stuffed with Crabmeat*; Sauce Rémoulade*;
    green salad; hot rolls
Fruit sherbet
Riesling

Poached Striped Bass* with Hollandaise Sauce*; green beans;
    Boiled New Potatoes*
Deep-Dish Rhubarb Pie*
Chablis

Cold Poached Striped Bass* with Herb-Flavored Mayonnaise*;
    cold rice salad with peas, garnished with cherry tomatoes;
    hot rolls
Lemon soufflé
California Pinot Chardonnay

Broiled Whole Striped Bass*; Broiled Tomato Halves*; Stir-Fried
    Green Beans*; hot French bread
Paris-Brest*
Pouilly-Fuissé

Chilled lemon soup
Broiled Fillets of Haddock au Gratin*; Broiled Zucchini*
Deep-Dish Blueberry Pie*
California Pinot Chardonnay

Artichokes* with Vinaigrette Sauce*
Pan-Fried Whole Fish*; baked potato
Profiteroles au Chocolat*
Muscadet

Broiled Sea Scallops*; boiled rice; sliced tomatoes; crusty hot
    French bread
Lemon Meringue Pie*
Corton-Charlemagne

Broiled Sea Scallops*; Cherry Tomatoes with Garlic and Herbs*;
  Spinach with Pine Nuts*
Cheese and fruit
California Pinot Chardonnay

Skewered Shrimp with Garlic Butter*; rice pilaf or boiled rice;
  Caesar salad; hot Italian bread
Cheese and fruit
Dry Orvieto or Chablis

Batter-Fried Vegetables* garnished with lemon wedges and parsley
Sautéed Shrimp*; boiled rice; hot Italian bread
Pears and Gorgonzola
Dry Orvieto

Antipasto
Sautéed Shrimp*; boiled rice; hot Italian bread
Chocolate Mousse Pie*
California Chablis

Deep-Fried Oysters*; Stir-Fried Green Beans*; hot French bread
Cheese and fruit
California Chablis or Muscadet

Deep-Fried Shrimp*; Stir-Fried Cucumbers and Scallions*;
  hot Italian bread
Lemon Meringue Pie*
Verdicchio

Deep-Fried Clams*; Stir-Fried Broccoli*; hot French bread
Lemon sherbet with raspberry sauce
Beer

Deep-Fried Mussels*; Stir-Fried Asparagus*; rice; hot French bread
Fresh strawberries in their hulls, powdered sugar
California Pinot Blanc

Artichokes* with Lemon Sauce*
Boiled Lobsters* with melted butter; French-Fried Potatoes*
Deep-Dish Blueberry Pie*
California Chablis

Asparagus* with Vinaigrette Sauce*
Cold Boiled Lobsters*; Dill-Flavored Mayonnaise*;
  hard-cooked eggs; hot rolls
Apple Fritters*
Muscadet

A Brace of Chickens, Stuffed and Roasted*; Cherry Tomatoes with
  Garlic and Herbs*; Stir-Fried Green Beans*
Coconut Layer Cake*
Corton-Charlemagne

Chickens Braised in Beer with Mushrooms*; boiled rice; green salad
Dessert Fritters with Apricot-Peach Sauce*
Beer

Chicken Sauté Paprika*; buttered noodles with caraway seeds;
  green salad
Deep-Dish Rhubarb Pie*
White Côtes-du-Rhône

Southern Fried Chicken*; Mashed Potatoes*; green peas;
  Baking Powder Drop Biscuits*
Southern Pecan Pie*
California Pinot Chardonnay

Southern Fried Chicken* at room temperature; potato salad;
  cherry tomatoes
Deep-Dish Blueberry-Peach Pie*
California Pinot Chardonnay

Poached Chicken with Ivory Sauce; buttered rice; peas;
green salad
Pêches Melba*
Graves*

Butter-Basted Chicken with a Pan Sauce; Broiled Zucchini*;
rice; crusty French bread
Paris-Brest*
White Burgundy*

Herb-Buttered Chicken; Broiled Mushrooms*; Mashed
Potatoes*; Italian bread; green salad
Walnut Torte*
Pouilly-Fuissé*

Chicken with a Deviled Topping; Broiled Tomato Halves*;
baked potato; crusty French bread
Orange Gingerbread Upside-Down Cake*
California Riesling*

Roast Turkey with Corn Bread Stuffing; Buttered Brussels
Sprouts*; Brown-Braised Onions*; French rolls; watercress
and endive salad
Almond Meringue Cake*
California Pinot Chardonnay*

Marinated Duckling with Orange Slices; kasha; spinach salad
Sliced pineapple and cookies
Alsatian Traminer*

Ducklings Braised in Hard Cider; Mashed Potatoes*;
puréed yellow turnips; green salad
Cheese, fruit, and French bread
Hard cider or California Riesling*

Roast Duckling with Liver Stuffing*; Stir-Fried Broccoli*;
   hot French rolls
Fresh fruit and petit fours
California Burgundy

Scaloppine al Limone*; buttered pasta with Parmesan cheese;
   Spinach with Pine Nuts*; Italian bread
Pineapple Cream Sponge Roll*
Soave

Émincé de Veau*; A Crisp Brown Potato Cake*; green salad
Lattice-Topped Cherry Pie*
Fendant

Batter-Fried Vegetables*
Breaded Veal Cutlets Milanese*; buttered pasta
Ripe pears and Gorgonzola cheese
Bardolino

Wiener Schnitzel*; buttered noodles; Broiled Tomato Halves*
Fresh fruit and cheese
Alsatian Riesling

Vitello Tonnato*, garnished with sliced tomatoes, scallions,
   hard-cooked eggs, black olives; crusty Italian bread
Liqueur-flavored or fruit soufflé
Soave or dry Orvieto

Braised Veal with Prunes and Madeira*; Boiled New Potatoes*;
   French rolls; green salad
Orange-Apricot Chiffon Pie*
Valpolicella

Braised Veal with Prunes and Madeira*; boiled rice; peas
French Cherry Custard Cake*
Zinfandel or chilled rosé

Hot boiled Artichokes* with melted butter
Filets Mignons with Mock Hollandaise Sauce*, garnished
    with watercress and cherry tomatoes; Broiled Mush-
    rooms*
Floating Island*
Médoc

Poached Fillet of Beef in the French Manner* with Béarnaise
    Sauce*; Boiled New Potatoes*; green peas
Strawberry Tart*
Médoc

Standing Rib Roast of Beef with Yorkshire Pudding*;
    Horseradish Sauce*; Buttered Brussels Sprouts*
Pineapple Cream Sponge Roll*
Nuits-St.-Georges

Asparagus* with Hollandaise Sauce*
Roast Sirloin Tip with Marchand de Vins Butter*; baked potatoes;
    green salad
Fresh strawberries
Cabernet Sauvignon or red Burgundy

Broiled Porterhouse Steak* with Parsley Butter*; Broiled
    Diced Potatoes*; green salad
Àpple Fritters*
St.-Émilion

Broiled Sirloin Steak* with Marchand de Vins Sauce*;
    Broiled Zucchini*; baked potatoes
Fruit Tart*
Cabernet Sauvignon

Steak au Poivre*; French-Fried Potatoes*; green salad
Strawberry Tart*
Red Bordeaux

Rib Steaks Florentine*; Broiled Cheese-Topped Eggplant*;
    Italian bread; green salad
Fresh pears and Gorgonzola cheese
Chianti Classico

Broccoli* with Hollandaise Sauce*
Pan-Fried Steak*; A Crisp Brown Potato Cake*; French rolls
Deep-Dish Rhubarb Pie*
Nuits-St.-Georges

Broccoli* with Hollandaise Sauce*
Broiled Marinated Flank Steak (London Broil)*; Broiled
    Diced Potatoes*
Fresh fruit or fruit compote
Red Côtes-du-Rhône

Broiled Flank Steak (London Broil)* not marinated; Cherry
    Tomatoes with Garlic and Herbs*; baked potatoes
Fruit Tart*
Red Côtes-du-Rhône

Broiled Ground Beef Steaks*; Broiled Cheese-Topped Eggplant*;
    green salad
Lattice-Topped Cherry Pie*
Beaujolais

Marinated Beef Shashlik*; boiled rice; Cherry Tomatoes
    with Garlic and Herbs*; hot French bread
Black-on-Black Chocolate Layer Cake*
California Cabernet Sauvignon

Braised Short Ribs with Kidney Beans*; boiled rice; green
    salad with avocado slices; hot French bread
Fresh fruit and cookies
California Pinot Noir or Beer

"Boiled" Beef* with Horseradish Sauce*; Boiled New Potatoes*
Fresh fruit
Beer

Oxtails Braised with White Grapes*; Boiled New Potatoes*;
   tossed green salad
French Cherry Custard Cake*
Beaujolais

Asparagus* with Vinaigrette Sauce*
Poached Leg of Lamb with Dill and Caper Sauce*;
   Mashed Potatoes*; mixed green salad
Southern Pecan Pie*
St.-Émilion

Artichokes* with Vinaigrette Sauce*
Boned Leg of Lamb Flamed with Gin*; Broiled Tomato Halves*;
   A Crisp Brown Potato Cake*
Profiteroles au Chocolat*
California Pinot Noir or a good red Bordeaux

Stuffed Hindquarter of Lamb*; fresh garden peas;
   Brown-Braised Onions*; crisp green salad
Strawberry Tart*
A fine red Bordeaux, Médoc or St.-Émilion, or a
   grand cru Burgundy

Broiled Boned Leg of Lamb with Lemon Sauce*;
   boiled rice; buttered green beans
Pineapple Cream Sponge Roll*
California Grenache rosé

Dill-Stuffed Double Loin Lamb Chops*; Broiled Mushrooms*;
   Broiled Tomato Halves*
American Apple Pie*
Red Côtes-du-Rhône

Marinated Shoulder Lamb Chops*; buttered rice; Spinach
   with Pine Nuts*
Chocolate Mousse Pie*
California Pinot Noir

Shoulder of Lamb with Spinach Stuffing*; steamed cauliflower;
   mixed green salad
French Cherry Custard Cake*
Beaujolais or Côtes-du-Rhône

Ground Lamb Steaks with Dill Butter*; Broiled Diced Potatoes*;
   Broiled Cheese-Topped Eggplant*; green salad
Lattice-Topped Cherry Pie*
Santenay

Marinated Lamb Shish Kebabs*; boiled rice; Broiled Cheese-
   Topped Eggplant*
Coconut Layer Cake*
California Pinot Noir

Baked Ham with Apricot Glaze*; Braised Belgian Endives with
   Buttered Walnuts*; baked potatoes; green salad
Profiteroles au Chocolat*
Graves or cider

Chicken Broth with fresh herbs*
Crown Roast of Pork with Apple-Sage Stuffing*; Brown-Braised
   Onion*; Braised Brussels Sprouts and Chestnuts*; Broiled
   Tomato Halves*
Orange-Apricot Chiffon Pie*
Chilled rosé

Pork Chops Braised with Bacon and Potatoes*; crisp green salad
   with orange slices, Vinaigrette Sauce*; hot rolls
Lemon sherbet
Beer

Fried Pork Chops; applesauce; Cabbage Quarters with Sour Cream
  and Nutmeg**
Orange Gingerbread Upside-Down Cake*
Cider

Fried Pork Chops*; Braised Red Cabbage*; Boiled New Potatoes*
Baked apples
Beer

Rolled Pork Shoulder with Sauerkraut; Mashed Potatoes*;
  Broiled Tomato Halves**
Fresh orange sections
Alsatian Riesling

Stuffed Spareribs; Brown-Braised Onions*; Stir-Fried
  Green Beans**
Lemon Meringue Pie*
Beer or New York State Riesling

Beef Tongue*; Spinach with Pine Nuts*; Mashed Potatoes*
Dessert Fritters with Apricot-Peach Sauce*
Beer

Broccoli* with hot clarified butter and lemon wedges
Sautéed Calf's Liver*; French-Fried Potatoes*; mixed green salad
Lemon Meringue Pie*
Beaujolais

Fried Calf's Liver*; baked potatoes; Spinach with Pine Nuts*
Chocolate Mousse Pie*
Chilled rosé

Batter-Fried Artichoke Hearts*
Fried Calf's Liver*; Boiled New Potatoes*; green salad
Cheese and fruit
Valpolicella

Sautéed Chicken Livers*; Broiled Tomato Halves*;
   buttered noodles
Coconut Layer Cake*
Chilled rosé

Gougère*; escarole salad with Vinaigrette Sauce*
Pêches Melba*
California Pinot Noir or red Burgundy

Deep-Fried Savory Turnovers*; green salad
Cheese and fruit
Volnay or a rosé

Ham Croquettes*; Stir-Fried Asparagus*
Fresh fruit
Beaujolais or a chilled rosé

Deep-Dish Chicken Pie*; green salad
Fresh fruit and cheese
California Pinot Chardonnay

New England Clam Pie*; green salad
Fresh fruit and cheese
California Pinot Blanc

Swiss Potato and Sausage Tart*; green salad
Fresh fruit
Alsatian Riesling or Rheingau

Ham and Cheese Tart*; green salad; hot French bread
Fresh berries
Vouvray or Pouilly-Fumé

Crabmeat Tart*; salad with avocado slices and Vinaigrette Sauce*
Fresh fruit
Muscadet

Pineapple Fritters*; grilled ham slices; Whipped Cream Biscuits*
Sandtorte*
Chilled rosé

Index

Aging
  of beef steaks, 145
  of lamb, 161
  of meat, term defined, 145
Almond meringue cake, 351–53
Altitudes, high. *See* High altitudes
Aluminum foil, heavy-duty, 9
American apple pie, 365–67
American white bread, 280–82
Appetizer(s)
  boiled shrimp (hot or cold), 40–42
  broiled mushrooms, 195
  Cheddar cheese rounds, 322
  cheese tartlets, 410–11
  crabmeat tartlets, 411–12
  deep-fried savory turnovers, 110
  gougère, 423–24
  Parmesan cheese fritters, 118–20
  sesame seed crackers, 320–22
  skewered shrimp with garlic butter, 205–207
  small puffs
    filled with curried tuna pâté, 418–20
    filled with herbed cream cheese, 420–21
Apple(s)
  cooking vs. "eating," for pies, 365–66
  fritters, 114–15
  as garnish for ducklings braised in hard cider, 228–30
  pie, American, 365–67
  -sage stuffing, crown roast of pork with, 255–57
Applesauce, date, and pecan ring, 333–35
Appliances, kitchen, 1
  See also Equipment, cooking

Apricot(s)
  glaze, baked ham with, 259–60
  jam, as glaze for strawberry tart, 405–407
  orange-, chiffon pie, 387–89
  -peach sauce, 120–21
  tart, 405–407
Arrowroot, as thickening agent for pie fillings, 357
Artichoke(s)
  boiled, 51–54
  buying, 51
  eating, 54
  hearts
    batter-fried, 116–18
    preparation of, for deep-fat frying, 117
  preparation of, for boiling, 52–53
Asparagus
  buying, 61
  preparation of
    for steaming, 61–62
    for stir-frying, 97
  steamed, 61–62
  stir-fried, 97–98
Au gratin dish, 3

Babka, 295–97
Bacon
  Canadian-style, for roasting, 243
  fat, for frying, 77
  and potatoes, pork chops braised with, 223–25
Baking
  butter in, 327
  dishes, 3
    See also Pans, baking; Soufflé dish
  high-altitude, 453
  pans. *See* Pans

Baking (*cont'd*)
  powder, 275, 443
    in cakes, 326
    drop biscuits, 314
    vs. roasting, 241–42
  sheets, 5
  soda, 275, 443
  substituting sweeteners in, 328
  techniques
    for biscuits, 314, 315, 317
    for breads, basic yeast, 279,
      283, 286, 289
    for breads, batter, 303, 304,
      306
    for breads, quick, 311, 313
    for breads, sweet, 294, 297, 300
    for bread tartlet shells, 403
    for cakes, 329, 331, 333, 337,
      341–42, 346, 349
    for chou paste, 417–18, 424, 426
    for crackers, 321, 323
    for ham, 259–60
    for meringues, 352
    partial, for tart shells, 396
    for pastry lids, 379–80
    for pies, 362–63, 365, 378
    for pies, double-crusted, 367,
      369
    for pies, lattice-topped, 372
    for pies, meringue-topped, 376
    for pie shells, 373–74
    for pizza, 292
    for popovers, 308–309
    for scones, 319
    for shortbread, 319–20
    for sponge roll, 339
    for tartlets, 410, 412
    for tarts, 397, 399, 400, 402,
      403, 405
    for tart shells, 392–93, 395
    for tortes, 344
Balloon whip, 7
Barding fat. *See* Fat
Barley, in basic vegetable soup, 37–
  38
Bass. *See* Striped bass
Baster, bulb, 9
Basting techniques
  for fish, 183
  for poultry, 174
  for vegetables, 192
Batter
  for batter-fried vegetables, 116–
    17

breads. *See* Breads
cake. *See* Cakes
for deep-fried shellfish, 108–109
Beans, kidney, braised short ribs
  with, 211–13
Béarnaise sauce, 432–33
  See also Sauces
Beaters, 7
  See also Mixers; Whisks
Beating techniques
  for egg whites, 328
  for meringues, 67, 352, 376
  See also Whipping
Beef
  "boiled," 19–21
  for boiling, 19–20
  for braising, 210
  brisket, fresh, for "boiled" beef,
    19
  chuck
    boneless, for "boiled" beef, 19
  filets mignons with mock hollan-
    daise sauce, 153–55
  fillet of, poached in the French
    manner, 23–25
  ground, for broiling, 147
    See also Beef steak, ground,
    below
  liver
    fried, 83–85
    sautéed, 124–25
  London broil
    carving techniques for, 157
    cuts for, 155
  marinades for, 156, 159, 202
  marinating, to tenderize, 147–48
  rib roast of, standing
    preparation of, for roasting,
      247
    with Yorkshire pudding, 246–
      49
  roast, serving amounts for, 243
  for roasting, 242
  shashlik, marinated, 201–203
  short ribs
    braised, with kidney beans,
      211–13
    in "boiled" beef, 19
    preparation of, for braising,
      212
  sirloin tip, roast, 245
  skewered, broiled, 201–203
  steak(s)
    aging of, 145

Beef, steak(s) (*cont'd*)
  au poivre, 130–32
  broiled, testing for doneness of, 149–50
  broiled, turning, 144
  broiling charts for, 150–51
  broiling timetable for, 148
  for broiling, 145–47, 155
  flank, broiled marinated, 155–57
  fried, turning, 81
  grading, federal, of, 146
  ground, broiled, 157–58
  marbling of, 145
  pan-fried, 85–87
  preparation of, for broiling, 147–48
  preparation of, for pan-frying, 86
  preparation of, for sautéing, 129, 131
  rib, Florentine, 158–60
  sirloin or porterhouse, broiled, 152–53
  strips, sautéed, in a Chinese sauce, 128–30
  temperature of, for broiling, 143
 stock. *See* Stocks
 tongue
  leftover, in croquettes, 105–107
  peeling, 22–23
  pickled, "boiled," 21–23
  smoked, "boiled," 21–23
  See also Oxtails
Beer, chicken braised in, with mushrooms, 226–28
Belgian endives, braised, with buttered walnuts, 235–36
Benne seeds. *See* Sesame seeds
Beurre manié, term defined, 443
Biscuits
 baking, 314, 315, 317
 baking powder drop, 314
 cutter, 7
 eggs in, 276
 ham and buttermilk, 315–16
 ingredients for, 274–76
 mixing, 314, 315, 317
 rolling and cutting, 316, 317
 whipped cream, 316–17
Blanching
 technique, for salt pork, 310
 term defined, 12

Blender(s)
 electric, 1
 pastry, 6
Blueberry pie, deep-dish, 380–81
Board(s)
 carving and cutting, 3–4
 pastry, 6
Boiling
 vs. steaming, for vegetables, 50
 techniques
  for artichokes, 53
  for broccoli, 55–56
  for cauliflower, 57
  general, 16
  for lobsters, live, 43–44
  for potatoes, 58, 60
  for shrimp, 41, 42
  for water, 14
 term defined, 12
 See also Simmering; Steaming
Boning technique, for leg of lamb, 26
Bouquets garnis, cheesecloth for, 9
Bowls
 chilling, 446
 mixing, 7
Braising
 fish for, 210
 meats for, 210
 "pot roasting" as, 209
 poultry for, 210
 techniques
  for beef short ribs, 212
  for Belgian endives, 235
  for Brussels sprouts and chestnuts, 237
  for cabbage, red, 238–39
  for chicken, 227
  for duckling, 229–30
  for lamb shoulder, stuffed, 220
  for onions, 234–35
  ordinary, 210
  for oxtails, 214–16
  for pork, 222–23, 224–25
  for salmon steaks, 232–33
  for sauerkraut, 222–23
  for veal, 217
  "white," 210–11
 term defined, 209
 vegetables for, 210
Bread(s)
 Babka, 295–97
 basic
  baking, 279, 283, 286, 289, 292

Bread(s), basic (*cont'd*)
  cooling, 283, 286, 289
  glazing, 283, 286
  See also Bread dough (yeast),
    below
  batter
    baking, 303, 304, 306
    mixing, 301–302, 304
    onion dill, 303–304
    rising, 294, 302, 304, 306
    rye, 305–306
    See also Bread dough (yeast),
      below
  brioche, 300–303
  corn, with cracklings, 309–311
  dough (yeast)
    freezing, 278
    gluten in, 274
    kneading, 276–78, 280
    mixing, 281–82, 284, 291
    rising, 274, 278–79
    rising, in high altitudes, 453
    shaping into loaves, 282, 285–
      86, 288
    See also Breads, basic *and* bat-
      ter *above*; Breads, sweet, *be-*
      low
  Gugelhopf, 293–95
  ingredients for, 274–76
  Irish soda, 311–13
  oat, 283–86
  onion-dill batter, 303–304
  popovers, 307–309
  quick, 307–13
    mixing, 308, 311, 312
  rye batter, 305–306
  scones, 317–19
  sweet
    baking, 294, 297, 300
    glazing, 297, 300
    mixing, 294, 296, 299
    Portuguese, 298–300
    shaping into loaves, 299
    unmolding, 294–95, 297
    See also Bread dough (yeast),
      above
  tartlet shells, 412–13
  techniques for making, 276–79
  white, American, 280–83
  whole-wheat, 286–89
  yeast in, 274
  See also Biscuits; Crackers;
    Pizza
Breading: *See* Coating

Brioche, 300–303
Broccoli
  boiled, 54–56
  buying, 54
  preparation of
    for boiling, 55
    for stir frying, 96
  stir-fried, 95–96
Broiler (chicken), term defined,
  445
Broiling
  chart(s)
    for beef steaks, 150–51
    for lamb, 163
  meat and poultry for, 141–43,
    146–47, 161–62
  vs. "pan broiling," 142
  safety, note on, 144–45
  skewer, 8
  techniques
    for beef, skewered, 202–203
    for beef steak, 148–51, 152–
      53, 156, 157–58, 159–60
    for chicken, 174–75, 176
    for duckling, 174–75, 180–81
    for eggplant, 197
    for filets mignons, 154
    for fish, 183–84
    for frozen foods, 162, 183
    general, 142–44
    for haddock fillets, 191
    for lamb, 164, 166, 168, 170,
      171, 203–205
    for mackerel, 190
    for mushrooms, 195–96
    for potatoes, 200
    for scallops, sea, 186
    for shrimp, skewered, 206–
      207
    for skewered foods, 201–207
    for striped bass, whole, 188
    for tomatoes, 193–94
    for tomatoes, cherry, 198
    for zucchini, 194
  term defined, 141–42
  times
    for beef steak, 148
    for lamb, 162, 164
Broth(s)
  canned, 35
    as substitute for stock, 456
  Scotch, 39
  See also Soups; Stocks
Brushes, pastry, 7

Brussels sprouts
buying, 62
and chestnuts, braised, 236–37
preparation of
for braising, 237
for steaming, 62–63
steamed, buttered, 62–63
Bulb baster, 9
Butcher's knots, making, 443–44
Butter(s)
-basted chicken with a pan sauce,
175–77
in cakes, 327
clarifying, 444
compound, term defined, 429–30
dill, 440
ground lamb steaks with, 170–
71
for frying and sautéing, 76
garlic, 441
for mushrooms, broiled, 195–
96
skewered shrimp with, 205–207
grading, federal, of, 444
herb
for chicken, 177
combination, 440–41
marchand de vins, 441–42
for sirloin tip, roast, 245–46
parsley, 439–40
for beef steaks, broiled ground,
157–58
for steak, broiled sirloin or porterhouse, 152–53
in pastry, 356
salt vs. sweet, 444
in baking, 327
substitutes for
in baking, 276, 327
in pastry, 356
tomato, broiled mackerel with,
188–90
Butterfish, suitability of, for broiling, 182
Buttermilk, 444–45
in cakes, 327
ham and, biscuits, 315–16

Cabbage
buying, 63
quarters with sour cream and
nutmeg, 63–64
red
braised, 238–39

marinade for, 238
steamed, 63–64
Cake(s)
almond meringue, 351–53
baking, 319–20, 331, 333, 337,
339, 341–42, 346
batters
mixing, 319, 328–29, 330–31,
332–33, 335, 337, 338–39,
341, 343–44, 346, 349
overbeating, dangers of, 328–
29
cherry custard, French, 335–37
chocolate layer, black-on-black,
345–47
cooling, 320, 329, 339, 342, 344,
349
flour, 326, 451
fruit (applesauce, date, and pecan
ring), 333–35
ingredients for, 326–28
molds, 5
See also Pans, cake
orange gingerbread upside down,
340–42
pans. *See* Pans
pound, sour cream, 331–33
racks, 7
sandtorte, 329–31
shortbread, 319–20
sponge roll, pineapple cream,
337–39
storing, 320, 329
tester, 7
torte, walnut, 342–44
unmolding, 320, 331, 333, 335,
339, 342
Calf's liver
fried, 83–85
sautéed, 124–25
Canadian-style bacon. *See* Bacon
Candy thermometer, 5
Caper, dill and, sauce, poached leg
of lamb with, 25–28
Carp, suitability of, for braising,
210
Carving
equipment for, 4
techniques
for beef, standing rib roast of,
248–49
for chicken, roast, 262
for duckling, roast, 268
for ham, baked, 260

Carving, techniques (*cont'd*)
  for lamb, hindquarter of, 254
  for London broil, 157
  for pork, crown roast of, 257
  for spareribs, stuffed, 259
  for turkey, roast, 265–66
Casseroles (cooking equipment), 2
Cauliflower
  boiled, 56–58
  buying, 56–57
  remolded head of, 56–58
Cheddar cheese rounds, 322–23
Cheese(s)
  Cheddar, rounds, 322–23
  cream, herbed, small puffs filled
    with, 420–21
  in gougère, 423–24
  graters, 4
  ham and, tart, 396–97
  Parmesan, fritters, 118–20
  tartlets, 410–11
  -topped eggplant, broiled, 196–97
  two, savory tart with, 402–403
Cheesecloth, 9
Cherry
  custard cake, French, 335–37
  tomatoes. *See* Tomatoes
Chestnuts
  Brussels sprouts and, braised,
    236–37
  dried, preparation of, for brais-
    ing, 236–37
Chicken(s)
  basting, 174
  braised in beer with mushrooms,
    226–28
  broiled
    testing for doneness of, 175
    timetable for, 174–75
    turning, 144
  butter-basted, with a pan sauce,
    175–77
  classification of, 445
  with a deviled topping, 178–79
  fried
    southern, 89–90
    turning, 81
  frozen
    broiling, 174
    thawing, 445
  grading, federal, of, 445
  herb-buttered, 177
  leftover, in croquettes, 105–107
  livers, sautéed, 136–37

pie, deep-dish, 382–84
poached, with ivory sauce, 29–31
preparation of
  for braising, 226
  for broiling, 173–74, 176
  for frying, 90
  for poaching, 29–30
  for sautéing, 126–27
  for stock, 36
quartering, 446
"ready-to-cook," 445
rice, and vegetable soup, 39
roast
  serving amounts for, 243
  stuffed, 260–61
sauté paprika, 126–28
selection of, for broiling, 172–73
stock. *See* Stocks
suitability of, for braising, 210
trussing, 445–46
types of, for roasting, 243
Chilling techniques
  for bowls, 446
  for pies, 387, 388
  for pastry
    tart, 390, 394
    tartlet, 408–409
  for tarts, fruit, 407
Chocolate
  cream filling, for almond me-
    ringue cake, 351, 353
  layer cake, black-on-black, 345–47
  mousse pie, 385–87
  in profiteroles au chocolat, 421–22
Chopping
  equipment for, 3
  technique, for parsley, 454
Chou paste
  baking, 424, 426
  in gougère, 423–24
  mixing, 415–16, 423
  in Paris-Brest, 425–27
  principle of, explained, 414
  shaping, 424, 426
  speedy preparation, importance
    of, 414
  storing, 416
  See also Chou puffs
Chou puffs
  baking, 417–18
  filling, 419
  fillings for, 418–19, 420
  glazing, 417
  in profiteroles au chocolat, 421–22

Chou puffs (*cont'd*)
  shaping, 417
  See also Chou paste
Chunks, fish, term defined, 451
Cider, hard, ducklings braised in, 228–30
Citrus peeler, 4
Clam(s)
  deep-fried, 108–110
  pâté, as filling for chou puffs, 418–20
  pie, New England, 368–70
Clarification technique, for butter, 444
Cleaning techniques
  for duckling, 173
  for fish, 183–84
Cloth, pastry, 6
Coating techniques
  for croquettes, 107
  for foods for frying, 78–79
  for pie pans, lined, 361, 365
Coconut
  fresh, preparing, 446
  layer cake, 347–50
Cod steaks, preparation of, for broiling, 183
Colander, 8
Compote, lemon, fresh, for roast duckling with liver stuffing, 266, 268
Compound butters. *See* Butters
Confectioners' sugar. *See* Sugar
Consommés, canned
  vs. canned broths, 35
  shortcomings of, as substitute for stock, 456
Cookie sheets, 5
  preparation of, for baking chou paste, 417, 423, 425–26
Cooking equipment and utensils, 1–9
Cooling techniques
  for breads
    quick, 313
    yeast, 283, 286, 289, 300, 303, 304, 306
  for cakes, 329, 342, 349
  for shortbread, 320
  for sponge roll, 339
  for tortes, 344
Corkscrew, 9
Corn
  bread

with cracklings, 309–311
  stuffing, roast turkey with, 262–66
  meal, 452
  syrup, 456
    in cakes, 327–28
Cornstarch, as thickening agent for pie fillings, 357
Court bouillon, term defined, 40, 446
Crabmeat
  red snapper stuffed with, 269–71
  tart, 398–99
  tartlets, 411–12
Crackers
  baking, 321, 323
  Cheddar cheese rounds, 322–23
  mixing, 321, 322
  rolling and cutting, 321
  sesame seed, 320–22
  storing, 323
  unbaked, freezing, 322
Cracklings
  corn bread with, 309–311
  preparation of, 310
Cream, 446
  sponge roll, pineapple, 337–40
  whipped
    biscuits, 316–17
    as border, 386, 387
    as filling, 421, 422, 426
    as topping, 341–42, 343–44, 378, 387, 389
  whipping, 342, 344, 422, 426–27
Cream cheese, herbed, small puffs filled with, 420–21
Croquettes
  ham, 105–107
  shaping, 107
Crown roasts
  paper frills for, 9
  See also Pork
Cucumbers
  preparation of, for stir frying, 98–99
  and scallions, stir-fried, 98–99
Currant jelly, as glaze for fruit tart, 405
Custard cake, French cherry, 335–37
Cutters, 6–7
Cutting
  equipment for, 3–4
  techniques
    for biscuits, 316, 317

Cutting, techniques (*cont'd*)
  for crackers, 321
  for pastry lids, 379, 380, 384
  for pastry, tartlet, 409
  for pastry, turnover, 113
  quartering, for poultry, 446, 447
  for scones, 318

Date, applesauce, and pecan ring, 333–35
Decorating techniques, for double-crusted pies, 362
Deep-dish pies. *See* Pies
Deep-fat frying
  equipment for, 1, 3, 100–102
  fats for, 74–77
    amount needed, 101
    heating, 101
    reusing, 101
    storing, 101
  heat control in, 102
  safety in, note on, 103
  seasoning foods for, 77
  techniques
    for batter-fried vegetables, 118
    for croquettes, 105, 107
    for fritters, 115, 119–20, 121
    general, 100–103
    for parsley, 110
    for potatoes, 104–105
    for shellfish, 109–110
    for turnovers, 113
  term defined, 74
  thermometer, 5
Deep fryer(s), 3, 100
  electric, 1
  See also Deep-fat frying, equipment for
Deglazing techniques
  general, 447
  for stocks, 34–35
Degreasing techniques, 447
Dessert(s)
  Floating Island, 66–69
  fritters. *See* Fritters
  Paris-Brest 425–27
  pêches Melba, 69–72
  profiteroles au chocolat, 421–22
  See also Cakes; Pies; Tarts
Dicalcium phosphate, in meringues, 375
Dill
  butter, 440

ground lamb steaks with, 170–71
and caper sauce, poached leg of lamb with, 25–28
onion-, batter bread, 303–304
-stuffed double loin lamb chops, 165–66
Discoloration of vegetables, preventing, 50
Doneness, testing techniques
  for beef steak, broiled, 149
  for fish, 184
  for lamb, broiled, 164
  for poultry, 175, 455
Double boiler, 2
Dough
  bread. *See* Bread
  scraper, baker's, 6
Draining techniques, for fried foods, 81, 102
Dressing methods for fish, 182–83
Drying
  of food, importance of, before broiling, 143–44
  technique, for meringues, 352
Dry ingredients. *See* Ingredients
Duckling
  availability of, 447
  braised in hard cider, 228–30
  broiled
    testing for doneness of, 175
    timetable for, 174–75
  cleaning, 173
  fat, rendering, 229
  frozen, broiling, 143
  livers, sautéing, 229
  marinades for, 179–80
  marinated, with orange sauce, 178–81
  preparation of
    for braising, 228–29
    for broiling, 173–74
    for marinating, 180
    for roasting, 267
  roast
    with liver stuffing, 266–68
    serving amounts for, 243, 447
  selection of, for broiling, 172–73
  suitability of,
    for braising, 210
    for roasting, 243

Egg(s)
  in cakes, 326–27
  grading, federal, of, 447–48

Egg(s) (*cont'd*)
  hard-cooking, 448
  in pastry, 357
  separating, 448
  whipping, 448–49
  in yeast breads and biscuits, 275–76
Eggplant
  batter-fried, 116–18
  broiled cheese-topped, 196–97
  preparation of
    for broiling, 196–97
    for deep-fat frying, 117
  suitability of, for broiling, 192
Émincé de veau, 132–33
Endives, Belgian. *See* Belgian endives
Equipment, cooking, 1–9
  electric, 1, 7

Fat(s)
  barding, term defined, 443
  in pastry, 356–57
  See also Butter; Shortening
Filets mignons. *See* Beef
Filets de sole amandine, 140
Filets de sole à la meunière, 139–40
Fillets. *See* Beef; Fish
Filling(s)
  for bread tartlet shells, 412
  cake
    chocolate cream, 351–53
    lemon, 348–50
  chou puff
    cream cheese, herbed, 420
    seafood, 418–19
  for deep-fried pastry turnovers, 111, 112
  pie
    apple, 366–67
    blueberry, 380–81
    cherry, 370–71
    chicken, 382–83
    chocolate mousse, 386–87
    clam, 368–69
    lemon, 375–76
    orange-apricot, 387–88
    pecan, 377
    rhubarb, 381–82
  tart
    cheese, 402, 403
    crabmeat, 398
    custard, 406–407
    ham and cheese, 396–97
    potato and sausage, 399, 400
    spinach, 401
    tomato and cheese, 404
  tartlet
    cheese, 410
    crabmeat, 411
Fish
  available forms of, 450
  broiled
    testing of doneness for, 184
    turning, 144, 187
  broiling, 143
  chunks, term defined, 450
  cleaning, 183
  cooking, by weight, 450–51
  drawn, term defined, 450
  dressed, term defined, 450
  dressing methods for, 182–83
  fillets
    preparation of, for broiling, 183
    term defined, 450
  fried, turning, 91
  frozen, broiling, 183–84
  overcooking of, 449–50
  poacher, 3, 23
  serving amounts of, 450
  split, preparation of, for broiling, 182–83
  steaks
    poached, 48
    preparation of, for broiling, 182, 183
    term defined, 450
  stock, for braising salmon steaks, 231–32
  whole
    broiled, turning, 187
    pan-fried, 91–92
    poaching time of, estimating, 45–46
    preparation of, for broiling, 182
    preparation of, for poaching, 46
    suitability of, for baking, 243
    suitability of, for braising, 210
    suitability of, for broiling, 181–82
  See also Names of individual fish; Shellfish
Flame-tamer, use of, in poaching or simmering, 16
Flaming technique, for ducklings, 229

Floating Island, 66–69
Flour(s)
  all-purpose, 451
  in bread, measuring for, 276
  cake, 451
  in cakes, 326
  gluten in, 275
  in pastry, 356
  rye, 452
  sifted vs. unsifted, 275
  sifter, 6
  as thickening agent for pie fill-
    ings, 357
  types of, 274–75, 451
  whole-wheat, 451–52
Fluting technique, for pie crust,
  362
Folding technique, for beaten egg
  whites, 449
Food(s)
  to be broiled, importance of dry-
    ing, 143–44
  fried, keeping warm, 81
  frozen, broiling techniques for,
    143
  graters, 4
  mill, 4
  processor, 1
Fork, two-pronged, 8
Freezing techniques
  for bread tartlet shells, 413
  for chou puffs, 418
  for crackers, unbaked, 322
  for stocks, 35
  for tart and tartlet shells, 393
  See also Storing
French frying. See Deep-fat frying
"Frenching," term defined, 167
Fritters
  apple, 114–15
  dessert, with apricot-peach sauce,
    120–21
  Parmesan cheese, 118–20
  pineapple, 115
Frosting(s)
  for black-on-black chocolate layer
    cake, 345, 347
  for coconut layer cake, 348, 350
  ingredients for, 327
Frozen foods. See Foods, frozen
Fruit(s)
  cake (applesauce, date, and pecan
    ring), 333–35

juices in pastry, shortcomings of,
  357
frozen
  for pie fillings, 358
  for tarts, 405
pies, deep-dish, fully baked pastry lid for, 378–80
preparation of, for fruit cake,
  334
See also Names of individual
  fruits
Fryer, deep-fat. See Deep fryer
Frying
  basket, for deep-fat frying, 101–
    102
  coating foods for, 78–79
  fats for, 74–77
  heat control in, 81
  kettle. See Deep fryer
  pans. See Pans
  preheating pans for, dangers of,
    81
  shallow, term defined, 74
  techniques
    for calf's liver, 85
    for chicken, 90
    general, 80–81
    for pork chops, 88–89
    for potatoes, 93–94
    for veal scallops, 82–83
  See also Pan frying; Deep-fat
    frying; Sautéing; Stir fry-
    ing
Funnels, 9

Garlic
  butter, 441
    See also Butters
  and herbs, cherry tomatoes with,
    197–98
  press, 8
Garnish(es)
  apple, for ducklings braised in
    hard cider, 228–30
  parsley, deep-fried, as, 110
Giblet sauce. See Sauces
Gin, boned leg of lamb flamed with,
  249–51
Gingerbread upside-down cake,
  orange, 340–42
Glass cookware, vs. metal, 2, 6
Glaze(s)
  apricot, baked ham with, 259–
    60

Glaze(s) (*cont'd*)
term defined, 452
See also Glazing techniques
Glazing techniques
for Babka, 297
for bread, 283, 286, 300
for chou puffs, 417
for gougére, 423–24
for ham, 260
for lamb, braised, 220–21
for Paris-Brest, 426
for pastry lids, 379
for pies
double-crusted, 362, 365, 367, 369, 384
lattice-topped, 371
for scones, 318
for tarts, fruit, 407
Gluten
development of, in dough, 274
in flour, 275
Gougère, 423–24
Grading, federal
of eggs, 447–48
of meat, 449
beef steak, 146
lamb, 161
of poultry, 445, 447, 449
Graham cracker pie crust. *See* Pies
Grapes, white, oxtails braised with, 213–16
Grater(s)
cheese, 4
food, 4
nutmeg, 8
Gratin, term defined, 452
Grating technique, for coconuts, 446
Green beans
preparation of, for stir frying, 98
stir-fried, 98
Grid, proper use of, for broiling, 142–43
Ground beef. *See* Beef steak, ground
Ground lamb. *See* Lamb steak, ground
Gugelhopf, 293–95
pan for, 5, 293

Haddock, fillets of, broiled, au gratin, 190–91
Half-and-half (cream), 446

Halibut
steaks, suitability of, for broiling, 183
suitability of, for braising, 210
Ham
baked, with apricot glaze, 259–60
and buttermilk biscuits, 315–16
and cheese tart, 396–97
croquettes, 105–107
preparation of, for baking, 259
suitability of, for roasting, 242–43
types of, 452
Hard cider. *See* Cider, hard
Hard-cooking technique, for eggs, 448
Heat control
for boiling, 15
in frying, 81, 102
for poaching, 15–16
for simmering, 15–16
Herb(s)
butter
combination, 440–41
See also Butters
-crumb stuffing, double rib lamb chops with, 166–67
-flavored mayonnaise, 436
See also Mayonnaise
garlic and, cherry tomatoes with, 197–98
High altitudes
baking at, 453
boiling temperature at, 14
Hollandaise sauce, 430–32
See also Sauces
Horseradish sauce, 437–38

Ice cream on pie, shortcomings of, 367
Icing
spatula, 8
See also Frosting
Ingredients, dry, sifting, 276, 328
Inspection, federal, of meat and poultry, 449
See also Grading, federal
Irish soda bread, 311–13
Italian minestrone, 39

Jelly
currant, as glaze for fruit tarts, 405
-roll pan. *See* Pans.

Kidney beans. *See* Beans
Kneading techniques, for bread(s)
  dough, basic, 276–77
    by hand, 276–77, 279–80
    by machine, 277–78, 280
  quick, 312
  sweet, 296, 299
Knife sharpener, 4
Knives, 3–4

Lamb
  aging of, 161
  for braising, 210
  broiled
    serving amounts of, 164
    testing for doneness of, 164
  broiling
    chart for, 163
    timetable for, 162, 164
  choosing, 161
  chops
    double loin, dill-stuffed, 165–66
    double rib, with herb-crumb
      topping, 166–67
    shoulder, for broiling, 167
    shoulder, marinated, 167–68
    stuffing, 166
  cuts for broiling, 161–62
    temperature of, 143
  frozen, broiling, 143
    timetable for, 162
  grading of
    by age, 453
    federal, 161
  ground. *See* Lamb steak, ground,
    below
  hindquarter of, stuffed, 251–54
  leftover, in croquettes, 105–107
  leg of
    boned, broiled, with lemon
      sauce, 168–70
    boned, flamed with gin, 249–51
    boning, 26
    poached, with dill and caper
      sauce, 25–28
    preparation of, for broiling,
      169
    preparation of, for poaching,
      26–27
    preparation of, for stuffing and
      roasting, 249–50
  marinades for, 167, 204
  marbling in, 161
  ribs (rack), for broiling, 161

  for roasting, 242
  in Scotch broth, 39
  shish kebabs, marinated, 203–
    205
  shoulder
    for broiling, 161–62
    preparation of, for stuffing,
      219
    with spinach stuffing, 218–21
    See also Lamb chops, *above*
  skewered, broiled, 203–205
  steaks, with dill butter, 170–71
    ground, for broiling, 162
  stock. *See* Stocks
Lard
  for frying, 76–77, 101
  in pastry, 356–57
  storing, 77
Larding
  needle, 8
  term defined, 453
Lattice topping for pie, 371
  See also Pies, lattice-topped
Lemon
  compote, fresh, for roast duck-
    ling with liver stuffing, 266,
    268
  filling, for coconut layer cake,
    348, 349–50
  meringue pie, 374–77
  sauce, 434–35
    See also Sauces
Liver. See Beef; Calf's Liver;
    Chicken; Duckling
Lobster(s)
  boiled, 42–45
  live
    boiling, 43–44
    buying, 42–43, 453
    storing, 42–43
  pâté, as filling for chou puffs,
    418–20
  serving amounts from, 453
  unsuitability of, for broiling, 182
London broil. *See* Beef

Mackerel
  preparation of, for broiling, 189
  suitability of, for broiling, 182
Madeira, braised veal with prunes
    and, 216–18
Marbling
  in lamb, 161
  of meat, term defined, 145

Marchand de vins butter, 441–42
  See also Butters
Marchand de vins sauce, 438–39
  See also Sauces
Margarine vs. butter, 453–54
  in baking, 327
  for frying, 77
  in pastry, 356
Marinade(s)
  for beef, 156, 159, 201–203
  for duckling, 179–180
  for lamb, 167, 203–205
  for red cabbage, 238
  See also Marinating
Marinating
  of lamb, 162, 249
  purpose of, 147–48
  techniques
    for potatoes, 60–61
    for red cabbage, 238–39
Mayonnaise, 436
  herb-flavored, 436
  for seafood, 40–47
Measuring utensils, 4–5
Meat(s)
  boiled, 18
  for braising, 210
  broiling, 142–43
  frozen, broiling, 143
  poached, 18
  roasted
    "resting," importance of, 245
    serving amounts for, 243
  simmered, 18
    turning, 16
  thermometer, 4–5
  See also Names of individual
    meats
Menus, 463–75
Meringue(s)
  baking and drying, 352
  beating, 67, 352, 376
  cake, almond, 351–53
  pie, lemon, 374–77
  poaching, 67–68
  "weeping" of, controlling, 374–75
Metal cookware, vs. glass, 2, 6
Metric equivalents of weights and
    measures, 459–61
Milk
  in bread, 276
  in cakes, 327
Minestrone, Italian, 39
Mixer, electric, 1

Mixing bowls, 7
Mixing techniques
  for batter(s)
    cake, 328–29, 330–31, 332–33,
      335, 337, 341, 346, 349
    frying, 109, 117
    sponge roll, 338–39
    torte, 343–44
  for biscuits, 314, 315, 317
  for bread(s)
    batter, 294, 301–302, 304, 305
    dough, 281–82, 284, 287, 291
    quick, 312–13, 311
  for chou paste, 415–16, 423
  for crackers, 321, 322–23
  for croquettes, 106–107
  for pastry
    pie, 359–60, 372–73, 379
    tart, 390, 394
    tartlet, 408–409
  for popovers, 308
  for scones, 318
  for shortbread, 319
Molasses, 456
  in bread, 276
  in cakes, 327–28
Molds, 5
Mousse, chocolate, pie, 385–87
Muffin pans. *See* Pans
Mushrooms
  broiled, 185–96
  chicken braised in beer with,
    226–28
  sautéed, 336–37
  suitability of
    for broiling, 192
    for skewering, 201
Mussels, deep-fried, 108–110

Needle(s)
  larding, 8
  sturdy, and kitchen thread, 9
New England clam pie, 368–70
Nutmeg
  grater, 8
  sour cream and, cabbage quarters
    with, 63–64

Oat bread, 283–86
Oils. *See* Olive oil; Vegetable oils
Olive oil
  for frying and sautéing, 76
  storing, 76

Onion(s)
  brown-braised, 233–35
  -dill batter bread, 303–304
  peeling, 454
  preparation of, for braising, 234
Orange
  -apricot chiffon pie, 387–89
  gingerbread upside-down cake,
    340–42
  sauce, marinated duckling with,
    179–81
Oven thermometer, 4
Oxtails
  braised, with white grapes, 213–
    16
  buying, 213
Oysters, deep-fried, 108–110

"Pan broiling" vs. broiling, 142
Pan frying
  seasoning foods for, 77
  techniques
    for beef steak, 86–87
    for fish, whole, 92
  term defined, 74
  See also Frying; Sautéing
Pan(s)
  baking, 3, 5–7
    correct size of, for bread, 279
    metal vs. glass, 6
  cake, 5, 329
    filling, 329
    preparation of, 330, 332, 334,
      336, 341, 343, 346, 348–49
  frying, 2
    using, 80–81
    See also Pan frying
  Gugelhopf, 5, 293
  jelly-roll, 5
  muffin, 5
    lining, for tartlets, 409
  pie, 5–6
    lining, 361, 365, 373–75
  pizza, 5
  popover, 5
  preparation of, for sponge roll,
    328
  sauté, 2, 122–23
  roasting, 2–3
  tart, 6
    lining, 391–92, 395
  See also Molds
Paper frills, 9
  making, 454

Paprika chicken sauté, 126–28
Parboiling, term defined, 12
Parchment paper, 9
Parmesan cheese fritters, 118–20
Parsley
  butter, 439–50
    See also Butters
  chopping, 454
  deep-fried, for garnish, 110
  flavor of, 454
Pasta, in Italian minestrone, 39
Paste. See Pastry
Pastry
  bag(s)
    and tips, 7
    using, 454
  blender, 6
  board, 6
  brushes, 7
  cutters, 6–7
  for deep-fried savory turnovers,
    111–13
  dough, term defined, 355–56
  lids, fully baked, 378–80
    baking, 379–80
    glazing, 379, 380
    use of, for deep-dish fruit pies,
      380–82
  liquids in, 357
  mixes, shortcomings of, 357
  pie
    filling, 361
    ingredients for, 356–58
    mixing, 359–60, 364, 372–73,
      379
  rolling, 360–61, 364
  scalloping, 373
  short, term defined, 455
  tart
    chilling, 394
    mixing, 389–90, 394
    rolling, 390–91, 394–95
    See also Tart shells
  tartlet
    chilling, 409
    mixing, 408–409
  wheel, 6–7
Pâte à choux. See Chou paste
Pâté, seafood, as filling for chou
  puffs, 418–20
Peaches
  frozen, in deep-dish blueberry
    pie, 380–81
  poached, in pêches Melba, 69–72

Peaches (*cont'd*)
  preparation of, for poaching, 70
  sauce, apricot-, 120–21
  tart, 405–407
Pecan(s)
  applesauce, and date ring, 333–35
  pie, Southern, 377–78
Pêches Melba, 69–72
Peelers, 4
Peeling technique, for onions, 454
Pepper mills, 8
Pie(s)
  American vs. English, 358–59
  apple, American, 365–67
  baking, general, 362–63
  chiffon, orange-apricot, 387–89
  chilling, 387, 388
  chocolate mousse, 385–87
  crust, graham cracker, 385
    uses for, 385–87
  deep-dish
    baking, 384
    blueberry, 380–81
    chicken, 382–84
    fruit, fully baked pastry lid
      for, 378–80
    pan for, 6
    rhubarb, 381–82
  double-crusted
    baking, 362–63, 365, 367
    decorating, 362
    glazing, 362, 365, 367, 369, 384
    model, 363–65
    sealing, 361–62, 365, 369, 384
    steam openings in, 362
  fillings
    packaged and canned, short-
      comings of, 357–58
    thickening agents for, 357
  fruit-filled, baking, 363
  ice cream on, shortcomings of,
    367
  lattice-topped
    baking, 372
    glazing, 371
    sealing, 371–72
  lemon meringue, 374–77
  meringue-topped, baking, 363,
    376
  pans. *See* Pans
  pastry. *See* Pastry
  pecan, Southern, 377–78
  shell, fully baked scalloped, 372–
    74

  uses for, 385–89
  single-crust, baking, 378
  techniques for making, 359–60
  See also Pizza; Tarts; Tartlets
Plastic wrap, 9
Pineapple
  cream sponge roll, 337–40
  fritters, 115
Pine nuts, spinach with, 64–65
Pizza, 289–92
  cutter, 7
  pan, 5
  sauce for, 289, 290
Poaching
  equipment for, 16
  vs. simmering, 13
  techniques
    for beef, fillet of, 24
    for chicken, 30
    for fish, 46–47, 48
    for lamb, leg of, 27–28
    for meringues, 67–68
    for peaches, 70–71
    for veal, 32–33
  term defined, 12–13
Popover(s), 307–309
  pans, 5
Pork
  for braising, 210
  chops
    braised with bacon and pota-
      toes, 223–25
    fried, 87–89
    fried, turning, 81
  crown roast of, with apple-sage
    stuffing, 255–57
  and dangers of trichinosis, 255
  fat, rendering, 219, 222
  leftover, in croquettes, 105–107
  roast, serving amounts for, 243
  roasting
    cuts for, 242
    temperatures for, 255
  shoulder, rolled
    preparation of, for braising,
      222–23
    with sauerkraut, 221–23
  See also Ham; Spareribs
Portuguese sweet bread, 298–300
Potato(es)
  cake, crisp brown, 92–94
  French-fried, 103–105
  mashed, 59–61
  new, boiled, 58–59

Potato(es) (cont'd)
  pork chops braised with bacon
    and, 223–25
  preparation of
    for broiling, 199
    for French-frying, 104
    for frying, 93
  and sausage tart, Swiss, 399–
    400
  starch content of, 455
  suitability of, for broiling, 192
"Pot roasting," as braising, 209
Pots and pans, 2–3
Poultry
  boiled, 18
  for braising, 210
  broiling, 142–43, 174–75
  drumsticks, paper frills for, 9
  frozen, characteristics of, 172
  grading, federal of, 455
  poached, 18
  preparation of, for broiling, 173–
    74
  roast, importance of "resting,"
    245
  shears, 8
  simmered, 18
  storing, 454
  temperature of, for broiling, 143
  trussing, 445–46
  See also Names of individual
    poultry
Powdered sugar. See Sugar, confectioners'
Preheating pans before frying, dangers of, 81
Pressure cooking vs. steaming, 13
Profiteroles au chocolat, 421–22
Prunes and Madeira, braised veal
  with, 216–18
Punching-down technique, for bread
  dough, 279
Pudding, Yorkshire, standing rib
  roast of beef with, 246–69

Quick breads. See Breads

Racks, cake, 7
Raspberry sauce, in pêches Melba,
  70, 71
Red cabbage. See Cabbage
Red snapper stuffed with crabmeat,
  269–71

Reducing techniques
  general, 455
  for sauté sauces, 122–24
  for stocks, 35
    fish, 233
Reheating techniques
  for cauliflower, remolded head of,
    58
  for lemon sauce, 435
  for sautés, 124
Rémoulade sauce, 437
  See also Sauces
Rendering techniques, for fat
  duckling, 229
  pork, 219, 222
"Resting"
  importance of
    for meats, 18
    for poultry, roast, 245
  technique, for roasts, 245
Rhubarb pie, deep-dish, 381–82
Rib steaks. See Beef steaks
Rice, chicken, and vegetable soup,
  39
Ricer, 4
Ring molds, 5
Rising techniques
  for bread dough
    basic, 278–79, 282–83, 285, 286,
      288, 289
    batter, 302, 304, 306
    sweet, 294, 296, 297, 299, 300
  for pizza, 291
Roasters (chicken), term defined,
  445
Roasting
  vs. baking, 241–42
  meats for, 242–43
  pans, 2–3
  poultry for, 243
  techniques
    for beef, 245–46, 247
    for chicken, 261–62
    for duckling, stuffed, 267
    general, 244–45
    for lamb, 253–54
    for pork, crown roast of, 257
    for spareribs, stuffed, 258
    for turkey, stuffed, 264
  term defined, 241–42
  timetable for, 244–45
Roasts, string for tying, 9
Rolling-out techniques
  for cracker dough, 321

Rolling-out techniques (*cont'd*)
  for pastry
    pie, 360–61, 364, 373, 379
    tart, 390–91, 394–95
    tartlet, 409
    turnover, 112–13
  for scones, 318
  See also Cutting; Shaping
Rolling pin, 6
  sleeve for, 6
Rolling-up technique, for sponge
    roll, 339–40
Roux, term defined, 455
Ruler, for measuring pastry, 9
Rye
  batter bread, 305–306
  flour, 452

Safety notes
  for broiling, 144–45
  for deep-fat frying, 103
Sage-apple stuffing, crown roast of
    pork with, 255–57
Salads, vinaigrette sauce for, 439
Salmon
  pâté, as filling for chou puffs,
    418–20
  steaks
    braised with wine and shrimp,
      230–33
    preparation of, for braising,
      232
    preparation of, for broiling, 183
  suitability of
    for braising, 210
    for broiling, 182
Salt, in yeast doughs, 276
Sandtorte, 329–31
Sauce(s)
  apricot-peach, dessert fritters
    with, 120–21
  bâtarde. *See* Sauce, hollandaise,
    mock, *below*
  béarnaise, 432–33
    for asparagus, steamed, 61–62
    for artichokes, boiled (hot),
      51–54
    for beef, fillet of, poached in
      the French manner, 25–28
    for broccoli, boiled, 54–56
    for lamb, leg of, poached, 25–28
    for shrimp, boiled (hot), 40–
      42
    for sole, fillets of, rolled, 48–49

Chinese, sautéed steak strips in a,
    128–30
dill and caper, poached leg of
    lamb with, 25–28
function of, explained, 429–30
giblet, for roast turkey with corn
    bread stuffing, 262–66
hollandaise, 430–32
  for artichokes, boiled (hot),
    51–54
  for asparagus, steamed, 61–62
  for broccoli, boiled, 54–56
  for shrimp, boiled (hot), 40–42
  for sole, fillets of, rolled, 48–49
  mock, 433–44
  mock, for beef steaks, ground,
    broiled, 157–58
  mock, filets mignons with, 153–
    55
horseradish, 437–38
hot cocoa, for profiteroles au
    chocolat, 421–22
ivory, poached chicken with, 29–
    31
lemon, 434–35
  for asparagus, steamed, 61–62
  for broccoli, boiled, 54–56
  for lamb chops, double loin,
    broiled, 156–66
  for lamb, leg of, broiled boned,
    with, 168–70
  for mackerel, broiled, 188–90
  for sole, fillets of, rolled, 48–49
marchand de vins, 438–39
  for beef steaks, 152–53, 157–58
pan, butter-basted chicken with
    a, 175–77
for pizza, 289, 290
raspberry, in pêches Melba, 70, 71
rémoulade, 437
  for red snapper stuffed with
    crabmeat, 269–71
  for sautés, 123
  reducing, 123–24
tuna
  for shrimp, boiled (hot or
    cold), 41
  for vitello tonnato, 31–33
vinaigrette, 439
  for artichokes, boiled (cold),
    51–54
  for cauliflower, remolded head
    of (cold), 56–58
See also Mayonnaise; Butters

Saucepans, 2
Sauerkraut
    preparation of, for braising, 222
    rolled pork shoulder with, 221–
    23
Sausage, potato and, tart, Swiss,
    399–400
Sauté(s)
    chicken, paprika, 126–28
    glaze and sauce for, 123–24
    reheating, 124
    See also Sautéing
Sautéing
    equipment for, 122–23
    fats for, 74–77
    glaze in, 123
    seasoning foods for, 77
    techniques
        for beef steak, 129–30, 131–32
        for chicken, 127
        for chicken livers, 136–37
        for duckling livers, 229
        general, 122–24
        for liver, 125
        for mushrooms, 227
        for shrimp, 138
        for sole, fillets of, 140
        for veal, 133, 135
    term defined, 74
    See also Frying; Pan frying;
        Sautés
Scallions
    cucumbers and, stir-fried, 98–99
    preparation of, for stir frying, 99
Scalloping technique, for pastry,
    373
Scallops, sea
    broiled, 184–86
    buying, 184
    deep-fried, 185
    pan-fried, 185
    preparation of, for broiling, 185–
    86
    suitability of, for broiling, 182
Scaloppine al limone, 134–35
Scissors, 8
    See also Shears
Scones, 317–19
Scraper, dough, baker's, 6
Seafood
    fillings for chou puffs, 418
    frozen, broiling, 143
    temperature of, for broiling, 143
    See also Fish; Shellfish

Sea scallops. *See* Scallops
Sealing techniques, for pies
    double-crusted, 361–62, 365, 369,
    384
    lattice-topped, 371–72
Searing method, for roasting, 244
Seasoning
    of fish for broiling, 183
    of foods for frying, 77
    of meat for broiling, 147, 162
    technique, for roasts, 244
Sesame seed(s)
    crackers, 320–22
    toasting, 321
Shaping techniques
    for breads, 282–83, 285–86, 288
    for chou paste, 417, 424, 426
    for crackers, 323
    for croquettes, 107
    for meringues, 352
    for shortbread, 319
    for whipped cream, 427
    See also Cutting; Rolling-out
Shashlik, beef, marinated, 201–203
Shears, kitchen or poultry, 8
Shellfish
    for broiling, 181–82
    deep-fried, 108–110
    suitability of, for baking, 243
    See also Names of individual
        shellfish; Fish
Shish kebab, lamb, marinated, 203–
    205
Shortbread, 319–20
Shortening, vegetable, solid, 457
    for deep-fat frying, 75–76
    in pastry, 356
    storing, 76
    See also Butter; Lard
Short pastry, term defined, 455
Short ribs. *See* Beef
Shoulder of lamb. *See* Lamb
Shrimp
    boiled (hot or cold), 40–42
    broiled, turning, 144
    cleaning, 41–42. *See also* Shrimp,
        preparation of, *below*
    deep-fried, 108–110
    frozen, broiling, 143
    pâté, as filling for chou puffs,
        418–20
    preparation of
        for sautéing, 138
        for skewering, 206

Shrimp (*cont'd*)
  salmon steaks braised with wine
      and, 230–33
  sautéed, 137–38
  selection of, for skewering, 205
  skewered, with garlic butter,
      205–207
  suitability of, for broiling, 182
Sieves, 8
Sifter, flour, 6
Sifting techniques, for dry ingredi-
      ents, 276, 328
Simmering
  vs. boiling or poaching, 12–13
  techniques
      for barley, 38
      for beef, 20–21
      for beef tongue, 22
      general, 15–17
      for water, 14
Skewers, 8
Skewering
  advantages of, for broiling, 200
  disadvantages of, in broiling
      vegetables, 192–93
  technique, for broiled foods, 200–
      207
Skimming technique, for stocks,
      16–17
Slab, cutting, 3
Sole, fillets of
  amandine, 140
  à la meunière, 139–40
  preparation of
      for sautéing, 139
      for steaming, 49
  rolled, 48–49
  suitability of, for broiling, 182
Solid vegetable shortening. *See*
      Shortening
Soufflé dish, 3
Soup(s)
  chicken, rice, and vegetable, 39
  minestrone, Italian, 39
  vegetable, basic, and variations,
      37–39
  See also Broths; Stocks
Sour cream, 455
  in cakes, 327
  and nutmeg, cabbage quarters
      with, 63–64
  pound cakes, 331–33
Southern fried chicken, 89–90
Southern pecan pie, 377

Spareribs, stuffed, 257–59
Spatulas, 8
Spinach
  buying, 64
  with pine nuts, 64–65
  preparation of, for steaming, 65
  stuffing, shoulder of lamb with,
      218–21
  tart, 401–402
Spoons, 4, 8
Squab chickens, term defined, 445
Squash
  batter-fried, 116
  preparation of, for deep-fat fry-
      ing, 117
Standing rib roast. *See* Beef
Steak. *See* Beef; Fish; Lamb;
      Salmon
Steamer, collapsible, 8
Steaming
  vs. boiling, for vegetables, 50
  vs. pressure cooking, 13
  techniques
      for asparagus, 62
      for Brussels sprouts, 53
      for cabbage, 64
      general, 17
      for sole, fillets of, rolled, 49
      for spinach, 65
  term defined, 13
  value of, for vegetables, 50
Stewing chickens, term defined,
      445
Stir frying techniques
  basic, 95
  for vegetables, 96, 97–98, 99
Stock(s)
  chicken, 36–37
  fish, for braising salmon steaks,
      231–32
  freezing, 35
  reducing, 35, 455
  skimming, 16–17
  storing, 35
  straining and degreasing, 34–35
  substitutes for, 34, 456
  techniques for making, 34–35,
      36–37
  See also Broths; Soups
Storing techniques
  for cakes, 329
      fruit, 333
  for chou paste, 416
  for chou puffs, 418

Storing techniques (*cont'd*)
for crackers, 323
for fats for deep-fat frying, 101
for fish, 450
for lard, 77
for lobsters, live, 42–43
for oil(s)
olive, 76
vegetable, 75
for poultry, 455
for shortbread, 320
for shortenings, vegetable, 76
for stocks, 35
See also Freezing
Strainers. *See* Sieves
Straining
cheesecloth for, 9
technique, for stocks, 34–35
Strawberry tart, 405–407
String, for tying roasts, 9
Striped bass
broiled whole, 187–88
poached whole, 45–47
preparation of
for broiling, 187–88
for poaching, 46
Stuffing(s)
apple-sage, crown roast of pork with, 255–57
for chickens, roast, 260, 261
corn bread, roast turkey with, 262–66
crabmeat, for red snapper, 269–70
dill, for lamb chops, double loin, 165
for lamb, boned leg of, flamed with gin, 249, 250
for lamb, hindquarters of, 252, 253
liver, roast duckling with, 266–68
for spareribs, 257, 258
spinach, shoulder of lamb with, 218–21
techniques
for chickens, 261
for duckling, roast, 267–68
for lamb, boned leg of, 249
for lamb chops, 166
for lamb, hindquarter of, 253
for lamb shoulder, 219
for pork, crown roast of, 256
for red snapper, 270

for spareribs, 258
for turkey, roast, 264
Sugar
in bread, 276
brown, 456
in cakes, 327–28
confectioners', 276, 456
shaker for, 9
in pastry, 357
superfine, 456
Sweeteners, liquid. *See* Corn syrup; Molasses
Sweet potatoes
broiled, 199–200
suitability of, for broiling, 192
See also Yams
Swiss potato and sausage tart, 399–400
Swordfish steaks, preparation of, for broiling, 183

Tapioca, as thickening agent for pie fillings, 357
Tart(s)
baking, 397, 399, 402, 403, 405
crabmeat, 398–99
filled and baked, freezing, 393
fruit, 405–407
chilling, 407
glazing, 407
ham and cheese, 396
pans. *See* Pans
pastry. *See* Pastry
potato and sausage, Swiss, 399–400
savory, with two cheeses, 402–403
shell(s)
baking, 392–93, 395
broken, repairing, 393
freezing, 393
fully baked fluted, 393–95
fully baked fluted, uses for, 398–99, 401–407
partially baked fluted, 396
partially baked fluted, uses for, 399–400
spinach, 401–402
strawberry, 405–407
tomato and cheese, 404–405
unmolding, 397, 399, 403, 405
See also Pies; Tartlets
Tartlet(s)
baking, 410, 412
cheese, 410–11

Tartlet(s) (*cont'd*)
crabmeat, 411–12
pastry. *See* Pastry
shells
bread, 412–13
bread, fillings for, 412
freezing, 393, 413
ummolding, 411, 412
See also Pies; Tarts
Tea kettle, 2
Temperature conversions (table), 460
Tenderizers, commercial, vs. marinades, for meat, 147–48
Tester, cake, 7
Thawing techniques
for chicken, frozen, 445
for duckling, frozen, 447
Thermometer(s)
candy, 5
meat, 4–5
oven, 4–5
Thickening agents, for pie fillings, 357
Toasting technique, for sesame seeds, 321
Tomato(es)
butter, broiled mackerel with, 188–90
and cheese tart, 404–405
cherry
broiled, 197–98
with garlic and herbs, 197–98
preparation of, for broiling, 198
suitability of, for skewering, 201
preparation of, for broiling, 193
suitability of, for broiling, 192
Tongs, kitchen, 8
Tongue. *See* Beef
Topping(s)
for broiled tomato halves, 193
deviled, chicken with a, 178–79
herb-crumb, double rib lamb chops with, 166–67
See also Cream, whipped
Tortes. *See* Cakes
Trichinosis, decreasing dangers of, in pork, 255
Trimming techniques
for beef steak, before broiling, 147
for lamb, before broiling, 162

Trout, suitability of
for braising, 210
for broiling, 182
Trussing
skewer, 8
technique, for chicken, 445–46
Tuna sauce. *See* Sauces
Turbot, suitability of, for braising, 210
Turkey
leftover, in croquettes, 105–107
preparation of, for stuffing and roasting, 263–64
roast
with corn bread stuffing, 262–66
serving amounts for, 243–44
suitability of, for roasting, 243
Turkshead mold. *See* Gugelhopf pan
Turning techniques
for broiled foods, 144, 187
for deep-fried foods, 102
for fried foods, 81, 94
for simmering meat, 16
Turnovers, deep-fried savory, 110–13

Unmolding techniques
for cakes, 331, 333, 335, 342
for Gugelhopf, 294–95
for shortbread, 320
for sponge roll, 339
for tartlets, 411, 412
for tarts, 397, 399, 400, 402, 403, 405
Utensils
cooking, 1–9
for measuring, 4–5

Veal
braised, with prunes and Madeira, 216–18
for braising, 210
characteristics of, 457
cutlets
Milanese, breaded, 83
preparation of, for frying, 82
Wiener Schnitzel, 81–83
grading of, by age, 457
preparation of
for braising, 217
for poaching, 32
for sautéing, 132–33, 134–35
roast, serving amounts for, 243

Veal (cont'd)
    for roasting, 242
    scallops
        preparation of, for sautéing,
            134–35
        in scaloppine al limone, 134–
            35
    stock. See Stocks
    in vitello tonnato, 31–33
Vegetable(s)
    batter-fried, 116–18
    boiled, 51–61
    broiling, 192–93
    color of, intensifying, 51
    discoloration of, preventing, 50–
        51
    oils
        for frying, 75, 101
        in pastry, 356
    peeler, 4
    preparation of
        for boiling, 50–51
        for steaming, 50–51
    shortening. See Shortening
    for skewering, 201
    soup
        basic, and variations, 37–39
        chicken, rice, and, 39
    steamed, 61–65
    stir-fried, 95–99
    suitability of, for braising, 210
    temperature of, for broiling,
        143
    See also Names of individual
        vegetables
Vinaigrette sauce, 439
    See also Sauces
Vitello tonnato, 31–33

Walnut(s)
    buttered, braised Belgian endives
        with, 235–36
    torte, 342–44
Warming techniques
    for fried foods, 81
    for hollandaise sauce, 432

Water
    in bread, 276
    as cooking liquid, 13–14
        acidulated, for vegetables, 50–
            51
        for seafood, 40
    iced, in pastry, 357
Wax paper, 9
"Weeping" of meringue, control-
    ling, 374–75
Weights and measures metric
    equivalents (table), 459–61
Whip, balloon, 7
Whipped cream. See Cream
Whipping techniques
    for cream, 71, 342, 344, 422, 426–
        27
    for egg whites, 448–49
    See also Beating
Whisks (whips), 7
Whitefish, suitability of, for broil-
    ing, 182
Whole-wheat bread, 286–89
Wiener Schnitzel, 81–83
Wine
    for cooking, 457
    and shrimp, salmon steaks
        braised with, 230–33

Yams
    broiled, 199–200
    See also Sweet potatoes
Yeast
    breads. See Breads
    characteristics of, 274
    dough. See Bread
    dry vs. compressed fresh, 275,
        457–58
Yorkshire pudding. See Pudding

Zester, 4
Zucchini
    broiled, 194
    suitability of
        for broiling, 192
        for skewering, 201